Development and Cities

Oxfam GB

Oxfam GB, founded in 1942, is a development, relief, and campaigning agency dedicated to finding lasting solutions to poverty and suffering around the world. Oxfam believes that every human being is entitled to a life of dignity and opportunity, and it works with others worldwide to make this become a reality.

From its base in Oxford, UK, Oxfam GB publishes and distributes a wide range of books and other resource materials for development and relief workers, researchers, campaigners, schools and colleges, and the general public, as part of its programme of advocacy, education, and communications.

Oxfam GB is a member of Oxfam International, a confederation of 12 agencies of diverse cultures and languages, which share a commitment to working for an end to injustice and poverty – both in long-term development work and at times of crisis.

For further information about Oxfam's publishing, and online ordering, visit www.oxfam.org.uk/publications

For further information about Oxfam's development and humanitarian relief work around the world, visit www.oxfam.org.uk

Development and Cities

Essays from *Development in Practice*

Edited by
David Westendorff and Deborah Eade

A Development in Practice Reader

Series Editor
Deborah Eade

First published by Oxfam GB in association with UNRISD in 2002

© Oxfam GB 2002

ISBN 0 85598 465 1

A catalogue record for this publication is available from the British Library.

Available from:
Bournemouth English Book Centre, PO Box 1496, Parkstone, Dorset, BH12 3YD, UK
tel: +44 (0)1202 712933; fax: +44 (0)1202 712930; email: oxfam@bebc.co.uk

USA: Stylus Publishing LLC, PO Box 605, Herndon, VA 20172-0605, USA
tel: +1 (0)703 661 1581; fax: +1 (0)703 661 1547; email: styluspub@aol.co

For details of local agents and representatives in other countries, consult our website:
http://www.oxfam.org.uk/publications.html
or contact Oxfam Publishing, 274 Banbury Road, Oxford OX2 7DZ, UK
tel: +44 (0)1865 311 311; fax: +44 (0)1865 312 600; email: publish@oxfam.org.uk

The Editor and Management Committee of Development in Practice acknowledge the support
given to the journal by affiliates of Oxfam International, and by its publisher, Carfax,
Taylor & Francis. The views expressed in this volume are those of the individual contributors,
and not necessarily those of the Editor or publisher.

Published by Oxfam GB, 274 Banbury Road, Oxford OX2 7DZ, UK

Printed by Information Press, Eynsham

Oxfam GB is a registered charity, no. 202 918, and is a member of Oxfam International

Contents

Contributors

Adriana Allen is Director of the Environmental Planning and Management Programme at the Development Planning Unit at University College London, and a visiting professor at several universities in Latin America.

Adrian Atkinson is associated with the Development Planning Unit (DPU) at University College London, where he developed courses in urban environment over many years. Currently, he acts as a consultant to various aid agencies, with a focus on South-East Asia.

Banashree Banerjee is an urban planner and associate staff member of the Institute for Housing and Urban Development Studies (IHS), Rotterdam. She was part of the core team of consultants involved in designing and overseeing the implementation of the programme described in her paper.

Erhard Berner is a lecturer in Local and Regional Development at the Institute of Social Studies in The Hague, and has taught at universities in the Philippines, Nepal, and Namibia.

Alison Brown is a consultant urban planner and part-time lecturer at the Department of City and Regional Planning of Cardiff University.

Diego Carrión is Dean of the Faculty of Architecture and Design at the Catholic University of Ecuador and a researcher at the Centro de Investigaciones CIUDAD in Quito, Ecuador. He is also chief adviser to the mayor of Quito.

P. G. Dhar Chakrabarti is a senior Indian Civil Servant. He held the post of Director in the Ministry of Urban Development in the Government of India when this article was written. This article is written in his individual capacity and does not necessarily reflect the opinions of his organisation.

Karina Constantino-David is Professor of Community Development at the University of the Philippines, former Secretary of Housing and Urban Development from 1998 to 1999, and a Philippine NGO leader.

Deborah Eade is Editor of the international journal *Development in Practice* and has written widely on development and humanitarian affairs.

Carlos García Pleyán holds degrees from the universities of Barcelona, Paris, and Havana. From 1970 to 1996 he was a town planner at the Instituto de Planificación Física in Havana. Since 1998 he has been Vice-President of the NGO, Habitat-Cuba.

Jaime Joseph is a member of Centro Alternativa, an action-research NGO that works in Metropolitan Lima, and is co-ordinator of the school for leaders and research.

Wilbard Jackson Kombe is a senior lecturer at the University College of Lands and Architectural Studies (UCLAS) in Dar es Salaam.

Amitabh Kundu is based at the Centre for the Study of Regional Development at Jawaharlal Nehru University in New Delhi.

Carlo Lavalle works at the Space Applications Institute, Strategy and Systems for Space Applications (SSSA) Unit in Italy.

Darshini Mahadevia teaches courses on housing and environment at the Centre for Environmental Planning and Technology in Ahmedabad and is currently working on urban poverty issues in India.

Fernando Murillo is an architect. Having worked the Middle East, Rwanda, and Nicaragua, he is currently Research Project Director in the Faculty of Architecture and Urbanism at the University of Buenos Aires.

Cesare Ottolini is the European representative of Habitat International Coalition (HIC), a founder member of the European Charter for Housing Rights and the Fight Against Exclusion, and president of the *Unione Inquilini* (Tenants' Union), one of Italy's most prominent associations of tenants and homeless people.

Geoffrey Payne is a housing and urban development consultant and a specialist on urban land tenure and property rights in developing countries. He is also an External Associate Adviser to the British Council on built environment subjects.

Hélène Rivière d'Arc, a geographer, is Director of Research at the Research and Documentation Centre (CNRS) in Paris, where she focuses on Latin America.

David Westendorff was a Research Co-ordinator at UNRISD from 1991 until 2001 and is now an independent consultant co-ordinating a series of international comparative research projects on urban governance. He will assume a faculty position at Tsinghwa University, Beijing, China in mid-2002.

Sponsoring organisations

N-AERUS

Founded in 1996, N-AERUS (Network-Association of European Researchers on Urbanisation in the South) is a pluri-disciplinary North-South network of researchers and experts working on urban issues in developing countries. N-AERUS is premised on an understanding that:

- cities are increasingly contributing to the development process;
- any interventions must take into account the social dimension of urban development, the cultural diversity of cities, and the diversity of urban areas;
- European research capacities and experiences in the urban sector are under-utilised.

N-AERUS channels its research findings to the EU, in order to render its technical assistance programmes and urban projects in the South more effective. N-AERUS also disseminates information, and seeks to develop, mobilise, and consolidate institutional and individual research and training capacities, and to provide sound intellectual backing to urban development projects.

For further information, visit www.n-aerus.org

European Science Foundation (ESF)

The European Science Foundation (ESF) is an association of 67 research councils and institutions devoted to basic scientific research, based in 23 countries. The scientific work sponsored by ESF includes basic research in the natural sciences, medical and biosciences, the humanities, and the social sciences. The ESF also seeks to be a catalyst for the development of science by bringing together leading scientists and funding agencies to debate, plan, and implement pan-European activities.

For further information, visit www.esf.org

IREC-EPFL

The Research Institute for the Built Environment (Institut de Recherche sur l'Environnement Construit, IREC) is based in the Department of Architecture at the Swiss Federal Institute of Technology in Lausanne (Ecole Polytéchnique Fédérale de Lausanne, EPFL).

IREC was founded in 1971 as an interdisciplinary team of researchers to analyse the built environment and urban phenomena in regional, national, and global development plans. The Institute contributes to improving the understanding of these structures and the economic, social, political, and cultural processes that shape them. The main thematic areas of its research include urban dynamics and metropolisation; construction, property, and real estate; development of housing conditions and the urban environment; spatial and social structures; urban migration and public space; technology, science, and society.

For further information, contact <Jean-Claude.Bolay@epfl.ch>

UNRISD

The United Nations Research Institute for Social Development (UNRISD) is an autonomous agency engaging in multi-disciplinary research on the social dimensions of contemporary problems affecting development. Its work is guided by the conviction that development policies will be effective only if they are based on an understanding of their social and political context. UNRISD attempts to provide governments, development agencies, grassroots organisations, and scholars with a better understanding of how development policies and processes of economic, social, and environmental change affect different social sectors. Working through an extensive network of national research centres, UNRISD aims to promote original research and strengthen research capacity in developing countries.

UNRISD's recent research on urban issues has focused on the role of community-based organisations in confronting urban social problems, and on the emerging forms of co-operation and interaction between such organisations and local authorities. In both areas, community-based researcher-activists and community groups have been intimately involved in the research alongside more traditional 'knowledge workers'. The purpose of this approach has been to create a 'grassroots perspective' on the problems and prospects for improving urban governance, and particularly the ability of marginalised groups to organise themselves to influence the flow of public and private resources to their benefit.

For more information, visit www.unrisd.org

Preface

Deborah Eade

This *Reader* is based upon the May 2001 double issue of *Development in Practice*, guest-edited by David Westendorff of the United Nations Research Institute for Social Development (UNRISD). Now based once again in China, he was from 1991 to 2001 a research co-ordinator at the UNRISD office in Geneva, where his work focused on the related themes of urban governance and civil society and social movements. Prior to this, he co-ordinated research projects on urban development and planning issues in Brazil, China, Mexico, India, Peru, South Africa, and the USA.

Among development agencies in general, and specifically in the NGO sector, there is a continuing reluctance to engage fully with issues of urbanisation. The prevailing attitude is either that cities are a problem in and of themselves and shouldn't be encouraged, or that their residents enjoy better facilities and so are less 'needy' than their rural counterparts, or that the challenges posed by rapid urbanisation are simply too big, too expensive, and too complicated to handle. A glance through the grants lists and literature of some of the best-known international NGOs suggests that, in part because of their short-term or project-bound focus, if they get involved at all, most find it easier to deal with the specific problems of specific population groups in the towns and cities of the South – street-children and sex-workers topping the list – rather than getting involved in the messier processes of urban management, such as housing or transport or public amenities. Ironically, the largest human settlements in which many NGOs take a more holistic approach to the planning and management of basic services are refugee camps – usually cramped and often squalid settlements that earn their description as 'rural slums' – but again their involvement is characteristically short-term rather than open-ended or processual.

Of himself, David Westendorff comments that his formal training – in architecture in the mid-1970s, and city and regional planning in the early 1980s – allowed him to ignore these topics until real-world experience began to show him who the real builders and planners were. In his introductory essay, he therefore underlines the importance of making discussions about sustainability in the urban sector accessible to those institutions of civil society that (potentially) have a pivotal role to play in influencing policy debates and shaping practice – the grassroots activists, community- or neighbourhood-based organisations, social movements, and NGOs, among many others. We, in association with UNRISD, are pleased to help in disseminating the enormous breadth of professional and practical experience, and cultural backgrounds, reflected here. We trust that this *Reader* will help to break down some of the barriers and prejudices that so often limit our understanding of and approaches to urban problems (and their solutions), and to stimulate new thinking in this area.

Sustainable cities of the South:
an introduction

David Westendorff

This *Development in Practice Reader* builds upon the May 2001 double issue of *Development in Practice*, which comprised approximately half of the papers initially prepared for presentation at the European Science Foundation's annual N-AERUS Workshop, held on 3–5 May 2000 in Geneva.[1] Its title, 'Cities of the South: Sustainable for Whom?', reflects concern within the N-AERUS and the host institutions – UNRISD and IREC-EPFL – that urban development processes in many cities of the North and South are being guided by superficial or misleading conceptions of sustainable development in the urban context. As will be seen in the contributions to this *Reader*, the aims of different groups proposing strategies for the sustainable development of cities tend to skew their arguments about what this means and how to achieve it. Environmentalists who see the pollution-free city as the only sustainable one may be willing to sacrifice the only affordable form of mass transport for poor people, or dirty low-tech jobs that provide them their meagre living. Those pursuing the globally competitive city may succeed in attracting foreign and domestic investments that boost economic growth and productivity, but which concentrate the benefits of growth very narrowly, leaving an increasingly large majority to live in penury at the foot of glass skyscrapers. Beleaguered bureaucrats attempting to improve or extend public infrastructure may adopt financing mechanisms that weaken poorer groups' capacity to benefit from the newly installed infrastructure, even though they bear a disproportionate share of the costs of paying for it. International organisations seeking to promote more effective governance of cities may encourage decentralisation processes that fragment responsibility in the absence of legal, administrative, and institutional frameworks to organise and finance governmental responsibilities at the local level. Such a vacuum may be filled by local bosses or other power brokers who have little interest in the common good.

In different ways, our various contributors focus on these contradictions.

The contributions are grouped into four partially overlapping categories. The first group comments on different aspects of the international challenges to achieving sustainable cities. In the second group, researcher-practitioners from Africa, Asia, and Latin America offer their understanding of the principles that would have to be followed in order to achieve sustainable development in their cities, and the current set of constraints against doing so. These chapters necessarily touch on the contested roles of international agencies and bilateral donors in shaping national strategies for urban sustainable development. The next five contributions discuss issues of housing and land-use management in cities of developing countries. The next group, comprising two contributions, provides updates on new information technologies that may play important roles in planning for sustainable development, whether in cities, their regions, or countries. This collection ends with a salutary reminder from **Hélène Rivière d'Arc** that planners' solutions to the problems of poor people have long been formed by a technocratic vision and expressed in a technocratic language. These rarely reflect the language or the approaches to the problems the marginalised groups themselves elect to use. The misapprehension of the meaning and role of 'community' remains a crucial 'dis-connect' for many planners and urban officials.

In the first of the two papers on the international context for urban sustainable development, **Adriana Allen** chronicles the impact of the increasing internationalisation of Argentina's fishing industry on the city of Mar del Plata. This process included the transition from small-scale producers catering for local markets to larger highly capitalised international fishing enterprises producing for export markets. As neo-liberal policies of deregulation pushed catches to unsustainable levels in the 1990s, Mar del Plata's native fishing and canning industries became progressively sidelined by foreign competitors operating in Argentinian waters. Over time, Mar del Plata's unions could provide less and less protection to workers, enterprises cut back on investments in plant and equipment, and the city's tax revenues began to fall, affecting its ability to provide infrastructure and enforce environmental standards in the port area, etc.. Today, the prospects for sustaining decent livelihoods and living conditions for Mar del Plata's residents are as uncertain as the fate of the fish from which it has drawn its sustenance for decades. In the second of these papers, **Amitabh Kundu** reviews the recent experience of a number of large Indian cities in financing infrastructure through domestic and international capital markets since the imposition of structural adjustment policies in the early 1990s. One of the author's major concerns is that the stringent mechanisms for assuring repayment of loans increasingly take decision making about the design and implementation of infrastructure out of the hands of local governments and place it with entities whose chief concern is an adequate rate of return to investors in the short run. This transfer of decision making is modelled largely on the experience of the USA and is being promoted through international institutions such as the World Bank and regional development banks, and with the support of like-minded bilateral donors. Its suitability to the Indian context is challenged because it appears to exacerbate intra- and inter-regional disparities in infrastructure and service delivery, thus reinforcing already unacceptably high levels of social segmentation.

The first of the six contributions discussing regional experiences in achieving sustainable cities is the review by **Wilbard J. Kombe** of efforts to revitalise urban planning and management in the Tanzanian capital Dar es Salaam during the 1990s by means of the Environmental Planning and Management (EPM) promoted by Habitat (UNHCS) and the United Nations Environment Programme (UNEP). The Sustainable Dar es Salaam Project was established in 1992 as the vehicle for guiding this effort. Kombe focuses on the functioning of two of the nine working groups established to propose solutions to the most pressing habitat problems in the city and to facilitate and monitor their implementation. The working groups were an important innovation in that they were designed to include all the parties that could materially affect the success of the proposed solutions. While both working groups appear to have mobilised new collective forms of problem solving, their most important proposals could not be implemented. Vested interests among stakeholders, institutional inertia, bureaucratic in-fighting, and a lack of political will at the central level all stood in the way. **Diego Carrión** then paints in broad brushstrokes how Latin American geo-political processes of democratisation, structural adjustment, state reform, including decentralisation, liberalisation of economies via privatisation, etc., are bringing about a sea-change in the way cities are governed. This transforms the processes for deciding how to proceed towards sustainable urban development. The author's particular concern is that civil society organisations (CSOs) – especially those at the grassroots – and local authorities are assuming many of the responsibilities for sustaining society and its habitat. To move in this direction requires that local authorities facilitate community participation in ways that have rarely been adopted before. Carrión proposes six principles to guide local authorities' efforts to include CSOs in the planning and implementation of new development strategies.

Jaime Joseph prefers the term 'sustainable human development' when discussing a better future for the residents of Lima's vast informal settlements. In this megacity, most housing is constructed by those who live in it. These same residents have often provided themselves with the necessary infrastructure to sustain their living conditions, even if only at subsistence levels. Repeated waves of structural adjustment in recent decades have made this a way of life for many. This must be a premise for efforts to achieve sustainable development in the city, i.e. they must take a decentralised approach, relying on grassroots organisations, their supporters in civil society, and the local authorities. But sustainable improvements in material and social life must be built upon a culture of development and democracy. This is being nurtured in Lima's 'public spaces', informal opportunities in which community organisations, NGOs, and sometimes local authorities, join in open debate about how to develop their neighbourhoods and districts. If properly supported with information, ethical practices in debate and decision making, and legislative support, the nascent process of political development will take root and flower. The environment for this is not optimal, however, as the Peruvian economy, weakened by structural adjustment and civil strife in the 1990s, is today further threatened by imports from a global economy that undercut employment opportunities for poor people in Lima and the rest of the country. Without a respite from this desperate competition, positive change may be stymied.

Karina Constantino-David's experience of attempting to bring decent housing and habitat to Manila's poor leads her to frame sustainable development in cities as a question of achieving 'sustainable improvements in the quality of life'. Standing in the way of this aim in the Philippines is the country's current model of 'parasitic' development – the blind pursuit of economic growth through global competitiveness and foreign investment. This process is driving the deterioration of the quality of life in Filipino cities. Five distinct but overlapping power groups – the state, business, the dominant church, the media, and international aid agencies – share responsibility for this. In Constantino-David's opinion, the only possible path out of this morass is to pay more attention to the earth's 'carrying' and 'caring' capacity. She furthermore highlights the often negative role that foreign assistance plays in curtailing attention to these issues in the Philippines.

Darshini Mahadevia reviews initiatives taken in India over the past decade to improve either urban development or the urban environment or the conditions of life for the cities' poor. These are a disparate range of initiatives undertaken by central and local government, civil society organisations, or the judicial system. Sometimes external assistance is involved, sometimes not. But these efforts are rarely conceived with a view to the possibilities of mutual reinforcement or synergetic interaction. Nor do they attempt to take a 'people-centred approach' in which the concerns of poor people take precedence in a model that relates all development concerns in a holistic manner. In his chapter on the growing urban crisis in India, **P.G. Dhar Chakrabarti** identifies several of the most important causes behind the failure of sub-national governments to halt the decay of living conditions in the country's cities. More important than the absence of funds for upgrading urban infrastructure and services is the lack of capacity of government agencies and authorities to use the resources available for this purpose. This absence of capacity continues despite constitutional amendments of 1992 which, in theory, give local authorities far greater powers to administer and finance their own affairs. Indeed, the kinds of reforms and improvements in local government capacity that were expected to follow the constitutional amendments have been abysmally slow. As evidence of their continuing weakness, the author cites the failure of local authorities to take up highly effective and affordable technologies for rainwater collection, sanitation, and building materials. He calls for a 'reform of the reform process' as a first step in the right direction.

At the mid-way point of this collection, **Adrian Atkinson** surveys the evolution of external assistance agencies' (bilateral and multilateral donors, UN agencies, the development banks and foundations, and international NGOs) support to programmes and projects in cities of the South. These agencies have only very recently taken on an explicit concern for 'urban sustainable development', and tend to reflect variable and often specious understandings of what the concept means. The main international urban co-operation programmes, such as in transport, sanitation, and water supply, have been fragmented and often politically, socially, and technologically unsustainable, even in the short term. New forms and approaches to external assistance are emerging, albeit slowly, tentatively, and on a small scale. The author highlights some of the most pertinent to urban sustainable development, but notes that they are being attempted in a particularly adverse international environment. For example, programmes and projects to alleviate poverty within cities may be being implemented within a political and ideological framework that tends to generate more poverty. **Banashree Bannerjee**'s paper on the Andhra Pradesh Urban Services for the Poor (APUSP) project describes a state-of-the-art partnership between a bilateral donor and the state government of Andhra Pradesh to promote sustained improvements in living conditions for the urban poor.[2] The project does not overtly promise to deliver the sustainable city in Andhra Pradesh, but it does acknowledge and require a series of inputs from other sectors of society that are necessary if not sufficient conditions for achieving this goal. The programme attempts to bring these inputs and conditions together by making explicit a framework for strengthening grassroots civil society and for creating incentives for municipal authorities to achieve the same. Indeed, AP-USP appears to have been formulated to address, among other concerns, the lack of planned synergy among existing anti-poverty and urban development programmes in India (see also Mahadevia in this volume), the weakness of local authorities in raising or using available resources and innovations to the benefit of urban residents (highlighted by Chakrabarti), the lack of effective grassroots participation in decision making, either because of weaknesses in CSOs themselves (referred to by Joseph and Constantino-David) or the failure of the process to be opened to representatives of low-income or marginalised groups (issues also raised by both Kombe and Brown).

In the first of five contributions concerned with urban housing and habitat, **Erhard Berner** argues that because the large majority of housing in cities in developing countries is self-constructed, government-run schemes to provide adequate housing are too small-scale to serve the growing demand, and its products are too expensive to be affordable for low-income groups. He presents two brief case studies of efforts to integrate practices of informal housing markets – particularly incremental structural upgrading by the residents – into government programmes. These were aimed at making the housing provided under government programmes more affordable. In the case of the Community Mortgage Programme in the Philippines, the programme succeeded for about two thirds of the residents in upgraded slums. The poorest third tended to be forced out, however, because they were eventually obliged to pay a rent in the upgraded neighbourhood that they could not afford. In a different approach attempted in Hyderabad, in Pakistan, the scheme worked well economically but failed for other reasons: namely, stiff resistance from those accustomed to profiting from informal and formal land markets. **Geoffrey Payne** approaches the question of the 'costs of formality' from a different angle. In many countries, some even within the European Union, a large proportion of housing is constructed outside formal regulatory frameworks, i.e. the dwellings are illegal to some extent. This is done to avoid the costs of meeting official standards that are deemed unaffordable by homeowners. Often these standards are remnants of a colonial past and were never intended to be applied to the population as a whole. In other situations, standards and bureaucratic formalities persist because they yield formal income (fees, service charges) and informal income (graft) to interested parties within the government. The author proposes that where standards are set artificially high, they should be lowered in order to help lower-income groups continue to provide and improve housing for themselves without threat of legal sanctions. Understanding what constitutes artificially or unnecessarily high standards in a given national context is a theme on which research is needed. In the following paper, **Alison Brown** shows that the continuing impact of apartheid land-use planning and regulations in Harare impedes convenient access by poor people to public spaces that provide both economic opportunity and affordable leisure activities. Planners need to recognise the limited alternatives available within the city for these groups and guide future changes in the urban fabric in a way that enhances opportunities for poor people to help themselves.

The last two contributions in this group describe innovative partnerships to bring about better and more affordable housing to the residents of the cities of Cuba and Buenos Aires in Argentina. In the first, **Carlos García-Pleyán** describes the process by which a consortium of Cuban architects, planners, and government administrators is attempting to assist in the transformation of low-income urban neighbourhoods and housing provision processes on the island. The group began developing its efforts in the 1990s as Cuba's economic and technological support from Eastern bloc countries disintegrated. This process stimulated new thinking about how to manage with existing resources the transitions needed in Cuban cities. For

Habitat-Cuba this means doing things that have not been done before: mobilising residents of low-income areas to participate in the trans-formation of their neighbourhoods; establishing economic, cultural, and environmental sustainability of proposed solutions; and stimulating both interaction and co-operation among all the social actors involved in the transformation processes. According to **Fernando Murillo** the approach to government-sponsored low-income housing provision in Buenos Aires could not be more different: with the encouragement and technical assistance of the World Bank, the city developed a programme, *Casa Propia*, that would rely on a public–private sector partnership to finance new low-income housing. Indeed, the private sector's contribution was to be large: scarce land for construction, the design and construction of the apartments, and the bulk of the mortgages. The city's contribution was to identify qualified 'low-income' buyers and to act as guarantor of their mortgages. In practice, the private developers of *Casa Propia* targeted the project to the top end of the low-income bracket, as higher-cost apartments would yield higher absolute profits than lower-cost apartments. Indeed, most of the buyers tended to be at or slightly above the income barrier separating the eligible low-income groups and the ineligible lower-middle income groups. True low-income households could not afford the monthly mortgage payments for *Casa Propia*. And while low-income families could not gain entry into the programme, many living in the communities in the immediate vicinity of *Casa Propia* were forced to leave because of rising rents in the area. Other nearby low-income residents lost their local green spaces, and experienced greater traffic congestion and other environmental inconveniences. These and other less positive outcomes forced the city and its private partners to reconsider the validity of this form of partnership, and to halt the project after only approximately a third of the total apartments planned had been built.

The debate on the capacity of information technology to help poor, marginalised, or isolated groups to leapfrog gaps in knowledge and hence development will continue for a long time to come. The two papers included on this subject discuss technologies that are undoubtedly of interest to the major actors in the sustainable development debate. From the perspective of both grassroots and formal sector urban planners and decision makers, Internet connectivity is proving a boon in the North, as **Cesare Ottolini** argues. However, the evidence of its use in developing countries is patchy and inconclusive, especially with regard to urban grassroots actors in the housing and local development fields. New research should be undertaken, involving these actors, to find out how the technology may become more accessible and useful to them. Earth observation technologies, on the other hand, have by virtue of their development costs been limited to use by Northern countries and even then by the better-resourced planning and development agencies. **Carlo Lavalle** *et al.* report on efforts by the European Commission (EC) Centre for Earth Observation of the EC's Directorate General Joint Research Centre to apply earth observation technologies to the understanding of urban development patterns and their consequences for sustainable development as defined by the EU. These efforts have recently been extended to the analysis of a number of cities in countries that will be joining the EU and megacities in several developing countries. The authors believe this technology will be useful and inexpensive for developing countries both because of its ease of use and the availability of EC funding for technology transfer.

While it is impossible to sum up the lessons to emerge from the collection in a few short sentences, certain points are repeated. The meaning of 'sustainable cities' or 'sustainable urban development' is frequently manipulated to meet the ends of the agencies or persons using the phrase. Yet most of the authors in this collection, and indeed attending the N-AERUS Workshop, tend to agree that the sustainable city is one:

- that genuinely pursues improvements in livelihood and habitat for all in the short, medium, and long run without damaging in the process the carrying capacity of the city's hinterland or other regions;
- in which decentralised governance, democracy, and non-exploitative community participation are necessary but insufficient conditions to move cities in this direction;
- in which adverse macro-economic environments – and especially unfettered international economic competition – are likely to retard movement in the right direction; and
- in which a strong, just state is an essential asset for pursuing true social, economic, and environmental sustainability.

Less clear are the value of external assistance (foreign aid) in promoting sustainable development when the basic needs of the population remain grossly unmet; the promotion of partnerships for implementing sustainable development strategies and programmes in the absence of a willingness on the part of the most influential partners to share power and information with the least powerful partners; and the decentralisation and privatisation of state responsibilities in the context of vacuums of power and capability at lower levels.

On balance, the reading of this volume suggests that sustainable cities in developing countries will have to be built upon broader and deeper local-level and national civil society organisations than exist today. These organisations will, moreover, need far more access to and preparation for participation in decision-making forums, including at the international level. While national and sub-national governments have a responsibility to heed the will of their people, and to prepare them for active citizenship, some countries' willingness to do so remains in question. It will therefore be crucial for agencies of international governance and for bilateral donors to assist countries in acknowledging their responsibilities in this regard and to ensure that as external actors their own actions do not hamper the development of vibrant CSOs in developing countries.

David Westendorff
United Nations Research Institute for Social Development (UNRISD)

Acknowledgements

The N-AERUS Workshop – for which drafts of these and other papers not included here were prepared – was supported by grants from the European Science Foundation (ESF), the Swiss Agency for Development and Co-operation (SDC), the French Ministry of International Affairs, and UNRISD. Special thanks are owed to SDC for its grant to enable participants from developing countries to attend the workshop, while the Institute for the Built Environment of the Federal Polytechnic of Lausanne and ESF also contributed intellectual and organisational support.

On a personal level, I would to thank my co-organisers, Alain Durand-Lasserve and Jean-Claude Bolay, for the collaboration, guidance, and collegiality they offered before and during the workshop. I would also like to thank colleagues at UNRISD who facilitated many aspects of the workshop and its follow-up: Wendy Salvo for her able handling of liaison with the United Nations Office in Geneva, where the meeting took place; Liliane Ursache for preparing multiple agendas, participant lists, and other essential documents, and for helping with logistical concerns; Janna Lehmann for administrative backup during and after the workshop; and Rachael Mann and Katy Agg who assisted in preparing the annotated resource list at the end of this *Reader*. I would also like to thank Deborah Eade for allowing N-AERUS, through the journal *Development in Practice*, and this *Reader*, to reach audiences whose contributions to promoting sustainable development in cities are increasingly crucial but who would not necessarily follow debates on the subject in more technically focused journals on urban planning or urban studies. Translations from French and Spanish where necessary were undertaken by Deborah Eade and myself. Last, but not least, I would like to thank all the contributors to the issue of Development in Practice on which this volume is based for their willingness to undertake the multiple and sometimes substantial revisions requested by me in my role as guest editor.

Notes

1   Network-Association of European Researchers on Urbanisation in the South (N-AERUS). A brief description of the ESF, N-AERUS, the United Nations Research Institute for Social Development (UNRISD), and the Institut pour Recherche sur l'Environnement Construit-Ecole Polytechnicque Fédérale de Lausanne (IREC-EPFL) – can be found on page ix.

2   For reasons beyond the control of the author and editor, this paper did not appear in the May 2001 issue of *Development in Practice*.

Urban sustainability under threat: the restructuring of the fishing industry in Mar del Plata, Argentina

Adriana Allen

Cities are increasingly recognised as the areas in which almost all of the environmental impacts of development are felt. It is also increasingly recognised that development strategies must ensure that today's gains do not result in cities that will need radical restructuring in the future because they need more resources and have too great an impact on the environment to be sustainable. However, a significant outcome of macro-economic restructuring is that the 'globalisation' process is generating social and environmental conflicts in specific localities. While it is clear why we should focus attention on the urban environment and sustainable development, the precise relationship between macro-economic strategies and the sustainability of contemporary urban development trends remains largely unexplored (Burgess *et al.* 1997).

The need to assess development in the light of its social, environmental, and political impacts is the central concern of this paper, which focuses on the emergence of a socio-environmental conflict resulting from the restructuring of the Argentinian fishing industry in the city of Mar del Plata. The experiences we shall describe are typical of those facing many medium- and small-sized cities in Argentina which, unlike the metropolitan areas, are finding it increasingly difficult to reposition themselves in an open economy. Recent macro-economic reforms in the country have had an impact not only on the local economy of such cities, but also on their political, social, natural, and physical sustainability.

Argentina's local fishing industry developed in the post-war period according to a Fordist model, whereby production processes and forms of labour organisation were standardised, but which sought to guarantee workers a living wage. This model was supported by a series of regulatory institutions, which included the principle of collective bargaining, the establishment of minimum wages, and formal contracts of work. These were backed up by a welfare state whose role was to assist all individuals to have access to the market. Since the 1980s, industrial production in Argentina, as in most of Latin America, has shifted from Fordism to liberal-productivism. But, as Lipietz reminds us, '[a]s with Fordism, liberal-productivism fosters a use of natural resources which makes no sense, as the ecological debt which past and present generations are handing on to future generations ... will have to be paid for in the next forty years' (Lipietz 1992: 321). The main difference between the two systems lies in the increasing domination by transnational markets of national and local political actors (Gould *et al.* 1996).

In Argentina, the shift from Fordism has been shaped by political changes, economic instability, heavy debt-servicing, and the dramatic reduction of public investment in social expenditure and infrastructure. Argentina's economic reform can be divided into two periods: stagnation and instability between 1976 and 1990, and a period of macro-economic recovery and economic growth since the 1991 Convertibility Plan. During the earlier period, the abandonment of the import-substitution culture and the process of trade reform were the initial catalysts of the conditionalities imposed by the World Bank in return for trade policy loans. These resulted in increased under-utilisation of industrial plant, sizeable reductions in productivity and real wages, and growing inequality in income distribution.[1]

During the second period, which started in 1991 and is still ongoing, import liberalisation went far beyond the requirements of the inter-national financial institutions and full liberalisation became part of a wide-ranging plan to deregulate the economy. Argentina's so-called 'New Economic Model' (NEM) consists of internal and external reforms dealing with macro-economic stability, opening up of the economy, fiscal reform, privatisation and financial liberalisation, technological modernisation, and the redefinition of the role of the state. These reforms rapidly stabilised and expanded the economy, and profoundly restructured national patterns of consumption and production. Such developments brought dramatic social and environmental changes in their wake, particularly in urban areas.

Since 1991, and after a decade of economic recession, urban-based manufacturing industries (particularly food industries) have been the most dynamic sector, shifting from the domestic market to export. However, this growth has not translated into higher incomes because of the lack of growth in formal employment and lack of capital growth per worker in the informal sector.[2] The economy of small- and medium-sized cities like Mar del Plata, where most such industries are based, relies increasingly on the exploitation of natural resources, processed or raw. In order to face the difficulties posed by the opening up of the economy, activities like the fishing industry have based their international competitiveness on the 'informalisation' of processing activities, unsustainable exploitation of the natural resources on which they depend, and externalising (i.e. disregarding) the environmental costs. The national government regards current social and environmental problems as an unavoidable consequence of economic growth and stabilisation that might eventually have to be tackled through investments to clean up the environment and through social assistance for the most vulnerable groups. But the prospects for even such narrow environmental and social policies are strongly constrained by the country's low rate of national savings.[3]

This paper will argue that contemporary processes of industrial restructuring that are prompted by neo-liberal macro-economic strategies not only accelerate competition over environmental resources but also promote the short-term maximisation of profits through socially and environmentally unsustainable mechanisms. As a result, not only are local livelihoods negatively affected and environmental conditions worsened but also existing regulations governing natural resources are transformed, which introduces new struggles between local and external stakeholders. This paper will first examine the social and environmental impacts of macro-economic strategies that, obsessed with growth, often overlook these dimensions of the development process. It will then look at the reconfiguration of local stakeholders, their power relations, behaviour, and rhetoric, and the institutional arrangements that emerge when industrial expansion goes beyond the limits of nature's resilience. In short, the paper examines how the intensification of environmental conflicts within specific localities results in new forms of governance, and asks whether the new regulatory frameworks effectively confront long-term power associations or simply perpetuate relations of dependence and depletion.

The sustainability of urban development: towards an analytical framework

Many discussions of sustainability invoke the idea of a 'three ring circus', in which sustainable development (SD) is about the intersection of encompassing social, environmental, and economic goals (see Figure 1). Although this model represents a great advance on previous perspectives, it perhaps does not go far enough for two reasons. First, it says little about the trade-offs and contradictions inherent in the pursuit of economic, social, and environmental goals. Second, it provides a picture that is still too abstract to explain how the relationship between growth, development, and environment unfolds at the urban level, and how macro-economic strategies and urban social and environmental problems relate to each other.[4]

Figure 1: The 'three ring circus' model of sustainable development (SD)

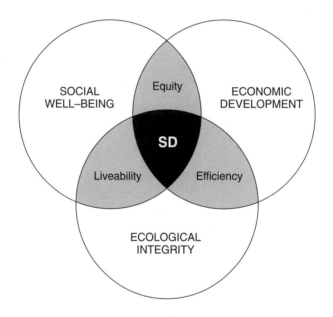

In order to assess whether contemporary processes of urban development are moving towards or away from sustainability, we must consider the way in which the concept of sustainability redefines the social, economic, environmental, and political performance of urban development. In cities, environmental performance is defined not only in terms of the use and appropriation of the natural resource base or natural capital but also in terms of the performance of the physical or built environment. Thus, assessing the sustainability of the urban development process will depend on the trends and challenges associated with the dimensions discussed below.

Economic sustainability (ES), defined as the ability of the local economy to sustain itself without causing irreversible damages to the natural resource base on which it depends, implies maximising the productivity of a local economy (urban or regional) not in absolute terms (e.g. increase of economic capital) but in relation to the sustainability of the other four dimensions and their respective capitals. In this sense, ES has to be pursued in the context of a bio-regional rationality, which ensures that a given region produces and consumes within the natural limits of its surroundings, and that it does not do this by exporting environmental degradation to other regions. Increasingly, economic globalisation is promoting competition among cities and between cities and the regions on which their production is based, and is thus reshaping urban economies. In this sense, the achievement of ES implies the need to fix a certain ceiling to the competitiveness of urban economies so that they do not improve at the expense of other areas or compromise the long-term use of their own natural resource base.

Social sustainability (SS) is defined as a set of actions and policies aimed at the improvement of quality of life, but also at the fair access and distribution of rights over the use and appropriation of the natural and built environment. SS implies the improvement of local living conditions by reducing poverty levels and increasing the satisfaction of basic needs. SS involves the consolidation of popular economic strategies, as a means of articulating the relationships between house-hold survival strategies and the strategies deployed by the public and private sectors. SS also implies addressing the regressive impacts produced by the process of economic globalisation through policies focused on reintegrating those who are marginalised by such a process.

Natural sustainability (NS) is understood as the rational management of natural resources, and of the pressures exerted by the waste produced by societies, which demands an integrated view of local, regional, national, and international development and environmental trends. Natural sustainability is linked to the potential of urban regions to extract natural resources, and the management of the productivity of these resources. In a context characterised by increasing pressures from a global economy, urban systems are less able directly or indirectly to maintain the sustainable use of their natural resources. The over-exportation of natural capital and growing inequity in the access to and distribution of rights in respect of the natural resources of a city or region increasingly compromise the sustainability of natural capital.

Physical sustainability (PS) is defined as the capacity and aptitude of the urban built environment and techno-structures to support human life and productive activities. Crises in natural and physical sustainability are strongly linked. In Argentina, rural–urban migration in the 1950s was connected with the failure of national policies to develop an intensive agriculture model and a network of agro-production services centres. Since the 1960s, the crisis of physical sustainability has been manifested in metropolitan and large medium-sized cities like Mar del Plata, through the imbalance between in-migration and the carrying capacity of these cities in terms of natural resources and technical infrastructure.

Political sustainability (PS) is understood as the democratisation and participation of the local civil society in decision-making processes. This concept refers to the sustainability of urban governance, that is, the ability of local society to use its political capital in regulating the relationship between the previous four dimensions. Again, the predominance of outside and market forces in bringing about global change is increasingly challenging this ability at the local level.

Figure 2 shows the relationship among these five dimensions of urban sustainability. While economic, social, natural, and physical sustainability are represented as four angles of the urban development process, political sustainability is represented as the governance framework regulating the performance of the other four dimensions. The circle represents the ecological capacity of the urban region to deal with the pressures of the four angles. The extent to which social, economic, natural, and physical performance is sustainable depends on whether these pressures are kept within the ecological capacity of the urban regional ecosystem.

Looking at current trends affecting urban sustainability, there is a growing polarisation between the two diagonals presented in Figure 3. On the one hand, urban sustainability is increasingly related to the processes of change governing the relationship between economic and natural performance through the 're-primarisation' of urban economies, i.e. the process by which local economies become ever more reliant on the exploitation of the resource base of their surroundings, so straining the limits of natural regeneration. On the other hand, social and physical performance are closely related in the experiences of large sectors of the urban population living in poverty and lacking adequate living conditions. This is related to the environmental conditions of urban systems as the living and working environment of a large

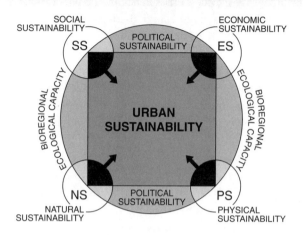

number of people and includes a specific concern for lower-income communities, which are particularly vulnerable to the negative impacts of urban development. At the same time, environmental problems affect the livelihood strategies of these communities and decrease their access to different types of assets (including access to natural resources such as land, water, energy, and so forth).

In terms of the level at which decisions are made with regard to these two critical trends, we see that the diagonal of economic and natural performance is increasingly dominated by decisions made externally, while the diagonal of social and physical performance is being shaped by the decentralisation of responsibilities and decisions from the national to the local level. Given that the decentralisation of the decisions related to these two dimensions is seldom accompanied by the resources needed to be able to respond in a meaningful fashion, this is often referred to as the 'decentralisation of the urban crisis' (Pirez 1995).

The following sections will examine the links between the decisions made at the four angles of urban sustainability and the political sustainability or governance framework that regulates their relationship.

The fishing industry in Mar del Plata

The coastal city of Mar del Plata,[5] in the province of Buenos Aires, has traditionally been the centre of national tourism and of the domestic

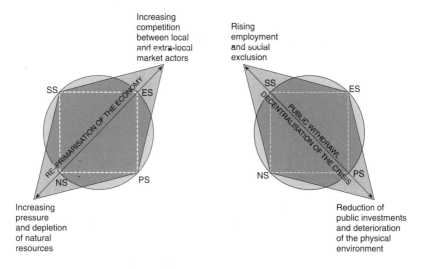

Figure 3: The impact of micro-economic strategies on urban sustainability

Increasing competition between local and extra-local market actors

Rising employment and social exclusion

Increasing pressure and depletion of natural resources

Reduction of public investments and deterioration of the physical environment

RE-PRIMARISATION OF THE ECONOMY

PUBLIC WITHDRAWL DECENTRALISATION OF THE CRISIS

fishing industry, which consists of processing fresh sea produce into frozen, canned, and fishmeal products. Both activities have been based on the city's natural comparative advantage – a long coastline with some of Argentina's best beaches, and easy access to the rich fishing grounds of the south-west Atlantic. Thus, national policies dating back to the late 1940s turned Mar del Plata into a favourite working-class holiday destination and a decade later into a dynamic industrial city, attracting thousands of migrants from the rest of the country.

Commercial fishing in Mar del Plata began in the early twentieth century with a small local market supplied by local fishermen. Towards 1915, immigrant communities contributed two essential elements to the development of maritime fishing: the incorporation of Europeans (who were traditionally fish consumers) and the settlement of people qualified in the trade. In 1922, the city's harbour was completed and the area became the working and residential centre of the Italian community.[6] Gradually, changes in technology and communications saw a shift from artisanal to industrialised production. Towards 1942, protectionist policies helped the local fishing industry to displace canned imports. National jurisdiction over the continental shelf was established in 1945, and from the 1960s the fishing industry was further promoted through various government policies and subsidies.

The introduction of the filleting process and the marketing of packaged fillets were central to the rapid industrialisation of fishing activities in the 1960s, when frozen fish displaced canned fish as the main product. Local firms were originally based on family enterprises, mostly of Italian origin, and simultaneously embraced the activities of fishing, industrialisation, and trade. The local fleet was mainly oriented to coastal fishing but local firms expanded during the 1960s and made significant investments in offshore vessels and land-based factories, where fresh fish was processed into fillets and fishmeal.[7] Thus, Mar del Plata consolidated its role as the centre of the national fishing industry.

Since then, the Argentinian hake (*Merluccius hubssi*) became the main commercial species and the focus of the local fishing industries. In 1973 the government adopted an Exclusive Economic Zone (EEZ) that extended 200 miles from the shore, establishing the exclusive right of Argentinian vessels to fish in the zone, which includes one of the world's largest continental platforms (1,164,500km^2). At the same time, national firms were encouraged to incorporate foreign factory and trawler vessels, and the fishing industry began to produce and export frozen merchandise. Despite this, production was still focused on the domestic market.

Restructuring of the fishing industry took place in two phases. The first began in 1976 with the military coup, when a dualistic approach was adopted towards the fishing sector. While the military régime reaffirmed national industrial interests and rights over the Argentine Sea, it also opened up to foreign fishing rights and investments. The second phase corresponds to the structural changes initiated in 1989 under the Menem administration and later consolidated with the 1991 Convertibility Plan. It was characterised by an aggressive attempt to insert Argentina's exports into a more competitive international economy, the liberalisation of business transactions, and the restructuring of labour relations including the 'flexibilisation' of terms and conditions. How did these two sets of structural changes affect the national and local fishing industry?

In 1976 the military régime created the Secretary of Agriculture, Cattle, Fishing, and Food (SAGPyA) and the National Institute for Research and Fishing Development (INIDEP). These institutions became the policy and scientific bodies for regulating fishing at the national level. With a view to decentralising fishing from Mar del Plata down to the southern coast of Patagonia, new policies granted special benefits to fishing exports from the latter region. In practice, this became an opportunity for foreign companies to form joint ventures with the Argentine fleet in order to gain access to the then under-exploited fishing grounds of the Argentine shelf. These new enterprises were granted special benefits, tax breaks, and rights to exploit the fishing grounds south of the 41° parallel. Hence, between 1976 and 1979 the total hake catch increased by 215 per cent, freezing and storing capacities increased by 210 per cent and 232 per cent, respectively, while fish exports rose by 220 per cent in tonnes and by 449 per cent in US dollar value (Pagani and Bertolotti 1991).

In 1982, the Falklands/Malvinas war ended with the British victory. The long-standing dispute over these islands was in fact a conflict over the adjacent fishing zone. The British government established an administrative fishing zone around the islands and granted fishing rights to foreign fleets, while Argentina signed agreements with Bulgaria and the Soviet Union over the same fishing grounds. Between 1982 and 1987 new and existing firms started to focus on the exploitation of squid in the region of Patagonia. Special support from the provincial governments saw the capacity of the region's fishing industry increase by 87 per cent. This shift was accompanied by changes in production, from the exploitation and processing of hake to other species; from national land-based factories to long-distance foreign factory ships; and from combined domestic and export-oriented enterprises to an almost exclusively export-oriented market. Figure 4 shows the close relationship between the growth of catches and exports.

Since 1991, the opening up of the economy, together with a series of changes in the regulations governing the fishing industry, led to a second transformation, which brought with it a new cadre of actors and new power relations.[8] With the expansion of fishing rights to the foreign long-range fleet and the creation of partnerships between European and national enterprises, catches doubled in a few years, leading to the collapse of the Argentine hake, until then the main commercial species.

Towards or against sustainability?

We now turn to the impact of the restructuring process on local fishing in Mar del Plata and on the development of the city.

Economic performance

The local fishing industry played a key role in the development of Mar

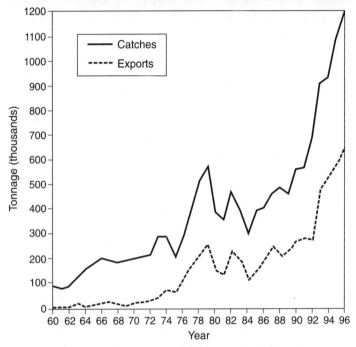

Figure 4: Evolution of fish catches and volume of exports, Argentina, 1960–1996

Tonnage (thousands)

Year

— Catches
---- Exports

Source: Based on national statistics collected by SAGPYA 1997

del Plata, generating a significant share of the urban economic output and constituting one of the main sources of employment. Over the last two decades, this sub-sector has undergone major restructuring in Argentina.[9] Despite significant changes in the number of industrial units and personnel employed over the period, in 1994 the fishing industry still accounted for 33.1 per cent of the total value of industrial production, 36.4 per cent of the total industrial employment, and 6.1 per cent of all industrial establishments.

The fluctuation in the number of fishing establishments is associated with the increasing competition of foreign fleets and firms operating in the south of the country, but also with the shift from the combined domestic and external market to almost exclusively the latter. Only 45,000 tonnes of fish was exported in 1973, compared with 270,000 tonnes in 1987. In 1996, the local fishing industry accounted for 93 per cent of total exports from the area, i.e. 12 per cent of the gross product of Mar del Plata (MGP 1997). Today, almost all the local fish production is for export, representing almost 40 per cent of national exports (Madaria 1999). Consequently, local firms have become increasingly dependent upon and exposed to fluctuations in the international market. At the time when the national market was opened to foreign capital, local firms were characterised by low productivity, low levels of diversification, and the inability to invest in new technologies in order to meet these challenges.

Between 1994 and 1995, industrial activity in the city diminished by 5 per cent and total industrial employment decreased by 3.8 per cent, one of the results of the Convertibility Plan on production previously geared to the domestic market. The fishing industry was the only sector that escaped the general economic recession, increasing its output by 13.6 per cent (Gennero de Rearte 1996). However, the dramatic drop in the number of firms and personnel employed witnessed in 1994 was never reversed. As foreign competition increased, many local companies closed down, and production became centralised in a few enterprises. Some large companies remained in business by moving to Patagonia or by forming new firms with foreign investors.

The surviving local companies continued operating with offshore trawlers and processing their catches in land-based factories. However, in order to reduce fixed production costs and to deal with the increasing competition of foreign factory vessels, these companies adopted a 'labour flexibilisation' strategy, reorganising their workers in co-operatives. Now, six large enterprises concentrate the local process of catching and trade, subcontracting most of the production processes to workers' co-operatives. Today, over 66 per cent of the industrial establishments, including the co-operatives, process fish provided by a few enterprises, and so are highly exposed to fluctuations in their demands (INIDEP 1998).

The strategy of decentralising by means of subcontracting aspects of production can be viewed as a 'renewed form of Fordism' (Lipietz 1992) whereby the firm reduces the costs of maintaining a labour force and gains the flexibility needed to respond to fluctuating demands. This in turn puts pressure on the subcontracted firms, who are forced to reduce their costs through providing more precarious working conditions. Thus, the risks of operating under increasing uncertainty are transferred towards the lowest links in the production chain. This has dramatic impacts on the organisation of production and on the relationship between capital and labour, squeezing labour and avoiding environmental regulations.

Social performance

Towards the late 1970s, the local fishing industry employed about 10,000 workers of whom almost 40 per cent were women.[10] By 1990, there were 7000 workers, and by 1992 there were only 3000.[11] By 1994, about one third of those who had lost their jobs in the larger industrial plants joined co-operatives, while the rest had become unemployed. By 1996 about 44 per cent of all workers in the fishing industry were based in co-operatives (INIDEP 1998), but the others who were made redundant in 1992 have not found work.

The organisation of the labour force into co-operatives took place over a period of four months between 1991 and 1992. The sheer speed of the process prevented workers from mounting a defence. Some workers continued working in the same factories, but lost their status as full-time salaried employees. In other cases, the workers who were made redundant formed new co-operatives, operating informally in small workshops and even households. According to the Institute for Co-operative Action (IAC), in 1999 only one third of such co-operatives were fully registered, while the rest operated in the so-called 'pseudo-co-operatives', without even the basic infrastructure required for performing their tasks safely and competitively.

Decentralising the processing phases outside the firms' legal and contractual responsibility did not respond to real principles of co-operativism, such as egalitarian organisation, collective negotiation and management of production, or equitable distribution of the benefits. In fact, the firms imposed this co-operative structure in order to avoid taxes and social contributions, as well as regulations concerning the local environment and working conditions In this way, they established a flexible contractual system, payments became directly related to productivity, and the risks inherent in a fluctuating demand were transferred to the workers. These workers lost many of the rights that had been won over decades of struggle, such as pension contributions, paid holidays, insurance, and collective bargaining. In addition, working hours became irregular, depending on the demand and availability of fish. When the demand goes up, workers will put in up to 12 hours a day, with no bonuses for working over public holidays or weekends (field survey).

The impact of this restructuring on workers needs to be examined in the light of what has happened to employment patterns over the last 20 years. Argentina has traditionally been a 'salaried society': full employment policies promoted the social integration of the working class as citizens with full social, political, and civic rights. With the dismantling of formal working conditions and the co-operativisation of the labour force in the early 1990s, the official trade union lost its 'clients' and bargaining power. A new *Unión Obrera del Pescado* (UOP) (Fishworkers' Union) emerged in the late 1990s as a parallel organisation, as did an association of women whose families were engaged in the fishing trade. The role played by these two groups in mobilising to defend the livelihoods of the local fishing community and against the depletion of hake, is discussed in the final section of this paper.

Natural performance

The national fleet had enjoyed unrestricted fishing permits that entitled vessels to fish as much as they wanted of any species. Until the 1980s, the Argentine Sea was among the few major fishing areas of the world with large unexploited potential. In the 1990s, fisheries expanded hugely and catches reached a historic maximum in 1997 at 1,341,077 tonnes (Madaria 1999). As noted earlier, the government took a schizophrenic approach to the industry, on the one hand tightening up the licensing regime, while on the other offering subsidies for the incorporation of new vessels and granting new fishing rights.[12] Within a few years, the fishing sector was over-capitalised and over-expanding: many fish stocks became fully exploited while hake became severely depleted. This process was further accelerated by an agreement signed in 1994 to promote Argentinian–European fishing joint ventures.

As discussed above, the fishing industry was focused on hake and structured around the offshore fleet and land-based processing plants for the domestic and external market. Until the mid-1980s, the offshore fleet accounted for the majority of hake landings while the factory and freezer fleet accounted for 15 per cent. The harbour of Mar del Plata had a share of 77 per cent of national catches in 1986, which declined to 35 per cent in 1993 and 31 per cent in 1998 (Madaria 1999). The lost hegemony of Mar del Plata during the restructuring process was due to the expansion of a long-range fleet of mixed and foreign companies which was established in Patagonia. Between 1991 and 1997, while the offshore fleet catches remained almost static, the long-range fleet quadrupled its catches, and almost all the total catch growth in recent years has been a direct result of the expansion of that fleet.[13]

In 1991, INIDEP warned the government that the reduction of hake biomass and high mortality levels were together rendering the hake fisheries unsustainable. Disregarding this, SAGPyA continued expanding the fishing rights over the Argentine Sea.[14] The 1994 agreement with the European Union established a total allowable catch (TAC) of 250,000 tonnes to be exploited over a period of five years by joint ventures between Argentinian and European companies or between European countries. In exchange, the newly formed companies received tax advantages to export their catches to Europe. The agreement responded to Europe's need to find new fishing grounds in order for its fishing industry to stay in business. The stated aim of the agreement was to modernise the national fleet and to diversify from hake to other species. However, under this agreement, the EU subsidised the incorporation of approximately 100 freezer trawlers, which were on average older than the national vessels they were supposed to replace, and focused on the species already over-exploited by the national fleet. In addition, the new joint ventures kept the supposedly 'replaced' vessels in operation, thus expanding the overall fleet. The fleet of freezer and factory trawlers added significantly to pressure on the fishing grounds, but generated no local jobs as all the processing was done on board.

Physical performance

The restructuring of the fishing industry brought not only negative social and natural consequences but has resulted in the deterioration of the city's environment, particularly the harbour area where the fishing activity was focused, as well as being the residential, social, and political centre of the community. Today, 85 per cent of the fishing industries are located there, taking up an area of 350 hectares (about 20 per cent of the total urban area). The area has the highest concentration of slums in the city, with 36 squatter settlements on private and public land.[15] Most of the slum-dwellers were part of the seasonal labour force of the fishing industry, but many are now without any work. In recent years, living conditions in the area have been worsened by frequent floods, due to the accumulation of industrial wastes blocking the drainage system. The area is also affected by foul-smelling emissions from fishmeal factories and by the stench of the putrid fish supplied to them.

Over the years, the harbour had affected the coastline, causing the erosion of the beaches located to the north of the city. In addition, sand accumulation in the harbour constrains the operations of the fishing fleet and demands regular dredging. During the 1960s and 1970s, there were significant public and private investments in urban infrastructure. Since the 1980s, the environmental conditions have deteriorated rapidly, both because the state has withdrawn from the administration of public utilities (through a combination of privatisation and decentralisation), and because the industries have cut costs at the expense of the environment.

During the 1980s, the state, which was historically responsible for the administration of the harbour, cut public investment in its improvement and maintenance, and announced in 1994 that the harbour would be privatised. The local government challenged this decision and, together with local fishing firms and trade unions, demanded a role for the local fishing community in the administration of the harbour. Consequently, a local consortium is now overseeing the process of privatisation. The local government views this as an opportunity to improve the infrastructure of the harbour for industrial purposes and to turn it into an international freight point in order to revitalise the local economy and the city itself. The plan includes the removal of the slums settled on public land in order to extend the regional railway system to the harbour. The proposal has been resisted by the slum-dwellers and the local government is now considering relocating the slum-dwellers to the outskirts, while it still seeks possible investors to modernise the harbour.

The restructuring process has also led to a chronic lack of private investment in maintaining facilities in the surviving industrial establishments. Added to this, fishing firms have increasingly tended to externalise their environmental costs by discharging their wastes directly into the sewage and drainage systems and also by sub-contracting parts of the production process to informal co-operatives. Wastewaters from fishing industries are rich in fats, blood, proteins, and other organic residues, and, to a lesser degree, chemicals used in cleaning the plant. Only the larger plants have primary treatment systems, and most of the co-operatives lack decanting tanks. Today, 60 per cent of the factories discharge their industrial wastewater through clandestine connections into the drainage and sewage networks or directly into the sea (INIDEP 1998). Since 1985, Mar del Plata has had a sewerage treatment station but, because of budget cuts made while it was being built, it only provides primary treatment: liquid and solid effluents are separated and then discharged directly into the sea. As a result, sea and beach pollution has also worsened during the last decade.

The fishing industry has also been associated with the recent over-exploitation of groundwater. The city's supply for domestic, industrial, and agricultural uses relies exclusively on groundwater sources. Fishing industries account for the highest consumption among industrial users. In the canning factories, water is used to wash raw materials and containers and for sterilisation processes. In the cold-storage factories the main uses are ice production, general hygiene, and fish processing. Over the years, the port has been particularly affected by the depression of groundwater levels and has suffered recurrent water shortages. Since the late 1980s, many factories have installed clandestine pumping systems to guarantee a supply of water, thus aggravating the situation. As a consequence, the wells that supply the area present a high level of salinisation (800–900mg/l) and also a high concentration of chlorites, reaching values of 6000mg/l, far above the maximum value recommended by WHO as acceptable for human consumption (700mg/l) (Allen 1999).

The body responsible for monitoring the quality of fish products is the National Secretary for the Auditing of the Food Sector (SENASA). The provincial government of Buenos Aires establishes the legal framework dealing with the control of atmospheric emissions and the municipal Parastatal Company for Water and Sanitation (OSSE), which was decentralised in 1985, regulates the emission and treatment of liquid and solid wastes. Since 1996, a new legal framework introduced by the provincial government demands the environmental auditing of all industrial activities. The municipality is responsible for enforcement while the provincial government assesses the environmental auditing reports. All fishing industries are requested to submit an environmental audit report in order to obtain a Certificate of Environmental Aptitude (CEA). In theory, no industry can operate without such a certificate. However, according to municipal records, in 1998 only 13 per cent of the fish processing plants had submitted an environmental audit report and only 10 per cent had obtained a CEA. These figures exclude the many pseudo-co-operatives and informal establishments of which the municipality has no records (field survey).

The environmental framework regulating the fishing industry has a poor level of enforcement owing to the dispersed and conflicting intervention of several agencies. The municipality has acquired a new role in the environmental management of the city, but this has squeezed its budget and institutional capacity. Within the local government, industrial monitoring and infrastructure management are still two separate spheres, just as the monitoring of fishing and processing are also regulated, respectively, by national and local bodies.

Conflicts in the aftermath of the restructuring process

The 'Fish War'

Following the collapse of hake populations, the government attempted to impose a system of closed seasons and quotas in defence of 'national interests'. The local state, firms, and workers of Mar del Plata formed a coalition, known as the Multisectoral Group, to fight the measure and demanded the expulsion of the foreign fleet. Under the leadership of the mayor of Mar del Plata, the Group included representatives of the trade unions, chambers of the national ship-owners, and land-processing factories supported by the provincial government of Buenos Aires. The mixed national-foreign capital firms responded by staking out their own claim to be part of the 'national fishing industry', and were supported in this by the regional governments of Patagonia, whose meagre economies had slightly improved through the revenues from the joint companies. Both sides were internally divided, but the proposed new management regime became the central focus of the conflict.

A new Federal Fishing Law was introduced in January 1998 with the aim of promoting the 'sustainable development of the fishing industry', defined as the preservation of natural resources, the promotion of increased value-added in fishing products, and the use of national labour. This law established a new division of powers, ratifying SAGPyA as the implementing authority and creating the Federal Fishing Council (CFP) as the main national policy-making body. Five representatives of the national government and one representative from each of the five provinces with interests in the Argentine Sea form the CFP. This was a significant change in the decision-making structure regulating the fishing industry, which shifted from being the almost exclusive responsibility of the national government to a collegiate body of stakeholders with representatives from the main fishing provinces.

In parallel with the creation of the CFP, local and provincial councils were organised in each fishing harbour and province, with representatives from the public sector, trade unions, and business chambers. These councils and the Multisectoral Group in Mar del Plata generated a new structure in the governance of the fishing activity and consolidated the alliance of local stakeholders voicing their demands before the national authorities.

The second innovation of the law was the abolition of the previous unrestricted fishing rights and the establishment of a new system of individual transferable quotas (ITQs) to be allocated to each vessel or enterprise within the maximum sustainable yield.[16] The system was to be implemented in 1999 but its enforcement was resisted by several pressure groups operating at the local, provincial, national, and international level. The main conflict was between the Multisectoral Group and the long-range fleet. One of the main fears was that the transferability of the quotas could open the possibility for the larger firms to acquire those granted to smaller companies in order to establish monopolies. The law explicitly banned the transference of fishing quotas to the freezer-factory fleet, and this was resisted by the joint ventures in Patagonia, where the majority of this fleet operated. A second concern was the strong reliance of the system on the control and regulatory capacity of the state to guarantee adherence to the quota system as well as the fulfilment of conservation measures.

While heated negotiations continued, thus preventing the implementation of the quota system, increasing uncertainty about the sustainability of hake populations resulted in a 'rush to fish', which aggravated their depletion. In response to another alarming report issued by INIDEP about the severe decline in the reproductive biomass of hake, in late April 1999 the CFP prohibited hake fishing from the beginning of June for an indefinite period. Leading the Multisectoral Group, the local government of Mar del Plata fought for the fishing quota to be allocated to the local fishing industry in order to avoid its collapse and the consequent social crisis. Over 100 vessels from Mar del Plata blocked the harbour of Buenos Aires in protest, while over 2,000 people demonstrated against the measure in front of the parliament building, demanding a Fishing Emergency Law. The protest was supported by demonstrations in other cities and received general public and media support. The draft Fishing Emergency Law established the displacement of the freezer fleet to the south of parallel 48° and outside the EEZ and postponed the enforcement of the quota system until December 1999. This was a short-term measure to defuse the conflict and gain time to negotiate the distribution of the quotas. In the meantime, the freezer fleet opposed the draft law and threatened to block the access of fuel supplies to the whole of Patagonia.

The national media gave massive coverage to the so-called 'Fish War'. The international fleet claimed that the Emergency Law curtailed their freedom and rights to operate in the country. This was supported by the Spanish government, which reacted in defence of Spanish investment. The Multisectoral Group argued for the nationalisation of the fishing industry on the grounds of defending the rights of national and local workers and enterprises to sustain their activity as stated in the National Constitution. Several environmental NGOs, including Greenpeace, demanded urgent measures to preserve the hake and the livelihoods of thousands of workers. Cedepesca, a local NGO, estimated that 5000 regular workers were to be affected by the closure of the harbour, plus a further 5000 if temporary workers and jobs indirectly related to fishing were included. The conflict was brought to a halt when a group of women from Mar del Plata disrupted a cabinet session and obtained the commitment of the president to enact the Emergency Law, granting the right to fish hake to the harbour of Mar del Plata. This took place just before the elections of October 1999, a decisive factor in inclining the final decision in favour of the local fishing industry.

However, after the approval of the Emergency Law, INIDEP revealed that there were only 50,000 tones of hake left to fish within the maximum sustainable yield (MSY). A rotating system of closed seasons was implemented to distribute the remaining TAC among the local offshore fleet. This was supposed to guarantee the regular supply of fish to the land-based processing factories and to mitigate the possibility of massive unemployment in Mar del Plata, but was insufficient to contain the crisis. The harbour of Mar del Plata experienced the highest level of inactivity in the history of the local fishing industry. Most industrial establishments worked only four months during 1999 and production was reduced to about one third of its average annual amount (field survey). The co-operatives suffered even more; many closed down and in those which survived work was down to less than eight days a month.[17]

A new local conflict arose over the distribution of the fish supply between the formal and informal processing sectors. Given that the supply of fish was controlled by the larger firms that owned the offshore fleet, the measure benefited these firms at the expense of the co-operatives and smaller establishments. Challenging the Multisectoral Group, workers went on strike demanding the regularisation of the pseudo-co-operatives, the return to a salaried regime, and measures of social containment and compensation to reduce the impact of the plants being inactive during closed seasons.

Cedepesca and the UOP fought for a monthly compensation of US$500 for the local workers. Instead, the government sent 6000 food parcels to be distributed among the worst affected workers by the trade union and the municipality. This measure was followed by violent demonstrations against the larger firms, the trade union, and the municipality; but they were ignored by the Multisectoral Group. Thus, the workers became still further marginalised.

Political performance

Table 1 summarises the changes experienced by the local fishing industry from its artisanal origins through its development in the 1960s and 1970s to its restructuring since then. Until the late 1950s, there was a balance between the four angles and decisions were made at the local level by the fishing community. During the second phase, the local fishing industry expanded at a dramatic rate but still within the limits of natural carrying capacity. The expansion of fishing fleet and land-processing plants played a key role in the local economy and had a significant impact on the generation of salaried employment and investments in infrastructure. The expansion and industrialisation of the activity was promoted by import-substitution policies and supported by national protectionist policies and subsidies. In this way, the governance of the fishing industry shifted from the local to the national sphere and was led by an alliance between capital, workers, and the state.

Following the trends presented in Figure 3 (p.19), the process of industrial restructuring transformed the economic, social, physical, and natural performance of the local fishing industry. This brought dramatic changes to the city but also to the political alignment of local, national, and international actors. Local versus national government, national versus foreign capital, formal versus informal workers, and land-based factories versus factory ships, were some of the issues of contention within and between the various parties within the coalition and its opponents. Initially, the state, firms, and workers were at one in defence of the local fishing industry but as the conflict evolved the alliance broke down. This section examines how the claims of local actors were organised around different interpretations of sustainability.

Hake populations were the only actor without a voice in this conflict. However, there were public calls to sustain the maritime ecosystems

Table 1: Evolution of the local fishing industry of Mar del Plata, Argentina

Development phases	Economic and technological changes	Social changes (livelihoods)	Natural changes	Built environment changes	Political changes
Up to1950s: Origins phase	• Artisanal fishing and processing techniques • Domestic market • Familiar organisation of production • Low added value	• Italian immigration • Establishment of the fishing community	• Low pressure on the natural resource base • Local catches within the micro-region	• Construction of the harbour • Settlement of the fishing community in the harbour area	• Local social contract regulated by cultural factors of the fishing community
1960–1970s: Consolidation and expansion phase	• Domestic and external markets • Fordist organisation • Expansion of capital investments in offshore fleet and land processing plants	• Expansion of local salaried employment • Incorporation of women in production • Access to social networks and financial capital (credit and savings)	• Increasing pressure but below MSY • Expansion of fishing area to regional grounds	• Capital-isation of the harbour • Investment in infrastructure and built environment improve-ments	• Corporatist social contract • National import-substitution policies • Unrestricted fishing rights
1980–1990s: Restructuring phase	• Shift to exports • Joint ventures with interna-tional investors • Relocation and downsizing of firms • Economic concentration • Vertical decen-tralisation of production	• Working con-ditions more precarious • Mass lay-offs • Emergence of pseudo-co-operatives • Worsening income and working conditions	• Unsustain-able • Generalised over-fishing and rush to fish • Increasing pressure over national fish-ing grounds • Depletion of hake	• Public and private dis-investment • Privatisation of the harbour • Negative impacts due to externali-sation of environmen-tal costs • Deterior-ation of local environment	• Macro-economic reforms • Breakdown of corpo-ratist social contract • With drawal of the national state • International versus local actors
Outcomes	• Increasing uncertainty • Disappear-ance of small and medium enterprises • Investments frozen due to economic and natural uncertainty	• Emergence of new disen-franchised workers and women's organisations • Increasing uncertainty • Welfarism	• Increasing natural uncertainty	• Uncertainty • Projects to improve efficiency and higher productivity of harbour • Relocation of slums	• Privatisa-tion of the sea (ITQs) • Local multi-sectorial coalition • Marginal-isation of workers' demands

made by several environmental NGOs who investigated the effects of over-fishing and informed the general public of the outcomes of similar international conflicts elsewhere. Cedepesca carried out several investigations into the illegal practices that, with the consent of national government, had allowed the expansion of the foreign fleet operating in the Argentine Sea in the 1990s and provided crucial evidence for the annulment of the agreement with the EU. NGO demands were made in defence of the sustainability of the natural resource but also of the livelihoods of the local fishworkers of Mar del Plata and other fishing harbours in Patagonia.

Firms focused on defending their economic viability and recognised this as being intimately linked to the sustainability of the hake ecosystems. In the words of the manager of one of the oldest and largest firms in the city:

> *The crisis of the fishing industry emerged because there are more fishers than fish. Someone has to leave the sea and it is only fair that the foreign fleet leaves. We have invested in this city and brought wealth to it for many years.*

When asked about the reorganisation of the labour force into co-operatives, he explains:

> *The co-operative system was the only way to reduce fixed costs to survive in an increasingly competitive system. It is unfortunate but it is the only way in which we could manage to become more flexible to the expansion and contraction of the market. The long-range fleet processes everything on board and lands its catches in foreign harbours, at least we bring work to the city, even if that is through the co-operatives.* (Fieldwork interview, December 1999)

The social dimension is thus reduced to 'sustaining a cheap and flexible labour force'. The physical dimension of sustainability is only expressed in terms of improving the efficiency of the harbour infrastructure through private investment, but is silent about environmental degradation, which is seen as another cost that has to be paid by the city in order to sustain the activity and its revenue.

The local government took as a starting point its role in managing the physical environment of the harbour and adopted a proactive approach to sustaining the natural resource base and the local fishing sector. Although invoking the rhetoric of 'saving the social capital of the city, the livelihoods of its workers, and the well-being of their families', the mayor focused on reorganising the social contract between enterprises and trade unions at the local level, using the same alliance that had been created to retain control over the harbour if it was privatised. Although the local government was in an ideal position to draw together the different dimensions of the conflict, its demands to the national government were almost exclusively focused on obtaining the maximum local benefit in how the quota system was to be allocated. It responded to social demands with reassuring rhetoric followed by weak welfarist measures, exemplified in the distribution of food to the families most critically affected by the closed seasons.

The social measures necessary to provide a meaningful response to the inevitable decline of the fishing industry were kept off the agenda. In the words of the mayor:

We need social compensatory measures for the expulsion of workers from the fishing industry but this falls to the national government. (Fieldwork interview, December 1999)

Similarly, the connections between the deterioration of environmental conditions in the harbour and the offloading of costs via the pseudo-co-operatives were not up for discussion. A senior officer from the Municipal Environmental Department explains why:

The municipality has inherited a long-term crisis and is doing its best to cover deficits in areas that lack basic infrastructure, the problem now is quantity, not quality. The port is deteriorating but at least it has basic infrastructure. We don't have the human resources to monitor efficiently who is polluting what and where, and even if we did, we would then face serious problems in enforcing the existing regulations. In a context of crisis, we cannot close down factories because they are illegally discharging blood and fat into the sewage or drainage system or even directly into the sea. We are forced to be flexible and to a certain point blind to avoid the worst consequences. (Fieldwork interview, December 1999)

Workers focused on defending their livelihoods and organised their demands outside the corporatist regime of the trade unions. They did not simply focus on improved incomes but on a more structural defence of rights as citizens and workers. Miguel, who worked in the fishing industry for 20 years, explains the motives behind their mobilisation:

We don't fight for a simple pay-rise. We don't want to bring bread to our families today and misery tomorrow. We don't want boxes of food.

We fight to make sure that the fishing grounds are sustained in the long
term and not just for the benefit of a few local and foreign companies.
We fight to abolish the perverse regime of the co-operatives and to regain
our rights. Ironically, we seem to be responsible for polluting the water
we drink, but we are forced to do so on behalf of those who get richer
on the back of our work and suffering. (Fieldwork interview,
December 1999)

This statement shows the position of citizens and workers with regard
to the social, economic, natural, and physical changes brought about
by the restructuring process. A clear connection is established between
these dimensions and also in relationship to how these changes are
managed.

Looking at the different claims, it is possible to understand the
rationale behind the coalitions and conflicts at the local level. It is also
possible to see that certain issues, such as the impacts on the
livelihoods of the fishing community and the deterioration of the
physical environment and habitat of the harbour, were marginalised in
the attempts to seek a political response to the conflict. Local actors
were polarised in their demands and were in fact fighting against
external actors in the economic–natural sustainability diagonal. In
doing so, they surrendered to the same logic that they were trying to
fight, the dominance of economic considerations over social, natural,
and physical ones.

Concluding remarks

The state was essential to the development of the local fishing industry,
as it guaranteed a monopoly over access to fish resources and protected
the domestic market through special regimes and subsidies. However,
in the 1970s this model faced a crisis, partly due to the penetration of
Argentina's domestic market by cheaper imports. In addition, there
was increasing competition among countries to attract international
investments on the basis of low salaries and free access to natural
resources. In this context, firms and governments tried to overcome
the 'rigidities' of the Fordist model through decentralising production
processes via subcontracted firms and the offloading of risks.

The social implications of this approach can be seen in the
reorganisation of the relationship between capital and labour under the
façade of the 'co-operative system'. Firms gained flexibility at the
expense of workers' stability and worsening environmental conditions.

Furthermore, most workers became disenfranchised and lost their legal protection and traditional mechanisms for collective action. The rationale behind this process was based on a static, zero-sum understanding of the relationship between economic interests and political institutions, promoted by the Menem administration. The assumption was that high wages, state-enforced controls over production, and rigidities in labour deployment constituted significant barriers to internal capital accumulation.

The process of industrial restructuring not only reinforced social inequalities but also exacerbated the depletion of the natural resources upon which the fishing industry as a whole relies. Increasing competition over the local and regional fisheries resulted in a crisis that became evident for all to see with the collapse of hake fisheries in the late 1990s. This turned the conflict into an environmental one, in that all sectors (state, private industry, and labour) became engaged in the search for ways to sustain the fishing grounds, although with rather different interpretations of what needed to be done.

In 1999, the governance of fishing resources became the subject of intense conflict and uncertainty owing to the depletion of hake, disagreements about a new fishing régime, and national elections. The future of the fishing industry and of the many who depended on it was trapped into a debate that was determined by sectoral interests in which the government failed to establish limits to avoid further depletion of the fishing resources. The introduction of a system based on the distribution of ITQs brought with it inevitable conflicts. This initiative opened the debate about the need for a long-term policy framework to guarantee the sustainable management of the fishing industry. However, this was not accompanied by measures to reduce or offset the social and economic impacts of a reduction in fishing, which left the industry with no certain future. Political decisions were torn between conserving fishing resources and maintaining policies to favour free trade, foreign investment, and export-led economic growth.

The fishing industry in Argentina was traditionally ruled by a coalition between the state, corporate capital, and labour organisations. Their interests were bound by the pursuit of continuous economic expansion and based on the assumption that the supply of natural resources was infinitely elastic. Hence, environmental considerations were marginal, and were felt only in a weak and centralised fisheries management régime, in which the preservation of fishing grounds lost out to the possibility of more catches. It was only with the advent of the hake crisis that most sectors became aware of the effect of over ten years of uncontrolled expansion. Not only did the traditional alliance between national capital and the state break down, but also new locally based coalitions were forged, shifting their claims from economic to environmental and social arguments. The local government of Mar del Plata took forward these claims at the national level through mechanisms such as public hearings and demonstrations, with overwhelming support from civil society. The Multisectoral Group that was formed in reaction to the crisis succeeded in taking a proactive approach, playing a key role in drafting new legislation and establishing a decentralised régime to discuss the future of the fishing industry. Two significant changes accompanied this process; first, alliances split between local and external actors, and, second, there were further splits between the local government, firms, and workers. The national government was trapped between these two constituencies and finally forced to prioritise local claims. But the workers' demands were marginalised in the process and subordinated to the corporatist coalition of local trade unions, firms, and the local government. It could be argued that the social and environmental claims put forward by the Multisectoral Group were something of a tokenistic fight against the increasing participation of foreign capital in the development of the fishing industry.

Unfortunately, local reactions were too late and too polarised to offset the consequences of the crisis. The local industry reaffirmed its exclusive rights over the fisheries at a time when the collapse of hake had already taken place. With little fish left for the local plants to process, the industry continues to decline and workers are still being laid off. The case of Mar del Plata's fishing industry could be the tale of many cities in the South. Increasingly, restructuring processes are leading to over-exploitation of certain areas and natural resources, leaving local firms and workers in a highly vulnerable position as they attempt to cope with the aftermath of environmental, social, and economic collapse.

Acknowledgement

This paper draws largely on the author's doctoral dissertation entitled 'Environmental conflicts and industrial governance in a time of economic restructuring. The case of the fishing industry in the city of Mar del Plata, Argentina'.

Notes

1   In the 1980s, per capita income fell dramatically and per capita investment levels fell by 70 per cent. Between 1949 and 1974, inflation averaged an annual 27 per cent. From 1975 until 1988, the annual average totalled 227 per cent and there had been two hyper-inflationary surges by 1991 (López Murphy 1996). The labour market also worsened significantly. In the 1980s, there was a strong trend towards increasing unemployment, the growth of micro-enterprises and informal activities, and a general drop in salaries and increased labour instability. A wider sector of the population was negatively affected by adjustment policies, and by the regressive impact of inflation on income distribution and on the country's economic activity (Beccaria and López 1996). Poverty became widespread and intense, as many middle- and lower-middle-class households experienced a significant reduction in their incomes.

2   Between 1980 and 1990, per capita income declined 11 per cent, the minimum salary dropped by 33 per cent, and urban unemployment increased from 3 per cent to 8 per cent. Non-agricultural employment in the informal sector grew from 39.4 per cent in 1980 to 49.61 per cent in 1992, while employment in large private firms decreased from 41.8 per cent in 1980 to 32.7 per cent in 1992. Incomes in the informal sector declined by 42 per cent and industrial salaries declined by 6 per cent (PREALC 1992).

3   Between 1991 and 1993 the accumulated deficit in the current account reached US$21.4 billion. If the funds used for accumulating international reserves are added, the total demand for foreign finance was US$29.5 billion.

4   The contradictory approaches that led the debate on environment, growth, and development over the previous decades were not overcome but rather intensified as SD came to the fore. The 1992 UNCED conference was a clear example of the political tensions that increasingly dominate the North–South debate. Since then, bottom-up initiatives in implementing Local Agenda 21 have spread, while multinational corporations have lobbied to add 'sustained economic growth' as a leading principle to SD. Progress in assessing and implementing the principles of SD is hampered by disagreements about the basic terms of reference.

5   The city of Mar del Plata has a resident population of 600,000, which rises to 1,500,000 in the tourist season.

6   In 1925, the city boasted about 140 steamships and 80 sailing boats, whose catches reached 12,000 tonnes (of the 16,000 tonnes for Argentina as a whole). This was entirely for the domestic market and the population of Buenos Aires City alone consumed half of it (Alvarez and Reynoso 1991).

7   In the 1960s, the development of the fishing fleet was based on the incorporation of offshore vessels built in the country as well as imported from abroad. In 1962, the national government supported the construction of 30 offshore fishing vessels financed by the Argentinian Industrial Bank. Legal reforms were incorporated to subsidise national shipyards and a tariff licence was introduced to import vessels (Alomar 1973).

8 Under other general economic regulations the rights of foreign and national investors merged, allowing freedom to establish anywhere in the country and to repatriate capital and utilities. The tax regimes for national and foreign companies were also similar, allowing the latter to create subsidiary branches in the country or joint ventures with Argentine or other foreign firms. A new mechanism established the regime of 'local enterprises of foreign capital', by which foreign firms could operate in the country through new companies in which they owned over 49 per cent of the capital (Madaria 1999).

9 In 1974, local production was shared by 30 large enterprises and 103 small and medium enterprises, which followed a Fordist production model. By 1989, the number of total industrial units operating in Mar del Plata had suffered a dramatic reduction as the recession had reduced the domestic and external markets. At that time many local companies suffered a debt and liquidity crisis, with huge stocks of inventory which they could not sell. This crisis was associated with the removal of national protection tariffs that enhanced the competitiveness of foreign products and caused a rise in imports. The fishing industry was the only industrial sector that survived this crisis without a massive reduction in the number of firms or employees.

10 Since the 1970s, women have had a significant role in the local fishing industry, particularly in processing activities such as canning and filleting. In 1996, over one third of the total number of workers in industry were women but they represented only 20 per cent of the workers organised in co-operatives (INIDEP 1998).

11 Records of the Fish Industry Workers' Union (*Sindicato Obrero de la Industria del Pescado* SOIP) 1995.

12 In the early 1990s, the legislature established that the fishing resources under Argentinian maritime jurisdiction were to be exclusively exploited by national flagged vessels authorised by the competent authority. Since then, fishing rights have been granted on the basis of individual fishing projects to be assessed by SAGPyA. The approval of each application depended upon the technical capacity of the applicant and could only be granted within the limits of the maximum sustainable yield (MSY) defined by INIDEP. Although fishing rights were granted to individual vessels and firms, they could be transferred to other companies.

13 The offshore fleet of Mar del Plata operates in the fishing grounds north of parallel 41°S, while the long-range fleets operate both north and south of parallel 41°.

14 In addition to the agreement with the EU, several resolutions from SAGPyA allowed national ship-owners to hire foreign vessels for the fishing of squid over a period of three years. Out of the nearly 200,000 tonnes of squid catches in 1995, half corresponded to the 71 foreign vessels incorporated under this provision. The accidental by-catch of hake by these vessels also contributed to the increasing pressure on the species (Godelman *et al.* 1999).

15 The settlements on private land alone account for 3209 inhabitants (Fernández 1996).

16 Fishing quotas were to be granted according to five criteria: the average catch of each enterprise between 1989 and 1996, the number of personnel employed, the investment already

made, the volume of production, and the record of previous offences committed by each company. The Law also established the right of the CFP to reserve and grant part of the annual quota to cases of 'social interest', as a mechanism to ameliorate the socially regressive impact of the system on the most vulnerable groups.

17 María, a 40-year-old woman with two sons, who worked with her husband in the fishing industry for 17 years, explains the situation affecting thousands of local workers:

We were not rich but nor were we poor. We worked hard but the effort was worth it. Over the years, we managed to build our own house and to send the kids to school. When the fishing seasons were bad, it was easy to obtain credit, nobody denied it to a worker from the fishing industry, now they laugh at you...I leave the house at 4 am ... at that time you can see hundreds of men and women walking around the port and checking one co-operative after another to see if there is any work. We have to walk because we cannot afford the cost of bus fares any more. Sometimes we don't get a table [to fillet] in the whole week, if we are lucky we work one or two days per week ... the rest of the time we just walk. My husband stopped seeking work because he is 50 and the plants only want young people. He does bits and pieces in construction, but with the fishing industry in crisis there is not much work in the city. (Fieldwork interview, December 1999)

References

Allen, Adriana (1999) 'Sustentabilidad productiva: ajuste político-económico estructural y efectos ambientales. El caso de la industria pesquera marplatense', in Fernández et al. (eds) *Territorio, Sociedad y Desarrollo Sustentable. Estudios de Sustentabilidad Urbana*, Buenos Aires: Editorial Espacio

Alomar, J. (1973) *El Crédito para Inversiones Privadas. La Pesca Comercial en Argentina*, Buenos Aires: Fundación de Estudios Marítimos

Alvarez, Adriana and Daniel Reynoso (1991) 'Las actividades económicas', in Alvarez et al. (eds) *Mar del Plata: Una Historia Urbana*, Mar del Plata: Fundación Banco de Boston

Beccaria, Luís and Nestor López (eds) (1996) *Sin Trabajo. Las Características del Desempleo y sus Efectos en la Sociedad Argentina*, Buenos Aires: UNICEF/LOSADA

Burgess, Rod, Marisa Carmona, and Theo Kolstee (eds) (1997) *The Challenge of Sustainable Cities. Neo-liberalism and Urban Strategies in Developing Countries*, London: Zed Books

Fernández, Roberto (ed.) (1996) *Habitat Mar del Plata. Problemática de Vivienda, Tierra y Desarrollo Urbano de Mar del Plata. Diagnóstico y Propuestas*, Mar del Plata: Programa ARRAIGO/Universidad Nacional de Mar del Plata

Gennero de Rearte, Ana (1996) 'Dinámica del Crecimiento de la Industria Local', unpublished report, Mar del Plata: Facultad de Ciencias Económicas y Sociales, Universidad Nacional de Mar del Plata

Godelman, Ernesto, Claudia Bruno, Eduardo Tamargo, Gonzalo Pidal and Fabián Gonzáles (1999) 'La política de subsidios pesqueros de la Unión Europea', *Comunidad Pesquera*, December

Gould, Kenneth, Allan Scnaiberg, and Adam Weinberg (1996) *Local Environmental Struggles: Citizen Activism in the Treadmill of Production*, Cambridge: Cambridge University Press

Instituto Nacional de Investigaciones para el Desarrollo Pesquero (INIDEP) (1998) 'Resultados Preliminares del Censo Nacional Industrial Pesquero 1996', unpublished report, Mar del Plata: INIDEP

Lipietz, Alan (1992) *Towards a New Economic Order: Post-Fordism, Ecology and Democracy*, Oxford: Oxford University Press

López Murphy, Raúl (1996) 'The feasibility of sustaining economic reform in Argentina 1995–2000', paper presented at ILAS conference 'Argentina Towards the 21st Century: Challenges Facing the Second Menem Administration', Institute of Latin American Studies, London, 1–2 February

Madaria, Edgardo (ed.) (1999) 'El Sector Pesquero Argentino', unpublished report, Buenos Aires: Escuela de Ciencias Politicas, UCA

Municipalidad de General Pueyrredon (MGP) (1997) *Mar del Plata en Cifras*, Mar del Plata: MGP

Pagani, Andrea and María Isabel Bertolotti (1991) 'La actividad industrial pesquera: análisis intercensal 1982–1987. Capacidades de producción por regiones y evolución de la incorporación tecnológica', in *Proceedings del V Simposio Científico de la Comisión Técnica Mixta del Frente Marítimo*, Montevideo (Uruguay), 7–8 December 1989, Vol. 9

Pirez, Pedro (1995) 'Actores Sociales y Gestión de la Ciudad', *Ciudades* special issue, October–December, Mexico DF: RNIU

PREALC (1992) 'Empleo y Transformación Productiva', Working Paper No. 369, Santiago de Chile: OIT-PREALC

Institutional innovations for urban infrastructural development: the Indian scenario

Amitabh Kundu

The processes of structural adjustment and decentralised governance in India are expected to generate rapid industrial and infrastructural development. Although the negative impacts of this policy package, launched in the early 1990s, are noticeable in the slowing of public investment and in reduced access to basic amenities for large sections of the population, its proponents believe that these are transitory. They believe that efficient and accountable governance will be the driving force behind the provision of more and better economic infrastructure and basic amenities. The public sector organisations that failed to provide these services in a cost-effective manner have instead blocked enormous capital resources of the state without yielding adequate returns. These, along with other parastatal agencies such as the Development Authorities, were created in the post-Independence period. They had taken over many of the functions of local bodies, and must, therefore, be dismantled.

The government and the Reserve Bank of India have already imposed a degree of 'financial discipline' on these agencies, forcing them to generate resources internally, borrow at high interest rates from development-cum-banking institutions, or raise funds in the capital markets. This has restricted the scope, if not the volume, of their activities. At the same time, financial sector reforms that loosen the directed credit system have brought about a decline in mandatory investments in social infrastructure by financial institutions. Further, many of the infrastructural services are gradually being transferred to private agencies or managed on commercial lines. A more complete remedial package is being urged on India by the World Bank. It includes reducing public sector intervention, ensuring appropriate prices for infrastructure and urban amenities by eliminating or reducing subsidies, developing capital markets for resource mobilisation, facilitating private and joint sector projects, simplifying legislative processes to promote optimal land use and location of economic activities, and so on (World Bank 1995, 1998; Expert Group on Commercialisation of Infrastructure 1996). Solutions are also being found in terms of transparent management of urban projects and innovative institutional arrangements.

With the passage of the 74th Amendment to the Indian Constitution (Ministry of Urban Development 1992) and corresponding legislation, amendments, ordinances, etc. at the state level, decentralisation has become the keyword in governance. People at municipal, district, and metropolitan region level should now be able to formulate programmes and schemes for meeting their own developmental and infrastructural needs, something that is impossible in a centralised regime. This, along with opening up of the capital markets, is expected to promote economic activity and better provision of basic services in urban centres.

The basis for this optimism, however, has not been examined empirically. This paper seeks to analyse initiatives that substantially affect the functioning of urban local bodies. It will first examine the efficacy and implications of the new system of maintaining municipal budgets in the context of devolving funds from state-level agencies.[1] This is followed by a discussion of the problems and possibilities of rating credit-worthiness of local bodies so that they may tap resources for investment in infrastructure, and by an examination of the implications of the Amendment Act for enabling the municipal bodies to undertake responsibility for development planning. The following section discusses the recent initiatives by these bodies to assign contracts to private agencies for the provision of basic services. An explanation for the limited success of the much-heralded slum networking projects is followed by an analysis of innovative systems adopted at the local level for mobilising resources from capital markets and institutional sources as well as the conditionalities imposed by lending agencies and financial intermediaries. The key question throughout is whether the proposed modifications will help to de-bureaucratise the local bodies, inject efficiency into their functioning, and improve accessibility of poor people to infrastructure and basic amenities. The final section summarises the results and conclusions, and reviews the validity of the development perspective behind the proposed solutions.

The new system of maintaining municipal budgets and devolution of state funds based on performance

Until recently, state governments supported local bodies in their budgetary expenditures through a gap-filling approach. This has been criticised for making the local bodies lax in resource mobilisation, tax collection, and efficiency, and in the era of globalisation, this policy is being discarded. The new approach is to promote infrastructural and industrial investment in cities and towns that can cover its own costs. The task for the national government is to create an institutional and legal structure that enables the 'most deserving cities' to access resources. Methodologies have been developed to determine worthiness based on 'objective measures' of local government performance, not merely when local bodies are seeking resources in terms of loans from national and international organisations or from bond offerings but also via transfers from the State Finance Commissions.

Unfortunately, there are serious conceptual and operational problems in establishing performance indicators using the budgetary data of municipal bodies and other local agencies. Most local bodies use a cash-flow-based single-entry accounting system. They are neither required to adhere to agreed accounting standards nor to be externally audited.[2] Further, as the concepts and categories used in the budgets and their coverage vary widely, identical ratios obtained for different organisations do not imply the same situation. Comparison of the indicators between municipalities would not, therefore, make much sense unless these concepts were standardised.

This lack of comparability can be found across several of the most important categories of municipal accounts, including capital earnings and expenditures (Narayanan 2000), current earnings and expenditures (NIPFP 1995), and earnings from assets. The Municipal Corporation of Delhi admits for 1996 that 'since compilation of arrears of property tax is a time-consuming process, exact figures can not be indicated' (MCD 1997).

What is urgently required, therefore, is that the definitions and coverage of the concepts be standardised, and that unambiguous indicators be established for the purpose of temporal and cross-sectoral comparison. However, the only clear-cut prescription to local bodies to assist them in garnering support from a large number of financial agencies has been to segregate the earnings and expenditure for different sectors and maintain separate accounts. This is often put forward as a prerequisite for cities wanting to mobilise funds from international sources or capital markets (domestic or international). The Indo-US Financial Institutions Reform and Expansion (FIRE) Project in India, for example, proposes that the Pune Municipal Corporation establish separate accounts not merely for capital and current expenditures but also for different sets of sectors (Mehta and Satyanarayana 1996). With accounts segregated this way, selected sectors may be pooled to create 'cost centres'. Proponents of such measures would then impose or enhance user charges and restrict intersectoral transfers, thus making certain economically viable sectors independent of the general municipal budget. It is argued that this would go a long way towards attracting capital investments.

The Mumbai Municipal Corporation agreed to such an arrangement as a precondition for obtaining a World Bank loan to improve its water supply and sewerage facilities. It now maintains accounts for these sectors on an accrual basis while its other budgets are maintained separately. There are cases where receiving a small loan from an international or national agency has constrained city governments from cross-subsidising 'economically unattractive' sectors or areas.

Credit rating of local bodies for market borrowing: the need for a development perspective

One significant development in the context of investment in infrastructure and amenities in India is the emergence of credit-rating institutions. As the financial markets become global and competitive and the borrowers' base more diversified, investors and regulators increasingly turn to credit-rating institutions when making their decisions. The rating of the debt instruments of corporate bodies and municipal enterprises is currently being carried out by institutions like the Information and Credit Rating Agency of India (ICRA), Credit Analysis and Research (CARE), and Credit Rating Information Services of India Limited (CRISIL). By the end of 1999, 20 cities and urban authorities had already been rated by these agencies and the cases of another 15 were being processed.

CRISIL, which has received technical support from USAID under the Indo-US FIRE (D) project for the development of methodology for credit rating, first assesses the feasibility of the proposed project(s). It then rates the debt instruments on the basis of historical trends and projections of the borrower's (a) current earnings and expenditures, (b) debts and savings profile, and (c) economic and social profile of the area governed by the entity.

Unfortunately, the indicators selected for these three dimensions and the weights assigned to them have neither been precisely defined nor made adequately transparent Indeed, difficulties arise in applying indicators to these dimensions, as they are subject to manipulation in budget or other policy documents by urban local bodies (ULBs) aspiring to raise resources from the capital market. Even the quantitative indicators considered by CRISIL when rating the urban local bodies– e.g. tax and non-tax receipts as percentages of total revenue, grants from state governments as percentage of revenues, total revenue deficit and overall deficit, debt-service coverage ratio, expenditure on core services and on wages and salaries as a percentage of total expenditure – have elements of subjectivity because budgetary information is compiled differently by different municipalities (Kundu *et al.* 1999).

More important than the data problem is the choice of development perspective. Any rating agency would have problems in deciding whether to go by financial performance indicators like total revenue or tax revenue (in per capita terms) or to build appropriate indicators to reflect medium- or long-term efficiency of management *and the economic strength of the service area*. One can possibly justify the former on the grounds that to service debts, what is needed is high income, irrespective of its source or managerial efficiency. However, if the agency wants to support projects that may have debt repayment problems in the short run but are likely to succeed over time, it would consider the level of managerial efficiency, structure of governance, or the long-term economic base. In such cases, the agency would use a different set of indicators. These might pertain to provisions in state legislation regarding decentralisation, stability of the government in the city and the state, per capita income of the population, level of industrial and commercial activity etc., all of which have a direct bearing on the prospect of increasing tax and non-tax earnings of the municipal body in the long run.

A review of the analyses done by CRISIL (e.g. CRISIL 1996) suggests that it has indeed not based its rating on a few quantitative indicators alone but on a host of other factors, including those pertaining to policy perspectives at the city and state level that are not easily measurable. The only problem here is that it has not specified all the factors or the procedures by which these qualitative dimensions enter the credit-rating framework and are aggregated with the quantitative dimensions.

Besides providing initial bond rating, the rating agencies also monitor the capacity of the issuer to make timely payments of principal and interest, throughout the term of the bond, and may upgrade or downgrade the rating on this basis. The continued monitoring of ULBs by a rating agency, which has been considered crucial for the 'effective operation of the secondary bond market', besides being a financial burden, may impose restrictions on the ULBs' functioning, particularly in undertaking activities to meet social obligations that do not have immediate financial return.[3]

Assigning planning responsibilities to local bodies

The 74th Constitutional Amendment has been hailed in India as a landmark in transferring powers to and creating an enabling environment for local bodies *to undertake planning and development responsibility.* The problem is that the local bodies are simply *not* yet equipped to take up such responsibilities, especially for capital projects (Joshi 1996). Indeed, considerable expertise is required to identify the infrastructural and industrial projects appropriate for the growth of a city or town, assess their environmental implications, and mobilise resources for them. Given their difficult financial situation, it is unlikely that these bodies will be able to strengthen their planning departments by recruiting technical and professional personnel in the immediate future. State government departments face similar constraints and are unlikely to be able to provide the technical assistance needed.

Instead, local bodies are resorting to the financial intermediaries and credit-rating agencies that have recently emerged with assistance from certain international organisations, as mentioned above. The principal concerns of these agencies and also of the companies likely to provide the finance are reflected in the preparation of the project. These include commitments by the borrowing agency to ensure cost recovery, legal and administrative restructuring for attracting private participation, etc.. Understandably, the 'investments which are clearly linked to enhanced revenues, are preferred' (Indo-US FIRE Project 1998a). The criteria proposed by the agencies thus impose financial perspectives and discipline on the local bodies that may not promote integrated development of the city or regional economy.

Assigning the responsibility of planning to local bodies does not automatically enable them to prepare projects based on a development perspective for the town or region. Preparing a long-term integrated plan to answer the needs and aspirations of local people in different social and income brackets and then breaking it down to a set of meaningful projects, is a different exercise from that of identifying projects with high credit rating that would attract corporate investment. In an era when obtaining funds for investment from the private sector or capital markets has become the critical factor, it is not surprising that the exercise of preparing master plans has been thoroughly discredited (Joshi 1996).

Given this emerging scenario, the option of going for project preparation in formal or informal consultation with interested companies or the 'stakeholders', and with the financial institutions acting as intermediaries, seems to be an easy way out. Indeed, local governments in large cities have found this hard to resist.

Management contracts for services to be provided by private agencies

Deficiencies in infrastructure and basic amenities in India have reached alarming proportions with the decline in investment and financial support from the central and state governments to local bodies and the limited capacity of the latter to replace them with resources of their own (see Chakrabarti in this volume). This is forcing ULBs to work out alternative institutional arrangements to bridge the gap. Private sector participation in management of municipal services is one such arrangement. Different forms of participation have been designed with varying levels of responsibility and cost sharing between private and public agencies. The most common form is contracting out management of one or a set of services by the municipal bodies to private companies. This is expected to reduce substantially the costs incurred by local authorities and, at the same time, open up business opportunities for the private sector. A crucial concern for government is then to ensure that subcontracting does not lead to the dilution of social responsibility and exclusion of poor people and vulnerable sections from the formal delivery system.

This requires new regulatory and supervisory arrangements for monitoring and enforcing agreements with private or joint-sector companies. Establishing and effectively implementing these is no small challenge, as it is well known that, under the old system of state control, public agencies failed to meet a broad range of social objectives, including catering to the needs of poor people. Many of the same state agencies are now being called upon to design and implement regulatory controls in a liberalised régime in which resources and responsibilities are more widely dispersed and less subject to direct control than before. Along with many other developing countries, India is receiving assistance from international agencies to lay a foundation for participatory management practices, including, for example, drawing up terms and conditions of contracts, increasing community participation in management, facilitating contacts with prospective enterprise partners and, often, negotiating contracts on behalf of local bodies.

Tables 1 and 2 list some of the cities that have entered into management contracts for provision of basic services. While not exhaustive, these illustrate the different sectors and management forms involving the private agencies that have gained currency in the past decade. The relatively recent nature of this phenomenon prevents systematic assessment of the costs and benefits of this form of privatisation. Reliable data on revenue and expenditure of local bodies before and after the subcontracting arrangement are not yet available. The same applies to the number of companies engaged in the provision of services and their profit levels. Even if such data were available, the ability of local bodies to reduce their financial burden through privatisation of services is in itself no indication of success of the arrangement. Such a judgement is possible only after the quality of the services and, more importantly, the extent to which these reach the urban poor, are known. No systematic data are available yet which cover these aspects at national, state, or local level. These would have to be obtained through field surveys at the micro level, and it gives cause for concern that such studies have yet to be conducted.

Existing studies on contractual agreements, progress reports, and other official documents reveal that there have been problems even at the level of the working arrangements and norms for day-to-day functioning. This is understandable because India does not have much experience in public–private partnerships at the municipal and sub-municipal levels. Many arrangements fell into serious difficulties after the formal launch of the projects. In Vadodara, for example, the arrangement with a private company to make fuel pellets from waste turned out to be uneconomic for the company because the waste it purchased from the municipal corporation had to be collected from sites that were too geographically dispersed. When the two parties could not agree on an alternative collection scheme, the company closed the operation. Similar difficulties have been encountered elsewhere.

Table 1: Management contracts for services in Indian cities in 1993

Services/tasks	Cities
Sanitation and public health:	
• Conservancy; drain cleaning; sanitation; maintenance of sewage treatment plant	Guwahati, Banglore, Jodhpur, Navi Mumbai, Ludhiana
• Construction and maintenance of toilets	Faridabad, Delhi, Hubli-Dharwad, Aurangabad, Kalyan, Jaipur, Cochi
Solid waste management:	
• Garbage collection and disposal; street cleaning	Guwahati, Ahmedabad, Rajkot, Baroda, Banglore, Cochi, Mumbai, Pune, Jalandhar, Amtritsar, Ludhiana, Jaipur
• Compost plant; solid waste conversion	Vadodara, Kalyan
Roads and streets:	
• Road construction	Ahmedabad, Cochi
• Road maintenance	Banglore, Cochi, Jaipur
• Street lighting	Ranchi, Rajkot, Faridabad, Jodhpur, Navi Mumbai
Water supply:	
• Maintenance of water supply system	Navi Mumbai
Tax collection etc.:	
• Collection of entry tax; other local taxes and charges	Guwahati, Navi Mumbai
• Parking lots and collection of charges	Guwahati, Pune
Gardens and parks etc.:	
• Development and maintenance of garden parks, playgrounds, sports centres, swimming pools, planetaria, traffic islands	Rajkot, Baroda, Bombay, Faridabad, Hubli-Dharwad, Banglore, Cochin, Ranchi, Aurangabad, Navi Mumbai, Kalyan, Pune, Amritsar, Ludhiana, Jalandhar, Jaipur
Social forestry, tree planting:	Baroda, Rajkot
Other:	
• Bus stations and shelters	Ranchi, Cochi
• Ward security	Ahmedabad, Rajkot
• Market development	Ahmedabad, Kalyan
• Maintenance of vehicles	Rajkot
• Land development	Faridabad
• Provision of libraries etc.	Faridabad
• Milk market	Hubli-Dharwad

Source: Meera Mehta (1993)

Table 2: Partnership in urban services and infrastructure: selected examples		
City	**Service/facility**	**Form of partnership**
Nasik	*Octroi* post	Auction
Panvel	By-pass	Turnkey
Pune	Solid waste (resource recovery)	BOT (Build-Operate-Transfer)
Jaisingpur	By-pass	Franchise
Baroda	Solid waste	BOT (co-operative society)
Chennai	Solid waste	NGO industry (Exnora)
Chennai	Waste water recycling	Private company
Tiruppur	Water supply	Private company
Hyderabad	Light rail transit system	Joint stock company
Vishakhapatnam	Water supply	Large private financing
Indore (Rau)	Link road (Rau Pittampura)	BOT
Delhi-Noida	Link bridge transport	BOT (privatisation of routes)

Source: NIUA (1997)

Solid waste management is one service where local bodies have shown great interest in involving the private sector. The method of collection often involves participation of citizens' groups and NGOs. Indeed, success stories from a number of cities suggest that many urban residents are willing to invest time and money in an improved system of garbage disposal. Evidence to date does not indicate, however, that the provision of basic amenities to poor areas or households increases after a private company assumes the responsibility. And, indeed, institutional and legal structures obliging companies to maintain the same level of commitment to poor people as that offered by municipal bodies have yet to be proposed or established.

Evidence from several states suggests that the progressive transfer of responsibility from state governments to the unprepared ULBs for infrastructure development and other capital projects such as for sewerage and garbage disposal, is being passed on quickly to enterprises through contractual agreements. Even in cities where innovative projects have been developed in these areas (for example the Slum Networking Project in Indore, described below), solid wast disposal coverage is less than 50 per cent. In situations such as these, excluded groups are unable to raise their voices or complain to the municipal body, as the latter tell them to take their complaints directly to the service provider. This has led to the fragmentation of responsibility and of the service-delivery system, with marginalised areas and people remaining under-serviced or unserviced. As a consequence, the risk of periodic epidemics touches the entire urban community.

It is difficult to assess the improvement or deterioration in the quality of the services in cities where subcontracting arrangements are in force. Nonetheless, the declining numbers of sanitation workers employed by the contracted agency should cast doubt on claims to improve services. Pre-subcontracting levels were already below the norms recommended by the Committee on Solid Waste. A survey conducted by National Institute of Urban Affairs (NIUA 1997) estimates the shortfall to be as high as 50 per cent. Yet, in most cases, after the subcontracting arrangement was launched levels fell still further. In a few cities, such as Pune, the number of sanitation workers is at 25 per cent of the recommended level. Even if residents assume some of this burden, it is clear that assessing and controlling the standards of services provided by these agencies would be extremely difficult unless the local community is actively engaged in the implementation process and unless strict norms of functioning evolve over time.

Involving community in infrastructure development and provision of services

Community participation gained currency as a component of development strategies in the 1980s as a consequence of the failure of public agencies to reverse worsening trends in the provision of basic amenities. It was argued that the community could help not only in social mobilisation but also in raising the financial resources that the local authorities needed badly. In many cases, it became possible to reduce project costs substantially if the prospective beneficiaries provided their labour free or at below market wage rates. Further, the pressure of peer groups under participatory arrangements resulted in better monitoring, more productive engagement of the beneficiaries in the project, and better recovery of development loans to individuals.

Today, community participation in urban development projects can be seen at different levels and in different forms. One of the most innovative forms of participation is occurring in the neighbourhood and slum improvement schemes launched by local bodies. These are being carried out by networks of community groups, enterprises, and city agencies with little financial support from the state or central government. Residents in the project area have been involved in all stages of the project, including monitoring and maintaining the services.

The Slum Networking Project (SNP) of Indore (1990–1997) is the most celebrated of these.[4] It involves provision of individual water taps and toilets connected to a sewage network, an integrated drainage and sanitation system, soft landscaping, and mobilisation of the community for monitoring the project. The underlying model recognises that participation does not mean leaving poor people to design and implement the project by themselves or simply to involve them in some mechanism of access to credit and loan recovery. The basic objective in a networking project is to make high-quality techno-engineering expertise available to the people, within the framework of community participation, so that slums are upgraded in a manner that integrates both the residents and their community 'into the fabric of city life' (Municipal Corporation of Ahmedabad 1998).

Although SNP Indore involved high-level engineering innovations, it was a low-cost solution: the sewer lines used the natural drainage system, the roads were designed for draining storm water, and both the sewer lines and roads were built at ground level. This substantially reduced the capital expenditure. More importantly, linking the slum sub-system with the city network promised to improve the quality of water around the city.

The SNPs in Indian cities have earned unprecedented acclaim nationally and are often internationally cited as examples of best practice. Yet, like many highly publicised cases of 'best practice', the reality on the ground is not always what it seems. Claims to 'dramatic transformation of the slums' through SNP remain to be demonstrated empirically. Moreover, the projects have yet to prove replicable on a large scale and therefore cannot be presented as an alternative to existing slum improvement strategies in the country.

Many of the assumptions of the model have not been met on the ground, thus limiting the project's achievements. The most important premise for the success of the underground sewerage system – that all households would take individual connections for water supply and sewage disposal – is far from reality. The 1997 Impact Assessment Survey found that only about 34 per cent of the households had taken toilet connections, while for water connections the figure was as low as 16 per cent. Many could not afford the connection, as they had neither the resources nor any access to credit and banks would not extend loans to households not possessing legal title to 'their land'. Further, the quality of water was poor, with one third of households with tap connections reporting contamination, and two thirds reporting the pressure of the water supply to be inadequate.

In the absence of sewer connections, a large number of households discharged sullage on to the roads. Indeed, roads were supposed to act as drains, but only for storm water. Open disposal of sullage thus created extremely unhygienic conditions, posing health hazards to the entire community. Also, the premise that the city had sufficient water supplies to operate a city-wide underground sewerage system turned out to be false (Verma 2000). Techno-economic surveys revealed that the sewerage system in the city became choked for lack of water. Understandably, no improvement could come through the water quality of local rivers and lakes.

The strongest criticism of the Indore project is the neglect of community development (CD) activities (Verma 2000). No serious effort was made to create community-level organisations and involve them in the preparation of the plan and its implementation. Towards the end of the project, the CD staff had lost their credibility as the drainage system became choked and they could offer no solution. Instead, preoccupied with their own job security and post-project postings following the termination of the project, they ignored people's grievances.

Another celebrated case of SNP, Parivartan (Change Project), is underway in Ahmedabad. It comprises similar objectives and tools of intervention to that of Indore's SNP, but has been designed to avoid the major problems encountered there. Perhaps the most innovative aspect of the project is its intended reliance entirely on local financing, i.e. from residents, NGOs, Ahmedabad municipal corporation (AMC), and the private sector. To keep down costs and ensure proper functioning of the sewer, water and toilet connections have been made obligatory. Community development activities receive high priority, with NGO partners being involved right from the beginning. To ensure maintenance of the sewerage system, a revolving fund has been established with a contribution of 100 rupees from each household. The difficulty of obtaining credit for slum households has been largely solved by the involvement of the SEWA (Self Employed Women's Association) Bank as a project partner (Dutta 2000).

The most disturbing aspect of the Indore SNP was that many of the slum residents were evicted within a few years of the upgrading To allay such concerns, AMC gave assurance to slum-dwellers right from the outset that they would not be evicted for at least ten years. Similar assurances have come from private owners of the plots and slum areas that are to be improved in the second phase. The plot-owners, in turn, have been assured that their land ownership rights would not be prejudiced as a consequence of the programme.

Despite all the safeguards, Parivartan is encountering serious difficulties. Differences of opinion among the partners emerged even in the pilot phase. Of the original four slums scheduled for upgrading, three have not gone ahead because of the reluctance of their communities to raise or contribute the required resources. Conflicts developed between the engineering wing of AMC and Arvind Mills, the private company involved in the construction component of the project, arising from differences in work culture and decision-making procedures.[5] This led to Arvind Mills withdrawing from the project after the pilot phase. More disturbing, no other private company has come forward subsequently to participate in the project and provide financial support.

Today the project is being implemented in a selective and less ambitious manner by the corporation, a few community groups, and NGOs. Consequently, the concept of integrating all the slums into the basic fabric of city life is now something of a pipe dream. AMC is hard-pressed for resources and is trying to raise funds from several central and state government schemes. If successful, AMC may be able to carry the work forward, but at the cost of going against the fundamentals of the SNP project: to make urban development self-financing.

Arrangements for raising resources from capital market and financial institutions

The ongoing process of globalisation has serious implications for most local bodies and urban development authorities making major invest-ments in infrastructure in India. By virtue of a host of domestic factors – the weak economic position of these bodies, uncertainties in the preparation and supervision of municipal budgets, and the lack of interest by the private corporate sector in partnership financing – urban local bodies are compelled to seek innovative financing methods for their projects. More and more, the kind of financing that is available comes from international lenders or domestic institutions whose first responsibility is to assure prompt repayment at adequate rates of return. The pursuit of such goals is bringing about a sea change in modalities of financing by forcing the conditions for securing loans. It is, in fact, altering the content and objectives of the projects themselves.

In the USA and Europe, revenue bonds have been the main source of capital financing for ULBs. Under this system, funds for repayment are generated through the projects themselves, which are launched using the debt amount. This option is not available in India since urban development projects generally do not yield the required rate of return. Other forms of borrowing, such as general obligation bonds that commit the total budget of the local bodies, would not be of much help as many of these have significant budgetary deficits. Structured debt obligations (SDOs), through which bonds are issued on the condition that the borrowing agency pledges or escrows (places in trust as a deposit or security) certain buoyant sources of revenue like *octroi* (a duty levied on certain goods entering the city), property tax, etc. for debt servicing, could be more feasible. By such means, the repayment obligations are given priority and kept independent of the overall financial position of the borrowing agency. SDOs are designed in such a manner that loans are repaid through the committed revenue sources, irrespective of the overall budget, which may be in deficit. Unfortunately, the level of financing needed to fill the enormous deficit in infrastructure exceeds the escrow capacity of most local bodies to meet the debt-service obligations. As a consequence, they are often required to pledge other sources of revenue and grants as well, which is done in the case of general obligation bonds. Thus, the bondholders enjoy the security of certain dedicated revenue streams and, in addition, are given the faith and credit pledge of the city, thereby making the issue an SDO as well as a general obligation bond, as noted in the case of Ahmedabad discussed above.

Issuing authorities are often required to adhere to certain additional conditionalities, such as maintaining an average debt-service to credit ratio, pledging municipal assets with a certain asset coverage ratio, creating a sinking fund, etc., particularly if they are seeking a high credit rating. In case of possible changes in macro policies that may affect the budgetary position of the concerned authority (such as the abolition of *octroi*), assurances of compensatory payment by state or central government have been stipulated. These are all precautionary measures to protect the interests of the investors.

This has not, however, discouraged a large number of ULBs from attempting to improve their credit rating, for the purpose of raising funds from the capital market. Achieving a budget surplus by cutting down, among other things, 'unremunerative social expenditures' is one of the preferred paths to this objective. However, as a consequence of stiff competition among the ULBs on one hand, and political and civil pressure to restore the level of social expenditure on the other, many ULBs are defaulting.

Organisations that mobilise resources by offering bonds or securities for sale to the public are also required to file a draft prospectus with the Securities and Exchange Board of India (SEBI). As many more ULBs seek to mobilise funds through public placement of the securities, SEBI approval will become common in the future. Such approval often involves additional conditionalities as well as modifications to the project structure and financing system.

Indeed, the general trend for protecting investors (purchasers of securities or bonds issued by ULBs and urban authorities) is in the direction of Europe and North America. Loans taken by subsidiary enterprises (of the ULBs) are to be clearly recorded, reported publicly, reduced to a minimum, or avoided altogether so that the contingent liability does not go beyond the repayment capacity. The role of trustees, whose responsibility it is to monitor ULBs' debt servicing and ensure that the borrowing agency does not have access to the pledged resources (both for the funds raised by it or by its subsidiary enterprises, until the loan is repaid), is to be reformed as well. This is to make trustees personally accountable to the bondholders, to reduce their wide discretionary powers 'to act in the larger social or community interest', and to insulate the trustees, as much as possible, from political influence. It is further proposed that the ULBs should rank their debt instruments in terms of priority so that the general public knows which obligation will have priority in repayment, in case of exigencies. All these arrangements would impose constraints in various ways on the normal functioning of ULBs.

Finally, attempts are being made to design a 'comprehensive debt limitation policy' at the state level. This would ensure compliance of ULBs to certain norms and set a ceiling on their borrowing capacity, based on their economic strength and repayment capacity. This system would speed approvals by removing the requirement to seek approval from the state government in every case. Market borrowing on the part of local authorities can, thus, be made 'independent of the state government'. It is proposed that a market-linked agency like SEBI can take up the regulatory role instead.

International agencies operating in the urban sector have stressed the need to keep the issuance of bonds outside the regulatory framework of government and have pleaded for the development of an independent capital market. The Indian experience in this regard, however, has not been very encouraging. The few cities that were able to float bonds had to depend ultimately either on the guarantee from the state government or on its approval.

A major impact of making the capital market for the development of urban infrastructure independent of government would be the accentuation of inequality across regions as well as in relation to the size of urban centres. Understandably, under the new policy, a few large cities with a growing economy and buoyant revenue sources, would be able to access the market, by-passing the bureaucratic hassle of going through the government. With the discontinuance of the practice of state guarantee, smaller towns, however, would be in no position to mobilise resources. Consequently, the greater dependence on capital markets in future would increase disparity between cities and towns in terms of per capita expenditure and, consequently, the level of amenities (Kundu *et al.* 1999).

Provisions under the Income Tax Act that exempt the income received from bonds issued to finance infrastructure from tax liability may further enhance these disparities. Similarly, under section 88 of the Act, a certain percentage of investment on 'qualified infrastructure' does not come under income tax. These and other exemptions for infrastructure may give a boost to investment in municipal facilities like water-supply and sanitation systems. But better-off states and cities are likely to benefit most from such concessions. Given the bias towards investment in a select group of large cities, small towns in disadvantaged areas are unlikely to receive investment unless certain special concessions are designed for them.

The overview provided here suggests that recent developments in the capital market would, while liberating local agencies from the control of central and state government, place the former under more stringent conditionalities of trustees, commercial banks, and the SEBI, etc. that are in turn controlled largely by pure market considerations.[6]

Financial power would shift from the state governments to financial institutions, international donors, and credit-rating agencies that, through various innovative and complicated arrangements, would control expenditure patterns.[7] They would also be in a position to determine the types of projects to be undertaken and in certain cases the management system of the municipalities. It would, therefore, be extremely important to monitor the problems faced by cities in handling their budgetary earnings and expenditures after accepting such terms and conditions for raising resources from capital markets.

The processes discussed above for evaluating and approving development projects funded through SDOs, i.e. review by SEBI, concerned credit-rating agencies, and trustees, give the impression that projects are rigorously formulated and monitored when capital market finance is involved. The fact that there have been considerable delays in many cities in launching the identified projects and utilising the bond proceeds – obtained at high interest rates – must therefore be taken seriously. In a recent case, also in Ahmedabad, 'the bond proceeds were not used in the first year since project designs and tenders were not ready' (Indo-US FIRE Project 2000). This happened despite extensive technical support to the AMC from USAID in preparing the proposal, CRISIL's awarding the highest possible rating to the proposal after a thorough examination, and the AMC's acquiescence following SEBI's review of the bond prospectus 'to appoint private project management consultants to facilitate the process of project design, approval, tendering, construction supervision, quality control, and payments'. Taken together, these factors suggest that procedural formalities were completed more for administrative or bureaucratic purposes than in order to examine the economic feasibility of the project and its implementation.

Were it not for an impending water crisis, AMC's use of the bond proceeds may have been delayed even further. Indeed, the AMC successfully implemented an emergency bulk water supply scheme – the Raska project – in a record time of five months (Indo-US FIRE Project 2000). Had the officials not been able to obtain clearance from a large number of organisations at the central, state, and local levels so quickly, the negative arbitrage implications (paying a higher rate of interest of 14 per cent to bondholders than the interest it was receiving on bond proceeds) would have been far more serious. The claims of AMC that it could get highly competitive tenders from private contractors, as it had huge cash flow due to delays in other projects, can, at best, be accepted as a hypothesis. As Ahmedabad is the state capital, and home to most of the state's economic and political élites, the likelihood that the project would be approved by the state government may be a better explanation of why competitive tenders were received than that the corporation had a large cash flow because of having been unable to undertake capital expenditure on schedule, after years of careful planning.

Conclusions and generalisations

This overview of the innovative methods of financing infrastructure development in urban India reveals that, given the resource crisis in the economy, projects have come to depend on capital market borrowing, privatisation, partnership arrangements, and community participation. These seem to be the only options available for providing infrastructure and basic amenities. Planners and policy makers have, in recent years, made a strong case to make parastatal agencies as well as local governments depend increasingly on their internal resources and institutional finance, in order to '[bring] in efficiency and accountability in their functioning'. Our analyses suggest that this changed perspective and the consequent decline in public investment are likely to accentuate disparity in the levels of amenities across the states and size class of urban settlements.

Furthermore, poor people are likely to be priced out of the various schemes that are being launched within the private and joint sector or through subcontracting arrangements. The companies participating in the schemes will ensure a change of perspective and force social objectives to be diluted. As a consequence, better-off colonies will tend to get more attention and a larger share of investable resources due to their higher disposable incomes and political patronage. The public sector schemes that have increasingly been made to depend on institutional loans and the capital market reflect similar tendencies. All these accentuate the gaps in the levels of basic amenities enjoyed in rich and poor areas of the city.

Efforts are underway to develop the capital market so that a few of the more efficient parastatal and local-level agencies can mobilise resources by issuing SDOs and other credit instruments. An analysis of the arrangements, worked out by financial intermediaries including the credit-rating institutions, for accessing the capital market, reveals that these can severely restrict the functioning of these ULBs and impede them from fulfilling their normal obligations. In several cases, local bodies have been forced to pledge their regular earnings from *octroi*, grants from the state, etc., as a guarantee for debt servicing.

Importantly, the projects that are likely to be financed through the credit market would, by their very logic, be commercially viable and ensure profitability to the investors and other stakeholders. However, if the projects fail to generate the desired rate of profit, a local body may be left with no funds even for general administration since much of its revenue earnings will be diverted to pay investors or to complete the project. It thus appears that the policy of liberating the local governments from the regulatory and legislative controls of the state would place them under the direct control of financial institutions. This may be desirable from the viewpoint of developing a few global cities, providing space for businesses, office complexes, and residences for the executive and entrepreneurial class, but it may not answer the need for basic amenities for the majority of urban poor.

Unfortunately, much of the subsidised infrastructure and amenities provided through governmental programmes during the 1960s, 1970s, and early 1980s went to a few large cities and benefited mostly the high- and middle-income neighbourhoods. Since the beginning of structural adjustment in the early 1990s, the scope for this form of subsidy has been drastically reduced. Ever more urban infrastructure projects are relying on combinations of locally generated resources, including cost-recovery pricing, subcontracting arrangements, borrowings from capital markets, and various forms of community participation. However, evidence is beginning to accumulate that this régime of service provision accentuates inequality across regions and between different sizes or class of urban settlements. It may also increase intra-urban disparity and lead to segmentation, particularly in India's metropolis and other large cities. This would have serious consequences for micro-environments, local health, and law and order, and possibly discourage foreign and private investment in and around these cities. The whole process of liberalisation and efforts to create a few global cities in India may then fall into jeopardy. Welfare arguments apart, even the validity of efficiency arguments behind the institutional innovations can be disputed by taking a slightly longer-term perspective on urban development.

Notes

1 Hereafter, 'state' refers to the second tier of government in India, i.e. that which functions directly below the federal or central government.

2 Only recently have several cities and one state taken initiatives to improve accounting and auditing systems in urban centres (Indo-US FIRE Project 1998a and 1998b).

3 'Regardless of the purpose, once a rating has been issued, continued surveillance by the rating agency is important to identify changing conditions and trends in performance.' (Indo-US FIRE Project 1999)

4 Capital expenditures for this pilot project were funded with a grant from the UK's Overseas Development Administration (now the Department for International Development).

5 'The delay and friction was caused by lack of a clearly defined role of the AMC functionaries ... the AMC engineer began to play a proactive supervisory role, despite the fact that SHARDA trust had employed the contractor and was supervising him. There was tremendous confusion on site.' (Chauhan and Lal 1999)

6 The agencies active in the capital market admit that 'such stringent requirements may place some burden on the development of a municipal bond system' (Indo-US FIRE Project 1998b).

7 Madhaya Pradesh government, for example, has admitted its ability to provide escrow cover to only a few of the proposed power projects, although a large number of applications are lying with them (*Economic Times* August 1998).

References

Chauhan, Uttara and Niraj Lal (1999) 'Public–private partnerships for urban poor in Ahmedabad: a slum project', *Economic and Political Weekly* 6–13 March

Credit Rating Information Services of India Limited (CRISIL) (1996) 'Credit Rating of Municipal Bonds', rating report on Ahmedabad Municipal Corporation, New Delhi: CRISIL

Dutta, Shyam S. (2000) 'Partnerships in urban development: a review of Ahmedabad's experience', *Environment and Urbanization* 11(2): 13–26.

Expert Group on Commercialisation of Infrastructure (1996) 'Infrastructure Report: Policy Imperatives for Growth and Welfare', Ministry of Finance, New Delhi: Government of India

Indo-US Financial Institutions Reform and Expansion Project (1998a) 'The Pune Water Supply and Sewerage Project: focus on private sector participation', *Project Notes* 9

Indo-US Financial Institutions Reform and Expansion Project (1998b) 'Emerging issues in India's municipal bond system: the need for regulatory control', *Project Notes* 10

Indo-US Financial Institutions Reform and Expansion Project (1999) 'Developing a municipal credit-rating system in India', *Project Notes* 20

Indo-US Financial Institutions Reform and Expansion Project (2000) *Lessons Learned: Ahmedabad Municipal Bond and Water Supply and Sewerage Project*, New Delhi: USAID

Joshi, R. (1996) 'Financial management in municipalities', *Urban India* 16(2)

Kundu, A., S. Bagchi, and D. Kundu (1999) 'Regional distribution of infrastructure and basic amenities in urban India: issues concerning empowerment of local bodies', *Economic and Political Weekly* 34 (28)

Mehta, M. and V. Satyanarayana (1996) *Pricing and Cost Recovery for Urban Services*, New Delhi: Community Consulting International

Ministry of Urban Development (1992) *The Constitution Seventy-fourth Amendment Act 1992 on Municipalities*, New Delhi: Government of India

Municipal Corporation of Ahmedabad (1998) *Slum Networking Project*, Ahmedabad: AMC

Municipal Corporation of Delhi (MCD) (1997) *Budget 1995–96*, revised estimates, New Delhi: MCD

Narayanan, E. (2000) 'Municipal debt financing for urban infrastructure development', in K. Singh and B. Tai (eds) *Financing and Pricing of Urban Infrastructure* New Delhi: New Age International

National Institute of Public Finance and Policy (NIPFP) (1995) 'Redefining State–Municipal Fiscal Relations', Volume I (mimeo.), New Delhi: NIPFP

National Institute of Urban Affairs (NIUA) (1997) *Scope and Practice of Privatisation of Urban Services in India*, Study Series No. 60, New Delhi: NIUA

Suresh, V. (1999) 'Options for urban infrastructure development in India', in *Papers of the International Seminar on Financing and Pricing of Urban Infrastructure*, New Delhi: Human Settlement Management Institute

Verma, Gita Dewan (2000) 'Indore's Habitat Improvement Project: success or failure?', *Habitat International* 24: 91–117

World Bank (1995) *India Transport Sector: Long-term Issues*, Report No. 13192-IN, Washington, DC: World Bank

World Bank (1998) *Reducing Poverty in India: Options for More Effective Public Services*, Washington, DC: World Bank

Institutionalising the concept of environmental planning and management: successes and challenges in Dar es Salaam

Wilbard J. Kombe

Over the last three decades, most Third World cities have experienced rapid growth accompanied by dwindling local and central government resources and management capacities. Traditional approaches to urban planning and administration, such as master plans or 'blueprints' for development, did not work and became increasingly obsolete in the 1970s and 1980s. Shortages of public finance and technical capacity within the local and central authorities that were responsible for controlling and directing urban development were exacerbated in the 1990s as the impacts of structural adjustment were felt. Urban planning and management approaches also suffered other shortcomings, including:

- failure to facilitate cross-sectoral co-ordination or inter-departmental and inter-institutional collaboration;
- insufficient mechanisms and tools for substantive participation by community-based stakeholders;
- absence of modalities for collaboration between the public and private sector;
- overemphasis on physical outputs rather than the process for achieving them (Majani 2000).

As a result, unmanaged urban growth, characterised by the poor quality or absence of basic public infrastructure, services, and facilities, increasing environmental degradation, and the depletion of natural resources, is the norm in most cities of the South. Dar es Salaam is no exception. During the same period, the capacity of urban planners to manage rapid urban growth has also declined (Post 1997: 347). Such factors prompted the Prime Minister of Tanzania to dissolve the Dar es Salaam City Council in June 1996 and replace it with a Commission

(Dar es Salaam City Commission, DCC) of centrally appointed members.[1] Until then, Dar es Salaam had been reasonably independent of central government. However, its powers to collect revenue and make decisions were subject to frequent intervention by central government, meaning that the city government has often been unable to fulfil its obligations to local citizens.

It was in response to these worsening urban management problems and conditions that Habitat (UNCHS), in collaboration with the United Nations Environment Programme (UNEP), developed and began promoting its urban Environmental Planning and Management (EPM) agenda. Underlying the EPM approach is the concern to create a harmonious balance between physical development and the environment in urban settings, and to involve those groups interested in and affected by urban development in seeking solutions to problems that may arise. EPM emphasises the interrelations between and among social actors and environmental issues and thus puts partnership among the key stakeholders at its centre. These partners or stakeholders typically include actors in the public, private, and popular sectors, civil society, and NGOs.[2]

An agreement to adopt the EPM in Dar es Salaam was signed by the government of Tanzania in 1992. That same year, the Sustainable Dar es Salaam Project (SDP) was established, becoming operational in 1993 in order to institutionalise the EPM in the functioning of the City Council.[3] The SDP mandated stakeholders to produce a Strategic Urban Development Plan (SUDP) for the city. This was to be accomplished with substantive inputs from working groups (WGs) composed of 'informed' representatives of key stakeholders, including grassroots representatives.[4] Their functions within local government were to be deliberative, consultative, strategic, and mobilisational.

In the EPM scheme, WGs result from stakeholder consultations whose purpose is to identify priority environmental issues at the city, municipal, or town level. In theory, the WGs open up channels for residents to influence decisions and contribute to the management of the city. WGs therefore may be seen as energisers and agents of change in the management style and decision-making processes in local government. They also facilitate and enhance the accountability of public institutions to local citizens.

This article chronicles the functioning, achievements, and failures of two such WGs, one on the management of informal (petty) trading activities and the other on the management of communal open spaces.

Most of the data were collected in interviews with key actors in the respective WGs and with representatives of the main institutions and relevant NGOs. These WGs were chosen from among the nine in existence because they were among the few that had analysed the issues, formulated strategies, and gone on to implement them.

Description of the EPM working groups

A city consultation meeting held in 1992 allowed stakeholders to develop a consensus on the priority problems of Dar es Salaam and how to address them. In accordance with EPM protocol, this consultation provided the mandate to establish WGs comprising key actors or stakeholders from public, private, and popular sectors. Each WG was required to prepare an action plan, identify the information/data required and other experts or other actors and institutions to be contacted or involved, and to determine the sessions to be held, and outputs or targets.

The WGs were also mandated to choose chairpersons and co-ordinators.[5] The latter were often appointed from among the SDP technical experts – that is they were persons knowledgeable about EPM – many of whom were officers seconded to the SDP unit from the central government ministries. Members of the WGs were intended to represent the stakeholders and were supposed to be chosen from among senior technical staff who could take decisions on behalf of their institutions. In practice, most institutions appointed less influential officers.

All nine WGs were constituted in response to the priority environmental issues identified.[6] While some DCC councillors became WG members, the day-to-day operations of the SDP unit were run by WG co-ordinators, headed by a project manager or co-ordinator.[7] Initially, Habitat appointed an expatriate technical adviser to set up the unit, but this post was later filled by a local expert. Since its inception in Dar es Salaam, the head of the SDP and now the Urban Authorities Support Unit (UASU) have been appointed from outside the DCC.

From the outset, the SDP has been a separate physical entity with its own assets and management structure. Currently, its only role is to support the institutionalisation of the EPM in three new municipalities in Dar es Salaam. Following a recent government decision to replicate the EPM elsewhere, the UASU has been formed to co-ordinate, monitor, and support this process.[8]

The SDP depends on Habitat and UNDP for financial, logistical, and technical support. Administratively, the SDP and UASU are accountable to the City Council and Ministry of Local Government, respectively. On technical matters, they are largely answerable to Habitat and UNDP: Habitat provides in-house expertise and short-term consultants, and UNDP is the main donor, though it does not fund the WGs' action plans or projects (see Figure 1).

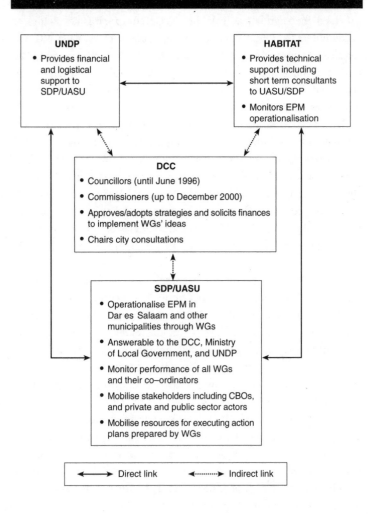

Figure 1: Institutional framework for operationalising the EPM in Dar es Salaam City

UNDP
- Provides financial and logistical support to SDP/UASU

HABITAT
- Provides technical support including short term consultants to UASU/SDP
- Monitors EPM operationalisation

DCC
- Councillors (until June 1996)
- Commissioners (up to December 2000)
- Approves/adopts strategies and solicits finances to implement WGs' ideas
- Chairs city consultations

SDP/UASU
- Operationalise EPM in Dar es Salaam and other municipalities through WGs
- Answerable to the DCC, Ministry of Local Government, and UNDP
- Monitor performance of all WGs and their co-ordinators
- Mobilise stakeholders including CBOs, and private and public sector actors
- Mobilise resources for executing action plans prepared by WGs

◄──────► Direct link   ◄┄┄┄┄► Indirect link

According to the plans, the participation of the DCC's functional officers and other technical staff in the WGs would eventually serve to integrate EPM into the routine functions of the DCC. The resulting changes would sustain collaboration between the local authority and other stakeholders in identifying environmental problems and developing and implementing strategies to address them.

Implementing EPM via the working group process

Case study I: management of informal trading activities[9]

The nature of informal (petty) trading activities: The extent, growth rate, and potential inherent in informal trade activities (ITAs) in Tanzania are difficult to quantify because the definition of what constitutes petty or informal trade activities is ambiguous, and local-level opportunities vary widely.[10] However, a study conducted in Dar es Salaam in 1995 estimated that there were about 350,000 informal businesses providing approximately 500,000 jobs (SIDO-GTZ 1995). The 1992 National Informal Sector Survey report estimated that petty trading engaged 64 per cent of the informal business sector in Dar es Salaam and provided employment to over 203,000 people.

The SIDO-GTZ study further showed that more than 90 per cent of these petty traders had no security of tenure to the land on which they were carrying out their activities, i.e. they were largely operating on areas not sanctioned or designated for trading by the local government. Despite this, ITAs have been flourishing and expanding rapidly and include activities such as selling fruit, vegetables, prepared foods, flowers, newspapers, used garments, and petty services.[11] In the absence of permanent premises and security of tenure, most vendors operate from makeshift tables or temporary sheds erected on open spaces or along roadsides. Many inner-city sites, including pedestrian malls and major road junctions, are lined with hawkers.[12] Most vendors are unemployed youth, although *mama lishe* (women food vendors) are more prominent among those selling food. In general, informal petty business is the employment of last resort for the most economically vulnerable city residents.

The regulation of ITAs has been haphazard, often leading to adverse effects on the traders' immediate surroundings. These include land-use conflicts and other problems resulting from the improper management of the waste from petty trading, obstruction of traffic movement, trespassing on private or semi-private premises (e.g. shopping verandas), etc.. Worse, because informal businesses are largely conducted on premises that have not been sanctioned for such use, some vendors pay exorbitant sums of money to operate there. That such payments usually end up in private pockets rather than in local government coffers (SIDO-GTZ 1995), in part explains the local government's concern to improve the way in which ITAs are managed.

Local authorities traditionally have a negative perception of informal petty trading, and this attitude has resulted in numerous crackdowns on petty traders by *askaris* (DCC militia), causing losses, injuries, and forced evictions or round-ups.[13] Yet despite such repression, and even prosecutions, ITAs have grown. Trade liberalisation and low salaries coupled with massive retrenchment, especially in the public sector, have accelerated such growth (Yusuph 2000). The ensuing conflicts and the increasing role that ITAs were playing in the city economy led to this being identified as a priority concern during the city consultation workshop in 1992.

Working group formation and performance: Given the magnitude of the conflicts, the complexity of the trading activities, and the diversity of interests and actors involved, the search for solutions required a multidisciplinary approach. Thus the WG on petty trading comprised 12 stakeholders including VIBINDO (Vikundi vya Biashara Ndogondogo, the Organisation of Small-scale Business Groups), DKOA (Dar es Salaam Kiosk Owners' Association), and the City Council Departments of Planning, Economy, Trade, and Legal Matters, as well as councillors and Ward Executive Officers, representatives of the key ministries (i.e. Labour and Youth, Trade and Industry), and representatives of important NGOs and government institutions, including SIDO (Small Scale Industries Organisation), GTZ (the German technical co-operation programme), Poverty Africa, and the ILO.

One of the first outcomes from the negotiations, which was carried by the WG in 1994, was the agreement to acknowledge informal (petty) traders as legitimate actors in the city. Thus, their activities would have to be supported by the city's development planning and management process. To accomplish this, the WG developed three guiding strategies:

- accommodation: support to vendors operating in uncontested areas;
- eviction: expulsion of vendors operating on prohibited or contested sites, including stalls or makeshift tables mounted in front of or within public premises such as school areas and around public office buildings and hospitals;

- relocation: establishment of new market facilities and expansion of existing ones to provide space for resettling petty traders operating in the overcrowded or undesignated areas, particularly in the city centre.

Of these, relocation was the main strategy, primarily because it helped hawkers to remain in their trade. This seems to have been an important precondition for bringing key actors together and forging consensus. This was certainly the case for VIBINDO, which repeatedly had to assure vendors that the WG intended to work with them and solve their problems in order to get their collaboration.

Further consultations and discussions were then conducted with various groups representing vendors and other informal sector operators in the city, to solicit their views, support, and co-operation. Explaining the problems associated with reconciling diverging interests, the WG co-ordinator recalled:

> ... the most difficult stage during the initial working group sessions was to evolve and agree on a common strategy. Often, differences emerged between vendors' organisations [e.g. VIDINDO and DKOA] as well as among WG members. It took us a lot of time and effort to come to an agreement.[14]

Ultimately, a consensus was reached including proposals for relocating vendors at two sites, Makumbusho and Sterio-Temeke. The relocation proposal included a sketch design for market sheds to accommodate vendors, drawn up by an architectural firm in consultation with the WG. Modest fees, to be paid by the vendors to the DCC, were also proposed. The global proposal was then submitted to the DCC for approval and eventual support in mobilising the necessary financial resources.

Unexpectedly, shortly after receiving the proposals, and without consulting the WG, the DCC resolved to evict hawkers from Congo Street, one of their strongholds in the city. This action was taken ostensibly because the street had to be reconstructed, and vendors were required to move to the two sites identified by the WG.[15]

The DCC then shelved the WG's proposal for modest market sheds. Through competitive bidding, another private architectural firm won the tender to prepare new design proposals for the market. Without consulting the WG, the firm proposed a modern market complex. This was approved by the DCC and subsequently built.[16] Asked why the design that had been generated in consultation with the WG was abandoned, one WG member who worked in the institution that financed the new market proposal responded:

*... I was an active member of two WGs, that is the petty trading and traffic
management group. Before the City Council was abolished in June 1996,
WGs were generally working closely with the various DCC Departments.
For instance there were staff from the City Council Departments
participating in our WGs. However, when the Commission took up its
duties, the link between WGs and the Commission waned. We [the funding
agency] only received a notice from the Commission saying that a new
design for the market was required because the sketch proposal submitted
by the WG did not meet requirements for a 'modern market', as it did not
provide for cold rooms, butchers, grocers etc.. In order to respect and meet
our clients' needs and interests we floated the tender for competitive bidding.
This is the standard procedure we used to award design as well as
construction contracts.*

Commissioners gave varying reasons on why the WG proposal was not
adopted by the DCC.[17] Some observed that:

*... the land designated for the relocation of vendors [markets] were prime
sites. The Commission therefore decided to put up structures which would
reflect the value of the land as well as enhance the visual outlook of the area.*

Another commented that:

*... what the WG had proposed did not take into account other factors such
as options which can generate the desperately needed revenue. The WG
was only concerned with the Machinga [hawkers] resettlement problem.
This is only one of the problems the Commission was facing.*[18]

Asked why they did not consult the WG when the decision to drop its
proposal was made, one Commissioner said that the DCC was not
obliged to seek WG approval for decisions taken by management.
Others said that because the SDP attended the DCC management
meetings, it was up to the SDP project manager to inform WG co-
ordinators and members of decisions made by the DCC.

The eviction of the hawkers from Congo Street without consulting
the WG or taking into account the WG proposals, and the decision to
set aside the WG's design for simple market sheds in favour of very
costly structures, challenged the central tenets of the EPM, namely
building partnership among stakeholders and ensuring their
participation in managing the city's development. Indeed, the WG
seems to have had little or no impact on this process.

The eviction of petty traders provoked skirmishes between the City
Council askaris and vendors and led to new invasions by hawkers on

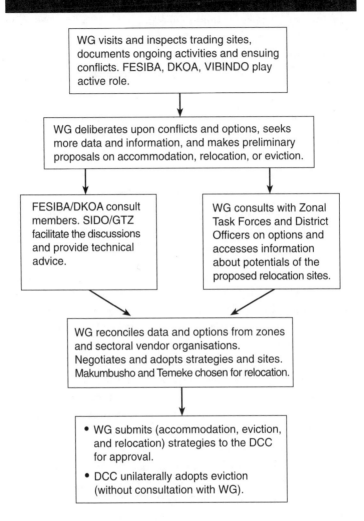

WG visits and inspects trading sites, documents ongoing activities and ensuing conflicts. FESIBA, DKOA, VIBINDO play active role.

WG deliberates upon conflicts and options, seeks more data and information, and makes preliminary proposals on accommodation, relocation, or eviction.

FESIBA/DKOA consult members. SIDO/GTZ facilitate the discussions and provide technical advice.

WG consults with Zonal Task Forces and District Officers on options and accesses information about potentials of the proposed relocation sites.

WG reconciles data and options from zones and sectoral vendor organisations. Negotiates and adopts strategies and sites. Makumbusho and Temeke chosen for relocation.

- WG submits (accommodation, eviction, and relocation) strategies to the DCC for approval.
- DCC unilaterally adopts eviction (without consultation with WG).

open sites elsewhere. More generally, the DCC's actions not only demoralised the stakeholders but also increased hostility between the local authority and the vendors.[19]

Most stakeholders who participated in the WGs expected to obtain some benefit. Vendors expected that through negotiation they would get a better deal, e.g. permanent and safe trading places. Others, such as VIBINDO and DKOA, wanted the city to adopt a more coherent and supportive approach to the petty trading problem.[20] The DCC, on the other hand, used its powers to ensure the adoption of an option that would above all boost revenue collection as well as improve the cityscape. But because the new Temeke and Makumbusho markets have been abandoned by the vendors (Yusuph 2000), the interests of neither the DCC nor the WG seem to have been met.[21]

Case study II: management of open space

The abuse and misuse of open spaces: The WG on the management of open spaces was also established in response to the 1992 city consultation and became operational in January 1994. It was charged with addressing problems such as:

- illegal occupation or invasion of open spaces;
- legal but dubious subdivision and changes of the use of open spaces by unscrupulous (DCC/MLHSD) officers; and
- underdevelopment and or misuse of open spaces.

The group comprised over 10 institutions and 13 members, including representatives from the local *Mtaa* (sub-ward)[22] and ward committees, the Ministry of Lands and Human Settlement Development (MLHSD), the National Environmental Council, the National Land Use Commission, the City Council Departments of Planning, Public Works (Parks and Gardens Section), and councillors appointed from the DCC committees. As with other WGs, institutional representatives were to be appointed on the basis of relevant skills, knowledge, or information about the subject in question, and a personal interest in it. A few additional resource persons were invited to join specific sessions.[23] The WG chose to focus on one of the most affected residential areas in the city, namely the planned high-density housing neighbourhoods close to the city centre. Six of the city's 52 wards were selected, two each from the districts of Kinondoni, Ilala, and Temeke.[24]

Evolving and inaugurating community-based open space management: This WG decided that local community leaders should be commissioned to manage open spaces. Describing how this strategy evolved, the WG co-ordinator said:

> We started with visits to the selected wards and Mtaa. We conducted several meetings with Mtaa, Ten cell, and at times Ward Executive Officers. We also had layout maps [scale 1: 2500] covering the areas we visited. During the visits to the wards and Mtaa, the community leaders took us [WG] round to observe the use of the public open spaces in their areas and

plot or confirm their location on the maps. It is from the discussions and experiences about the community's achievements and flaws in trying to check the abuse and misuse of open spaces that the idea to involve local leaders emerged. For instance, from the informal discussions with a ward leader in Mwananyamala Ward, we learnt that [the] Mtaa leader in Kambangwa street in the ward, had filed a case in the court against an unscrupulous builder who invaded and erected a house on community open space.

Later, the observations and views collected during local visits were discussed in WG sessions and incorporated into the strategy that was adopted. However, because the Public Recreation Grounds Ordinance does not mandate communities or private individuals to manage and develop public open spaces, the WG had to seek the DCC's approval to legalise the proposed arrangement.[25]

Predictably, community resistance to invasions of recreational open spaces was already the most common response to the problem. Thus, the WG's strategy of empowering the local community to play a meaningful role in the development and management of open spaces did not require much mobilisation or extended negotiations with grassroots leaders. However, a contract had to be drawn up to define roles, stipulate conditions, and, most importantly, formalise agreements between the local government and the respective community leaders, corporate bodies, or private individuals, as necessary.[26]

Apart from formulating this contract, the WG also initiated an awareness-creation campaign that aimed to mobilise support from residents. This involved the Commission, the three City District Commissioners, ward, and *Mtaa* leaders. According to WG co-ordinators, local community leaders were excited and enthusiastic about the new approach these campaigns proclaimed. Many of them felt that gradually their role in the city management process was being acknowledged.

Marked improvements have been made in the wards where community leaders and private companies were contracted to develop and manage open spaces. For instance, communities in Mwananyamala, Ward 14 Temeke, Makurumla, and Ilala wards have taken initiatives not only to protect open spaces against invaders but also to develop them by planting trees, providing leisure facilities, and undertaking routine cleaning. This approach has tapped resources from private companies to improve open spaces in other areas such as Mnazi Mmoja, Mwananyamala B, and Temeke Wailesi. Furthermore, several private companies have sought DCC consent to manage and develop

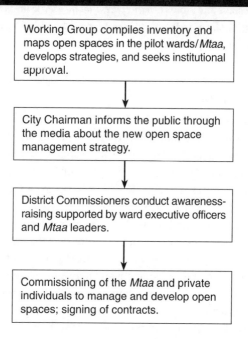

Figure 3: Inauguration of community-led strategy for managing open spaces

Working Group compiles inventory and maps open spaces in the pilot wards/ *Mtaa*, develops strategies, and seeks institutional approval.

City Chairman informs the public through the media about the new open space management strategy.

District Commissioners conduct awareness-raising supported by ward executive officers and *Mtaa* leaders.

Commissioning of the *Mtaa* and private individuals to manage and develop open spaces; signing of contracts.

areas such as Biafra open space along Kawawa Road in Kinondoni, a playground at Namanga shopping area, Oyster Bay beach area, and Mbagala Kibonde Maji open space in Mbagala Ward. These initiatives suggest that the community and private sector are willing to collaborate with the public sector in order to supplement the latter's weaknesses.

These positive developments must be set against less positive trends, which most notably include the DCC's waning commitment to integrating the WGs in its routine functions. Grassroots actors' enthusiasm for and contributions to the management of open spaces has also declined. This is attributed to a number of factors, chief among them the DCC's failure to honour the agreement to delegate management of open spaces to local community leaders. Local leaders in Sinza, Buguruni, and Magomeni Wards complain that zonal or city authorities have not responded effectively to their request to restrain invasion or encroachment on open spaces. They also complain that invaders often collude with officials at the DCC or the MLHSD. The officials change the use of open spaces without consulting community leaders, suggesting that the officers responsible have vested interests.[27] There have also been instances of *Mtaa* leaders attempting to evict invaders from open spaces, only to be restrained from doing so by the DCC. Working group co-ordinators claim that their attempts to follow up appeals forwarded to the DCC by ward and *Mtaa* leaders often received a cold response, signalling the institution's unwillingness to co-operate.[28] In other words, despite the proclaimed intention of involving local community leaders to play active roles in the management and development of open spaces, and the exemplary results from the pilot wards, some DCC bureaucrats have continued to operate as if nothing had changed, or as if community leaders or WG roles do not much matter.

The DCC's insensitivity to proposals and appeals for support from community leaders has demoralised and weakened the WG members, particularly the local representatives. This, coupled with lack of logistical support to facilitate WG sessions, seems to have undermined the partnership spirit of the EPM approach. Owing (among other things) to 'vested interests', the belief that roundtable 'consensus' reached through the EPM would push those in powerful or decision-making positions to adopt and support partnership with stakeholders, is in jeopardy. Discussing the rise and fall of government–community partnership for urban development in Sri Lanka, Vidler and Russell (2000: 85) caution that entrenched government institutions and power structures could undermine sustainable partnership. This observation may also explain the flagging nature of the collaboration between DCC, bureaucrats, and local communities in enhancing the management of open spaces in Dar es Salaam.

An overview of past and recent trends of the working groups

The overall performance and extent to which WGs were deployed in the decision-making processes and resolution of environmental problems in the city since the inception of the EPM is outlined below. This account is based on interviews with 18 individuals, among them SDP co-ordinators, WG members, heads of DCC departments, as well as three City Commissioners and two former DCC councillors.

Overall, the DCC has benefited from the innovative strategies developed by the WGs, particularly in relation to the improvement of solid waste collection, the establishment of a city-wide Geographic Information System (GIS) Unit, traffic management in the city centre, and partnership arrangements for improving basic infrastructure in informal housing. However, while the DCC has implemented a number of WG proposals, these have mainly been those that contributed to accomplishing its own short-term agenda. It would appear that it has been one thing to access or implement proposals from WGs, but quite another for the DCC to take steps to change working norms for routine urban planning and management functions. As depicted in Figure 4, WGs were deployed increasingly between 1991 and 1996, but this trend declined in early 1997.

The nature of activities and conditions that contributed to the rise and fall of their deployment are also shown. As we have already seen, the general observation is that during the City Council's period, WGs were generally extensively deployed, but much less so during the Commission's era.

The working group approach: lessons and challenges

It may be too early to assess the degree of institutionalisation or extent of reforms that the EPM approach has contributed to the routine planning and management systems of the City Council. It is also difficult to generalise from the achievements and flaws observed to date. However, the evidence suggests that unless the challenges which have arisen in the course of implementing the two EPM programmes are addressed, the sustainability of the concept in reforming planning and management in Tanzania will be jeopardised.

This is not to question the need for an alternative planning and management approach or to suggest that its implementation ought to have been a straightforward task. In fact, because the implementation of EPM inevitably involves cross-sectoral and cross-jurisdictional issues, as well as a multitude of institutions and actors, achieving a breakthrough in reforming urban management and planning practices is likely to take time. However, it is worth recapitulating those factors which have adversely affected implementation of the EPM so that we can build upon the experiences of Dar es Salaam.

Insensitive culture of governance and transition from City Council to Commission

The EPM approach encourages partnership between local government institutions and other stakeholders in urban development. At the centre of this partnership is the question of power-sharing between the local government officers and other stakeholders. But without any legal

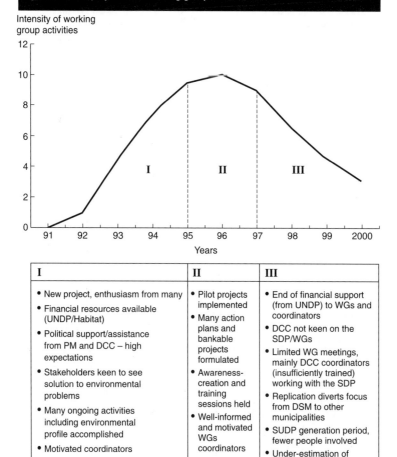

Figure 4: The deployment of working groups, 1992–2000

Intensity of working group activities

Years

I	II	III
• New project, enthusiasm from many • Financial resources available (UNDP/Habitat) • Political support/assistance from PM and DCC – high expectations • Stakeholders keen to see solution to environmental problems • Many ongoing activities including environmental profile accomplished • Motivated coordinators	• Pilot projects implemented • Many action plans and bankable projects formulated • Awareness-creation and training sessions held • Well-informed and motivated WGs coordinators	• End of financial support (from UNDP) to WGs and coordinators • DCC not keen on the SDP/WGs • Limited WG meetings, mainly DCC coordinators (insufficiently trained) working with the SDP • Replication diverts focus from DSM to other municipalities • SUDP generation period, fewer people involved • Under-estimation of grassroots leaders • Action plans prepared but not implemented; WGs demoralised

or structural position in local government, WGs essentially act like voluntary pressure groups. Local government officials ask 'Who are these WGs, with whom we must share decision-making powers?' The situation in Dar es Salaam was further compounded by the replacement in 1996 of the elected council with a team of bureaucrats (commissioners) appointed by central government. This seems to have short-circuited local demo-cratisation processes, especially the participation of stakeholders and representatives of civil society in the management of city affairs which, in turn, seems to have made it harder for the EPM to be institutionalised.[29]

The ongoing process of democratisation in Tanzania, including political pluralism, local government reforms, and calls for more transparency in the dealings of the public sector, are yet to have any significant impact on the management style of local governments. Discussing how centralised power and decision making in the DCC Chairman has affected solid waste management in the city, Majani (2000) asserts that the lack of delegation led to higher transaction costs. For instance, decisions were often delayed or could only be made after the DCC Chairman had sanctioned them.[30]

Emphasising the omnipotence of the City Commission, Majani further notes that the practice at DCC was ' ... what has not been seen (i.e. sanctioned) by the Chairman has not been seen by the Commission'. Suffice it to say that the climate at the DCC was not conducive to empowering functional officers to take decisions. It is no wonder actors from outside the DCC, such as WGs and community leaders, faced obstacles in their path as they tried to influence decision-making processes.

Immature transition to multi-party democracy

The adoption of participatory urban planning and management is taking place at the advent of multi-party democracy in Tanzania. The EPM concept and multi-party democracy ought to be mutually reinforcing, yet this does not seem to be the case. Multi-party democracy is new and has yet to mature. And, as all plans are ultimately political statements and all attempts to implement them are political acts (Rondinelli 1983), partisan politics in the context of multi-party competition may even be slowing the implementation of EPM, as bureaucrats may distrust WG members because of their affiliation to certain (opposition) parties.[31] This tends to reinforce traditional administrative centralism that is so dominant among some local government bureaucrats and especially in an unelected local council and that disregards other parts of the urban administration and is insensitive to the 'principle of subsidiarity'. This context seems to have been one of the main constraints on institutionalising the EPM in Dar es Salaam (Majani 2000).

Frequent change of top leadership and priorities

The frequent change of the chief executives of the DCC – six in eight years – adversely affected the process of institutionalising the EPM. Every time a new city executive was appointed, the SDP had to re-establish links with the new leadership, and had to make repeated efforts to gain each successive executive's support for the EPM approach. In addition, because of lack of continuity in the DCC administration, a number of training sessions had to be held to inform new incumbents about the new city management and planning concept.

Since the EPM was adopted in Dar es Salaam, the city authorities, including the mayor and later the DCC Chairman, have repeatedly made public statements in support of fully incorporating EPM into the city management system. These statements were seldom backed by action. For instance, none of the proposals submitted to the City Council or Commission seeking a financial contribution to facilitate WG sessions was granted, despite numerous promises (Kombe 1999b).

The change of priorities, and especially the expectation of immediate outputs, during the Commission tenure seems to have undermined the adoption of the EPM within the DCC. Discussing the criteria for evaluating the ability to implement plans, Rakodi and Devas (1993: 60) caution that those in power have somehow to accept them. Although the DCC was interested and did sometimes use WG outputs, at the same time it seemed reluctant to address the constraints to the generation and flow of outputs. In the end, the low priority given to the SDP is reflected in the government's failure to meet its pledge to provide matching funds for the national sustainable cities programme over the 1996–2000 period. By May 2000, only US$75,000 of the promised US$1,200,000 had materialised (Burian 2000).

Furthermore, priorities and decisions during the DCC's term largely focused on areas where quick results could be obtained. By and large, the City Commission tended to adopt WGs' contributions only if these fitted into and/or gave immediate tangible outputs. Thus, in the months following the formation of the City Commission, the WGs started to wither, as did the relationship between the DCC and the SDP (depicted in Figure 4).[32]

Overemphasis on physical outputs, and insufficient knowledge

In Tanzania, where the tradition of master planning remains influential, the term 'project' is largely understood to mean the construction of infrastructure and the like. Thus, when the SDP was established, many at the DCC assumed that it was a project along the lines of sites and service or squatter improvement initiatives, and they expected the SDP to channel funds to tackle problems such as poor roads, lack of storm water drains, the lack of trucks for emptying cesspits, or insufficient housing plots. Changing that perception among councillors and bureaucrats took time. According to an SDP co-ordinator, 'Often it has been difficult to get support from some of the commissioners because they perceived the EPM as a project that ought to fund development programmes of the DCC. When funds for such purposes were not forthcoming, many bureaucrats lost interest.'

These misconceptions about the SDP and the EPM approach, how it should operate, and what its outputs should be persist among some officials to this day. Unless those who are expected to put the EPM into practice truly understand its aims, the sustainability and institutionalisation of the approach are likely to founder.

Semi-autonomous status of the SDP

The EPM in Dar es Salaam is handicapped by the fact that the agent of change, the SDP, was established as a semi-autonomous unit outside the DCC. This caused various problems, including weak communication between the staff of the two bodies.[33] The physical separation between the SDP and the DCC, coupled with the comparatively better remuneration and working environment enjoyed by the generally more junior SDP staff, also fostered some ill-will and so hampered working relationships that could have facilitated the adoption of the EPM norms in the routine operations of the DCC.[34] This was exacerbated by the fact that all project managers and co-ordinators were appointed from outside the DCC. Former SDP co-ordinators noted ' ... the EPM concept seems to have been over-mystified. Throughout its existence the head has been appointed from outside the DCC, and not from among us. We do not know why.'[35] Since all project managers and co-ordinators were appointed on merit, such remarks probably represent petty grudges. But the underlying message is clear.

Elitism and distrust of working groups

The EPM approach requires bureaucrats and politicians to be open and responsive to ideas from stakeholders.[36] But while DCC departments were represented in the WGs, the experiences recounted in the case studies above show that DCC officials typically received proposals from the WGs with reservation, if not outright scorn. The VIBINDO Executive Secretary noted:

> Both the former City Council and the Commission have done little to solve the Machinga [hawkers] problem except to harass them and evict them. They believe they have solutions to problems even when their actions do not

work. They cannot provide employment to the youth, but they destroy their initiatives. The major problem is that the relationship between City Council or Commission and us [non-council persons] is poor. They think we [VIBINDO] are lay-persons and thus have no [skills] or good ideas, which can address local problems. They ignore us because they think we cannot speak the same language.[37]

It is no surprise that views and ideas from below are looked down on by those in power. Bureaucrats often tend to treat people from outside the local government system as uninformed lay-persons who cannot make meaningful contributions towards solving community problems (Kombe 1995). Such attitudes may frustrate the establishment of partnerships with private and community actors, and undermine the EPM approach.

Conclusion and recommendations

- EPM implies cross-sectoral co-ordination and consensus-building among many stakeholders often with diverse interests. It must, therefore, proceed slowly. If it takes too long to deliver tangible outputs, the approach is likely to be criticised by those who expect fast results. Indeed, its time-consuming nature may imply costs that stakeholders are unwilling to pay. Some stakeholders may well abandon the approach in favour of existing, though often unsustainable, fast-track options. It is therefore essential that WGs become more efficient and output oriented. This may be accomplished initially by choosing smaller pilot study areas where the pressing environmental issues require strategic inputs from WG stakeholders. The WGs should not attempt, however, to manage routine local government tasks.

- Changing power relationships and norms, rules, and procedures is a slow and complex process, particularly because self-interest may inhibit such changes. To consolidate the radical changes in the local institutional setting envisaged by the EPM will take time, endurance, and ongoing nurturing of the approach, as well as tolerance on all sides.

- The present role and position of WGs in local government is ambiguous, since they have neither a statutory nor a structural position in the administration. Their position as an operational arm of the EPM should be defined, including a mechanism to convey feedback from the local authority to the WG members. While WGs ought to facilitate partnerships, they should be dissolved once their specific tasks are accomplished and not become permanent structures within the local government. However, the institutional framework for deploying and responding to WGs should be developed at all levels of urban governance.

- Local governments should play a leading role in implementing the EPM, particularly by convening WG sessions. Local government is in a position to foster confidence in the WGs among local bureaucrats, increase WG accountability to local government, and mitigate or eradicate the power-sharing problem. Organised local communities, including those at the ward and *Mtaa* level should be assisted to adopt and form their own WGs to link with those operating at the local government level.

- Sustained partnership requires that all parties share benefits as well as costs. This is important in order to help establish a recognition of (monetary) value of the WGs' outputs as well as fostering their accountability to the local authorities.

The shift from bureaucratically controlled to substantive stakeholder participation in urban planning and management can improve the handling of problems facing our cities and towns, whether through mobilising resources or in order to promote environmentally friendly urban settlements. The EPM's impacts on and contribution to sustainable development in Dar es Salaam are already being felt in the gradual adoption of multi-sectoral approaches to planning and management in the City Council; the implementation of an effective traffic management system; the training of central and local government staff as well as community (civil society) leaders in the three municipalities; and the increased participation of residents (both community members and professionals) in urban governance.

So far, the UASU has concentrated on the nine new municipalities and the city of Dar es Salaam. Little has been done to support, build capacity, and put in place a policy and legislative framework for monitoring long-term replication and implementation of the EPM process elsewhere in Tanzania. In addition to the recommendations above, the future prospects of EPM in the country also hinge on the ability to explore and build the capacity to propagate and monitor the adoption of the EPM at a pace that meets the anticipated demand nationwide. This will happen only if the key ministries responsible for urban development management and planning, as well as key training institutions in the country, are fully involved in promoting the EPM strategy.

Notes

1 Most DCC bureaucrats are appointees of the council; commissioners are appointees of the central government. Local communities in the wards elect councillors, who often have different socio-economic or training backgrounds from those of the commissioners or DCC bureaucrats.

2 UNCHS (Habitat) and UNEP launched the Sustainable Cities Programme (SCP) in August 1990, as part of the Urban Management Programme. Its main goal is to ensure that fast-growing cities and towns remain economically, socially, and environmentally sustainable. For more details see SCP Source Book Series, Habitat/UNEP; see also UNCHS 1995, 1997.

3 Institutionalisation here refers to a process whereby the participatory principles and instruments inherent in the EPM approach are adopted in the routine decision-making process. This implies that EPM norms become stable and legitimate within local government structures.

4 'Informed' in the sense that the selection of stakeholders' representative groups is *inter alia* made from persons with knowledge of, and interest in, the specific environmental issue of concern.

5 The emphasis on partnership primarily arose from the increasing acknowledgement of the fact that neither the central, local government, popular sector, donor communities, nor private sector alone has sufficient wherewithal to address problems posed by unprecedented urban population growth.

6 Priority environmental issues which were identified and agreed upon are: solid waste management, liquid waste management, air quality management and urban transportation, open space management and urban agriculture. Others are upgrading unplanned and unserviced settlements, managing urban expansion, managing urban renewal, managing coastal resources and managing the urban economy and integrating petty trading in the urban economy.

7 SDP co-ordinators or project managers were appointed on merit by a panel constituted of officers from the Ministry of Local Government and Regional Administration, the city (Commission) council and Habitat.

8 UASU, like SDP, continues to operate as a separate entity and maintains a financial accounting and management system separate from that of the local governments it supports.

9 Management of informal activities or businesses entailed organising the actors and their activities, providing premises, and formalising their operations by registering them and issuing licences.

10 Petty trading is a part of the informal sector operations. It is estimated that the informal sector could employ about 65 per cent of the annual increase in the labour force while the formal sector can absorb only 8.5 per cent (URT 1997).

11 Some activities including vegetable and food vending as well as service activities such as carpentry, garages, and tailoring have fixed premises,

but these have often not been sanctioned by the local government.

12 The location of informal (petty) trading in the city is often influenced by the expected flow of buyers from surrounding areas.

13 For instance, it is estimated that forced eviction of petty traders in Congo Street in Dar es Salaam City resulted in a loss of over 30,000 businesses and property worth more than TShs 500 million (SIDO-GTZ 1995).

14 Discussion with Anna Mtani on 26 March 2000.

15 Discussion with the WG Co-ordinators and a former head of the DCC department.

16 The reported cost of building the Sterio-Temeke market was TShs 480 million (US$600,000).

17 Interviews conducted with some of the former DCC commissioners and the programme officer for the organisation which financed the design construction of the two markets, the National Income Generation Programme (NIGP), invariably argued that this was a decision by the DCC management.

18 The respondents preferred to remain anonymous.

19 In a discussion with Mr Michael (WG Co-ordinator) on 24 March 2000 and VIBINDO Secretary General on 28 March 2000, both asserted that WG morale deteriorated sharply and animosity between vendors and the DCC followed the DCC's decision.

20 Discussions with VIBINDO Secretary General and Chairman, 28 March 2000.

21 Yusuph (2000) reports that because of the high charges levied on the stalls erected at Temeke Street market, vendors have abandoned the stalls. Meanwhile, the government-owned newspaper, *The Daily News* (5 June 2000) characterised Makumbusho market as 'A sleeping giant' and reported that despite the call on petty traders (*Machingas*) by the President of Tanzania on 26 September 1997 to make full use of it, the complex remained sparsely occupied with only 65 of 350 stalls being used. This market complex is reported to have cost TShs 370 million (US$500,000).

22 *Mtaa*, or sub-ward, is the smallest administrative unit of local government and comprises several Ten Cell Units or agglomerations of ten houses (though in practice the number varies from eight to 15 dwellings).

23 For instance, during some of the WG sessions, local leaders (*Mtaa* and Ten Cell leaders) who had been involved in initiatives to protect and monitor the use of open space in their respective areas were invited to share their experiences with the WG members. Some architects from private and public offices in the city were also invited.

24 The selected wards were Mwananyamala and Makurumla; Ilala and Tabata; Ward 14 and Mbagala; in Kinondoni, Ilala, and Temeke Districts, respectively.

25 The amendment was effected through Government Notice No. 167, 1994.

26 The signatories to the contract include the City Chairman, the Solicitor, the respective ward and *Mtaa* leaders and the corporate body, or private individual as the case may be.

27 This refers to, for instance, changes of communal open spaces in Block A in Sinza and invasion of a school plot in Magomeni.

28 Discussions with WG Co-ordinators on 26 March and 28 March 2000.

29 Primarily because the grassroots, including wards, were not represented in the Commission.

30 In a discussion between the author and those who have been closely involved in the EPM promotion activities in Dar es Salaam and else-where in Tanzania, they suggested that the strong mandate given to the Commission, and overall management style, contradicted the EPM spirit (personal communication from B.B.K. Majani, A.G. Kyessi, and T.J. Nnkya).

31 This may happen despite the fact that national legislation requires that civil servants remain non-partisan in executing their duties.

32 Majani and Halla (1999), discussing solid waste management in Dar es Salaam, reiterate this, noting that one of the pitfalls of the City Commission is that it focuses on short-term results. Initially the Commission term was only one year; later it was extended by two more years.

33 This includes interpersonal clashes between the DCC bureaucrats and the SDP staff (personal communi-cations from Dr Burian (UASU Co-ordinator), Mr Lubuva (former City Commission Secretary, now Ilala Municipal Director), and Mr Salewi (Engineer, National Income Generation Programme [NIGP]).

34 SDP co-ordinators felt that some of the DCC bureaucrats were resentful of the SDP staff because the latter enjoyed better working conditions, despite being junior to them, views echoed by some of the former heads of departments interviewed.

35 The respondents wished to remain anonymous.

36 The fact that the current generation of bureaucrats in the local govern-ment system was largely trained and employed before the EPM was adopted might inhibit the adoption of changed working practices, while some bureaucrats may shy away because of ignorance about the EPM.

37 Discussion with the VIBINDO Secretary General, Gaston Kikuwi, 28 March 2000.

References

Burian, B. (2000) 'Sustainable Development in an Urban Tanzania Context', presented at N-AERUS international workshop, 'Cities of the South: Sustainable for Whom', 3-6 May, Geneva

Dar es Salaam City Commission (1996) 'Summary of the Proceedings of the Workshop on Preparation of the Strategic Urban Development Plan', 15-17 October, Karimjee Hall, Dar es Salaam

Dar es Salaam City Council (1993) 'Proceedings for the City Consultation on Environmental Issues', DCC: Dar es Salaam

Kombe, W.J. (1995) Formal and Informal Land Management in Tanzania: Case of Dar es Salaam City, Dortmund: SPRING Publication, No. 13

Kombe, W.J. (1999) 'The Synthesis of the Contentious Sustainable Urban Development Plan (SUDP) Issues', working paper prepared for the Dar es Salaam City Commission and UASU, Dar es Salaam

Majani, B. (2000) 'Institutionalising Environmental Planning and Management: The Case of Solid Waste Management in Dar es Salaam', doctoral research, University of Dortmund

Majani, B. and F. Halla (1999) 'Innovative ways for solid waste management in Dar es Salaam: towards stakeholder partnerships', Habitat International 23(3): 351–61

Post, J. (1997) 'Urban management in an unruly setting, the African case',

Third World Planning Review 19(4):
347–66

Rakodi, C. and N. Devas (1993) *Managing
Fast Growing Cities: New Approaches
to Urban Planning and Management
in the Developing World*, Harlow:
Longman

Rondinelli, Dennis A. (1983) *Development
Projects and Policy Experiments: An
Adoptive Approach to Development
Administration*, London: Methuen

SIDO-GTZ (1995) 'Security of Land
Tenure for Informal Sector: A
Proposal Submitted to the Steering
Committee for the Settlement of
Informal Sector Business', unpublished
report, Dar es Salaam

UNCHS (1995) *First Evaluation Report for
the Sustainable Dar es Salaam Project*,
Nairobi: UNCHS

UNCHS (1997) *Second Evaluation Report
for the Sustainable Dar es Salaam
Project*, Nairobi: UNCHS

United Republic of Tanzania (URT)
(1997) *National Employment Policy*,
Dar es Salaam: Ministry, Labour and
Youth Development

Vidler E. and S. Russell (2000) 'The rise
and fall of government–community
partnerships for urban development:
grassroots testimony from Colombo',
Environment and Urbanization 11(12):
73–86

Yusuph, K.A. (2000) 'Relocation of Petty
Traders, a Strategy for Management
of Informal Activities in Dar es
Salaam City: a Case of Temeke Sterio
Market', unpublished dissertation,
Department of Urban and Regional
Planning, Dar es Salaam: UCLAS

Democracy and social participation in Latin American cities

Diego Carrión M.

Democratisation, structural adjustment, state reform (including de-centralisation), and liberalisation of the economy (including privatisation) have brought about dramatic changes in the nations, societies, and cities of Latin America and the Caribbean (LAC). As central governments devolve greater responsibilities to them, local governments are obliged to perform new roles and strengthen their managerial capacity to cope with increasing urban problems and popular demands. In response to the state's inability to address local problems, there has been a flourishing of civil society organisations (CSOs) engaging in self-help initiatives, building social networks and mutual support groups in order to meet their basic needs (see article by Joseph in this volume; McCarney 1996). To deepen democracy and promote popular participation in resolving urban issues calls for clear guiding principles and methodologies. These should be based on the wealth of experience Latin American cities have acquired over the years.

Re-reading the context

Modernisation

Within the new global scenario, a series of social, economic, and political changes have spread across the planet. *Modernisation* has brought with it the reorganisation of both capital and the state. This is being achieved through the so-called *flexibilisation* of labour, which seeks to eliminate legal and trade-union-based forms of protection for workers, and through market *deregulation*, which seeks to stimulate commercial activity and allow private business to fix prices and determine the quality of products.

The state is being reorganised around the redistribution of a series of functions and responsibilities among non-governmental actors. Privatisation policies mean that the more profitable functions are being sold cheaply to large national and multinational companies, while unprofitable social policies are handed over to municipalities, the churches, NGOs, and citizens themselves. This is accompanied by the streamlining of the state, which includes lay-offs as well as reductions in public spending and investment in the social sector. Meanwhile, the state's reproocive apparatus its mechanisms for controlling the population, and political patronage networks, remain intact.

Globalisation

The key to this scenario is the process by which national economies are becoming internationalised. Foreign trade is increasing, and a global economy is consolidating as transnational corporations grow stronger and develop new strategies. Countries and cities now depend to a greater degree on the dynamics and behaviour of the global economy, in which the movement of capital, information, and physical inputs determine the patterns of production and consumption. Yet the various macro-economic adjustments – the new rules for local markets and the dismantling of forms of social protection – benefit only a few and bring about the growing impoverishment of the majority.

Latin America and the Caribbean: an increasingly urban region

One component of this scenario in the LAC region is the tendency towards urbanisation. The region now has more than 500 million inhabitants (more than Europe), with 70 per cent of them living in urban areas. Currently, it has 36 cities with populations of over one million, two of the five largest cities in the world, and eight of the world's 50 largest cities. Populations are concentrated in one or two major cities in each country, but medium-sized cities are growing rapidly.

The 16,000 municipalities in the LAC region form a highly hetero-geneous set of cities and towns. Even within countries, cities differ markedly in size, location, economic and productive functions, history, culture, and relationships with external environments and markets. It is thus difficult to speak about *the* Latin American city. But where cities differ least is in their concentration of populations whose basic needs are unmet and whose quality of life is deteriorating. And cities lack the capacity to receive new population influxes in the short or the long term.

The phenomenon of urban growth in the midst of economic recession has meant that cities do not have the necessary resources to maintain, much less to improve, basic infrastructure and services (see article by Allen in this Reader). In addition, unemployment is rising, poverty is growing, private investments have dropped, and the norms of neighbourliness and co-existence are giving way to various forms of violence. Meanwhile, low-income groups face increasing problems of access to housing and urban services. It is no easy matter to promote equitable, democratic, efficient, and environmentally sustainable forms of urban development against such a backdrop.

Consolidating democracy and citizenship through local governments and civil society

A central issue in the current reform of the state involves the transfer of powers from national to local governments, principally in order to relieve pressure on national government institutions and to transform the municipality, assigning it roles and functions so that it can provide better services. The challenge here is also to transfer decision making, technical capacity, financial resources, and administrative autonomy in a way that facilitates democratic management of local affairs.

The problems of Latin American cities create new demands on, and challenges to, the international community, national governments, local bodies, and local society. These go beyond current administrative, technical, and financial policies and capacities for managing urban development. The challenges require a broadening and strengthening of the capacities of social organisations and institutions. It is thus important to recognise the specific competences and dynamics of national government and municipal institutions, as well as those of NGOs and communities. Arenas for consultation, co-ordination, interrelation, and co-operation among all these actors are vital, for it is here that the conditions and guiding principles necessary for local development are negotiated.

Guiding principles for local development

- *Constituting a new realm of sustainable development:* The objective would be to balance human welfare with nature, based on the values of democracy, equality before the law, and social justice, for present and future generations; without discrimination based on gender, creed, ethnicity, economic, social, or political status.

- *Broadening the democratic management of cities:* This would entail forms of planning, building, operating, and governing cities that are based on the participation of and control by all social actors and local social institutions, where the common good would prevail, with respect for local cultural values and attention to the need for long-term sustainability.

- *Constructing citizenship:* Inhabitants and their organisations would exercise their rights and would fulfil their obligations in full. Decisions would be based on consensus, multilateral dialogue, negotiation, and political will, in a context of transparency, public consultation, and adequate information and knowledge of the affairs related to the management of the locality.

Local governments, democracy, and citizenship

Local governments are the institution of government closest to the everyday lives and problems of citizens, and they exercise partial governance over the city.[1] This points to the need to broaden and strengthen citizenship as a starting point for deepening democracy, while at the same time assisting the municipality in managing the affairs of the city. It is in the meeting place between citizens and the state that progress can be made in building broader forms of democratic government, that is, *good government.* It is, therefore, vital that the municipality is strengthened through effective decentralisation and de-concentration, and through the existence of a free and active civil society (Rodríguez and Winchester 1996).

NGOs and popular organisations: initiating processes and influencing policies... the quality of life in cities is not a matter which only involves the state or which is exclusively conditioned by the market. In fact, civil society has exercised the right to intervene in the city. (Ediciones Sur 1996: 7)

Resolving the problems of cities and the urban habitat in Latin America is enormously difficult within traditional frameworks of government practice and formal market mechanisms. Bureaucracy, corruption, political patronage, and lack of creativity on the part of the state have been obstacles to addressing the needs of low-income groups. The private sector, because of its profit-seeking logic, is not geared towards low-income populations. Popular and grassroots actors have, therefore, developed their own strategies and mechanisms for fulfilling these needs and for some years now, NGOs, community-based organisations, and other popular organisations have played a role in habitat-related activities.

While acknowledging the limited reach and impact of their programmes, NGO-supported popular processes often reinforce the principle of:

ensuring that projects contribute to the development of autonomous social subjects, capable of representing themselves, capable of promoting their own interests in aspects which concern them, capable of interacting from a favourable position with other actors and agents each of which responds to its own logic. (Unda 1996)

Thus:

In the neighbourhoods of Latin America's cities, social organisations and non-governmental organisations do many things: they design and build housing, roads, streets, and pathways; they install potable water, sewage, and electrical services; they renovate neighbourhoods; they confront emergencies – earthquakes, floods, economic crisis, civil wars; they attend to food and health needs; they give courses and technical training in the development and management of socially oriented projects; they formulate proposals and develop studies; they revitalise neighbourhood-level economic networks; they hold meetings, broadcast the problems of the city, demand solutions, collaborate in forming groups, in linking institutions, in promoting spaces for multilateral dialogue and negotiation; they design, articulate, and manage socially oriented projects together with governmental agencies and institutions; they incorporate public and other available resources; and they seek to develop replicable processes. (Ediciones Sur 1996: 36)

The thousands of efforts of this kind around the world show that it is indeed possible for society to move forward, serving to initiate genuine political processes and influence public policy. Such efforts often inspire others and are replicated, transferred, and disseminated. As such, they offer a ray of hope. But to achieve their full potential, these organisations must be free to set up and initiate actions for and with residents, and to have the full moral support of local authorities in doing so.

Challenges for Latin American cities: obstacles and opportunities

In moving towards local development that is guided by the principles listed above, Latin American cities will face a series of major challenges in order to:

- alleviate poverty;
- raise the efficiency and competitive strength of the urban economy;
- improve urban environmental quality;
- develop and consolidate democratic governance;
- increase the efficiency of urban management and service delivery; and
- strengthen respect for cultural values and diversity.

Several major obstacles lie in the path, but there are also opportunities that may help us to build a new kind of city, and both the obstacles and the opportunities demand creativity in our handling of them. The obstacles include:

- the fact that neither urban planning, improvisation, nor clientelistic practices have been successful;
- shortage of financial resources in local governments, high turnover of local government officials, political and economic instability, and corruption;
- dreams of a city that we cannot build and manage (e.g. Singapore, San Francisco, Barcelona);
- property speculation spurred by liberalisation and deregulation.

The opportunities include the following:

- the democratisation process occurring in the region may help to strengthen local governments and increase community participation;
- decentralisation may deepen democracy, given the emergence of local government as an important actor;
- existing social capital in LAC societies may introduce innovative ways of dealing with urban problems;
- globalisation might favour those LAC cities with a comparative advantage in the world market.

An alternative approach to managing Latin American cities

The city is an integrated and complex system, whose management, among other things, has to deal with issues of building, development, and maintenance. How urban growth and development take place and are managed, and the availability of adequate land for residential areas and the provision of housing and services, are matters of collective social concern, and are not the monopoly of the political and intellectual élites.

People's participation in planning and in decision-making processes is indispensable to handling complex urban affairs in a democratic fashion. As we often see in Latin American cities, unilateral decisions are the basis of an inegalitarian and authoritarian society and need to be addressed head-on.

Among the greatest obstacles to be overcome are the perceptions and influence of what we might call the economic pragmatists. Particularly misguided is the view that social infrastructure and services in human settlements are 'non-productive' investments, and so should be made only if resources are remaining after 'productive' investments have been made. The simplistic use of econometric models, based on the primacy of economic growth, obscures the complex intersectoral connections in the development of human settlements. In so doing, such positions diminish the possibility of placing human settlement processes at the centre of social and economic change.

Increasing poverty is one of the LAC region's greatest problems today. Neither poverty, hunger, nor the lack of housing and services, constitutes a problem in itself. The problem arises when hunger is not followed by access to enough food; when the need for shelter is not satisfied by good-quality houses; when basic facilities are either inadequate in themselves, or in insufficient supply. The contradiction between needs and their satisfaction is seen in the poverty that is caused through the exploitation of low-income groups. It is impossible to overcome urban problems in such a situation. Key structural reforms need to be introduced to allow new initiatives to develop. These need to address: the reorientation of national priorities to resolving the problems affecting poor people; reforms to develop the democratic management of cities; mechanisms to increase popular participation in the cities; institutions, politics, and social action for processes of decentralisation to the grassroots; and establishing a just equilibrium between participation of the state, the private sector, and civil society. These issues are discussed in greater detail below.

An urgent change in priorities: the fight against poverty

The challenge we face in the LAC region can be met only if we face it fully. This means *urgently shifting priorities* towards attending to the substantive problems and needs of Latin America's low-income groups. First and foremost, the problem is poverty. If we fail to address this, the prospects for strengthening democracy will disappear and existing social unrest will certainly rise. Confronting and resolving the problem of poverty will have to be sustained by changes in four areas, each constituting a pillar of support to a new democratic approach to improving the living conditions of the urban poor. The result of such changes will be a 'city for all', which assures egalitarian access to land, housing, and services – not just a watered-down and formalistic version of democracy.

Towards democratic city management

In Latin America, the shadow of totalitarianism is ever present. This constitutes a threat to democratic processes, which are already difficult enough to get off the ground. Totalitarian regimes are seldom concerned with solving the problems of poor people; rather, they usually reproduce a more intense and generalised form of poverty, which may be witnessed in the form of increasing social and spatial segregation in the cities. Such segregation perpetuates differential access to land, housing, and services, according to whether one lives in the legal or the illegal city. Reversing these trends requires far more than the right to elect government representatives. In Latin America, the ballot has, to date, offered little alternative to vertical governmental structures and procedures that are usually both bureaucratic and lack mechanisms for popular participation. Indeed, low-income and marginalised groups do not feel their interests are represented by national or local representatives.

The responsibility for democratising society overall, and the management of cities in particular, ultimately lies with popular organisations, provided that their autonomy and dynamics are respected by government. However, democratic management at the local level also requires some complementarity on the part of national institutions. Municipal governments, with popular support, will need appropriate levers and instruments for demanding that central governments assure them the means to secure resources for public works, service provision, and effective popular participation in regional and national structures of governance.

Other aspects of complementary democratisation will be needed in relationships between majorities and minorities; between local governments and people's organisations; among mayors, officers, and councillors; and between the executive body of local government and its legislative structure. If it is not possible to converse and debate openly with all local actors then the advance of democracy will be an uphill struggle.

Popular participation

Strong social organisation is indispensable to the democratic management of cities. This often begins with low-income groups organising around efforts to improve their material conditions. But processes such as these can and often do promote broader democratisation within society. The chances of this happening are better when local authorities and popular organisations develop a mutual appreciation and respect for the other's field of action. This can be promoted best by establishing a legal framework for promoting and protecting the existence and functioning of local civil society organisations, developing the political will within local authorities to work with them, and making it possible for CSOs to access the resources they need to participate more fully in decision-making processes. An indicator of success in democratising local governance would be CSO participation in defining urban policy priorities after municipal elections. Finally, democratisation is a process of building up social dynamics, starting from the base of society – the community – and ascending to the national level. But local-level democracy cannot be established without it first existing at the national level.

Decentralisation from a popular perspective

Popular participation must operate within a properly decentralised state if it is to contribute to democratic urban management. The common argument that the decentralisation of the state will, in and of itself, enhance democratic urban management and people's participation is based on a myth. Recent experiences in Latin America show that local societies and cities often remain in the power of traditional local élites and national authorities even after some forms of decentralisation have been implemented.

From a community perspective, it is imperative that different local groups (neighbourhood or community associations, local planning groups, etc.) are capable of expressing their demands and defining alternative approaches to their own problems. Local governments play a central role in this, given that they are the nearest form of power with which community groups will have contact. But, in order for them to channel popular participation, their structures must be adapted to allow and promote such participation and to be sensitive to the demands emerging from it. Above all, the kind of decentralisation process we need is one that distributes power, decisions, and allocation of resources democratically and on a long-term basis.

Democratic decentralisation means, for example, rethinking external debt, especially debt contracted by local and national governments to provide housing and services. If new loans are needed because of a lack of local financial resources, these should be made according to local and national priorities and under terms that do not cause social dislocation to the majority low-income population (see the article by Kundu in this volume).

Decentralisation has the potential to fragment the initiatives either of the people or of the local authorities. For example, the creation of too many local authorities or agencies could lead to ineffective planning and a lack of co-ordination regarding broader regional or national problems. Thus, what is needed is a dual perspective in which local problems and actions are approached with an understanding of macro-level context. Decentralisation should be based on the recognition that some problems cannot be resolved at the local level alone but have national or global ramifications: for instance, inflation, technological change, mass media, external debt, and international co-operation.

A new equilibrium between state, private sector, and community-based actors

Whether poor people can acquire assured access to land, housing, and basic urban services, and attain better living conditions, depends on achieving a more equitable equilibrium among three interdependent sets of social actors: the state, the private, and the popular (community) sectors.

In highly simplified and idealised terms, the three sectors concern themselves with the following functions. The state is society's regulatory agent, so it has to be strong enough to manage the economy and international relations, guarantee social peace, and provide basic services while allowing broad participation of all social groups in state structures and operations. Among its regulatory functions, the most important is to strengthen democracy. The private sector's major concern is to earn profits and its importance to the national economy cannot be underestimated. However, in recent decades its forms of operation have tended to undermine the capacity of the state to mitigate the unequal distribution of wealth. The community sector, which until now has been marginalised from decision making, has demonstrated an increasing dynamism and capacity to offer solutions to society's problems. From its position of economic and social disadvantage, this sector presses for democratic development processes.

With the state increasingly adopting the private sector's orientation towards profitability as a criterion for public investment, the possibility of providing social services to the broad majority is diminishing daily. Thus, housing and urban facilities for poor people continue to deteriorate at an alarming rate. So, too, do the prospects for integrating those who live and work in the informal economy into a comprehensive programme of social development.

Overcoming this persistent injustice is the collective responsibility of the state, civil society, and the private sector. But this must begin with the state's reassertion of its central role in planning national and local development. Without this there is no way to attain a healthy balance among different social groups and their interests. Harnessing the market for social development does not require transforming market relations. But it does require overcoming the market's incapacity to distribute wealth equitably enough to allow low-income groups to earn sufficient to pay for the services and facilities to which, as citizens, they have rights.

Civil society, and especially organisations of low-income groups, must also be given a role in planning and decision making. At present, the conditions for their effective participation in such activities are often weak. Meeting their own survival needs absorbs most of the time and energy of poor people. Both improvements in living conditions and the establishment of more direct channels of participation in decision making are precursors to achieving a better equilibrium among the state, civil society, and the market.

Criteria for popular participation in community development and management programmes

When designing and implementing elements of popular participation in community development and management programmes some basic criteria need to be followed:

- *Sense of totality:* Consider the city as well as the social group as a whole. Initiatives that are conceived and developed as isolated actions reproduce individualism at the community level and a dislocation between policies and actions more generally.

- *Political sense:* Consider the general political scenario. Programmes or projects that are conceived and designed without a careful analysis of the political context might fail because of unanticipated external constraints.

- *Sense of autonomy:* Support efforts of the community to acquire capacities and establish conditions for making autonomous and critical decisions about what matters to them. Support training processes that transfer knowledge, which is a step towards gaining power.

- *Sense of reality:* Avoid paternalistic and artificial conditions when conceiving and developing programmes or projects. The likelihood that a popular housing process will succeed lies precisely in the degree of long-term self-sufficiency that can be developed by the group involved.

- *Sense of continuity:* Understand that the housing processes of poor people are 'endless' and changeable. Interventions should be based on an understanding of the notion of process that is embodied in the development of popular neighbourhoods.

- *Sense of respect:* Be extremely respectful of people's commitments and behaviour. External agents, including progressive NGOs, are involved only temporarily; the people living in the community are permanent. If external agents are to work in a community they should respect the nature and the dynamics of the people, their organisations, and their leaders.

Conclusion

As the urban habitat deteriorates, so too does the quality of life for its residents. The poor majority are most severely affected by the quality of their habitat so, if we wish to improve their situation, we need an integrated approach to improving their habitat. This requires nothing less than building and maintaining an equitable and democratic city, a city that makes healthy living conditions equally accessible to everyone through effective participatory decision making.

To realise this 'utopian city for all' that offers access to land, housing, and urban services on an egalitarian basis, depends on there being genuine democracy throughout society – as a whole and in the management of urban issues. In the third millennium, most human beings will live in cities and towns; thus we must learn to live and let live. Twenty-first-century human society will require democratic and governable peoples who are prosperous and efficient, who express solidarity and justice, who are healthy and who support life, who feel safe and respect the rights of others, who share collective identities and a creative culture. Society has a historic responsibility to construct cities and towns that meet these conditions. Creating the social and political will to enable everyone to join in efforts to achieve these ideals is the task ahead.

Note

1 'Governance' is used to refer to the way in which power is exercised in a society. The concept of governance recognises not only that authorities govern society, rather that they are part of a complex network of interactions between institutions and groups. Governance is that network of interactions. The citizenry is established when people are incorporated into and actively influence this network (Rodríguez and Winchester 1996).

References

Ediciones Sur (1996) *Patrimonio societal e intervenciones urbanas. Trece experiencias en América Latina*, Santiago de Chile: Ediciones Sur

McCarney, P. (ed.) (1996) *The Changing Nature of Local Government in Developing Countries*, Center for Urban and Community Studies, Toronto: University of Toronto Press

Rodríguez, A. and L. Winchester (1996) 'El municipio: lugar de la ciudadanía', in *Revista Ciudad Alternativa* no. 12, Centro de Investigaciones, Quito: CIUDAD

Unda, Mario (1996) Las redes, los lazos y los hilos sueltos, Quito: CIUDAD

Sustainable development and democracy in the megacities

Jaime Joseph

In looking at sustainable development from the perspective of the cities of the South, we shall focus on Lima. We believe that the megacities in the Third World are a thorn in the side of strategies for building democracy and sustainable, human development. Indeed, the development occuring in these megacities seems the least human and sustainable. What can 'sustainable' mean in such a context? Our concern here is to find ways in which community-based organisations (CBOs) can continue to respond to basic material needs, but in such a way that their efforts are part of sustainable and integrated development processes and not limited to poverty relief and environmental clean-up projects. This concern is at once a social, political, and an ethical enterprise.[1]

The first part of this paper reflects on the concepts and theoretical framework for 'sustainable' development in the contemporary world, particularly in the light of the impact of neo-liberalism and poverty on the minds and hearts of people who live in Southern megacities. We argue that democracy and development must be inseparable if development is to be sustainable and fully human.

In the second part, we suggest that a central problem in the search for human sustainable development is *fragmentation,* as people's capacities and needs are treated as separate and unrelated issues. Moreover, we argue that, in the megacities, a democratic approach to development must be decentralised to the areas where most of the urban poor actually live. We end by reviewing some initiatives in Lima that might well inform strategies which would allow us to break out of our crisis and to promote and sustain processes of democratisation and development.

Sustainable: for whom and how?

The concept of sustainability as applied to development has a history. In 1983 the General Assembly of the United Nations set up the World

Commission on Environment and Development. Four years late under the presidency of Gro Harlem Brundtland, the Commissio published *Our Common Future*, which defined sustainable development as 'a development which satisfies the needs of the present without compromising the ability of future generations to satisfy their own necessities'. The essence of 'sustainable' seems to be to limit development. Instead of 'more is better', a slogan was launched claiming that 'sufficient is better'. What was not clear was what mechanisms – who and how – should be used to *'limit'* development. This is not principally a technical question but rather an ethical and a political problem that still remains unsolved.

The 1992 Earth Summit was organised as alarms were going off – and they continue to sound – all of them telling the planet that resources are limited, especially the resources that underpin our present model of development. What is even more alarming is that we may destroy the very conditions necessary for human life even before the resources run out. Global warming, holes in the ozone layer, and overpopulation are a threat to life in general. At the Earth Summit, 179 countries, North and South, made a commitment to construct their own Agenda 21 for sustainable development. And since then, 1300 local authorities have responded by designing their own action plans (ICLEI 1996).

The First World seems to be pressuring the Third World to do the limiting: reduce population, preserve rain forests, conserve water, etc.. It is not easy, then, to reflect on *sustainability* from the perspective of the urban poor who make up a large part of Southern megacities and for whom many basic needs remain unmet. There is in fact some discomfort with the topic, as 'sustainability' is in many ways an induced concern in urban poor communities who are struggling to satisfy the basic material needs essential to their own personal and social development.

'Environment and sustainability' are two of the many urgent issues or concerns that have sprung up in the North and have migrated to the South. In addition to environment, we have become aware of gender, human rights, especially those of children, citizens' rights, workers' rights, the freedom of sexual preferences. All of these, which indeed are essential and urgent world concerns, have become part of an agenda in the particular historical context of free-market, capitalist development in the West. Without denying their importance, we must ask ourselves if these issues mean the same in the South as in the North.

This precaution perhaps appears mistaken when environment and the limits of our planet are such universal concerns. However, it was not so long ago that the countries in the South were described as 'underdeveloped', and it then seemed quite obvious that they had to make efforts to move ahead on the same development road the North had followed. Today, we want to make sure that sustainability is an essential component of our development process and not either an add-on or a limiting factor.

It is difficult to imagine that the West could have achieved its own capitalist economic development if from the outset the emerging productive, financial, and commercial classes had been obliged to limit their use of natural resources, avoid pollution, pay just wages, provide safe and healthy working conditions, respect the rights of women and children, and not exploit foreign workers or workers from particular ethnic groups. The Third World peoples, trying to move ahead on the road to development, are being asked to carry the additional load of these major issues. This apparently puts the Southern countries, and especially their cities, in a bind: either we must accept our 'under'-development and deprive ourselves of the goods which other societies enjoy in excess, or we will inevitably bring about the destruction of the planet. Obviously we must find a third option.

This special issue of *Development in Practice* is dedicated to reflecting on this 'gap' between the accepted meanings of sustainable development in cities, both in the North and in the South. This gap does not reside principally in differences of definition but rather in the different contexts, processes, and systems in the North and the South.

Change the terms of reference: a new and ethical approach to development

It is now clear that the neo-liberal model of economic development is creating more poverty and widening the poverty gap, as well as proving incapable of curbing the overexploitation of the planet and its resources. The UNDP *1996 Human Development Report* tells us that 89 countries are worse off economically than they were a decade earlier. The *New York Times* article on that report (dated 15 July 1996) headlined its story: 'UN Survey Finds World Rich–Poor Gap Widening' (Morris 1996).

In the face of this undeniable reality, a new item was tacked on to the neo-liberal model: poverty relief and redistribution measures. It might even be argued that the nation-state, so weakened by transnational economics and globalisation, has survived and even prospered in its ability to relate to (or manipulate) the growing numbers of poor populations in Third World countries thanks to its role in administrating these programmes. For example, in September 1996, the head of the Inter-American Development Bank organised a forum to study the Washington Consensus in which its author, John Williamson, recognised that the measures had often been applied too strictly as if following a neo-liberal bible. He underlined the importance of the state in providing technological support, credit, information, and, above all, redistribution.

Grassroots organisations have been quite successful in reducing the negative effects of the neo-liberal model and the structural adjustments which have been imposed on all countries to put them on the 'reductionist' development track. But as David Morris (1996) has stated, it is not enough 'to add a dollop of humanitarianism to orthodox development policies already in existence, as seems to be what is happening currently among official donors'. Unfortunately, 'structural adjustment with a human face' implies that rapid GNP per capita growth remains the basic objective, and social improvement must be a by-product. If development is to enhance human well-being, it must be designed in such a way that improvements that raise the quality of life indicators are actively interacting with, even driving, the strategy for economic growth. We would add that it is not enough to add the adjective 'sustainable' to the same market-driven model.

Ethics and development

Ethics and development is not a new topic. The discussion is at least as old as Weber, who was writing in the late 1950s. Denis Goulet (1995) is one of the recent pioneers in this field. In South America, Manfred Max-Neef was one of the most important intellectuals to make clear that economic development was not the same as human development, that *having* (material goods) was not the same as *being* (a full human being). 'Development refers to persons not to objects ... The best development process will be that which permits raising the quality of life of the persons' (Max-Neef *et al.* 1986: 25, author's translation).

Amartya Sen also centred the strategies of human development in the development of the human capacities, freely determined (Sen 1983). 'If in the last analysis, we consider development as the expansion of the capacities of the population to achieve activities freely chosen and valued, then it would be entirely inappropriate to consider human beings as "instruments" of economic development.' (Sen 1999: 600)

Sen (1997) has stressed that ethical principles and human values are essential for development, pointing out that while Adam Smith argued that self-interest was behind the motivation for interchange, he never said this interest was enough. Confidence, interest and concern for others, what Smith called 'sympathy', 'generosity', and 'public spirit', were also essential. Sen (1997: 2) goes on to argue that, 'Capitalism could not have survived on seeking personal benefits alone.' Values are essential to the process from the very beginning.

Ethical and human concerns often enter the scene after the event; once structural adjustment has happened and the damage in terms of poverty and marginalisation has been done. We do not want an approach to development and ethics that is hemmed in by the very ideology that is at the basis of the crisis itself, for this will inevitably mean that ethics and human values only enter the scene at the end of the process. They will be used to give a facelift to and to curb neo-liberalism's chain of negative effects: poverty and inequality, unemployment, environmental destruction, exclusion, violence, *anomie*, and authoritarianism. Our question is whether and how ethical principles can help us break out of the ideological chains in which we have wrapped our approach to development, and replace this with new, effective, and sustainable approaches.

Democracy and development

'Sustainable for whom?' is a question not so much about what type or model of development is pursued, but how development decisions are made and who makes them. We understand 'sustainable' as comprising more than the environmental goals. The *Oxford English Dictionary* defines it as 'capable of being upheld or defended'. So, how can development – which must be 'freely determined', as Sen says –be upheld in a diverse and conflict-ridden urban society? According to Marcuse (1998: 105):

> Sustainability is a treacherous [formulation of goals] for urban policy because it suggests the possibility of a conflict-free consensus on policies, whereas, in fact, vital interests do conflict: it will take more than simply better knowledge and clearer understanding to produce change.

'Sustainability', like 'participation', can be a camouflaged trap. Both terms – highly respectable – can be used to maintain the status quo, focusing on particular 'issues' and covering up deep-rooted, structural problems. When 'sustainability' is applied as a limiting principle, and 'participation' is limited to poverty relief programmes, these concepts can hide the authoritarian hands and the power behind the control of major decisions in development, and cover up the real nature of the model itself.

The megacity as a scenario for sustainable development

From my own point of view – both personal and professional – one of the important positive results of the Earth Summit has been to place cities, especially Third World cities, back on the agendas of nation-states and multilateral agencies. In the 'Manual for Local Planning of Agenda 21, 1996' of the International Council for Local Environmental Initiatives (ICLEI), Elizabeth Dowdeswell, then Executive Director of the UN Programme for Environment, pointed out that there are 213 cities in the Third World with more than one million inhabitants. 'The future of cities', she says, 'will increasingly determine not only the destiny of the nations but also of the planet.' (ICLEI 1996: iii)

This is an important change since the main concentrations of people in the Third World, especially the megacities, that had been pushed to the margins of national and international concerns, are getting back on to the agenda. This is not so much owing to a concern for the massive and endemic poverty and injustice present in these cities. Unfortunately, there has been a common belief that everyone who lives in a megacity somehow benefits from the concentration of wealth and power found there, and so does not need priority attention.[2] Our cities are receiving attention now because they are a threat to the planet. Their demands for services are a threat to sustainability and therefore we need an 'approach entirely different for planning and providing services' (ICLEI 1996). We might say that the urban poor are getting on to the agenda through the back door but, whatever the reason, it is important that they be on that agenda. However, we would argue for a more positive view of the megacities, a view grounded in the potential and the practices of the urban poor.

Maurice Strong, president of the Earth Council, expresses a more positive approach to our Third World cities. '[U]rban areas present the concentration of our worst social, economic and environmental problems, and also offer opportunities for some of the most effective solutions.' (ICLEI 1996) He refers to social, economic, and environmental problems, but does not mention the essential and key aspect, which is building democratic politics.[3] Our argument here follows a simple but solid logic. First, it will only be possible to attend to the needs and demands of poor people with justice and equality if ethical values predominate in the basic decision-making process. Second, that in our complex modern societies the only way in which ethical principles can be the foundation of decision making is through democratic politics.

Yet, nowhere in the Third World has the social and political basis for sustainable development been so weakened as in our megacities. For instance, in Lima, especially in the low-income areas, development initiatives are reduced to survival tactics: nutrition, employment at any cost, health, and security in the face of violence and delinquency. Thus, extreme individualism tends to override the ethical considerations such as justice and equality and respect for cultural values, especially solidarity, that were always an essential element of community-based organisations (CBOs). Furthermore, the direct intervention of central government agencies and the overt manipulation of poor people in poverty relief programmes are undermining the basis for democratic politics.

Fragmented dreams and fragmented people in the megacity

We would argue that *fragmentation* is a growing problem for human sustainable development and for the democratic political systems that can make such development possible (Joseph 2000). Our concern is therefore with the scenarios and practices that can help to overcome the widespread fragmentation that we find even in our own strategies and programmes. For example, the survival of small businesses often depends on child labour, the denial of social benefits, and extremely long hours. Programmes devoted to building citizenship and promoting 'civic participation' or 'local democracy' often leave aside the concern for the *contents* of the decisions made (Joseph 2000). Such compartmentalisation has fragmented these issues and closed them off from any possibility of more synergetic strategies. In so doing, it has also closed them off from integral and sustainable approaches.

Of even greater concern is that this fragmentation of issues affects the social actors themselves. Each group or organisation, often each person, has their own specific area of interest, and this has seriously weakened the urban popular organisations. By focusing on a single issue and not trying to build common interests and goals, CBOs are less likely to interact and enter into dialogue with organisations which have different, and perhaps conflicting, interests. Such an outlook leads to conflict, distrust, and a zero-sum logic. In addition, issue-centred programmes tend to be confined to the short term, in an immediate response to essential needs. The longer or wider perspective that is necessary for development to be sustainable is therefore lost. The resulting sensation of being 'defeated' weakens the vision and the will on which sustainable development strategies depend.

It is often said that the grassroots organisations have disappeared. This is simply not true. In fact, with structural adjustment, the number and types of such organisations have grown, especially in the cities. New organisations have sprung up to face, collectively, problems that previously had been solved privately, by individuals or in the family: food, health, and employment, among others. Similarly, new organisations have been formed to cover responsibilities that the downsized state is unable or unwilling to face: environment, security, and even criminal justice.

However, grassroots organisations have lost much of their capacity to relate to and co-ordinate with different sectors. In the past, various CBOs in Lima were co-ordinated through the central 'Neighborhood Committee'. Previously, such co-ordination took place at a political level (urban popular confederations worked with trade unions and peasant movements) and CBOs were thus involved with political parties and political campaigns. With the weakening of political parties and the virtual breakdown of the democratic political systems, CBOs no longer work together in the same way. They have lost the common ground – explicit paradigms and political scenarios – upon which common proposals, common interests, and common values and principles can be built. They have also lost their power to influence public opinion and political decisions.

NGOs have also been part of this fragmentation of issues and actors, partly in response to accusations of being merely the tool of radical political groups (Joseph 2000). Let us mention just a few of the problems and traps that NGO strategies must grapple with. For one, we must address the basic question posed by contributors to this special issue: *whose* sustainable development? In other words, is it possible democratically to build a common ethical basis for human development when dealing with such diverse cultures, ethnic groups, and religions? This is a classic problem in modern ethics and political philosophy. The most effective form of ethical domination today is the imposition of the one-thought world, the *pensée unique* that has been spread around the globe (Joseph 2000). The increasing respect for individual freedoms and rights to choice seems to be leading to chaos, violence, and anomie. However, on the other end of the ethical spectrum, the greater risk is that ethical principles, values, and norms are imposed on people along with the common good supposedly represented by neo-liberalism. Or, where the neo-liberal model has not been fully successful, authoritarian or fundamentalist regimes are trying to impose their own 'alternative' ethical systems. Is there a real basis for building a common good that can avoid the risks of anomie, imposition by the powerful, or the tyranny of the majority in a democratic system, as was feared by so many liberal thinkers?

A second major trap – this one more on the political level – is often found in strategies designed to approach poverty relief and environmental programmes through different forms of 'participatory democracy' for local development. On the social level we face other problems as we seek to establish a more global strategy of development and democracy. Increasing, massive, and prolonged poverty as well as the widening gap between rich and poor, tend to weaken people's moral fibre and to encourage a savage individualism. The poor, especially those living in the megacities, have absorbed much of this neo-liberal discourse. At the same time, however, they are well aware of the tremendous disadvantages they face and know that it is impossible for them to compete in a market which is *free* or *liberal* only in name.

An essential difference between the world of the urban poor 20 years ago and their world today is that the people, and their political and social organisations, were then on the rise, were building their cities, and were part of a social and political movement that sought to change the world. Today, much of this vital force has been lost, and there is a growing feeling of defeat, of the sheer impossibility of getting out of this hole through one's own efforts.

Poverty and exclusion, limited democracy and authoritarianism, as well as social, cultural, and ethical fragmentation are the central problems we must face in order to move ahead towards sustainable human development. But how and in what scenarios can ethical principles be discussed and developed in such a way that they can guide the development process? How can this be done in a democratic system so that the tyranny of the majority or the manipulation by powerful minorities can be checked and overcome? How can a planned process of human development be made to work in an adverse economic and political context? In particular, how and in what scenarios can people who are immersed in poverty and excluded from most forms of power in an increasingly unequal and unjust social system become vigorous social and political actors? We are faced with a triple task: to consolidate the individuals and their organisations, which are the point of departure and the goal of any human development process; to place ethical, human values at the centre of the development process; and to build a democratic political system which can make these principles effective. Our search takes us to the Third World megacity.

Megacities of the South

'Megacity' is a concept that can be understood in different ways. From the European context, Peter Hall defines it as an urban agglomeration of ten or more millions of inhabitants, and points out that the megacity is growing in importance in developing countries (Hall 1998). In 1960, only 9 of the 19 megacities were in developing countries. Now, this is where 50 of the world's 60 megacities are to be found. However, although the number of inhabitants is an important factor in the definition, we believe that it is neither the only one, nor the most important. The megacity draws our attention because of its impact on society, development, and the state.

There is another important difference between most of the megacities in Third World countries and the modern megacity. Modernity has not only produced globalised cities linked through the highways of information networks (Castells 1996), but a different type of megacity has started to appear, which is more an *urban agglomerate* than a *city*. These agglomerates do not integrate the urban population, but are instead a physical expression of exclusion and disintegration. Such disintegrated and segregated cities are more common in poor countries, though there are growing indications that the megacities in the North are facing similar problems that weaken the possibilities of consolidating a democratic political system at the service of development.

Some analysts go further, and feel that we are witnessing the death of the city as defined by Jordi Borja:

> ... that physical, political and cultural complex, European and
> Mediterranean, but also American and Asian, which we have
> characterised in our ideology and in our values as a concentration
> of population and activity, a social and functional mixture, the ability of
> self-government and a place of symbolic identification and civic
> participation. City as encounter, exchange, city that means culture
> and commerce. City as a place and not a simple space for flows
> (of traffic and people). (Borja 1997: 2, author's translation)

Lima, the capital of Peru, is an example of a megacity in the process of disintegration. It is a megacity, not in terms of numbers, but because it concentrates a large population in both relative and absolute terms. It has over 7 million inhabitants, representing one third of Peru's total population and 44 per cent of its urban population. It also concentrates economic powers (production, finance, commerce), information, and political powers, something that had increased over the ten years of the authoritarian régime of Fujimori. However, in comparison with modern megacities in the North, or the global megacities, Lima is not an urban centre that links and integrates either its own population or that of the other regions of Peru. This is an important factor in explaining why the movements for decentralisation have anti-Lima overtones and often are explicitly opposed to the megacity.

CBOs and sustainable development

The question about sustainable human development is particularly complex in the context of a disintegrating urban agglomeration like Lima. For the last 20 years, a period of political, social, and economic crisis in most Third World countries, of structural adjustment and the one-thought world, our NGO *Centro Alternativa* focused its strategies on the popular urban CBOs. It is well known that Lima's urban poor have organised and found solutions – even if at the survival level – to their basic material needs. In a real sense, the inhabitants of Lima's *barriadas*, or poor neighbourhoods, have built their city.

However, the situation in the megacities in the Third World has changed, as has the reality of the popular urban organisations. These changes are what led the United Nations Research Institute for Social Development (UNRISD) and the United Nations Volunteers (UNV) to ask us to participate in a study of the situation of the CBOs in the megacities. The purpose was to evaluate CBOs' potential for participating with local governments in integral, sustainable development processes.

Our study (Joseph 1999) confirmed our basic strategy (and option) to work with the urban CBOs and enabled us to fine-tune our strategies for moving towards sustainable development in Lima, building on the strengths of the people and their organisations, but not ignoring the increasing obstacles to reaching our goals. We are currently trying to refine a decentralised approach to development and government in the megacity.

Here we can only briefly summarise the positive aspects of the urban organisations, which have demonstrated great creativity in solving their basic material needs. This was the case from the very beginning of the urban expansion around metropolitan Lima in the early 1950s, in what are now known as the 'cones' – north, east, and south. The urban squatters organised every stage in developing their habitat: invasion, urban design, basic services, and legalisation. There has been much praise, and rightly so, of the solidarity and co-operation which made this achievement possible. In these scenarios, women began to play a central role in community life and later in political life. Women's organisations, even more than the family, were the starting point for addressing gender issues in a comprehensive manner.

The following decades (1960–80) were also very vibrant in both the social and political arenas. The workers' movements grew in number and strength due to industrial expansion and to the support initially given by the military dictatorship to labour unions between 1968 and 1975. The peasant movement experienced similar growth and strengthening when the takeovers of land from the *haciendas* (large land-holdings) were followed by the agrarian reform. The popular urban organisations were also federated in Lima and at a national level. All of these social movements were part of a growing political activity, especially on the part of left and popular parties such as the various Marxist groups and the APRA party. The popular organisations seemed to be part of a movement that would lead to a more just model of human development, based on one or another form of socialism.

From 1980, this reality changed radically. For the purposes of this discussion, we would highlight structural adjustment which began in Peru in more subtle forms from 1975, the beginning of the second phase of the military government. The Fujimori government, which assumed power in 1990, later applied the mandates of the Washington Consensus 'without anaesthesia', as has been said. This meant a tremendous reduction in the purchasing power of the poorer urban families, and job losses in factories and public institutions. The loss of jobs also meant the loss of social benefits, especially in healthcare.

As mentioned above, the urban poor responded to the new situation with the same strategies and mechanisms that they had used to build their habitat: courage, creativity, organisation, solidarity, and a sense of justice and dignity. However, if we step back and take a broader look at what has taken place, especially in the last two decades, we find that not only have the grassroots urban organisations dropped off the news agenda but also the worker and peasant movements have been greatly weakened. This is due in part to structural adjustment in which labour laws have been made 'more flexible' in order to cut production costs and reduce government spending. Any union leader who becomes a nuisance can be quickly thrown into the growing ranks of the unemployed. And the peasant movement has been hard hit by the break up of community lands, the lack of technical and financial aid, and the individual struggle for survival within an ideological context of neo-liberalism and a strictly market-driven agricultural strategy.

Nor are CBOs a profitable commodity in the market-driven mass media. A good scandal, the more sordid the better, has much more chance of making the news than does the fact that hundreds of thousands of urban poor defy social statistics and are not only surviving, but becoming involved in alternative development processes. The problem is not just the media, for these are essentially a barometer of what is happening in society. In terms of politics, for instance, often the best way to be elected in Peru is to be the best clown. In the recent parliamentary elections, candidates have had to jump off cliffs in hang-gliders, dress up as Batman, and use all possible means to get press coverage. Issues of substance have been pushed off the media agenda.

Our approach to sustainable development has gone, and has had to go, far beyond the simple conservation of natural resources. We believe that the conservation of the planet depends not so much on limiting – cutting back on – the use of natural resources, especially in countries where basic material needs are still unsatisfied; rather, it depends on adopting a new, ethical approach to development, in which the economic dimensions and material aspects – the 'having' – are seen as means to 'being', to a high quality of life, to the unlimited expansion of our individual and social capacities. And we need to build a political system that makes such development possible. We have come to understand that in complex modern societies that are built on individual freedoms, ethics can only be brought into development through democratic politics.

A stable structure for sustainability

It is increasingly clear that achieving 'stability' in terms of integral human development is a complex challenge and must be seen as a social (especially educational), political, and economic process. Even if we were to limit the scope of 'sustainable' to the environmental aspects, it is obvious that without a democratic political system concerns about our planet and its limited resources will have no effect on the decisions taken. We would summarise the different aspects to be taken into account as follows:

Social level

Our point of departure and return in the development process is people and their communities. Development is concerned, as many have said, with people's needs and capacities, and with building communities which permit the highest quality of life. In the urban areas where poor people live, sustainable development must be based upon the ethical mandate to provide the basic human conditions that give each person a just opportunity to develop his or her capacities. This goes beyond mere survival tactics to ensuring that programmes for poverty relief and attention to basic human needs are seen as part of an integral development process. Obviously, this also covers initiatives to improve environmental living conditions in urban areas, such as water supply, solid waste management, and parks and green areas.

Integral development

Efforts to relieve poverty and protect the environment cannot remain at the level of ensuring basic survival. It is also becoming clear that with the levels of massive poverty and the prolonged economic crisis brought about by the application of neo-liberal policies, redistribution measures are even more necessary, but in themselves are not sufficient. It is also plain – and please excuse the repetition – that redistribution, poverty relief, and environmental programmes must be part of an integrated developmental strategy. Development will not be sustainable if this is not achieved.

We must also understand the context in which we are approaching integral and sustainable development, or we run the risk of promoting oversimplified solutions. An example of this is the importance now given to the *informal* economic sector. There has been much emphasis placed on small or micro-enterprises as the magic solution in offering economic development for the urban poor. Our work over the last 20 years with small businesses, which are multiplying in the megacity, shows that most of them are simply survival tactics with little or no chance for accumulation. Larger enterprises have more possibility for growth, but their markets are limited and increasingly invaded by cheap imports.

If we look at the purchasing power of the inhabitants of the northern cone of Lima, however, we do find a possible market for economic growth. This area has a population of nearly two million. That means two million pairs of shoes, socks, trousers, etc.. It also means furniture, building materials, medicines (natural medicines), and services such as education and recreation, nutrition ... the list is very long. It is not unrealistic to project that local producers could satisfy up to 80 per cent of there demands. However, the monopolistic and transnational production system, the concentration of commerce in a few shopping malls, a financial system which siphons out the savings of poor people, and a free-market policy which offers no protection for emerging enterprises, conspire against the economic dimension of a sustainable development strategy.

Political level

Democratic politics is essential for sustainable development. All our strategies and programmes with the urban poor must be evaluated in relation to their impact on building a democratic, institutionalised (sustainable) political system, which people regard as their principal instrument for moving towards human development. This is another gigantic and complex area, but one which we cannot afford to ignore. Our strategies here must address three basic aspects. The first is rethinking and reforming the state. There is no justification for imposing on all countries a 'one-size-fits-all model' that was designed for other realities and other tasks. We need a state that can make development sustainable for the people in poor urban areas. It must do more than 'level' the playing field. It must strengthen the players, give them the tools they need and, especially while they begin to grow, protect them from other oversized players who invade their pitch.

Second, the complex societies of the Third World need much more than simple referendum or plebiscite democracies. To be sustainable, our political systems require professional political actors, both individuals and political parties. Many analysts have placed the blame for the political debacle in Peru exclusively on the political parties, both right and left. The voters seem to share this assessment and continue to punish the parties and their leaders. However, after 10 years of an 'independent' government we are becoming aware that without professional political actors, the aspirations and proposals of the people cannot be translated into viable political proposals. Rather, independent rule has meant domination and manipulation and, most alarming, the collapse of people's wish to participate in politics. It is almost certain that in Peru, after an electoral process whose validity was questioned the world over, there will be a swing back to party politics.

The question is how this process will take place and what types of political parties will result.

A third and central aspect concerning the political level, and the one which is closest to our work and concern, is the building of a solid civil society and strengthening of citizens who have a positive approach to politics and a will to participate. Much effort and many resources have been dedicated to programmes – mostly educational – designed to build citizenship and to strengthen 'civil society' (Joseph 2000). However, our strategy must centre principally on actors and processes at the sub-national level. In the megacities this means decentralised strategies; so, in the case of metropolitan Lima, for example, we are working on ways to surround the 'cones'. Within that sub-national urban context, we have focused on what might be called emerging 'public scenarios' or 'public spaces' where, we believe, conditions are developing for building a new political and popular élite and new forms of linking democracy to development.

'Public spaces': a decentralised approach to development and democracy in the megacity

In the UNRISD and UNV study (Joseph 1999), we examined the evolving experience of *concertación* which is occurring in the popular neighbourhoods and is becoming something of a buzzword in Peru. According to the *Local Agenda 21 – Peru*:

> The concept of concertación is difficult to translate. It goes beyond
> consultation and brings the different stakeholders around the table
> so that solutions can be negotiated and responsibilities assigned.
> This includes conflicting interests where these exist.
> (Miranda and Hordijk 1998: 71)

Concertación does not exactly mean debate, discussion, or consultation, although it includes all of these practices. In a process of *concertación*, different – often conflicting – actors and interest groups sit at the planning table, analyse problems, design solutions, and, when possible, participate in putting these plans into practice. According to Grompone and Mejía, *concertación* refers to 'the integration of different actors in a system of negotiation and in the construction of public agendas'. This situation requires that each of the participants be recognised as a legitimate social and political actor (Grompone and Mejía 1995: 217). In these processes and scenarios the actors and institutions involved must be open to making compromises and concessions.

Concertación is taking place in public spaces in which organisations of different natures, with different and often opposing interests, are learning to recognise the others at the table as persons and social players with legitimate rights and interests. They are learning to plan together, to build common interest, and, we believe, to incorporate ethical values and cultural principles into the development planning process, which is essential if development is to be human as well as sustainable. Our major hypothesis, which is also a strategy, is that in these experiences we can find the seeds and ideas for a new democratic system that is an instrument for sustainable development.

This hypothesis is based on the positive aspects we find in the following experiences:

- The new experiences create favourable conditions for discussing development and for broadening the interests of the popular organisations. They also allow concrete demands and needs to be linked in synergetic strategies, and enable people to look beyond the short term to medium- and long-term planning. The process leads to a more integral and human focus on development.

- Through interchange and discussion in the planning processes, the social actors learn to do more than express demands for the things they *lack*. In so doing, they become more aware of their capacities, needs, and interests and they learn to express and defend these in dialogue with others. This self-recognition of interests and aspirations helps the participants to recognise the legitimacy of others' interests, which is essential for building a shared solution.

- In these public spaces it is possible openly to discuss ethical principles and values and to incorporate these in the planning process. It is also possible to broaden and strengthen the basis of trust and solidarity that are essential for building a democratic political system and for development. It is becoming evident that the 'post-material' values can be important factors and may be incorporated into development planning even when the actors are faced with crucial material deficits.

- In these public spaces the social actors begin to value and appreciate the dignity and role of democratic politics, understood as a human activity that is based not only on power but also on discourse, i.e. systems, symbols, and common values.

- A new understanding of, and new relations with, public agencies and local governments are established, thus overcoming the exclusively conflictual relations that tend to predominate.

These are the reasons why we are betting on a strategy that is centred on the strengthening of the poplar urban actors, CBOs, and local government and in consolidating the public spaces for *concertación*. In Peru and many other Third World countries, these 'participatory planning' processes, or 'concertations' have drawn a lot of attention and raised considerable expectations, although we are also aware of the need for caution in this regard (Joseph 2000).

Political culture and development

Within the new experiences of 'concertation' that are occurring in these emerging urban public spaces we have begun to focus on the social actors themselves, especially the community leaders, the grassroots urban élite. This is not out of any wish to leave aside the other actors such as local government, political parties, NGOs, and foreign development agencies. Nor do we mean to ignore the adverse economic and political context. We are focusing on the social actors, especially the popular urban leaders, because successes in the other areas depend primarily on these people (Joseph 2000).

Our research into the 'political culture for development' will be based on interviews, focus-group discussions, and direct observation. Our questions and findings fall into three central categories:

- individual and community;
- vision of development; and
- vision of politics.

The first category is the study of grassroots leaders and is centred on the process by which people perceive themselves as individuals. What we are finding is a positive correlation between self-esteem and self-awareness and respect for others and for political processes (Joseph 2000). The converse is that when people and communities have low self-esteem, their values of solidarity and confidence are usually restricted to primary relations (e.g. family, place of origin, religious faith). It is obvious that in planning and evaluating our involvement with the urban communities we must include actions to strengthen individuals and the kinds of relationships and values at work in the community. Likewise, we should include indicators that measure progress or regression in this regard.

The second category includes the working vision of development found in the leaders, assessing whether this is merely short term in focus or more inclusive and long term. We are also seeking to establish how far social actors appreciate the role of community in achieving personal and community development, or whether progress is understood as being only the result of personal endeavour and competitiveness (Joseph 2000).

The third category of ideas encompasses the political perspective and the construction of 'public spaces'. As we see it, opportunities for reconstructing the 'public domain' and a democratic political system exist primarily at the sub-national or regional level and not only in the megacity (Joseph 2000). We are finding that there is a correlation between the vision of development – more or less human and integral – and the will to participate in the emerging forms of democratic politics.

We would insist, therefore, that these topics – individual and community, sustainable human development, and democratic politics – become part of our common agenda, North and South. We need to do and share more research on the social and political actors, especially in the urban 'public spaces'. Such research needs to be linked to our own work in promoting sustainable development and, in a context such as that of Peru, also linked to promoting good governance within a decentralised strategy.

One final thought is to say that we would do a great disservice to the urban poor communities and leaders if we were to motivate them to participate in the complex processes of democratisation and development without also offering them the opportunities for the kind of education these processes demand. It is not enough simply to 'train' people in techniques for addressing isolated needs and *issues*. They also need the theoretical tools which will allow them to understand themselves, their organisations, democracy, ethics, and development, and the importance of these to sustainable development practices and planning. For this reason, we are also beginning to take on the shared task of building educational opportunities, methods, and materials the leaders require. But telling that story will have to wait for another occasion.

Notes

1 This article is based on the paper presented at the May 2000 conference: 'Cities of the South, Sustainable for Whom?' hosted by UNRISD, N AERUS, and the Federal Polytechnic of Lausanne. It also draws heavily on a paper published in *Development in Practice* (Joseph 2000), and reprinted in Deborah Eade (ed.) (2001) *Debating Development: The Future of NGOs*, Oxford: Oxfam.

2 For example, in Peru the 'Cities for Life Forum' prides itself on 'not giving priority to Lima ... [in order] to contribute to the strengthening of the capacities of those who really need them most' (Miranda and Hordijk 1998).

3 Not to have sewerage, water, or streetlights is quite a different thing in a shantytown compared with a rural area. If we included quality-of-life indicators such as the number of persons who were victims of violence or robbery, pollution levels, and so on in the last six months, the poverty maps of the megacities would be quite different.

References

Borja, Jordi (1997) *Significado y Función en el Espacio Urbano Moderno*, Barcelona: Centro de Cultura Contemporánea de Barcelona

Castells, Manuel (1996) *The Information Age: Economy, Society, and Culture*, Oxford: Blackwell

Goulet, Denis (1995) *Development Ethics: A Guide to Theory and Practice*, New York: The Apex Press

Grompone, Romeo and Carlos Mejía (1995) *Nuevos Tiempos, Nueva Política*, Colección Mínima 32, Lima: IEP

Hall, Peter (1998) 'Megacities, world cities and global cities', in *Megacities Lectures*, available at: www.megacities.nl/lecture@hall.htm

ICLEI (1996) *Manual for Local Planning of Agenda 21*, Toronto: ICLEI

Joseph, Jaime (1999) *Lima Megaciudad: democracia, desarrollo y descentralización en sectores populares*, Lima: Centro Alternativa and UNRISD

Joseph, Jaime (2000) 'NGOs: fragmented dreams', *Development in Practice* 10(3&4): 390–401

Max-Neef, Manfred, Elizalde Antioni and Martin Hopenhayn (1986) 'Desarrollo a escala humana', *Development Dialogue*, special issue

Marcuse, Peter (1998) 'Sustainability is not enough', *Environment and Urbanization* 10(2): 103-11

Miranda, Liliana and Michaela Hordijk (1998) 'Let us build cities for life: the national campaign of Local Agenda 21s in Peru', *Environment and Urbanization* 10(2): 69–103

Morris, David (1996) *The Changing Condition of the World's Poor, 1960–1990: Some Development Policy Implications*, Rehoboth, MA: Brown University

Sen, Amartya (1983) 'Los bienes y la gente', *Comercio Exterior* 12: 1115-23

Sen, Amartya (1997) 'Valores y prosperidad económica Europa y Asia', Conferencia en Cataña, www.iigov.org/pnud, Cataluña España 7

Sen, Amartya (1999) 'Teorías del desarrollo a principios del siglo XXI', in Louis Emmerji and José Nuñez del Arco (eds) *El desarrollo económico y social en los umbrales del siglo XXI*, Washington, DC: InterAmerican Development Bank

Unsustainable development:
the Philippine experience

Karina Constantino-David

In 1960, less than 50 per cent of the world's 19 megacities were in developing countries. Today, more than 80 per cent of its 60 megacites are in the South. In just four decades our cities have grown to spectacular proportions. Every country in the South can boast at least one major city that serves as the centre of governance and commerce as well as newer cities that are also developing at an alarming rate. While the presence of modern amenities marks our cities, a large segment of the urban population has barely the basic necessities for survival. The urban poor, residing on the edges of the rich enclaves, eke out a living in the midst of affluence, scavenge from the remains of our cities' consumerist lifestyle, and are systematically excluded from urban development.

For decades we have known of the spread of urbanisation and its concomitant ills. But our governments chose to prioritise 'development' even as countries of the North are already exhibiting the negative characteristics of unplanned growth. We set our sights on emulating the patterns of more developed countries, blindly importing and transplanting images of cities from the more affluent parts of the globe into what were essentially underdeveloped nations.

Parasitic development

The problem with development is that it implies movement towards a goal. Through the years, this movement has focused primarily on economic growth. The hope and the promise were that growth would 'trickle down' to the poor. Towards the second half of the 1980s, the concept of sustainable development was introduced, and was meant to correct the flaws of developmental thinking by mitigating the effects of the gods of economic growth with the foresight of generations to come. But this kept us essentially on the same development path, except that the importance of the environment we share has come to the forefront.

However, even with the grudging acceptance of the need for sustainable development by governments and multilateral agencies, the realities have not changed for the masses in the South. We have a parasitic form of development. It is a development that blindly assumes that human and natural resources are inexhaustible. It sacrifices the poor and the environment on the altar of the market and its promises of economic growth.

Economic growth and its consequent patterns of consumption cannot be equated with an improvement in the quality of life. In fact, while the pursuit of economic growth has indeed produced increases in trade, investment, and output in general, it has also resulted in widening disparities and inequalities between people and nations. The transactional and utilitarian nature of the market has further disempowered large numbers of people and marginalised their environments.

The unquestioned development paradigm and the rush of our governments to compete in the global market have had disastrous results. While our cities have grown to attract foreign investments, our rural areas have stagnated. Finding no way out of poverty, rural folk migrate to the cities in search of waged work. But for an under-developed country to attract foreign investment, one prerequisite is low wages. These migrants swell the ranks of the urban poor, engaging in low-paid contractual jobs, surviving through the informal economy, and residing in informal settlements. The irony of our cities is that they develop, quite literally, at the expense of the poor and our environment.

The reasons for poverty are complex. The primary causes are of a political, economic, structural, and social nature, abetted by a lack of political resolve and erroneous attitudes regarding public policy and the deployment of resources:

- At the individual level, people are handicapped by lack of access to resources, skills, or opportunities to make a decent living.

- On the societal plane, the major causes are inequalities in the distribution of resources, services, and power. These inequalities may be institutionalised in terms of land, capital, infrastructure, markets, credit, education, information, and advisory services. The same is true for the provision of social services: education, health, clean water, and sanitation. Inequality of services leaves rural areas the worst off, so that it comes as no surprise that an estimated 77 per cent of the developing world's poor live in rural zones. Yet the urban poor are mired in even worse conditions (ICPQL 1996: 22).

A more appropriate direction would be towards a 'Sustainable Improvement in the Quality of Life', which would allow us to focus on the needs of the poor and the environment within the realities of each country without compromising the ability of future generations to meet their own needs. The needs of the present must be viewed from the perspective of the poor, the needs of those who have been abused most by the current development path. The goal of sustainable improvement in the quality of life allows countries and sectors to define directions that can accommodate subjectivity and cultural diversity in an ever-ascending spiral.

'Sustainable Improvement in the Quality of Life', as proposed by the Independent Commission on Population and the Quality of Life, requires us to respect the limits of the globe's 'carrying capacity' while at the same time taking responsibility for the needs of people and the environment, in other words our 'caring capacity'. The antithesis of care is power and control, abuse and aggression. But in order to take this new path, we must recognise that the continued parasitism of society on the misery of the poor and the degradation of the environment will inevitably become the basis for the unsustainability and breakdown of our cities.

Patterns of parasitism in Philippine cities

Fifty-one per cent of the population of the Philippines, roughly 38 million people or 6.5 million families, lives in urban areas. The country has one of the highest rates of urban growth in the developing world, at 5.1 per cent over the past four decades. This has been due to a high birth rate of approximately 2.3 per cent per annum, rural-to-urban migration, and the reclassification of rural areas as urban due to their increasing population densities. It is significant to note that while rural-to-urban migration is still a major source of the increasing urban population, especially in newer cities, second- and third-generation migrants are now greater in number in areas like Metro Manila. Migration is obviously testimony to the continuing poverty in the countryside that forces the poor to seek a better means for survival in the cities.

Of the urban population, approximately ten million live in Metro Manila, which has an annual growth rate of 3.3 per cent. This area accounts for more than 30 per cent of the gross national product, but at least 3.5 million people can be categorised as urban poor. Ten thousand families live along the Pasig River alone, 32,000 families by the major tributaries, 45,000 families beside the railway tracks, and the rest in pockets of urban decay that range from communities of a handful of families to slums of tens of thousands of people.

The 'brown' environment has long been abused – air, noise, and water pollution, inadequate waste disposal, and congestion. The 'carrying capacity', or the maximum sustainable load that can be imposed on the environment before it loses its capacity to support human activity, is in peril. Motorised transport accounts for 94 per cent of the total organic gas in the air, 99 per cent of the carbon monoxide, and 83 per cent of nitrogen oxide emissions. Industries release massive amounts of sulphur dioxide into the atmosphere, and domestic and industrial waste is indiscriminately dumped into the city's waterways and streets. Apart from this, environmental degradation can be seen from the frequent disasters that occur: traffic pollution, flooding, homes destroyed by landslides and other earth movements, and death of wildlife in the rivers and seas.

Even as we strain the carrying capacity of the metropolis, the inadequacy of our own caring capacity is obvious. Metro Manila, where economic activities are centred, is home to the best urban amenities in both the business districts and in the rich residential suburbs. But security services are booming, protecting these areas from the assault of those who have far less. Tertiary healthcare and education are concentrated in the metropolis. But the primary health services accessible to the urban poor pale in comparison with those in rural areas: there is one primary health unit for every 10,000 people in the countryside compared with one for every 50,000 people in the urban centres. Even though primary and secondary education may be of a slightly higher quality in cities, the 1: 50 teacher-to-pupil ratio makes basic education unsatisfactory. At the college level, the scene is dominated by private universities, which overcharge for substandard education. And while the seats of government, the media, and the church are situated in Metro Manila, the basic minimum needs of the urban poor remain unmet.

Despite respectable economic growth and the proliferation of urban amenities, quality of life in Metro Manila has deteriorated. Economic growth that hinges on belief in globalisation has been achieved on the backs of the poor and at the expense of the environment. Unless drastic steps are taken, this very model is likely to discourage the much sought-after foreign investments. Inevitably, quality of life will deteriorate further and even the few who benefit from this kind of parasitic development will end up with less than they have today.

Which actors and what factors make or break cities?

No amount of dreaming can result in an alternative future as long as the major actors and factors that can make or break a city remain unchanged. In the case of Metro Manila and other urban areas in the Philippines, these can be categorised in two distinct groups: those who wield power and those who are powerless.

There are five distinct but overlapping power groups – the state, business, the dominant church, the media, and international aid agencies – which, although they are not monolithic, share responsibility for the deteriorating quality of life in cities. The model of development that underpins their actions is economic development through global competitiveness, with foreign investment as the engine of growth. But while sustainable development, equity, and pro-poor rhetoric are standard fare, there have been but minimal improvements in the lives of the urban poor. Secure shelter, sanitation, potable water, and pollution remain grave problems.

In the Philippines, the present administration, hounded by inefficiency and corruption, doggedly pursues the same economic policies as previous governments, despite a pro-poor campaign line that ushered it into power.[1] The poor, who put their faith over-whelmingly in President Estrada, were buoyed by initial promises. The business community and the dominant church nervously awaited clear directions on economic policy, fearful of growing cronyism and flip-flopping decisions. Media exposés of the inadequacies of the government range from the sublime to the ridiculous. Foreign agencies like the IMF baulked at what seemed to be a partial declaration of autonomy by some government economic managers as, for example, the insistence that interest rates be lowered.

But while charges of graft and mismanagement have remained, the economic directions seem to have settled back to the same development paradigm. In the Housing and Urban Development Department, which we headed for 15 months, the following radical changes in policy were undertaken:

- situating shelter within a broader national urban policy framework;
- allocating 80 per cent of government budgetary allocations for housing for the poor;
- expanding options for the lowest-income households through efficient rental markets;

- strengthening co-operative housing and the Community Mortgage Programme;[2]
- housing finance reforms;
- localising and decentralising urban and shelter policy, with an emphasis on ecological balance;
- ensuring effective participation of the poor;
- redefining public and private sector roles to ensure a better distribution of responsibilities and risks.

These changes were met with angry protests from a portion of the real estate business sector whose short-term interests were threatened. While most of the top-level government decision makers, as well as foreign aid agencies, welcomed these policy shifts, they were diffident about confronting the self-interest groups. It was more comfortable for government functionaries to keep away from the fray, while foreign aid agencies refused to take a proactive stance by hiding behind the convenient excuse of 'non-interference', although they were willing to voice their frustrations in private. Only a division of the World Bank took the bold step of immediately suspending negotiations for a major housing programme. Since the early 1990s the World Bank had taken a critical stance regarding past government housing policies. Our radical revisions in policies, especially in the field of housing finance, were basically consistent with the Bank's perspectives. As such, a grant-loan package was in the final stages of approval at the time. In the final analysis, however, the political will for change gave way to the temptations of corruption and image building.

Civil society – NGOs, people's organisations, academia, left-wing political groups, and other voluntary organisations – were powerless in the face of these attempts to protect the status quo and resist the reforms. First, the micro-perspective of the poor allowed them to view the changes only within the limited perspective of their immediate needs. Second, NGOs could not keep up with the policy debates, especially those that were systemic rather than concrete in nature. Third, some ideological activists could not wean themselves away from a consistently oppositionist stance to anything emanating from government. Fourth, academics did not seem to take much interest in either policy or research. Finally, there was a yawning gap between civil society demands (which were either very concrete or supremely conceptual) and the day-to-day requisites of change.

Pasig River rehabilitation

The case of the Pasig River Rehabilitation Commission provides a concrete illustration. The Pasig River is the major waterway of Metro Manila, covering a 27km stretch with dozens of tributaries that were once the centre of transportation and economic and cultural activity. Today the river is dead. It is the dumping ground for domestic and industrial waste, the largest septic tank in the country. Ten thousand informal settler families live on its banks, in houses built on stilts in the river, and underneath its bridges. Every previous administration for the past 40 years has tried to revive the river, and each has failed. The Estrada government decided to embark on an ambitious but achievable programme to resurrect the river (dredging, revetment walls, minimising water pollution, etc.), relocate the settlers within the ten-metre easement, restore it as a viable means of alternative transportation, and create open spaces along the banks.

The determination to succeed where others had failed miserably meant creating a commission composed of cabinet members who would orchestrate the entire programme. Apart from government resources, DANIDA (the Danish government aid agency) and the Asia Development Bank (ADB) provided support. A crucial element was dealing with the settlers. Past attempts had resulted in protests and forcible and inhumane relocation to distant sites – and ultimately the return of about 50 per cent of the settlers.

Work with the commission started in January 1999. A Housing and Resettlement Group (HRG) (which I chaired) was immediately established. It included representatives from each of the affected local government units and representatives from the informal settlers and their NGO counterparts. The HRG arrived at a consensus on a framework to govern resettlement, jointly revalidated a 1977 family census, and agreed on uniform parameters on the process of relocation, identified appropriate sites, scheduled each area for resettlement over a two-year period, and set up a monthly bulletin to provide accurate information to each of the communities. Among the innovations introduced were:

- voluntary relocation;
- giving priority to in-city, then near-city, relocation;
- providing communities with various options rather than just one site;

- taking whole communities to the sites before they made their decisions;
- the setting up of a graduated lease-purchase scheme, starting at less than US$10 a month;
- encouraging Local Government Units (LGUs) to keep the settlers within their boundaries or to contribute a set amount to the receiving LGUs if the settlers could not be accommodated within the city;
- making every effort to ensure that basic amenities and facilities – utilities, transportation, schools, health clinics, employment – were present in each of the resettlement areas;
- ensuring transparency, by asking the private sector to submit already developed potential resettlement sites for consideration, and over which (apart from technical evaluations) the prospective resident had the final decision;
- providing settlers with the option to submit their own resettlement plans.

Ten months later, despite what seemed like a slow start because of the participatory nature of the process, almost 2000 families had moved into new homes of their choice. These were medium-rise buildings along a major highway or terraced houses on the edge of Metro Manila. Relocation was voluntary, there were no acrimonious protests, and the cost of the sites was 15–35 per cent lower than the market value. In one area where the schools were not completed, relocation was limited only to those families that could be accommodated, even though 2000 more houses were ready for occupancy.

With hindsight, we could have done better. One major problem was with funding. The time that the ADB needed to process applications meant that funds would only be available by the year 2000. And yet President Estrada demanded action based on an extremely tight schedule. At the same time, some communities that wanted to ensure getting the site of their choice also wanted to move even while the schools were still being built. Within six months of my resignation, there was already restiveness in both the relocated communities and the communities still to be resettled. The HRG has been effectively disbanded. The poor no longer have access to decision makers. The sites identified for the Pasig River resettlers have become areas for other communities that have been forcibly relocated, the promised facilities have not been completed, and the people no longer have a say about the sites to which they would be transferred.

Not all the problems throughout this process came from government and foreign agencies. Academics were completely absent, when they could have provided much-needed assistance through research and fresh insights. Some political groups attempted to derail the process by stirring up all sorts of fears. But the participatory nature of the HRG ensured that leaders of the urban poor and NGOs could contain any disinformation because they themselves were part of the decision-making body. Although it was well worth it, the process was at times tedious and repetitive due to initially unreasonable demands, for example on-site relocation with free land, or a lack of understanding of the complexities of resettlement.

The role of foreign aid agencies: the seven deadly sins

The noble rationale for foreign aid is altruism, the responsibility of more developed countries to assist those with less, as an expression of concern as well as recognition that we share the same planet. But, in reality, much foreign assistance has degenerated into expressions of power and control and the dividing line between aid and business has become blurred. It is the reproduction of old colonial relations framed within the hypocritical rhetoric of democracy and philanthropy.

Undeniably, foreign aid agencies promote economic development as their highest priority. Some espouse it openly while others hide behind the platitudes of sustainable development. Countries of the South that are in desperate need of funds are thus placed in the ironic situation of having to thank lenders and donors for funds that ensure the South develops according to the paradigms of the North. This integrates them into a global order in which poor countries, like the poor of their own nations, are powerless.

With rare exceptions, foreign aid is premised on one view of the world. The identification of projects and programmes is largely left in the hands of the 'giver' with the recipient having the illusory option to accept or reject. Countries of the South are in a double bind – short-term gains for long-term pain or short-term pains for long-term gain. Within a democratic political system each administration invariably chooses the former, if only for political survival. And in the final analysis, it is the poor and the environment that suffer.

But, when viewed within the context of a government that has almost lost the capacity to care for the poor and the environment, beyond the basic issues of the development model that underpins foreign aid are practical realities that make the relation between 'givers' and 'takers' more onerous. The seven deadly sins are as follows:

- *Project pushers:* The cycle begins with a mission then moves to technical assistance usually by means of grants which appear to be altruistic attempts at assistance. But the agenda is largely set by the aid agency and the country is hooked to the loans that follow. And yet aid-givers have no accountability for the failures and the misery that may result from such projects.

- *Bureaucratic straitjackets:* The bureaucracy that has developed around aid is inflexible and expensive. No matter how much work has been put into consultations and project planning, foreign aid agencies require recipients to run the gauntlet of evaluations and project forms. At every step, the premise seems to be an underlying suspicion that the officials in the recipient country are either incompetent or cheats.

- *Parasitic expertise:* Much money is spent in hiring foreign consultants who tap local expertise as their workhorses instead of establishing collaboration on an equal footing. And yet much of the paperwork is simply a rehash of previous studies and plans. In many instances, government officials need to spend hours in briefing sessions in order to produce instant foreign experts on the Philippines, who are paid by the day more than we earn in a month.

- *Cultural blindness:* Many foreign aid personnel and consultants regard the South as a homogeneous entity, perhaps believing in the omnipotence of their paradigm, the infallibility of their expertise, and the uniform nature of their subjects. As such, countries of the South are forced to face an aid bureaucracy that is bereft of insight into our own uniqueness, which is grounded in centuries of history.

- *Insensitive conditionalities:* Because projects must run according to predetermined schedules and patterns, it is the poor and/or the environment that are ultimately sacrificed. Like the structural adjustment programmes that insist on bitter pills that further compromise the quality of life of the poor, some urban projects dismiss the needs of the poor in order to meet demands of foreign funders.

- *Negative acculturation:* Because most foreign aid agencies work through and with government, these agencies have learned to work the system. Instead of insisting on professional relations, they have learned the arts of patronage and pulling strings in the background.

- *Direction without risk:* Foreign aid agencies have the luxury of imposing projects while shielding themselves from any risks. On the financial side, loan repayments are, after all, guaranteed. On the human side, it is not they who will suffer the consequences. On the political side, they hardly earn the wrath of those whose lives are negatively affected since it is the in-country government that takes the flak.

There are certainly many cases in aid programmes where these sins are avoided. I have had the benefit of working directly with people from foreign agencies who undeniably have had the best interests of the Philippines at heart. While there is much that can be done to reform foreign aid, it is still the countries of the South that must bear the burden of change.

The challenges ahead

A shift in our development paradigm is urgently needed. I do not refer to earth-shattering upheavals, but to the simple resurrection of the importance of the rights of people and nature. In our frenzied rush towards economic development, our macro-economic policies and the short-term nature of political decision making have strained the carrying capacity of the earth and forgotten our caring capacity for the rights and needs of the poor. But beyond the platitudes that regularly mark our public statements, there are practical initiatives that can be introduced or strengthened.

Most of our governments have highly centralised systems for deciding national policies, allocating resources, and implementing programmes. Although we can all hope for national governance that is more responsive to the rights of the poor and the environment, we also know that the pressures of the dominant development paradigm are also stronger at this level. The specific realities on the ground are also more distant from national agencies, despite the presence of local structures. Consistent with a bottom-up approach, and because of the growing complexity especially of urban life, decentralisation to the local government level has the greatest potential to turn the situation around. This requires that central government lay down the general directions, policies, and regulatory framework while local government units play a more proactive role in planning and implementation.

Allow me to mention a few of the actions that local governments could undertake immediately:

- *Minimum quality-of-life indicators:* Social policies are the visible expressions of a caring government. We can start by creating measurable and verifiable parameters for non-negotiable minimum quality-of-life standards for each of our cities. Indicators must be formulated with the active participation of civil society. Indicators that are able to measure outcomes can serve as a social contract between local authorities and their constituencies because they relate to concrete action and defined accountabilities. For example, from baseline data on existing realities, quantifiable targets for the improvement of minimum quality-of-life indicators on housing, potable water, sanitation systems, welfare, employment, education, and health can be regularly monitored. Instead of the rhetoric of promises, it is a challenge to responsible local officials to submit themselves to regular assessment based upon clear indicators of performance. But, more than this, minimum quality-of-life indicators with a defined timetable can lay the foundation for ensuring that the poor and the environment are given the highest priority in governance.

- *Learning from the poor:* Expertise very often takes on an unconscious arrogance. Most public policy is formed without the participation of the poor. Many of our political leaders and technocrats unfortunately perceive the engagement of the poor as messy. On the other hand, civil society organisations tend to romanticise the poor as having all the answers. Social policy can only be effective if decision makers draw from the wealth of knowledge and skills of the technical experts and also of the poor. In the final analysis, a participatory approach is the best guarantee for success.

- *Maximising innovative initiatives:* We do not need to reinvent the wheel. There are many innovative initiatives that can be mainstreamed and further strengthened. The Sustainable Cities Programme of the United Nations Centre for Human Settlements and the United Nations Environment Programme and the City Development Strategies of the World Bank, although implemented in only a few areas, have had some positive results, especially in the area of participation. In the Philippines, the Community Mortgage

Programme, which allows informal settlements to negotiate with landowners and purchase the land on which they live, has accomplished significant results. More than 100,000 families have benefited, with repayment rates significantly higher than the usual low-cost housing packages. Various micro-enterprise initiatives and co-operative movements in Asia have also shown that, given the chance, the poor can manage their own economic development. In the field of health and education, many NGO-initiated programmes are testimonies to successful alternative interventions. It is also worth emphasising that all the successes can be traced back to the level of organisation found in urban poor communities. Organising and the accompanying increase in knowledge, attitudes, and skills of the urban poor is the base upon which poverty can most effectively be overcome.

- *Making the market work:* In this era of globalisation, it is naïve to dream of poverty eradication without addressing the market. Business and finance have long been viewed as the antithesis of poverty. But, in much the same way as we have learned that we all share a finite earth, business has also come to accept the reality that massive poverty is not good for business. The past few decades have seen a slowly emerging trend whereby more business conglomerates have moved from an almost total lack of concern, to charitable endeavours, to involvement in social issues, to self-imposed quality-of-life standards. Governments must speed up this development by providing the climate that would encourage access to the market by the poor. This can be done through enhancements like guarantees of and incentives for credit to the poor as well as through transparent subsidies so the poor can afford the market.

- *Focusing on newly emerging cities:* If our megacities developed into monstrosities due to lack of planning and simple neglect, we have the opportunity to avoid the same mistakes in the newer cities. At the same time, dramatic technological advances, especially in mass transit and electronic communication systems, make it possible to create centres of governance, business, and culture that need not be congested within tightly confined geographic areas. It is therefore imperative that local authorities in newly emerging cities muster the political will to anticipate the future and plan their cities beyond their terms of office.

We are fortunate to be leaders at the beginning of a new century. We can repeat the mistakes of the past or we can help to shape the future. I am confident that local authorities, with the effective participation of business and civil society, can make a difference for the poor and our environment. With the assistance of multilateral institutions along with urban researchers, all it takes is the political will to go against the grain of tradition and the daring to care for the poor, the environment, and the future.

Notes

1 This paper was completed before the campaign to impeach President Estrada had commenced.

2 The Community Mortgage Programme is an innovative system whereby informal settlers, with the assistance of an intermediary called an originator, negotiate with the landowner. Once an agreement has been reached between the parties, the land is mortgaged to the government, the landowner is paid in full, and the people amortise to the government over a period of 25 years at 6 per cent interest. For a fuller description and assessment of this programme, see the article by Berner in this volume.

Reference

Independent Commission on Population and Quality of Life (ICPQL) (1996) *Caring for the Future: Report of the Independent Commission on Population and Quality of Life*, Oxford: Oxford University Press

Sustainable urban development in India: an inclusive perspective

Darshini Mahadevia

People-centred development, or sustainable human development, has gained increasing acceptance over the last ten years. It emphasises that development should be broad-based and bottom-up; redistributive and just; and empowering and environmentally sustainable, seeking to meet the needs of the present generation without compromising the ability of future generations to meet their own needs (WCED 1987). In 1992, Agenda 21 (UNCED) outlined programmes that go beyond ecological sustainability to include other dimensions of sustainable development, such as equity, economic growth, and popular participation. Indeed, sustainable human development and Agenda 21 are converging.

The concept of 'sustainable cities' derives from that of sustainable development. The world is becoming increasingly urban and urbanisation is shifting to the South. To date, urbanisation has coincided with, and been accompanied by, increased consumption and ecological degradation across the globe. The ecological impact of the shift to the South on the quality of its urban environment has become a major justification for the concept of 'sustainable cities'. This concept is an amalgamation of various independent processes: the urban environmental movement, the decentralisation of local governance, and Agenda 21 followed by Habitat II in 1996. Prior to Habitat II, urban environmental issues were addressed by very few international efforts, namely: the Sustainable City Programme (SCP), the Urban Management Programme (UMP), the Urban Environment Forum (UEF), the International Council for Local Environmental Initiatives (ICLEI), the Local Initiative Facility for Urban Environment (LIFE), and the UNCHS (United Nations Centre on Human Settlements) Best Practices awards.

The pursuit of sustainable development and 'sustainable cities' is set against the backdrop of an increasingly globalised world in which the North dominates the South in economic terms. Most countries of the South have become part of the global economy through conditionalities and a development model imposed by the multilateral funding agencies under the general régime of structural adjustment programmes (SAPs). These have had adverse impacts on social sectors (Cornia *et al.* 1987) and on the environment (Reed 1995). In the urban context, SAPs have meant privatisation and commercialisation of infrastructure including social sectors, deregulation, and some withdrawal of the state from welfare responsibilities under the guise of decentralisation and popular participation (Stubbs and Clarke 1996; World Bank 1990; WRI *et al.* 1996).

Some have questioned the possibility of achieving sustainable development while the interests of capital dominate over those of people (Clow 1996). The same applies to the concept of 'sustainable cities', and this paper will review the current debate on the subject and then look specifically at the nature of the urban crisis in India and at how this is being addressed in the context of SAPs. India does not have a specific 'sustainable cities' programme, and policy documents refer to this only in the context of the urban environment. The government's failure to address urban environmental issues has led to spontaneous grassroots action and this paper will also review the effectiveness of civil society movements in moving the 'sustainable cities' agenda to centre stage. The final section presents the 'inclusive approach' and suggests the main outstanding issues and immediate action required in order to create 'sustainable cities' in the South.

Unravelling the concept: sustainable cities in the South

'Sustainable development' and 'sustainable cities' are central terms in the rhetoric of development policy making and debates. However, there is little consensus as to what has to be sustained, and how this is to be done. The WCED (1987) definition of sustainable development is considered the most comprehensive by some (Redclift 1992; Vivian 1992; Choguill 1996) and mere 'environmental managerialism' by others (Clow 1996). Stren (1992) suggests that the very ambiguity of the term attracts a wide range of political and intellectual currents across fragmented environmental movements. Chambers (1988) pegs the concept on its ability to create or support sustainable livelihoods for the rural populations of the South. This points to the fact that it is unsustainable development, which emanates from excessive consumption in the North and from the wealthy of the South, that has eroded rural livelihoods, so that the rural poor then migrate to towns and live as urban poor.

Making a structural criticism of the concept of sustainable development, Clow (1996) argues that the current global system is organised around the expansion of capital. This endeavour is intrinsically unsustainable. Clow holds that the 'environmental considerations cannot be "tacked on" as an afterthought to a "for profit" economy' (1996; 7). Even UNDP's concept of sustainable human development has been criticised for being 'economistic', for having ideological underpinnings (as it is supposed to take place in a global system where the North dominates the South), and for not having made the development process gender sensitive (Hirway and Mahadevia 1996; 1999). Nicholls (1996) criticises the approach for skirting round the issue of existing power structures at global, national, and local levels and for seeking to achieve sustainable development within structures that in themselves prevent true bottom-up, participatory, holistic, and process-based development initiatives; and for ignoring the reality of self-interested development actors, to be found at every level, who would perpetuate these unequal power structures.

Huckle (1996) groups these diverse definitions of 'sustainable development' into two categories, terming one 'weak sustainability' and the other 'strong sustainability'. The former is supported by conservative and liberal political ideologies, works towards sustainable development within the existing global structure, accepts the free-market ideology, individual property rights, minimum state regulation and intervention, and looks for techno-managerial solutions. Such solutions suit the official development aid agencies, including the World Bank and UNCHS. 'Strong' sustainable development accommodates various approaches, namely those of deep ecologists, 'greens', social ecologists, ecofeminists, postmodernists, political economists, and others. They reject the idea that nature and social systems are at the service of economic development, arguing that this bolsters capital rather than people in the development process. Some of them see sustainable development as a political process while others view it from a moral perspective, suggesting that self-discipline is required to achieve such development.

The concept of 'sustainable cities' can be approached in much the same way. However, there is widespread uncritical acceptance, even in the South, of various UN 'sustainable cities' programmes. In the early 1980s, UNCHS and the United Nations Environment Programme (UNEP) decided to prepare joint Environmental Guidelines for

Settlements' Planning and Management (or EPM) for cities. In the early 1990s, this initiative was converted into the joint SCP. The SCP, launched as a vehicle for implementing Agenda 21 at the city level, works towards building capacities in urban environmental planning and management, and promoting a broad-based participatory process. The aim is to incorporate environmental management into urban development decision making and to strengthen local capacities for doing so through demonstration projects. This is a techno-managerial approach.

The way in which 'sustainable cities' has been understood in the North has led to environment-friendly cities or 'ecological cities', where: (i) economic and environmental costs of urbanisation and urban development are taken into account; (ii) there is self-reliance in terms of resource production and waste absorption; (iii) cities become compact and energy efficient; and (iv) the needs and rights of all are well balanced (Haughton 1997). Proponents of this line of thinking view urban environmental issues in the South through a Northern lens, and so emphasise the reduction of resource consumption, local waste absorption, and the use of renewable resources, but ignore the critical issue of meeting basic human needs (Satterthwaite 1998).

Hardoy et al. (1992) hinted at numerous environmental problems in the cities of the South – as one Indian saying puts it 'a weak cow has many bugs'.[1] Many of these problems are the result of poverty and the inability of national and local governments to create institutions to provide sustainable solutions to poverty. They are also the result of a flawed development model, SAP conditionalities, and the pressure to achieve rapid economic growth at any cost. In India, the goal of increasing the rate of economic growth has resulted in the acceptance of many types of investment, some of them highly polluting;[2] and the granting of permission to transnational companies, such as Toyota, Ford, and Mercedes, to produce diesel cars for the Indian market[3] despite the fact that these produce 10–100 times more particulate matter than petrol engines and will lead to more pollution in the already congested cities of the South (Down to Earth 1999). The pursuit of economic growth also creates the need for new infrastructure, and hence investment, which in turn leads to privatisation and commercialisation, as the city governments are unable to raise new resources. Instead, they direct their resources to new commercial ventures, the poor are excluded, and the subsidies dry up. The urban environment will not be improved, essentially because globalisation is not conducive to sustainable development in cities of the South.

The SCP and other techno-managerial approaches to sustainable urban development treat the concept of 'sustainable cities' as a partnership among diverse interest groups. Satterthwaite (1996) sums up the Habitat-II consensus to move towards sustainable cities and sustainable human settlements as 'at best an illusion, as different groups gave different meaning to the terms', which allowed the 'international agencies to claim that they were the leaders in promoting sustainable cities, when in reality they have contributed much to the growth of cities where sustainable development goals are not met' (1996: 31). For cities to be genuinely sustainable would mean 'considering the underlying economic, social, and political causes of poverty or social exclusion' (ibid.: 32).

The move towards a 'sustainable city' in the South has to be an 'inclusive approach' based on four pillars:

- environmental sustainability;
- social equity;
- economic growth with redistribution; and
- political empowerment of the disempowered.

This holistic approach incorporates all dimensions of development, including the interests of the poor and the disempowered. It would challenge the existing unequal systems, from global to local, that have led to unsustainable development. In its place it would generate an equitable system to achieve sustainable human development that is employment generating, resource recycling, waste minimising, socially sustainable, and politically just. These four dimensions have to be approached simultaneously in the process of development and not, as at present, with one dimension taking precedence over the others within a fragmented and sectoral approach to sustainable development.

Urban crises in India: the context of structural adjustment programmes

India has a low level of urbanisation (26 per cent in 1991 and expected to reach 33 per cent in 2001), a large urban population in absolute terms (about 330 million in 2001), three of the 20 largest cities in the world (Mumbai, Calcutta, and Delhi) and 23 cities of one million-plus inhabitants, housing one third of the total urban population in 1991 (NIUA 1995). Its urban settlement pattern is concentrated in the western and southern parts of the country (Shaw 1999), and there is a high incidence of urban poverty – one person in every three overall (Dubey and Gangopadhyay 1998; GOI 1997), and one person in five in the metropolitan cities (Dubey and Mahadevia forthcoming).[4] Large cities are the focus of urban policies and programmes (Mahadevia 1999a), although poverty is concentrated in the small towns (Dubey and Gangopadhyay 1999; Dubey et al. 2000), which also have lower levels of basic services than the large cities (Kundu 1999).[5] The latter are integrated into the global system and the smaller towns into the local economy, with no continuum between the two (Kundu 1999). Urban employment has become more informal since the early 1980s (Kundu 1996) as the manufacturing sector has become increasingly capital intensive, leading to a decline in formal, secondary sector jobs. Researchers attribute the declining rate of urbanisation during the 1980s to this phenomenon (Kundu 1996; Mohan 1996). Finally, the urban sector contribution to the national economy increased from 29 per cent in 1951 to 55 per cent in 1991 (Suresh 2000).

In 1991, India began implementing its SAP and consequently the urban development strategy shifted to supporting rapid economic growth in place of balanced regional development.

> In the era of economic reforms, liberalisation and globalisation, cities and towns are emerging as centres of domestic and international investment. Within this framework, urban development policy calls for an approach that aims to optimise the productive advantages of cities and towns, while at the same time minimise or mitigate the negative impacts of urbanisation. (NIUA 1998: xiii)

The Ninth Five Year Plan (GOI 1998) thus proposed to address existing regional inequalities by funding infrastructure development in the undeveloped regions through raising resources, either from the financial institutions or from the commercial market. It is also proposed to fund social infrastructure in the same way.

In the post-SAP period, the focus has been on urban infrastructure. The India Infrastructure Report (Expert Group on the Commercialisation of Infrastructure Projects 1996) states that Rs2803.5 billion (US$74 billion, or US$7.5 billion per year at 1994 prices) will be required in order to meet all urban infrastructure needs by 2005. In 1995, a total of only Rs50 billion per year was available, so a strong case was made to privatise the building and maintenance of urban infrastructure.

With respect to urban land, deregulation is underway. The Urban Land Ceiling and Regulation Act of 1976, which sought to socialise urban land, was repealed in 1999. Land regulations are being gradually relaxed in some cities (Mahadevia 1999b). It is argued that the best way to make land available to the urban poor will be through efficient land markets.

While the government is passing responsibility for urban development to the market and the financial institutions, urban governance has been decentralised through the 74th Constitutional Amendment Act of 1995. This Act allows for local communities to participate in local development processes, but it also legitimises the transfer of responsibility for development to lower levels of government. If only those city governments that can raise market funds will be able to promote development, opportunities to participate in the process will vary across regions and different urban classes. This legislation may therefore increase existing inequalities in urban systems.

Finally, an urban poverty alleviation programme, *Swarna Jayanti Sheri Rojgar Yojana* (SJSRY, Golden Jubilee Urban Employment Programme) was introduced in 1997. The SJSRY has two components: self-employment and wage employment. The former consists of financial and training assistance to individuals to set up gainful self-employment ventures, and to groups of poor urban women to set up collective ventures within the so-called Development of Women and Children in the Urban Areas (DWUCA). Financial help takes the form of microcredit from scheduled banks. Wage employment is to be generated through the creation of public assets by local bodies. If the SJSRY succeeds in generating regular wage employment, poverty may decline; this is less likely if such employment is in the casual sector. Throughout the urban sector, poverty is highest among households supported by casual wage labour and self-employment (Dubey and Mahadevia forthcoming). The self-employment component of SJSRY depends on the poor taking out commercial loans from the official banking system on the recommendation of local governments. This does nothing to reduce bureaucracy. And the eradication of poverty through self-employment implies far more than simply providing credit, but includes access to markets and reasonably priced raw materials, and favourable terms of trade for the products. The SJSRY does not address these issues and thus represents a limited approach to urban poverty.

Macro development processes after 1991 encourage economic growth of a certain kind, but do not facilitate the reduction of social and economic disparities or of poverty, nor do they promote sustainable livelihoods, empowerment, or social justice. Yet this is the context within which environmental programmes for sustainable cities have been undertaken.

Official programmes towards the sustainable city: limited vision

Chennai, Hyderabad, Banglore, Delhi, and Calcutta have been directly connected with the SCP. While Chennai was the only Indian partner for SCP activities, other cities joined the Urban Environment Forum (UEF) that was set up with the SCP as a primary partner (SCP 2000). Some cities have received UNCHS Best Practice Awards, and three belong to the IULA. All these efforts are the initiatives of city governments, as there is no national programme, only fragmented policies and programmes that come under the 'sustainable cities' umbrella, as well as some city-level initiatives.[6]

Table I shows the official programmes and the spontaneous efforts to create 'sustainable cities'. The former are mainly centrally designed programmes. Only a few of the local or state government efforts are mentioned here, and only the environmental programmes listed here will be discussed below.

Legal initiatives

The first law to address urban environmental aspects was the Water Pollution (Prevention and Control) Act passed in 1974. This was followed by the Air Pollution (Prevention and Control) Act in 1981 and the Environment Protection Act of 1986. The latter deals with rules for hazardous material and its disposal, toxic waste handling, and bio-genetic material handling. In 1998, Bio-Medical Waste (Managing and Handling) Rules were introduced to deal with hospital waste.

Another recent piece of legislation is the Motor Vehicles Act (MVA) (1998), which is being strictly implemented in the large cities. It requires that vehicles obtain regular 'Pollution Under Check' certificates to monitor levels of suspended particulate matter (SPM) and noxious gas emissions. The Act also stipulates the retirement of old vehicles (as defined by the local government) and the manufacturing of motor vehicles according to European standards. In Delhi, vehicles older than 12 years are banned, while Hyderabad has fixed the level at 15 years. Mumbai now insists that diesel-run taxis be converted to petrol as a condition of registration. Taxi drivers challenged the legislation declaring they could not afford the expense of conversion, but the High

Four pillars	Official efforts	Spontaneous actions
Environmental sustainability	Legal initiatives	Legal initiatives
	Sustainable City Programme (SCP)	Protests for environmental protection
	Infrastructure projects	Community-based efforts
	Environmental management	Private sector initiatives
Social equity	Affirmative policies	Rights movements
Economic growth with redistribution	Poverty alleviation	Community-based programmes for addressing poverty
	Housing and shelter programmes	
Political empowerment	Urban governance decentralisation	NGO-led capacity-building activities

Note: The above listed are not recognised as programmes for 'sustainable cities'. They would come under the 'sustainable city' concept if the definition were expanded and made inclusive.

Court gave them six months to do so. In Delhi, loans have been offered to enable taxi drivers and three-wheeler drivers to convert old engines. However, banning these polluting vehicles brings with it the fear of job losses. There is a real conflict of interests here: improvement in air quality for all versus employment for drivers. The solution lies in better city planning, the development of efficient and affordable public transport, job-creation schemes for taxi and three-wheeler drivers, and the retirement of such vehicles from the road.

However, to judge by the pollution levels in Indian cities, this legislation has had only limited impact. For instance, citizens' groups have gone to the higher courts to obtain injunctions against water-polluting activities,[7] but the Water Act is of limited effect as industrialisation in some states is based on industries that cause water pollution. Similarly, the MVA can only be partially effective because while diesel vehicles are the main culprits of airborne pollution, the government is permitting Indian foreign companies to produce and market diesel vehicles locally.[8] So, although environment legislation exists, it will have little impact if economic growth continues to be based on polluting activities.

Sustainable City Programme (SCP)

The first city in India to join the SCP UNCHS/UNEP was Madras (now renamed Chennai) in 1995. The programme aims to promote local initiatives for environment management, and to improve the ability of individuals and organisations to identify, understand, and analyse environmental issues and incorporate them into sectoral programmes in an integrated manner. This effort resulted in the preparation of the 1997 Environmental Profile, based upon city-level consultation, and the framing of the Environmental Planning and Management (EPM), *Madras Vision 2000*. The resulting consensus for improving the infrastructural situation was produced in collaboration with the World Bank.

In Hyderabad City, an EPM was carried out while the *Master Plan 2011* was being designed and urban environmental issues were identified for incorporation into the Plan. The Plan proposed the spread of urbanisation throughout the state by decentralising economic development. To this end, the development of small ports and improvement in the financial position of local bodies was proposed, to be funded via an Urban Finance and Infrastructure Development Corporation. Two SCP programmes in India have concluded that more funds should be sought for city-level infrastructure, but of the 23 metropolises, only two have carried out EPM exercises.

Bangalore and Calcutta are members of the UEF due to their past efforts to take up environmental management programmes. In Bangalore, from 1984 onwards, some slums have successfully been relocated with community participation and local NGO help. The Calcutta Metropolitan District (CMD) Environment Management Strategy and Action Plan was prepared with the help of the British ODA in the early 1980s.[9] The top priority was the management of solid waste. A pilot project was begun in each of the eight participating municipalities, which entailed collection, transportation, and disposal of solid waste through the active co-operation of beneficiaries and local bodies. These pilot projects were successful, and the programme has been extended to other municipalities.

Infrastructure projects

Infrastructural development is considered to be key to improving the urban environment. For example, the construction of flyovers and the widening of roads are expected to ease congestion and reduce air pollution. Water supply and sanitation infrastructure are supposed to reduce water pollution. These projects are usually funded by international loans. Since only large cities are able to prove that they are creditworthy, they have been the main recipients of these loans.

The World Bank has been supporting urban infrastructure projects throughout India since the early 1970s, principally urban development projects and water supply and sanitation projects. Cumulative credit to date totals US$1809.6 million (NIUA 1998) and, in some cities, nearly half the capital budget consists of a World Bank loan (for Ahmedabad see Mahadevia and D'Costa 1997). Recently, the Asian Development Bank (ADB) also entered the urban arena and committed itself to support projects in Karnataka[10] and Rajasthan (in six cities), give technical assistance for the Calcutta Municipal Environmental Improvement Programme (under consideration), and set up the Urban Environmental Infrastructure Fund.[11]

Some foreign agencies advocate the direct participation of the private and commercial sector. For example, USAID sponsors:

1 The Financial Institutions Reform and Expansion (FIRE) project which would increase private investment in India's long-term debt market. This also puts emphasis on making the urban environmental infrastructure finance system commercially viable and improving the capacity of local government to plan, operate, maintain, and recover the costs for basic urban services. Under this project, USAID has pledged US$125 million from the US Housing Guarantee Fund to be channelled through the financial institutions (NIUA 1998) on condition that matching funds are raised locally;

2 The Technical Assistance and Support Project which gives grants to organisations engaged in economic policy analysis;[12]

3 The Programme for Advancement of Commercial Technology;

4 Trade in Environmental Services and Technology that would work towards addressing industrial pollution in India; and

5 The Centre for Technology Development (Technical Services US–AEP 1997).

The internationally funded Healthy Cities Programme (HCP), supported by WHO, was started in the 1990s to build the local capacity required for integrating environmental health concerns into all major urban policies and programmes, including the Mega City Scheme, and taking up HCP pilot projects in the five megacities, namely Bangalore,

Calcutta, Chennai, Hyderabad, and Mumbai.[13] The estimated cost of the project is US$125 million, but its benefits will accrue only to these five cities.

All large cities in India are keen to take up infrastructure projects to improve the urban environment, an area on which funding agencies concentrate. Interestingly, the sums pledged or invested by various donor agencies are insignificant compared with those available from India's internal sources or even the demand projected by the *India Infrastructure Report*. But these international agencies nevertheless exert a strong influence on official programmes; for example, the FIRE project is already mentioned in urban policy documents as an important option for raising resources (NIUA 1998). The urban problem is framed in such a manner that lack of finance is viewed as the major impediment to improving urban infrastructure and hence the urban environment. However, the capacity of cities to repay commercial loans and the impact of such loans on equitable development within the cities, find no mention.

Increased debt does not lead to sustainable development. Cities that borrow at commercial rates have to invest in projects that give immediate returns. Basic services projects, incorporating the interests of the poor, cannot give the same returns as commercially viable infrastructure projects. Debt-ridden cities will end up diverting their funds and project-handling capabilities to deliver the commercially viable projects, while the poor continue to live in degraded environments. Since cities have just begun to borrow, most of it from international agencies, the impact of such loans remains to be seen.

Environmental management

Solid Waste Management (SWM) projects dominate among environmental management efforts in India. Some local governments have tried to elicit the support of communities, NGOs, and private agencies for such projects. In both Ahmedabad and Mumbai, a private company is contracted to compost part of the city waste; in Mumbai, Bangalore, and Chennai, NGOs are involved in the collection and disposal of waste on behalf of the city government; in Pune, the local government has encouraged the housing colonies to decompose their organic waste; and in Rajkot, the city government is efficiently collecting the solid waste (HSMI/WMC 1996). All these projects began in the early 1990s. In Ahmedabad the World Bank donated Rs38 million to modernise SWM practices and the collection consequently increased by three to four times, though cases where the NGOs and community groups are participating in composting garbage include only a few hundred households (HSMI/WMC 1996). In Andhra Pradesh, the municipal administration has contracted out solid waste collection to the women's groups formed under SJSRY (Rao 2000). This is a holistic approach whereby local communities and government are participating to address environment and poverty issues together. However, such initiatives are rare.

Limited official vision

While local governments continue to provide basic city-level services, our discussion here has focused only on special programmes. The Government of India (GOI) has an important role in framing policies and programmes for sustainable cities, particularly because the very concept is multisectoral, multidepartmental, and comprehensive. However, this is not the GOI perspective. First, the official vision of sustainable urban development is limited to seeing this as an environmental issue, which is then linked to the development infrastructure through independent funding (GOI 1998). This is a simple, reductionist approach to the sustainable development of cities. To pay for it, the GOI has approached the multilateral and bilateral funding agencies and sees nothing wrong in doing so. In the process, some government programmes have been influenced by the funding agencies, something to which the GOI apparently has no objection.

The GOI approach does not recognise the other three pillars of sustainable development, despite the fact that poverty, the disempowerment of the majority, and poor basic services are serious urban problems. It does not regard these problems as being interrelated or as affecting the quality of the urban environment. The poverty-alleviation programmes and decentralisation of urban governance are not viewed as leading to sustainable urban development because urban development is approached sectorally. That is, poverty alleviation is viewed independently of infrastructure programmes, the decentralisation of governance is not linked with financing of urban development, and so on. Most of the international funding agencies also approach development programmes in a sectoral manner. Given this shared outlook, it is easy for the funding agencies to support sectoral programmes without regard for their impact on other sectors. It may not be far from the truth to say that many of the multilateral and bilateral agencies have taken the opportunity provided by the term 'sustainable cities' to open up new avenues for business in India in the name of improving the urban environment. We see evidence for this in the fact that Chennai and Hyderabad are demanding more financial support, and that the FIRE project has been accepted as the official GOI programme for raising commercial funds for urban infrastructure.

Legislation for improving the urban environment has either not been implemented seriously (as with pollution control laws), in part for fear of driving away new investment, or threatens the interests of certain low-income groups. In legal interventions to improve the urban environment, for example the MVA, techno-managerial solutions have been advocated because the issue is seen in one-dimensional terms. For example, after drivers in Delhi were compelled by law to change their car engines, some fitted engines that run on compressed natural gas (CNG). Demands that industries shift to non-polluting technologies have led USAID to promote US imports under its Trade in Environmental Services and Technology component.[14] Legal solutions are only partial and leave aside the question of what would constitute an appropriate and sustainable model of development. The legal approach to dealing with environmental pollution is neither holistic nor sustainable.

Spontaneous efforts towards sustainability: fragmented efforts

While government efforts are restricted to a few sectors, and the focus remains on improving the urban environment and infrastructure, living conditions are becoming intolerable and problems of the urban poor are not addressed. This situation is leading to spontaneous actions (see Table 1), some of which are discussed below.

Legal initiatives

Many Public Interest Litigations (PILs) have been filed by individual citizens or citizens' groups seeking legal remedies for industrial pollution (Mahadevia 1999c). The relocation of 9038 of the 100,000 industries in Delhi, ordered by the Supreme Court, is a landmark judgment in response to a PIL (Shrivastava 1995). The Ganga Action Plan to clean the River Ganga is the result of a PIL filed in the 1980s. Similar plans have since been drawn up elsewhere. In Calcutta, the fishing co-operative, which has been in existence since 1961 and is involved in managing the wetlands that recycle city waste and support fishing, filed a PIL to halt constructions that were diminishing the size of the wetlands, and won (Development Associates 1996). In addition, individual citizens have filed suits in the State High Courts and the Supreme Court of India against local urban bodies for neglecting mandatory responsibilities such as enforcing the prohibition of non-conforming land uses (mainly polluting industries) in the city master plans. The shifting of polluting industries out of Delhi is an outcome of such a PIL. Individual citizens' groups have used PILs on the grounds that the local government is failing to stop squatters from defecating on public roads. Environmental groups in Mumbai obtained an eviction order against squatters living in Borivali National Park, in an effort to protect the ecosystem. Having recourse to the law has become a way of protecting the urban environment when government systems have failed. This is an important dimension of the urban environmental movement in India, and the examples cited here are by no means exhaustive.

However, some of the PILs filed by citizens' groups have also been directly or indirectly against the interests of the poor, as illustrated above. And, as we have already seen, legal initiatives have only limited impact.

Grassroots protests for environment protection

Protest or resistance movements are important means by which affected populations make their voices heard in policy making. In India, there are many well-known rural environmental movements that protest against the diversion of essential resources for urban and industrial use and the dumping of urban and industrial waste in rural areas. There have also been collective actions in urban areas, such as the PILs described above.[15] Other protests take the form of direct action. For instance, 'People for Clean Air' in Delhi asked the government to act against industrial and vehicular pollution. In Udaipur City (known as the city of lakes) in Rajasthan, local citizens have organised under the *Jheel Sanrakshan Samiti* (Lake Protection Committee) to protect the lakes from pollution and putrification caused by economic activities on the lakefront, mainly connected with tourism, and to stop a new hotel being built (Anand 1994). In Bhopal, different citizens' groups and academic and research institutions joined to protest against the pollution of Lake Shahpura, an important source of drinking water, and subsequently to clean it (Development Associates 1996). There are many similar examples throughout the country.

Community-based efforts

There is a long history of community-based efforts and experiments in urban India, but our focus here is on community-based efforts to manage the urban environment, especially the city's solid waste. One successful NGO experiment is Exnora in Chennai. This started in 1989, when citizens expressed concern about deteriorating environmental conditions and drew up an action plan to collect garbage through placing new containers in the street, followed by an awareness-raising campaign. The rag-pickers, renamed city-beautifiers, were given loans by Exnora to purchase tricycles for door-to-door garbage collection and street cleaning. They received monthly salaries from the residents, from which they repaid the loans. Today, the city has 1500 Exnora units, each servicing 75 families or 450,000 people. Many Exnoras have now branched into other environmental activities such as monitoring the pollution of waterways, canal desilting, tree planting, rainwater harvesting for aquifer recharge (Chennai has severe water crises), environmental education in schools, public information campaigns on the environmental impacts of industrial development, slum upgrading, and converting degradable waste into manure. Exnora projects are thus multisectoral and address a wide range of issues (Anand 1999).

Other cities have started similar activities. In Vadodara City in Gujarat, Baroda Citizens' Council, a local NGO, started garbage collection in 1992, engaging local unemployed young people and rag-pickers in garbage collection at a monthly salary of Rs300–400 (US$7–10), paid by the residents. The recyclable waste (paper, plastic, metal containers, etc.) is carried away by the rag-pickers and sold. The degradable waste is converted to manure, and the rest is dumped as landfill. With the support of USAID, this project has been extended to cover 20,000 households, i.e. 100,000 people in a city of some 1.2 million (Cherail 1994). Similar experiments are being carried out in some areas of Delhi with input from local NGOs such as *Vatavarn* (environment) (Malik 1998). All these efforts address environmental and employment issues simultaneously, but they are limited to a few cities and a few localities within these cities.

Fragmented and localised efforts

The urban environmental movements in India have three basic approaches: direct protest, protest through litigation, and concrete development activities. All of these fit well within Local Agenda 21.

In the case of development activities, the stakeholders themselves participate in the development process and the NGOs act as catalysts. But these are generally localised efforts and their replicability on a larger scale remains a problem: they are simply too few in number and touch only a very small fraction of the city's population (Exnora being an exception). These fragmented efforts address one dimension of development, but their sustainability and wider impacts remain unknown. However, the macro context in which they take place is not favourable to the environment and marginalised sectors of society.

The protest movements or resistance to the prevailing development paradigm are just as important, but do not act in synergy. Development activities are generally fragmented and seldom touch the structural issues. The protest groups, which are engaged in political action, do not convert any gains into policies and programmes for concrete development work. In short, there is fragmentation, lack of synergy, and a dichotomy between protests and spontaneous development initiatives, and also among these initiatives themselves. There is therefore a long way to go in making bottom-up urban development sustainable.

An inclusive perspective from the South

Experience from India suggests that very little conceptual or practical research exists on 'sustainable cities', a term often confused with the SCP and other UN programmes. While 'sustainable development' has been critiqued from a Southern perspective, the same is not true of the concept of 'sustainable cities' which, in practice, is viewed as an environmental concept that is techno-managerial in nature, with aspects such as participation, decentralised governance and so on, regarded as subservient to improving the urban environment. In India, there is major government borrowing in order to build urban or 'environmental' infrastructure, first from international aid agencies, and now from the commercial sector. This creates indebtedness and in the long run excludes the poor from the urban development process. Some of the new infrastructure, such as wide roads, flyovers, and bridges (supposedly to decongest the roads and reduce air pollution), are themselves generated by the flawed development model being pursued. The GOI does not view the role of official aid agencies in this light, however, and is keen to seek funding from them.

Since 'sustainable cities' is understood in such a limited manner, other national initiatives in India, such as poverty-alleviation programmes and decentralisation, are not viewed as falling within its framework. As a result, there is no synergy between these various efforts, and the lack of convergence in thinking and in action reduces their cumulative impact. (The exception is in Andhra Pradesh where SWM and employment-generation efforts have been simultaneously addressed by the state government, by drawing on two otherwise separate initiatives.)

The Indian urban environmental movement is still nascent and, as we have seen, its three components – direct protests, litigation, and constructive development activities (the latter usually promoted by NGOs) – are fragmented, localised, and too small scale to make a noticeable impact. Seldom do development activities address the multidimensional nature of urban development or succeed in working at a city-wide level. Environmental and citizens' groups tend not to look at the wider development issues, so that their campaigns risk harming the poor. Development groups often ignore environmental issues, while protest movements and community-based development initiatives rarely work together. Hence, the protests are not translated into policies and programmes, while the benefits of community-based development efforts are not sustainable because they fail to address the macro context.

In India, mainstream debates on the subject look at either urban development or at sustainable cities, and tend to overlook people-centred approaches. Urban development and economic growth are regarded as synonymous, with cities viewed as economic entities that contribute to overall economic growth. Efforts to create a clean, liveable environment and to reduce social inequalities are subsumed into this efficiency paradigm.

Outstanding concerns in India

The sustainable development of cities in the South is possible only when the prime development issues are addressed, including steps to protect the environment. In India (and elsewhere in the South), issues that require immediate attention are:

1 secure housing rights;
2 provision and access to civic amenities, and a clean, safe, and healthy living environment for all;
3 adequate provision and access to adequate public health facilities, basic education, safe and sufficient drinking water, and food security;
4 freedom from violence and intimidation on the basis of social identity;

5 sustainable livelihoods; and

6 adequate and appropriate provision of, and access to, social security programmes.

It is possible to address these concerns while also protecting the environment only within a favourable macro development model in which the government can play a significant role. Some of the main requirements are (i) effective government policies to reduce overall inequality in the cities, and between the rural and urban areas; (ii) democratic urban development processes that meet the needs of the disadvantaged, not only those of businesses or funding agencies, and institutions through which the most disadvantaged participate in macro decisions; (iii) economic growth through activities that are non-polluting; (iv) a sound regulatory mechanism to check unsustainable activities through the participation of civil society; and (v) government responsibility for promoting human development.

Inclusive and synergetic approach

The approach to 'sustainable cities' in the South has to be inclusive, placing the vision of the poor and marginalised urban sectors at the centre of urban policy making. Thus, development processes, programmes, and projects need to be multidimensional and multi-sectoral. The term 'inclusive' implies the inclusion of all citizens and all dimensions of development, the convergence of thinking and action and of different aspects of development. This is the only sustainable way in which to address the major concerns listed above, and the only way in which to achieve sustainable human development. In other words, development and empowerment of the poor have to take place in such a manner that the environment is protected. If the urban environment deteriorates, it is the poor who are most affected. The role of the government, especially local government, is to see that synergies are built between development programmes and their various stakeholders – government and civil society, micro- and macro-level institutions, and so on.

This is no straightforward matter, as many conflicting situations need to be addressed at once. For example, if polluting industries whose employees belong to a marginalised group are closed down, then this raises issues of social equity and employment. These contradictions have to be addressed simultaneously, as to look at the pollution problem in isolation will not lead to a sustainable solution.

Similarly, the improvement of urban air quality does not simply mean getting rid of the polluting vehicles, but also creating alternative employment for those who lose their livelihoods as a result, developing a public transport system, discouraging private vehicles, and suspending car production so that even the better-off shift to public transport.

More critical still is a macro development climate that is pro-people, pro-women, pro-poor, and pro-environment so that any achievements will be sustained. Equally important is that organisations of civil society work together – the protest groups, development groups, and environmental groups – so that each builds a holistic vision of development and does not inadvertently harm the interests of the poor. However, in India today, partial (sectoral) vision and a techno-managerial approach exclude the poor.

At the start of this paper, we argued that the concept of 'sustainable cities' rests on four pillars, all of which need to be addressed simultaneously in development processes, programmes, and projects. For example, environmental programmes should link in with employment, poverty alleviation, and social equity programmes. Micro-level initiatives should be linked with wider strategies. Political empowerment has to be comprehensive and not only at the local level, as envisaged by the current urban governance approach. Environmental sustainability is not just about 'managing' the environment but also about finding a development model that does not generate unmanageable waste, an impossibility when there is such inequality between the North and the South and within the North. Inequality generates unsustainable consumption levels – too low among the poor of the South and unsustainably high among the rich of the South and the North in general. An inclusive approach to 'sustainable cities' in the South addresses development and sustainability in a holistic manner at every level, from the global to the local.

Acknowledgement

The author has benefited greatly from the comments by David Westendorff on the first draft and is grateful to him.

Notes

1 The proverb is in Gujarati.
2 For example, in the state of Gujarat, the second most industrialised state of India, from 1991 onwards, 79 per cent of new investment is generated by polluting industries (Mahadevia 1999c).

3 Diesel cars are cheaper to run than petrol cars. By giving permission to increase the production of diesel cars, the government wants to increase the purchases of cars, which will in turn improve the growth statistics.

4 In India, varying estimates of poverty, rural as well as urban, derive from disagreements on how to calculate the poverty line. The poverty ratios are calculated on the basis of consumer expenditure surveys. These figures are for 1993–4, the last year such consumption expenditure surveys were available.

5 Small towns are defined as having fewer than 50,000 inhabitants.

6 There is no national urban policy document. Urban policies can be discerned from the Five Year Plans, annual reports of the Central Ministry of Urban Development, and national-level urban policy and research institutes such as the National Institute of Urban Affairs. The Ninth Five Year Plan (GOI 1998) treats urban development under Land, Housing, and Basic Services, and is concerned with the growing gap between the demand and supply of basic services. The NIUA document mentions Agenda 21 as a global action plan to 'integrate environmental considerations in the development process' (NIUA 1998: 131). It identifies the importance of promoting sustainable human settlement and the initiatives of local authorities. The latter is of particular interest as it calls for interaction, participation, and involvement of the community and local authorities in the planning and management of the urban ecosystem. The action areas identified are environmental management, pollution control, and environmental protection. The vision of urban development here states that cities and towns have to be economically efficient, socially equitable, and environmentally sustainable (NIUA 1998: xiii). The focus is thus on the urban environment rather than on sustainable cities.

7 In Gujarat, citizens' groups have been very active in approaching the Gujarat High Court, seeking legal remedies for water pollution (Mahadevia 1999c).

8 This is partially effective because new vehicles, including the diesel ones, arrive with new technology (Reddy 2000).

9 Now the Department for International Development (DFID).

10 The Project costs US$132 million (ADB loan US$85 million) and the main focus is to decentralise economic growth from the rapidly expanding Bangalore city to four selected towns.

11 This is to assist the GOI to develop urban and environmental infrastructure, to leverage private sector and external resources for urban development and environmental improvement, and to prepare suitable projects involving public–private investment for financing under the Fund.

12 One of the programmes is support to the Centre for Environmental Planning and Technology (CEPT), an academic institution, to assist city governments to prepare their baseline reports and develop strategies for solid waste management. USAID took the opportunity arising from an Expert Committee Report prepared at the behest of the Supreme Court that gave guidelines for SWM in 300 Class-I cities in India in April 1999.

13 The Mega City Scheme is applicable to Bangalore, Calcutta, Chennai, Hyderabad, and Mumbai and would

make loans available from the fund set aside by central government.

14 One initiative is the signing of the Indian–US treaty, to which the Confederation of Indian Industry was party, for the import of environment-friendly technology from the USA (Banerji 1995).

15 For example, in the state of Gujarat, a number of PILs were filed by individuals against chemical pollution from industrial estates. The High Court of Gujarat in most cases directed the estates to set up Common Effluent Treatment Plants (CETPs). The CETPs dilute the industrial waste but do not treat the toxic and hazardous chemicals it contains. Such CETPs are therefore not the solution to the pollution caused by the rapid growth of chemical industries in the state (Mahadevia 1999c).

References

Anand, P.B. (1999) 'Waste management in Madras revisited', *Environment and Urbanization* 11 (2): 161–76

Anand, R. (1994) 'Churning the stilled waters', *Down to Earth* 3 (10): 22–3

Banerji, R. (1995) 'Environmental trade-off', *Down to Earth* 4 (1): 15

Chambers, R. (1988) 'Sustainable Rural Livelihoods: A Strategy for People, Environment and Development', Discussion paper, Sussex: Institute of Development Studies, University of Sussex

Cherail, K. (1994) 'Haul your own garbage', *Down to Earth* 3 (8): 10

Choguill, C.L. (1996) 'Toward sustainability of human settlements', *Habitat International* 20 (3): v–viii

Clow, M. (1996) 'Sustainable development: our next path of development or wishful thinking', *British Journal of Canadian Studies* 11 (2): 1–10

Cornia, G., R. Jolly, and F. Stewart (1987) *Adjustment with a Human Face: Protecting the Vulnerable and Promoting Growth*, Oxford: Clarendon Press

Development Associates (1996) 'NGOs/Civic societies and urban environmental advocacy', in B.N. Singh, S. Maitra, and R. Sharma (eds) *Urban Environment Management: The Indian Experience*, New Delhi: Housing Settlement Management Institute, and Rotterdam: Institute for Housing and Urban Development Studies

Down to Earth (1999) 'Licence to Kill', *Down to Earth* 8(2): 36–7

Dubey, A. and D. Mahadevia (forthcoming) 'Poverty and inequality in Indian Metropolises', *Indian Journal of Labour Economics*

Dubey, A. and S. Gangopadhyay (1998) *Counting the Poor: Where are the Poor in India?*, Sarvekshana Analytical Report No. 1, Government of India: Department of Statistics

Dubey, A. and S. Gangopadhyay, (1999) 'Poverty and occupational structure in size class of towns in India', *Regional Development Dialogue*, Nagoya

Dubey, A., S. Gangopadhyay, and W. Wadhwa (2000) 'Occupational structure and incidence of poverty in Indian towns of different sizes', *Review of Development Economy* 5 (1)

Expert Group on Commercialisation of Infrastructure Projects (1996) *The India Infrastructure Report: Policy Imperatives for Growth and Welfare*, Government of India: Ministry of Finance

Government of India (GOI) (1997) *Estimate of Poverty*, New Delhi: Press Information Bureau, Perspective Planning Division, Planning Commission, March

Government of India (GOI) (1998) *The Ninth Five Year Plan (Draft) 1997–2002*, New Delhi: Planning Commission

Hardoy, J., D. Mitlin, and D. Satterthwaite (1992) *Environmental Problems in Third World*, London: Earthscan

Haughton, G. (1997) 'Developing sustainable urban development models', *Cities* 14(4): 189–95

Hirway, I. and D. Mahadevia (1996) 'Critique of gender development index – towards an alternative', *Economic and Political Weekly* 31(43), 26 October

Hirway, I. and D. Mahadevia (1999) *The Gujarat Human Development Report*, 1999 (draft), Ahmedabad: Gandhi Labour Institute

HSMI/WMC (1996) 'City-wide best practices in solid waste management in collection, transportation and disposal', in B.N. Singh, S. Maitra, and R. Sharma (eds) *Urban Environment Management: The Indian Experience*, New Delhi: Housing Settlement Management Institute, and Rotterdam: Institute for Housing and Urban Development Studies

Huckle, J. (1996) 'Realising sustainability in changing times', in J. Huckle and S. Sterling (eds) *Education for Sustainability*, London: Earthscan

Kundu, A. (1996) 'New economic policy and urban poverty in India', in C.H. Hanumantha Rao and H. Linnemann (eds) *Economic Reforms and Poverty Alleviation in India*, New Delhi: Sage

Kundu, A. (1999) 'A Perspective on Urban Development and Emerging System of Governance: The Indian Case', paper presented at the National Workshop on Urban Agenda in the New Millennium, School of Planning, Centre for Environmental Planning and Technology and UNNATI, Ahmedabad, 23–24 July

Mahadevia, D. (1999a) 'Urban Policies in India: Critical Overview Towards Agenda in the New Millennium', paper presented at the National Workshop on Urban Agenda in the New Millennium, School of Planning, Centre for Environmental Planning and Technology and UNNATI, Ahmedabad, 23–24 July

Mahadevia, D. (1999b) 'Land and Housing Rights For All: A New Approach', paper presented at the National Workshop on Urban Agenda in the New Millennium, School of Planning, Centre for Environmental Planning and Technology and UNNATI, Ahmedabad, 23–24 July

Mahadevia, D. (1999c) *Economic Growth and Environment in Gujarat*, New Delhi: Research Foundation for Science, Technology and Ecology

Mahadevia, D. and W. D'Costa (1997) 'Poverty and Vulnerability in Ahmedabad', unpublished report, Ahmedabad: Oxfam (India) Trust

Malik, I. (1998) 'Waste management efforts in Delhi', *Shelter* 1(4): 59–60

Mohan, R. (1996) 'Urbanisation in India: patterns and emerging policy issues', in J. Gugler (ed.) *The Urban Transformation of the Developing World*, Oxford: Oxford University Press

National Institute of Urban Affairs (NIUA) (1995) *Handbook of Urban Statistics*, New Delhi: NIUA

National Institute of Urban Affairs (NIUA) (1998) *India's Urban Sector Profile*, New Delhi: NIUA

Nicholls, L. (1996) 'From Paradigm to Practice: The Politics and Implementation of Sustainable Human Development – The Example of Uganda', Research Paper 2, The Centre for the Study of Global Governance, London: London School of Economics

Rao, K.R. (2000) 'Clean and green cities: participation of communities/ neighbourhood committees', *Shelter* 3 (1): 50–3

Redclift, M. (1992) 'Sustainable development and popular participation: a framework for analysis', in D. Ghai and J.M. Vivian (eds) *Grassroots Environmental Action: People's Participation in Sustainable Development*, London: Routledge

Reddy, C. M. (2000) 'Vehicle emissions: beyond technology', in *The Hindu Survey of the Environment, 2000* 115–19

Reed, David (ed.) (1995) *Structural Adjustment, the Environment, and Sustainable Development*, London: Earthscan

Satterthwaite, D. (1996) 'For better living', *Down to Earth* 5 (5): 31–5

Satterthwaite, D. (1998) 'Environmental problems in cities in the south: sharing my confusions', in E. Fernandes (ed.) *Environmental Strategies for Sustainable Development in Urban Areas: Lessons from Africa and Latin America*, Aldershot: Ashgate

Shrivastava, R. (1995) 'A question of industry', *Down to Earth* 3(23): 18–9

Stren, R. (1992) 'A comparative approach to cities and the environment', in R. Stren, R.White, and J. Whitney (eds) *Sustainable Cities: Urbanisation and the Environment in International Perspective*, Boulder, CO: Westview

Stubbs, J. and G. Clarke (1996) *Mega Cities Management in the Asian and Pacific Region*, Volume I, Manila: Asian Development Bank

Suresh, V. (2000) 'Challenges of urban development in the new millennium', editorial in *Shelter* 3(1): 3–4

Technical Services US–AEP (1997) *US–AEP Country Assessments*, Washington, DC: Technical Services

Vivian, J.M. (1992) 'Foundations for sustainable development: participation, empowerment and local resource management', in D. Ghai and J.M. Vivian (eds) *Grassroots Environmental Action: People's Participation in Sustainable Development*, London: Routledge

World Bank (1990) *Urban Policy and Economic Development: An Agenda for the 1990s*, Washington, DC: World Bank

World Commission on Environment and Development (WCED) (1987) *Our Common Future*, Oxford: Oxford University Press

World Resource Institute (WRI), UNEP, UNDP and World Bank (1996) *World Resources: A Guide to the Global Environment – The Urban Environment*, Oxford: Oxford University Press

Urban crisis in India:

new initiatives for sustainable cities

P.G. Dhar Chakrabarti

India no longer lives in villages. At the dawn of the new millennium, 300 million Indians lived in its nearly 3700 towns and cities, in sharp contrast to only 60 million in 1947 when the country became independent. During the last 50 years the population of India has grown two and half times, but the urban population has grown nearly five times. In absolute terms, India's urban population is the second largest in the world after China's, and is almost twice the combined urban population of France, Germany, and the UK.

Yet, in relative terms India is still one of the least urbanised of the developing countries, with less than 30 per cent of its population living in towns, compared with 80 per cent in Brazil, 45 per cent in Egypt, and 35 per cent even in neighbouring Pakistan. But this scenario is changing fast.

While the rate of growth of population in the country is declining (from 2.16 per cent in 1991 to 1.9 per cent in 1999) the urban population is increasing more quickly (from 3.1 per cent in 1991 to 3.6 per cent in 1999) and demographers believe that it may grow even faster in the coming years. The urban population is expected to swell to 410 million in 2011, 550 million in 2021, and 800 million in 2041 when it will surpass that of China. At that point urban India will be larger than the total population of the whole of Europe (NIUA 2000).

This explosive situation has not been adequately appreciated at the national and international level. It is important, however, to focus on certain disturbing features of India's urban experience in order to highlight the implications of this growth in terms of sustainability.

For instance, there are large imbalances and disparities in the spatial patterns of urbanisation as measured by inter-regional and size–class distribution. While the western states of Maharastra, Goa, and Gujarat are nearly 40 per cent urban, the eastern states of Orissa and Bihar lag far behind at 13 per cent. This has been both a cause and a consequence of inter-regional migration. Surplus labourers from the relatively impoverished regions are crowding into urban centres in search of work and will continue to do so unless employment opportunities are created in the rural areas of the so-called backward states. Slightly over 40 per cent of urban growth in India has been a result of migration from the rural areas (NIUA 1988) and much of it has been dictated more by the absence of opportunities in these areas than by the presence of opportunities in the urban areas. Instead of contributing to urban growth as such, this has only impoverished the urban centres (Singh and Steinberg 1996). Therefore, the sustainability of urban growth in India is thus very strongly related to the development of rural areas, especially the backward pockets.

The imbalance in size–class distribution is another factor contributing to the abnormal growth of bigger cities. And while many of these are on the verge of collapse, many smaller cities lack adequate impetus for growth. Intra-city migration from smaller to bigger cities is continuing along with the migration from rural to urban areas. The government's Integrated Development of Small and Medium Towns scheme (IDSMT) has not been able to reverse this trend. Table 1 indicates the growth pattern of cities in India.

The percentage share of population living in Class I cities has increased sharply from 44.6 per cent in 1951 to 65.2 per cent in 1991, but has also declined in all other sectors, except in Class II towns, which have remained more or less the same. Again within the Class I cities, the share of population in metropolitan (1 million or more inhabitants) and megacities (10 million or more inhabitants) has been disproportionately higher. About one third of urban India is already living in metropolitan cities and this figure is expected to increase to 60 per cent

Table 1: Classes of Indian cities by size of population							
Year	Class I 100,000+	Class II 50,000– 99,000	Class III 20,000– 49,999	Class IV 10,000– 19,999	Class V 5000– 9999	Class VI less than 5000	All classes
1951	27.5 m (44.6%)	6.1 m (10%)	9.7 m (15.7%)	8.4 m (13.6%)	8 m (13%)	1.9 m (3.1%)	61.6 m
1991	139.1 m (65.2%)	23.4 m (11%)	28.1 m (13.1%)	16.6 m (7.8%)	5.5 m (2.6%)	0.6 m (0.3%)	213.3 m (100%)

Source: Census of India (1991)

in the next two decades. Of the total increase in the country's urban population of 58 million between 1981 and 1991, 44 million were added to Class I cities alone, 28 million of which joined the metropolitan cities. The number of metropolitan cities in the country has grown from one in 1901 to five in 1951, and to 23 in 1991. It is estimated that it will further increase to 40 by 2001, 52 by 2011, and 75 by 2021 (Singh and Steinberg 1996). Similarly, the number of Indian megacities will double from the current three (Calcutta, Delhi, and Mumbai) to six by the year 2021 (new additions will be Bangalore, Chennai, and Hyderabad), when India will have the largest concentration of megacities in the world.

The unplanned and uncontrolled growth of large cities has had negative effects on urban dwellers and their environment. The provision of infrastructure and services required for large and concentrated populations lags far behind the pace of urbanisation. Consequently, the urban environment, particularly in large cities, is deteriorating rapidly. Cities and towns are facing serious shortages of power, water, sewerage, developed land, housing, transportation, communication, and other facilities.

Imperfections in land and housing markets and exorbitant increases in land prices have left the urban poor with virtually no alternative except to seek housing in the mushrooming slums. About one third of urban dwellers live below the poverty line and in subhuman conditions in such slums, without access to the basic minimum facilities of drinking water, sanitation, medical care, and public hygiene (CSO 1997). The disparities in living conditions between slums and other areas are a potential cause of crime and social unrest in the large cities, which are no longer considered safe.

According to official statistics, 85 per cent of the urban population has safe drinking water. The average availability is less than four hours per day, however, and in some areas water is supplied only for one hour on alternate days (ADB 1997). Many people are forced to draw water from unsafe sources, which leads to widespread waterborne diseases like diarrhoea, hepatitis, roundworm, etc. The effect on public health and hygiene is telling. A recent study has indicated that about 30.5 million Disability-Adjusted Life Years (DALYs) are lost each year owing to the poor quality of drinking water and the absence of sanitation facilities.[1] The financial loss in terms of productivity has been quantified at Rs360 billion (US$9 billion) annually (MUD 2000b).

Only 49 per cent of the population in the cities have sanitation facilities and the rest use either dry latrines or defecate in the open. Out of 3700 towns in the country, only 72 have partial sewerage facilities and 17 have some form of primary treatment facilities before final disposal.

About 39 million tonnes of solid waste is generated in the urban areas every day. Of this not more than 60 per cent is collected daily, which leads to the accumulation and decomposition of waste in public places with its adverse effects on public health. There is no arrangement for the processing of waste except in a few cities where composting is done on a limited scale.

Road space per Passenger Car Unit (PCU) is declining steadily in all cities. Traffic congestion is assuming critical dimensions in many metropolitan cities owing to a massive increase in the number of private vehicles, inadequate road space, and lack of public transport. This extreme congestion results in ever-slower speeds, an increasing accident rate, fuel wastage, and environmental pollution. Air-pollution-related health problems are reaching disturbing proportions in some cities:

> India's urban centres are becoming lethal gas chambers. Most of the air quality standards in India are considerably more lax than those of the World Health Organisation. The WHO has rated Delhi the fourth-most polluted city in the world. (CSE 2000)

Unless a massive investment is made to improve urban infrastructure and living conditions significantly, most of the cities in India are heading for a major crisis. The Ninth Plan Working Group has estimated the investment requirement for housing in urban areas at Rs528 billion for the next five years (Planning Commission 1998). The annual investment needed for urban water supply, sanitation, and roads is estimated at approximately Rs280 billion for the next ten years (CPHEEO 1996). The Central Public Health Environmental Engineering Organisation (CPHEEO) has estimated the requirement of Rs1729 billion for total coverage of the urban population with safe water supply and sanitation services (DEA 1986). Estimates by Rail India Technical and Economic Services (RITES) indicate that the amount required for urban transport infrastructure investment in cities for a population of 100,000 or more during the next 20 years will be of the order of Rs2070 billion (RITES 1997). Against this, the combined investment of central, state, and local authorities from budgetary as well as institutional sources (both domestic and foreign) in housing, water supply, sanitation, and transport is approximately Rs80 billion annually, or less than 10 per cent of the requirement (Planning Commission 1998). This sums up the enormous urban problem in India, which assumes more critical dimensions with each passing day.

Sustainable cities: philosophy and context

What would a sustainable city mean in the context of the urban crisis, which has brought the large cities to breaking point? The *Oxford English Dictionary* defines sustainable as 'the ability to be maintained at a certain rate or level'. This implies that there is no fixed standard of sustainability since it varies according to the context in which it is defined. The standard of sustainability differs from country to country according to its level of development. Environmentalists propose a more neutral and stringent standard of sustainability as 'the conservation of an ecological balance by avoiding depletion of natural resources' (UNCHS 1998). In the urban context this would mean the resources of pure air, water, soil, flora, and fauna.

The environmental definition of sustainability is both too wide and too narrow: wide in the sense that it takes pristine nature as its standard, something that would by definition render three quarters of existing human settlements unsustainable; narrow in the sense that it ignores complex issues that have led human development to the state it is in today. Since human development has not followed a uniform pattern, it is futile and unrealistic to set a uniform standard of what constitutes a sustainable city, irrespective of the level of development.

A more pragmatic and realistic definition of a sustainable city is one that maintains the physical, human, and environmental standards it has set for itself and has the capacity, resources, and capability to achieve these. This calls for sustainability of governance and for sustainability of resources without which 'the sustainable city' is only a slogan.

The cities of India are facing the accumulated effects of past neglect when their affairs were not left to the citizens but to the extraneous forces of party politics and bureaucratic interference, when state control and the proliferation of parastatal agencies marginalised city governments, when cheap populist measures overshadowed sound financial considerations, when a kind of urban *laissez-faire* prevailed over discipline and control, when a culture of subsidy and concession was allowed to rule over cost effectiveness, when responsible and capable urban leadership was not allowed to develop, and when developing the capacity of urban managers was not a concern. Urban crisis in India is an accumulation of years of neglect of the local urban bodies. A sustainable city cannot be built on the basis of direction and control from provincial or state governments; it has ultimately to rest on the initiative and efforts of local citizens, the involvement and commitment of the local community, the vision and understanding of local leaders, and the capacity and capability of local managers.

All these are the essential ingredients of successful local self-government, but unfortunately, despite India's strong and vibrant democracy at the provincial and national level, city-level democracy has not really been allowed to flourish. City governments were treated more as an appendage of provincial government than as governments in their own right. This is ironic, as the institutional machinery of India's city governments was set up as early as the mid-nineteenth century and some of the great national leaders in pre-independence days were apprentices of leaders in city governments.

Initiatives for urban reform

The first model of city government in India was set up by the British. The considerations were twofold, to allow the 'natives' to rule over their own local affairs as a strategy to absorb dissent, but to allow only limited autonomy for maintaining 'control' over the larger policy issues. The statutes governing the city governments underwent change after independence, but 'control' of the urban local bodies continued. Provincial governments were given overriding powers to sanction municipal budgets, to approve municipal taxation, to take away municipal functions, to set up parastatal organisations to deal with such functions, and even to suspend and dissolve municipal governments for an indefinite period. The result was that city governments lost their importance and ability to take decisions and became an appendage of state governments. Party politics at the state level were passed down to the city level and city-level consensus on the major issues was not allowed to develop. In short, the citizens remained alienated from governing.

The first major initiative to reform urban governance was taken in 1992 when the Constitution of India was amended (74th Amendment) to incorporate certain revolutionary changes in the organisation, powers, functions, and jurisdictions of the urban local bodies. For the first time, city governments were given a constitutional status and released from the shackles of provincial governments. The Constitution of India formally recognised the city government as the third tier of government below the state and central governments.

Second, the powers of state governments to suspend or dissolve city governments were abolished. If a city government is to be dissolved, fresh elections must be held and a new elected body must be in place within a period of six months from the date of dissolution.[2] The era of prolonged suspension of city governments has come to an end.

Third, the Constitution provided that, apart from the city-level councillors, wardens are also to be popularly elected at the ward level and Ward Committees set up to interact with the citizens. These changes institutionalise the role of the grassroots in city governance.

Fourth, the Constitution defined the powers of the civic bodies and appended a separate schedule of their functions as follows:

- urban planning, including town planning;
- regulation of land use and construction;
- maintenance of roads and bridges;
- supply of water for domestic, industrial, and commercial purposes;
- public health, sanitation, conservancy, and solid waste management;
- provision of fire services;
- urban forestry, protection of the environment, and promotion of ecological aspects;
- slum improvement and upgrading;
- urban poverty alleviation;
- planning of social and economic development;
- safeguarding the interests of weaker sections of society, including the physically and mentally disabled;
- provision of amenities and facilities such as parks, gardens, and playgrounds;
- public amenities, including street lighting, parking lots, bus-stops, and public conveniences;
- regulation of slaughter houses and tanneries
- promotion of cultural, educational, and aesthetic aspects; and
- collection of key statistics, including registration of births and deaths.

Finally, the Constitution stipulated that every state is obliged to assign city governments such taxes, duties, and tolls that are levied, collected, and appropriated by them and ensure that the city governments are not discriminated against in the allocation of resources. The Constitution further provides that every state shall constitute a State Finance Commission (SFC) to decide which resources will devolve to the city governments in order to enable them to discharge their functions.

All these revolutionary changes will revitalise the city governments in the long run, but the pace of implementation has been so abysmally slow that their impact is yet to be felt. Elections to urban local bodies have been held in all but two states. Most of the state governments have either enacted a set of new municipal laws or amended the existing laws to bring them into line with the constitutional changes. Reports of many of the SFCs have also been brought into line, but considerable confusion persists with regard to the functions and jurisdictions of the city governments. A host of parastatal bodies set up in each state to deal with important functions like water supply, sewerage, urban planning, housing, etc. have not been brought under the jurisdiction of the civic bodies.[3] Similarly, the line departments of the state government continue to deal with many of the functions that have been assigned to the cities. On the financial side, there has not been much devolution of resources, primarily because there has not been much devolution of functions and responsibilities. Therefore, the amendment to the Constitution notwithstanding, the status quo prevails largely because parastatal bodies already have their own statutory character and expertise, which civic bodies do not.[4] Yet no significant effort has been made for building the capacity of civic bodies.

The urban reform agenda of taxation and financial reform, institutional reform, 'unbundling' of services, privatisation, etc., that should have followed the constitutional changes, has not taken place at all in most cities and been initiated only at a slow pace in a few. The status quo is that of continuing poor governance in most of the cities.[5]

There is considerable scope for generating sizeable resources from the cities through reforms in the system of property tax assessment and collection, and rationalisation of utility charges. However, there is no incentive for city governments to take such unpopular measures since most of the utilities are managed at state level, and managed so inefficiently that it will take real courage to break the coterie of vested interests that run them. The will and vision to do so are not forthcoming.

A truncated urban government cannot be expected to push the reform agenda and transform cities into self-sustaining and sustainable units of governance. What is required is 'a reform in the reform process' before it is too late.[6] If the push does not come from the top it will have to come from the bottom, as is now occurring in many dispersed initiatives (see Mahadevia in this volume).[7]

Sustainable technology

Despite the constraints of poor urban governance, there has been some advance made in adopting and propagating a few innovative, low-cost, and environmentally sustainable technologies for solving some of India's pressing urban problems. This has been made possible through the effort of a few individuals and organisations, and by grants from central government and soft credit from international financial institutions. Three major initiatives in this regard are the techniques of low-cost sanitation, low-cost housing, and rainwater harvesting. But the spread of these technologies has been severely restricted because of poor urban governance, an inefficient delivery system for extending the incentives, and the non-involvement of civil society in any meaningful manner in terms of creating awareness of the benefits and efficacy of these technologies. These observations are based on my decade-long experience of urban management in India.

Low-cost sanitation

The low-cost sanitation movement has made some progress not only to provide an affordable solution to the problem of open defecation in the cities but also to do away with the demeaning practice of manual collection of human excreta, which has traditionally been carried out by low-caste groups. Mahatma Gandhi had started his political career with a campaign to liberate the scavengers, but it was not until 1993 that manual scavenging was declared illegal by an Act of Parliament and since then the Government of India (GOI) has taken up a massive programme of conversion of dry latrines into pour-flush latrines in the urban areas and rehabilitation of the scavengers.

The pour-flush latrine consists of: (a) a specially designed squatting pan, (b) a trap with a 20mm water seal to prevent the emission of odours and fly and mosquito nuisance, (c) two leaching pits which retain solid matter and allow liquid to leach and gases to disperse into the ground, and (d) an interconnecting system between pits and trap. The excreta are carried into subsurface leach pits through pipes or covered drains and one pit is used at a time. The liquid seeps into the soil through the holes in the pit lining. The gases also disperse into the soil so a vent pipe is not necessary. When the one pit is full, the excreta are diverted automatically to the second pit. The filled chamber can be conveniently emptied after a rest period of 18 months, during which time pathogens are activated and the organic matter decomposed. Thus, the two pits can be used alternately and continuously (UNDP 1992).

A five-user pour-flush latrine costs as little as Rs4500 (equivalent to US$100), while a ten-user unit costs Rs8000.

The pour-flush water seal latrines are low in cost but involve high technology. They comprise a collection, transmission, and treatment system all within one on-site facility, which is hygienic, safe, and satisfactory. In addition, the technology is internally and externally upgradeable, meaning that the toilet interiors can be upgraded to accommodate improved systems such as the incremental flush. Furthermore, the system can be externally connected to sewers, if enhanced water-supply levels and sewerage can be afforded (HUDC 1988).

Since 1989–1990, the GOI has been supporting this low-cost sanitation technology with a mixture of subsidies and soft loans, which vary in scale according to the paying capacity of the user (see Table 2).

The scheme – called the 'Liberation of Scavengers' – has been taken up on a 'whole-town basis' so that the problem is solved for the town once and for all and the scavengers do not return to their original occupation. Simultaneously, a massive rehabilitation and training programme for scavengers has been launched to help them to pursue alternative vocations, and this is backed up with soft credit to set up microenterprises (MUD 1999).

In most towns, the survey and identification of dry latrines, the location and design of pour-flush latrines, and supervision of construction have been entrusted to the engineering wing of the civic bodies. NGOs, community-based organisations, and self-help groups have been involved in a few cities, but more as implementing agencies than as partners or stakeholders of the programme.

Table 2: Forms of GOI support for low-cost sanitation technology			
User category	Subsidy (%)	Loan (%)	User contribution (%)
Economically weaker sectors	45	50	5
Low-income groups	25	60	15
High-income groups	Nil	75	25

During the decade since the scheme began, 900,000 low-cost sanitation units have been constructed, and 30,000 scavengers liberated from the inhuman practice of manual scavenging. But this does not mean that the problem has been solved, as 6,300,000 more dry latrines have yet to be converted into pour-flush latrines and, until that has been done, the problem of manual scavenging will persist despite the legal restrictions. The problem remains one of both resources and management. It is estimated that a subsidy of Rs25.2 billion and soft credit of Rs63 billion will be required to convert all the dry latrines. Against this, the government allocates annually Rs270 million in subsidies and Rs1080 million in loans. The irony is that even this meagre amount is not fully deployed, and an accumulated unspent subsidy of Rs1 billion will reportedly have accrued by the end of financial year 1999–2000 (MUD 2000b). This points to the abysmal capacity of the urban local bodies and the low involvement of civil society in implementing such socially and environmentally sustainable schemes.

Low-cost housing

The Indian Building Centre movement for the promotion of low-cost housing technology is another example of how technology can mitigate the problem of having only few resources. High land prices and construction costs have driven as many as 100 million urban poor to seek refuge in the proliferating urban slums, although these are dangerously lacking the basic amenities of sanitation, drinking water, drainage, etc.. In many long-established slums, the emphasis has been to take up *in situ* development of basic amenities. In most other places, city agencies have resettled slum-dwellers on alternative sites at subsidised rates. The GOI has set a target of construction of 700,000 additional houses every year for the economically weaker sectors and low-income groups in the urban areas.

Much research has gone into the development of low-cost construction and design technology in order to permit poor people to own their houses. The thrust of this initiative has been to recycle various forms of industrial, agricultural, and domestic waste to provide new building materials that are affordable, sustainable, and environmentally friendly. Some of the new materials are listed in Table 3.

These new materials are not only energy efficient and environmentally friendly, but also cost effective: up to 25–30 per cent cheaper than conventional materials and 15–20 per cent more energy efficient to manufacture and use.

Table 3: Materials developed for low-cost construction	
Waste materials	**New building materials**
Industrial waste	
Fly and bottom ash from thermal power plants	Bricks
Cement factory waste	Asbestos
Basalt, slate, and laterite stone waste	Blast furnace slag
Coal washery waste	Copper/ferro-alloy slag
Gypsum mine waste	Iron railings
Limestone waste/lime sludge	Low-grade aggregates
Mica scrap	Phosphogypsum
Red mud/bauxite waste	Steel-making slags
Agricultural waste	
Rice husks, jute stalk, bagasse	Insulation boards, panels, roofing sheets
Domestic waste	
Used paper, cartons, plastic bags	Fence posts, roofing sheets

The GOI is attempting to stimulate production of low-cost building materials by exempting the Building Centres' production of materials and components from excise duty. It also offers a 25 per cent exemption in the organised industrial sector, a reduction in the customs duty on imports of equipment, machinery, and capital goods required to produce building materials that require fly ash (a by-product of coal) and phosphogypsum, and a total exemption of excise duty on doors, windows, etc. made from aluminium, steel, plastics, and other materials that will reduce the exploitation of India's forest resources.

Much research has also gone into the development of small machines for producing building materials on a small scale. An autonomous organisation called the Building Materials and Technology Promotion Council (BMTPC) was set up with the responsibility for co-ordinating research efforts in this area. The Council has developed a number of machines that have become quite popular. The machines make reinforced concrete construction doors and window frames, stabilised mud-blocks, sand-lime fly ash bricks, clay fly ash bricks, red-mud jute polymer door shutters, a coal stoker system for conventional brick kilns, a finger-jointing and shaping machine for plantation timber, a machine for making corrugated roofing sheets based on bamboo, and so on (BMTPC 1996).

Innovative building designs, such as interlocked cluster housing, organised common spaces, and incremental house design, have been introduced to minimise ground coverage, and reduce construction costs, while at the same time enhancing the aesthetic qualities of low-income housing.

Recognising that the propagation and extension of new cost-effective and energy-efficient building technologies at the grassroots requires innovative approaches, the GOI began setting up a national network of Building Centres in 1988–1989. So far, 400 such centres in district towns promote new cost-effective building materials by providing a variety of services to prospective producers and users. These include: disseminating and demonstrating cost-effective technologies; training artisans, entrepreneurs, and small contractors; advising householders; and producing low-cost materials and components to meet local housing needs. A number of centres are also producing new building materials and components. Encouraged by the results of these efforts, the GOI has now decided to establish similar centres in rural areas in every district of the country. Many of the newly trained artisans have set up production units to cater for local needs.

Despite these initiatives, low-cost housing technology has not replaced the conventional construction technology for poor households. An Expert Group set up to study the working of the Building Centres estimated in 1992 that of the total housing stock of economically weaker sections, not even 10 per cent had adopted the new technology and materials (MUD 1992). Things have not changed much since then.

Rainwater harvesting

Excessive extraction of groundwater and the limited open space for recharge in some of the cities have resulted in a sharp decline in the water table. This is manifested by the failure of tube wells, deterioration in groundwater quality, and saline water ingress. The problem has become acute in some cities, especially during summer, when drinking water has to be carried from distant sources, resulting in high costs and strict water rationing. Water strife and riots have become regular features in some of the towns of western and southern India during the summer months, and in Rajkot, for example, the police have been asked to supervise the distribution of the water to avoid violence and clashes among residents.

In the National Capital Territory of Delhi only 2.8 million m³ of water can be supplied per day for domestic use while the daily demand is for 4.88 million m³. The available surface water from the Yamuna River is grossly insufficient and must be made up from groundwater. Unplanned withdrawal of groundwater has resulted in a drop in the water level and a deterioration in the quality of groundwater in many places. Ironically, the 600mm of rainfall Delhi receives during monsoons drains mostly into the river. Recharge to the subsurface is minimal because most of the surface is occupied by buildings or roads.

The Central Ground Water Board (CGWB), in collaboration with the Indian Institute of Technology Delhi, has been conducting Experimental Artificial Recharge Studies (EARS). Based on the results of its experiments, a viable and sustainable technology for recharging groundwater is now available in deficit areas. This technology is ready to be applied, and a few water-deficit cities have already begun doing so (CGWB 1998).

The Madras Metropolitan Development Authority has made rooftop rainwater harvesting (RTRWH) mandatory for all institutional and public buildings, in order to augment subsurface storage. More and more private building owners in deficit pockets are also adopting this technology which is simple, affordable, and can be adopted at the neighbourhood or even the building level. The rooftop rainwater can be channelled into abandoned wells or abandoned or working hand pumps. Alternatively, a recharge pit, shaft, or trench with appropriate specifications can be dug at a corner of the house or a group of houses. It has been found that groundwater recharge from houses of 100m² of rooftop in average monsoon condition will be 55,000 litres per year, which is sufficient for a period of four months for a five-person family. This is a simple and innovative technology, and appropriate to the context of cities in developing countries which lack the adequate resources for mega-schemes or an assured water supply. This technology has yet to be adopted on a large scale in Indian cities, however, and there is to date no central scheme or incentive to propagate it.

Summary and conclusion

This paper has attempted to describe the rapidly deepening and urgent nature of the urban crisis in India. The failure to provide adequate livelihoods in rural areas is pushing larger numbers of people into the cities than ever before. Informal work and desperately unhealthy living situations in slums await most of the new entrants into the city.

Perhaps as much as a third of India's urban population of 300 million share this fate.

Urban infrastructure and services are abysmally bad and getting worse. Their long neglect and mismanagement by state-level institutions, development authorities, and parastatal bodies was supposed to have come to an end from the early 1990s with the implementation of the 74th Constitutional Amendment. This Amendment created the legal basis for expanding the authority of urban local bodies (city governments) in planning, managing, and funding the development and maintenance of their cities. The Amendment was also intended to encourage and empower civil society organisations to participate more fully in the governance of the city.

In the eight years since the Amendment came into force, the urban local bodies remain constrained in their ability to improve conditions through investments to upgrade infrastructure and services. Even very low-cost, highly efficient technologies for handling human waste, producing building components for housing from recycled materials, and replenishing groundwater supplies are not being widely taken up by the urban communities which so desperately need them.

This situation is a result of the continuing inability and incapacity of urban local bodies effectively to promote investments on the use of these and other appropriate technologies for improving living conditions in the cities. However, a deeper look into the matter shows that state-level institutions, development authorities, and parastatals are still too deeply involved in governance at the local level, and have little incentive and capacity to promote the kinds of initiatives that are needed. Hence, any fundamental change for the urban poor awaits a reform of the reform process begun with the 74th Amendment: that is, to implement more speedily and thoroughly the transfer of authority, initiative, and resources to urban local bodies and local civil society.

Notes

1   Disability Adjusted Life Years (DALYs) are a composite measure of the burden of each major health problem. The DALYs for a given condition are the sum of years of life lost due to premature mortality and the number of years of life lived with disability, adjusted for the severity of the disability. DALYs for different conditions can be aggregated into a single measure of the impacts of all conditions detracting from full health. They therefore provide a means for policy makers to prioritise health threats and challenges, though the concept has many critics (Anand and Hanson 1995).

2 A city government can be dissolved by the state government for a number of reasons: for example, when no party or group of parties command majority support in the municipal council, or when the council itself has passed a resolution recommending dissolution and early election.

3 The term 'civic bodies' has been used as a synonym for 'city governments'. It includes various forms of city governments such as notified area committees in small towns, municipal councils in medium towns, and municipal corporations in metropolitan towns.

4 Most of the parastatal bodies have been constituted by the laws enacted by the state legislatures, giving them an autonomous character. These are accountable to the state governments, and not to the city governments.

5 The state of urban governance in the post-1992 reform phase has yet to be studied in depth, but is reflected in the reports of the many SFCs. Mismanagement of many of the parastatal bodies is reflected in the huge subsidies they receive from the state governments and the poor level of satisfaction of the citizens. Very few state governments have the courage to withdraw the subsidy from the supply of water and power from urban consumers or to privatise the distribution systems. The political considerations of potential voter dissatisfaction that could follow such measures in the short term have prevailed over considerations of sound financial management. Similar considerations have prevented any significant reforms of the property tax systems in the urban areas. The classic example is the Delhi Rent Control Act which was passed in parliament and had received presidential assent, but was not notified in the official gazette owing to opposition from traders who successfully stalled the Act and forced the GOI to introduce legislation which significantly compromised the original idea of reforming urban rent laws by encouraging private investment.

6 This phrase has been coined to describe the post-1992 urban reform in the country. Those who are responsible for pushing urban reforms are themselves extremely cautious about such reforms. The fear of antagonising the urban middle class and the poor who may be affected in the short run by such measures have stood in the way of introducing these reforms.

7 Many such citizen initiatives are reported from various parts of the country. One such citizen's group has recently approached the Supreme Court of India for directions on improving the management of solid waste in the cities. This important Public Interest Litigation is expected to open a new chapter on solid waste management in the large cities of India.

References

Anand, S. and K. Hanson (1995) 'Disability-Adjusted Life Years: A Critical Review', Working Paper 95.06, Cambridge, MA: Harvard Center for Population and Development Studies

Asian Development Bank (ADB) (1997) *Urban Infrastructure in Asian Countries*, Manila: ADB

Building Materials and Technology Promotion Council (1996) *Low Cost Building Materials and Technology*, New Delhi: Government of India

Central Ground Water Board (CGWB) (1988) *Rooftop Rainwater Harvesting for Augmenting Ground Water Storage*, New Delhi: CGWB

Central Public Health Environmental Engineering Organisation (CPHEEO) (1996) *Meeting the Needs of Drinking Water in Urban India*, New Delhi: CPHEEO

Centre for Science and Environment (CSE) (2000) *State of India's Environment*, Citizen's Fifth Report, Chapter 5, New Delhi: CSE

Central Statistical Organisation (CSO) (1997) *Compendium of Environment Statistics*, New Delhi: CSO

Department of Economic Affairs (DEA) (1986) *India Infrastructure Report*, report of the Committee constituted under the Chairmanship of Rakesh Mohan, Ministry of Finance, New Delhi: Government of India

Housing and Urban Development Corporation (1988) *Guidelines for Sanitation Schemes*, Technical Circular No. 177, New Delhi: HUDC

Ministry of Urban Development (MUD) (1992) *Report of the Expert Group to Undertake a Study of the Working of the Building Centres*, New Delhi: Government of India

Ministry of Urban Development (MUD) (1999) *Solid Waste Management in Class I Cities in India*, report of the Committee constituted by the Supreme Court of India, New Delhi: Government of India

Ministry of Urban Development (MUD) (2000a) *Policy Paper on Urban Infrastructure*, New Delhi: Government of India

Ministry of Urban Development (MUD) (2000b) *Annual Report: 1999–2000*, New Delhi: Government of India

National Commission of Urbanisation (NCU) (1988) *Report of National Commission of Urbanisation*, New Delhi: NCU

National Institute of Urban Affairs (NIUA) (1988) *State of India's Urbanisation*, New Delhi: NIUA

National Institute of Urban Affairs (NIUA) (2000) *Urban Statistics Handbook*, New Delhi: NIUA

Planning Commission (1998) *Report of the Working Group of the Ninth Plan on Urban Development*, New Delhi: Government of India

Rail India Technical and Economic Services (1997) *Financing India's Urban Transport*, New Delhi: RITES

Registrar General of India (1991) *Census of India*, New Delhi: Government of India

Singh, Kulwant and Florian Steinberg (eds) (1996) *Urban India in Crisis*, New Delhi

UNCHS (1998) *Sustainable Cities Programme*, Nairobi: UNCHS

UNDP (1992) *Technical Guidance on Twin Pit Pour-Flush Latrines*, New Delhi: UNDP

International co-operation in pursuit of sustainable cities

Adrian Atkinson

Sustainability in the context of development is now generally understood to mean primarily *environmental* sustainability. This is rightly so, because environmental and, above all, resource problems of the future are issues that must be faced today. This paper, however, focuses attention more on the sustainability of the approaches adopted by external support agencies (ESAs) in their efforts to support projects and programmes in urban areas.[1] Of course, this does not exclude environmental sustainability which shares with the narrower concept a concern that successful urban programmes and projects should continue to yield results well into the future. But the intention here is to stimulate debate around the role of ESAs in their urban engagements, with the concept of environmental sustainability as a backdrop to the discussion.

The paper starts with a critical review of past attempts of international and bilateral agency to intervene in urban development. The recent refocusing of attention on urban development within the framework of 'sustainable development' has led to new kinds of initiative that are reviewed in the second part of the paper. As yet, however, these do not add up to anything like a coherent approach to support for urban sustainable development, and the third part of the paper attempts to identify new approaches and initiatives which relevant agencies might adopt to improve their performance. It will also be necessary for agencies to look seriously at 'bad practices' from the past that persist to a significant, if not overwhelming, degree among their activities in support of urban development. This is done with a view to undertaking thoroughgoing reform, not simply implementing a few 'best practice' projects that mask the realities of support for urban development. This issue is discussed in the final section.

Past problems in development agency support for urban projects

Northern 'development urbanists' and others involved in addressing problems in the cities of the South are generally aware that they are operating at the margins of the broad field of development. This seems increasingly perverse given that rapid urbanisation everywhere will lead to a situation within the foreseeable future where the majority of the world's population lives in urban areas and where urban problems become increasingly serious.

In the early years of what is now referred to as development work, in the context of the UN Charter and Bretton Woods agreement, it seemed clear that most attention should be focused on rural development. The majority of the population of the 'underdeveloped countries' lived in rural areas and the opportunities for improving their living conditions appeared to be great. Private international investment, as well as both public and private local investment, seemed to be concentrated in the cities (referred to at the time as 'urban bias') whereas the presumption – not without its detractors – was that improvements in rural productivity would be the foundation for a progressive development process.

Clearly, in this context little attention was paid to problems in urban areas. Many ESAs maintained a complete ban on urban projects and those that did fund them did so initially on an *ad hoc* basis in response to political exigencies. The first move towards recognising that urban problems also needed to be addressed by the ESAs was the 1976 Habitat conference, which led to the establishment of UNCHS (United Nations Centre for Human Settlements, or Habitat), a *very* small addition to the UN family. There was little impact, however, on the policies and priorities of existing agencies. Arguably the most significant bilateral agency initiative was that of USAID in establishing Regional Housing and Urban Development Offices (RHUDOs). UNDP also became a presence in the field of urban planning and management, and World Bank projects were started up in the larger cities of some countries.

However, in spite of the world having changed radically in terms of the geographic location of populations and the economic development process as a whole, urban interventions have remained stubbornly on the margins of development assistance. According to Chapter 8 of 'Agenda 21', as recently as 1988 only 1 per cent of UN funding was assigned to projects relating to human settlements. Of course, a greater amount was being spent in urban areas, but such funding (e.g. in health, education, roads, and energy supply) was not disbursed with any awareness of the particularities of planning and managing projects relating to urbanisation or in the urban context.[2]

Given this lack of interest in what might be the special characteristics of programmes and projects associated with urban areas, it is little wonder that the few activities that were supported encountered many problems. The tendency was for agencies encountering such problems then to retreat from involvement in the urban sector rather than increase resources to find out why projects weren't working and what might be done to improve matters. Essentially, funding decisions were based on internal agency prejudices about what was needed and who should be involved in determining how things should be done.

The first source of problems stemmed from the legal framework of the UN Charter, which required programmes and projects to be agreed, and generally controlled thereafter, by central government agencies. The centralised nature of most Southern governments, which inevitably meant that local authorities had little say in what was done – and other local actors even less – was a rather obvious reason for poor project performance: not only did corruption siphon off resources and distort priorities, but there was also a fatal lack of local knowledge on the part of responsible officers and, symmetrically, a lack of local understanding of why decisions were taken in the way they were.

There was an assumption among responsible staff and consultants that a significant reason for poor project performance was a lack of training of local authority staff, and some effort thus went into what were considered to be relevant training programmes. But in practice many of the staff knew well enough what to do in theory, but lacked motivation in situations in which they had little if any power to determine their own way of solving local problems.

In fact, until recently, ESA staff involved in urban programmes overwhelmingly assumed that what was needed was the consistent application of technocratic approaches to urban planning and management like those that had been successful in transforming European cities at the end of the nineteenth and beginning of the twentieth century. These included the development of mechanisms to plan cities, the design and management of integrated urban traffic and transport systems, the installation of piped water supply and sewerage systems, the introduction of technically sophisticated solid waste removal and disposal systems, and so on.

Upon introducing these techniques to cities in the South, compromises were made to accommodate obvious differences, mainly stemming from what was perceived as lack of financial resources to implement the expensive approaches taken in Europe to solving urban problems. Ineffective management structures and processes, usually treated peripherally and often completely disregarded as a component of urban projects, were an ongoing weakness of these projects. Little or no thought was ever given to the possibility that cities might be fundamentally different organisms in different geographic and cultural contexts, and that they would therefore require, in large measure, locally developed approaches to solving urban problems.

Indeed, ESA urban development professionals appear to have been universally ignorant (or they decided to disregard the significance) of the way in which effective urban planning and management in European cities emerged from hard-fought political battles. In Europe, improved 'techniques' developed progressively on the back of social movements from the 'public health movement' in the 1850s in the UK, through the turn-of-century 'progressive movement' in the USA, to the current environmental movements and their insistence on raising standards to eliminate urban pollution. In this light, it makes little sense to import techniques unless there is genuine local demand and a deep political commitment to them.

The second major source of problems underlying such interventions was the assumption that governments were in control of the urban development process but that the laws and regulatory mechanisms were not yet working very well (i.e. in time, the development process would yield more effective controls). However, although the modern world insists that all countries be overseen by governments with a certain appearance of legal structures and administrative organs, in practice governments in different cultural contexts are different kinds of organism.

In practical terms, what this means in relation to urban development in many countries of the South (and we can draw a distinction between more coherent approaches to urban planning and development in cultures that have a longer history of urbanisation than in those with little such experience) is that governments have had relatively little control over the urban development process.

In few countries of the South has urban planning had much more than a marginal effect in guiding the development of cities. The placement of infrastructure has had a more significant impact in that development is easier where there are, for instance, paved roads. But even the formal development sector has been able to disregard rules and follow its own path to profits, regardless of what might make a more pleasant and workable city for citizens as a whole. Meanwhile, a large proportion of urban development has been 'informal', following its own rationale – sometimes with harassment of governments and private landowners, but increasingly in a context of 'benign neglect' or even with some *post hoc* government and ESA assistance. 'Informal settlement upgrading' has by now joined the portfolio of a number of ESAs – although we should not exaggerate the extent of resources going into such projects, which nowhere reach even 5 per cent of official development assistance (ODA).

At the conceptual level, virtually no effort went into trying to understand the underlying processes and forces which created such cities and hence to discover what might be truly effective approaches to guide their development for the benefit of all. The overall concept seems to have been 'one day they will be like us', with a series of fragmented and contingent ways of dealing with the fact that these Southern cities and the processes of urbanisation were, rather obviously, *not* like those of the North.

New approaches in ESA support for urban development

Since the early 1990s, however, there seems to have been a gradual change of heart and understanding of what ESAs need to do to help improve conditions in cities of the South, and a growing commitment to becoming involved in supporting urban programmes and projects. Some agencies have produced policy documents that recognise the reality of rapid urbanisation in the South and the consequences of this in a situation of inadequate resources, powers, and capacities to guide the process. The best known of these are those produced by the World Bank (1991) and UNDP (1991). These were followed by many more policy and research publications by these agencies, including the World Bank Urban Management Programme (UMP) series, which was concerned with urban finance, land management, infrastructure, and the urban environment.

A number of bilateral ESAs, including those of Germany (BMZ 1995), Switzerland (SDC 1995), and Sweden (SIDA 1996) produced urban policy documents indicating a new interest in providing more coherent assistance in urban development in the South. Habitat II in 1996 prompted many ESAs to focus attention on urban issues and to put out policy positions, led by the substantial *Global Report on Human Settlements* (UNCHS 1996).[3] The World Bank, which picks up different themes in each report, focused major attention on urban development issues in 1999–2000 (World Bank 1999).

Urban research

There is evidence that ESAs are now looking for more detailed information that will help them to become more effective in supporting urban projects.[4] Over a longer period, a number of Northern institutions have carried out research and published on issues relating to urbanisation and cities in the South. The International Institute for Environment and Development (IIED) and the Stockholm Environment Institute (SEI) are well-known examples – even if their work on urban issues is but a small part of their overall research activity. There are also academic institutions in the North that have long focused attention on urban problems in the South although, responding somewhat to the market, the focus has been mainly on training and practice, with little attention to research needs. In the South itself, there are many academic and research institutions that have been undertaking urban research, sometimes in collaboration with, or financially supported by, Northern institutions.

In the late 1990s, this area of activity has been opening up. A major review of urban research in the developing world under the title of Global Urban Research Initiative (GURI), funded by the Ford Foundation and co-ordinated by the University of Toronto, produced a string of papers and substantial books on Asia, on Africa, and on Latin America, plus a thematic volume (Stren 1995).[5] Some of the bilateral ESAs have also expanded their research around urban themes. The focus of this research has varied greatly: from attempts to gain more coherent regional perspectives (e.g. the German Development Ministry's effort to analyse the state of play in participatory initiatives in sustainable urban development in Asia, see Samol 1999), to research programmes on approaches to understanding the processes of urban–rural interactions in the South (e.g. the Club de Sahel research into urban–rural interactions in West Africa, see Court 1998), to the DFID-funded peri-urban interface research programme, see DPU 1999).

The GURI programme focused attention on urban research being undertaken in the South, and aimed to strengthen networks among such research groups. This, and the work of the UMP, while more oriented towards the immediate needs of practitioners, remained exceptional in their attempt to be coherent across a range of research areas. Most of the research carried out by Northern institutions and consultancies on urbanisation and urban issues in the South has been fragmented with inadequate dissemination (some of it for lack of translation) and poor networking among researchers.[6] The Network Association of European Researchers on Urbanisation in the South (N-AERUS) was established to improve communication precisely in this area.

There has been an increase not only in general policy development and research, but also in assistance to relevant national agencies in certain countries, with a view to developing national urban policies and research capacity. UNDP and UNCHS have been the most active in this regard but there has also been some bilateral agency assistance. Clearly, such policy frameworks are important in order to facilitate a more coherent approach to ESA support for urban work, both to ensure support from the national government and also as an informational basis for providing perspective on the current situation and how assistance might be most effective.

'Good governance'

Until quite recently, the term 'governance' was rarely used and esoteric. Some would say it is still esoteric. Indeed, although it has become very widely used in development circles – many ESAs have adopted the achievement of 'good governance' as a major policy goal in development assistance – there is still a considerable lack of clarity as to what should be done under this heading. Perhaps this has to do with shyness about approaching the issues implicit in the term in a more direct manner, given that it points to direct interference in the politics of countries of the South. However, it ends up with agencies carrying out very different activities under the same rubric, and perhaps avoiding the ostensible aims of such support.

At one end, it has been assumed that the privatisation of public services and enterprises, which has also been an important policy goal of some agencies – especially USAID – is part of the more general promotion of good governance. This stems from the apparent 'inefficiencies' of government monopolies, which privatisation programmes are supposed to replace with 'more efficient' services provided by private businesses. While there are certainly success stories in, for instance, water supply and solid waste disposal in Southern cities, there are also limits to the possibilities.

On the one hand, ineffective regulation and corruption (see below) easily vitiate the whole purpose of privatisation, simply making profits for those companies that manage to obtain contracts to supply goods or carry out services, without necessarily improving matters. On the other hand, the supply of services to poor urban neighbourhoods (In many cities of the South, these constitute the majority of households) does not lend itself to privatisation in the usually accepted sense. Community self-help is proving to be a more effective approach here. Finally, although productive enterprises are the main focus of privatisation programmes, a simplistic division of public and private obviously cannot be equated with a distinction between efficient and inefficient. It is well known that in some Asian countries it is precisely the close connections between government (and not uncorrupt governments at that) and private enterprise that have proved the key to economic success – notably in Japan and South Korea and more recently China and Vietnam. In the end, the drive to privatise has more to do with ideology than an improvement in governance or real proven benefit to urban citizens.

In some cases, equity and particularly gender programmes fall under, or are seen as closely related to, ESAs' governance programmes. Certainly, it is difficult to talk of good governance in a situation where large sections of the population are *de facto* excluded from the benefits of development: where self-help is the predominant mode of provision of goods and (urban) services, governance is evidently not fair in the way that it looks after the needs of all citizens. Perhaps 'poverty alleviation' (or, nowadays, 'poverty elimination') *should* be seen as essentially a governance issue.

In reality, it would seem that the central concern of good governance programmes is the issue of corruption. Some ESAs have programmes specifically to address this question, but it is the political sensitivity of the issue that leads to the tendency to avoid addressing the matter directly. One problem is that ESAs have, in fact, colluded in corruption, albeit usually indirectly (e.g. their contractors have to pay officials to facilitate their development activities). For instance, in Indonesia, after the fall of the Suharto régime, the agenda was for reform and against corruption, collusion, and nepotism (locally 'KKN'). The fact that the World Bank had colluded in corruption became open knowledge and the Bank had to respond – which it did by 'estimating' that perhaps 30 per cent of its loans had been siphoned off into accounts other than those that produced the intended goods and services (Manning 1999).

In fact, 'corruption' is rarely the result of individual acts of graft and extortion. Most of it is systematic and a real part of the way that not only governments but also societies work. The relative 'good governance' to be found in Europe today resulted from social movements of a century and more ago which separated 'public service' from personal – or extended family – interests. In many, if not most, countries of the South, extended family or other 'patronage' or 'clientelist' networks are still the 'real' way that politics and social relations work. Unless these are uncovered and unless social movements arise to push for transparency, things will remain as they are. Social and political changes *are* in motion – and it is clear how changes in the government, for instance in South-East Asia, have been a function of the changing nature of the societies (Atkinson 2000). In this perspective, it is difficult for ESAs to mount 'good governance' programmes that go to the heart of the matter and expect to have the governments acquiesce where this potentially means their own demise, given that these are precisely the people who benefit from the continuance of corrupt practices!

Participatory approaches

One of the problems which led in the past to the under-performance of ESA-supported urban projects was that they were run through central government agencies rather than local government. Part of the new approach to supporting urban projects and programmes involves ESAs funding projects in which local actors are more directly involved in project development and implementation. Various mechanisms are being employed to do this, some of which are described below.

First, some funding is being channelled more or less directly to NGOs working in urban areas. This includes the funding of Northern NGOs to collaborate with local NGOs and community-based organisations working at the local level. Some resources – the UNDP LIFE programme being a good example – are going directly to Southern NGOs working at the urban level. Such projects are always small in terms of resources, in most cases addressing specific local problems predominantly in poor areas, but in some cases adopting a broader community development approach.

A second approach, sometimes referred to as 'decentralised co-operation', is a mechanism through which Northern municipalities co-operate with their Southern counterparts (Douxchamps 1997;

Ringrose 1999).[7] This has grown out of the 'twinning' (or *jumelage*) movement by which many Northern towns and cities became linked with one another in the decades following the Second World War. Increasingly, Northern towns and cities are twinning with Southern towns and cities (and sometimes institutions within these are forging links) with the intention of exchanging experiences and, in the process, attempting to improve the development processes of rapidly growing Southern cities. Some national municipal associations – notably in Canada, France, The Netherlands, the UK, and the USA – are providing advice and assistance to develop such links, and some ESAs are also funding such initiatives. The European Commission-financed URBS programmes (which promote co-operation between European and Southern local authorities) are a notable example of the latter.

Third, ESAs are finding ways of organising programmes and projects more directly with local authorities and communities without going through central government agencies. There are various formulas for this which include relatively traditional urban planning and management assistance projects, often focusing on particular sectors, lasting one or two years and operated by foreign consultants, but now working directly with local agencies. There has also been an increase in the number of longer-term urban projects that are developing in a more flexible way through local organisations and institutions. This new approach is not only being pursued by certain bilateral ESAs and UN agency programmes (such as the WHO Healthy Cities programme and the URBS programme), but most recently also by the regional development banks, including the World Bank. In all these cases, the watchword is 'participation'. There has been a broad realisation of the need to involve 'stakeholders' more directly in projects in order to elicit a greater sense of commitment and 'ownership' of project outputs.

A final point about 'participation' concerns the way in which initial decisions are taken about programmes and projects. Traditionally, development co-operation starts through bilateral negotiations, whereby delegations from donor agencies discuss what activities should be financed with relevant government officials in 'recipient' countries. In practice, the tendency is that 'he who pays the piper calls the tune': donor agencies are able to influence matters in favour of their own priorities, rather than those of the receiving countries. Furthermore, government officials who happen to be part of the negotiating process are likely also to favour projects that suit them, rather than representing broader constituencies.

Back in 1970, when the Canadian government created the International Development Research Council (IDRC), it experimented with providing a budget directly to a board, half of which was made up of representatives of Southern countries, which would determine the content of the programme. Later, similar arrangements have been attempted by other agencies including the Swedish Agency for Research Co-operation with Developing Countries (SAREC) (since absorbed into SIDA), the Dutch (for example, the Urban Waste Expertise Programme), and recently the French programme *Gestion Durable de Déchets et l'Assainissement Urbain*. The above-mentioned European-funded URBS programmes similarly are overseen by boards made up of experts from relevant participating regions. It cannot be said, however, that there is any rapid move to adopt such decision-making mechanisms.

Sustainable urban development

A further high-profile shift in priorities of ESAs has been to focus attention upon problems associated with the urban environment. This is often linked to a concern that, in future, projects must conform to the requirements of 'sustainable development'. This has had various, not necessarily linked, consequences. First, it should be noted that in many cases 'environment' is little more than a new term for certain kinds of traditional urban projects. When the environment came to the fore of public concerns in the late 1980s, it came associated particularly with fears about global pollution and the loss of resources such as tropical rainforests and fisheries. Those who had been working with urban infrastructure projects in the past feared that, yet again, budgets that should be spent in urban areas would be hijacked for non-urban projects aimed at addressing the newly urgent global environmental problems. Efforts were made, therefore, to ensure that the urban environment would also be seen as an important issue. The World Bank Urban Division coined the term 'brown agenda', asserting the importance of financing urban infrastructure projects, including (clean) water supply, sanitation and solid waste management, and air pollution controls, over the demands of the global environmental lobby.

On the other hand, growing out of the deeper concerns of the environmental movement and in particular the process emerging from the 1992 UN Conference on Environment and Development – specifically 'Agenda 21' – some ESA funding has gone into 'Local

Agenda 21' programmes and projects. In practice, these exercises look much like any other participatory urban development project concerned with improving living conditions and 'empowering' local communities. They do, however, effect a certain shift in focus towards environmental matters and attempt to link into 'Agenda 21' and its concern for environmentally sustainable development.

Despite the new rhetoric of environment and sustainable development, there is no clear indication that more funding is going even into traditional urban (environmental) infrastructure projects (Atkinson and Allen 1998). Further, projects explicitly concerned with sustainable cities (including 'Local Agenda 21' projects) have remained few and small (see articles by Kombe and Burian in this volume).

Contextual issues

In the light of these observations about the reorientation of ESA attention towards the field of urban development, it is useful to stand back and see how this relates to broader trends. The first thing is that, in spite of the apparently greater interest in urban problems and awareness of the need for more attention to be focused on addressing these, there is as yet no statistically significant shift in funding priorities of ESAs towards urban activities. Given that it is almost ten years since the World Bank and UNDP policy papers were circulated, and almost five years since Habitat II, we might have expected to see some change.

The second point concerns the rhetoric regarding ESA support for urban projects. Most agencies state as their first priority (or one of the first priorities) that they wish to contribute to the alleviation – or, more recently, the elimination – of poverty, which is in fact in many countries growing considerably faster in urban than in rural areas (UNCHS 1996). The channelling of resources to NGOs working at community level and the significant attention paid by some agencies to projects concerned with upgrading informal housing areas would seem to stem from this. However, little or no attention is paid to the way in which the wider conditions are undermining local efforts to alleviate poverty. In particular, the promotion of neo-liberal macro-economic policies and structural adjustment programmes (SAPs) have had the effect of increasing poverty in a way that cannot be meaningfully addressed by urban community programmes (UNRISD 1995).

Given the varied impacts of neo-liberalism and the diversity of urban projects in different countries it is perhaps somewhat specious to take just one example to illustrate the above point. Nevertheless, it is useful to provide some illustration and for this we shall draw on the author's own experience in Indonesia, which for many years has been the subject of a significant amount of attention paid to urban development by ESAs.[8] This is reasonable given the rapidity of urbanisation in Indonesia, indicated the fact that by 1990 as many as ten metropolitan areas had populations of over one million.

Official figures show a steady reduction of poverty to a level of around 11 per cent in early 1997. However, with the collapse of the economy in July that year, poverty levels rose steadily over the following 18 months to over 50 per cent of the population. The immediate cause was massive speculation against the currency following deregulation of the exchange rate. There is certainly no proof that in the long run the exchange rate deregulation will lead to the enrichment of the Indonesian people: this action was carried out according to the ideology of global liberalisation.

Interestingly, it was realised immediately by the development agencies that the impacts of the sudden rise in poverty would be particularly evident in urban areas – and, indeed, many industries immediately came to a halt. Tens of thousands of urban workers were laid off, which affected them, their families, and all those supplying them with goods and services (Lee 1999). The ESA community reacted quickly, with most agencies present in Indonesia mounting emergency programmes (BAPPENAS/UNDP 1998), a significant number of these explicitly directed at alleviating urban poverty.

Most significant among these was a series of World Bank initiatives involving a programme of supporting community organisations to disburse funds to support local activities including infrastructure, health, and environmental improvement initiatives. There was much pragmatic logic to these programmes: to inflate the currency by inserting large amounts of dollars; to go directly to poor communities in order to by-pass that layer of corruption that could export illegal takings; and to go into urban areas because more money could be spent there more quickly than in rural areas.

In other words, an apparent conversion to decentralised urban community initiatives was actually mainly about macro-economic manipulation in an attempt to compensate for the dire effects of liberalisation. Implementation of these programmes ran far more slowly than envisaged (thereby presumably losing much of the intended macro-economic impact). However, implementation was rapid enough to necessitate a very loose attitude towards the creation of local structures of accountability, and ran the risk of simply 'decentralising corruption' rather than creating any genuine community development or empowerment.

This attention to the context within which urban projects and programmes are implemented is however, new and exceptional. Hitherto, these have been organised, as noted earlier, in a manner that was blind to the differences in the social, cultural, and political contexts into which they were being inserted. They were also insensitive to the way in which the wider political and indeed ideological context determined priorities both within and beyond the project in ways that might not, in the end, be in the interest of putative project beneficiaries.

Essentially, although a new orientation appears to have been entering into the definition of urban projects supported by ESAs, there has been relatively little reflection on the ideological context within which the new approaches are unfolding and the contradictions inherent in these. Nor has there been much reflection on the need to develop a more consistent 'paradigm' that will make sense of the new initiatives and provide a robust framework for evaluating the likelihood of success.[9] It is no good supporting urban sectoral projects or even community development (or 'empowerment') projects unless steps are taken to combat a macro context that consistently leads to further impoverishment of local communities. At the same time, it seems that far more serious thought needs to go into the meaning of sustainable development and how to achieve it in relation to the ongoing process of urbanisation in the countries of the South.

Consistency in ESA support for urban programmes and projects

Below, we offer some thoughts in the direction of a new paradigm for ESA support for urban development programmes and projects. These grow out of our earlier critique, although we recognise that elements of a new paradigm are already evolving. Of course, we have selected particular themes and avoided or rejected others, with the aim of stimulating discussion.

Increasing ESA support for urban programmes and projects

This paper is premised on the view that a greater proportion of ESA resources should go into addressing urban problems, so no attempt is made here to argue the point in any detail (Atkinson and Allen 1998).

It is worth noting, however, a couple of points concerning the resistance of ESAs to making the necessary shift in resources.

The first reason seems to have to do with inertia within the agencies. Having been born in a world that demanded rural development, they find it difficult to adjust to the new realities. The experience and knowledge of the corps of senior professionals relates overwhelmingly to rural development or to sectors which do not relate directly to urban development as such, and they are not prepared to move into the unknown.[10] The argument is reiterated that urbanisation is nothing but a bundle of problems and that rural development should be supported in order to keep people on the land.[11]

A further reason is illustrated by cases where urban projects have been attempted by ESAs, but the complexity of working in this context, with the greater number of affected and involved actors and increased sensitivity to social and environmental impacts of even small interventions, has resulted in a decision to avoid developing projects in cities.

What general approach should be taken to developing urban programmes and projects?

Urban programmes and projects require a different orientation from the traditional short project with definite physical outputs. Here is a sketch of how an ideal type of urban programme developed by an ESA might look:

- It is extremely difficult to insert a narrowly defined sectoral project into an urban area without being involved in wider aspects of the way in which the city works. Urban projects need to be multi-dimensional. If they try to avoid being so, they are almost guaranteed to yield sub-optimal outputs with respect to their main aims.[12]

- It is also difficult to make a positive sustainable impact in a short period (short-term insertion of technical infrastructure, for instance, almost always ends in sub-optimal usage and management or even in outright failure). Urban projects need to be flexible and open-ended in terms of duration and scope, developing confidence and complex working relationships, and deciding what needs to be done. The project can then evolve and grow according to needs identified as it develops; alternatively, if insuperable difficulties arise, then the project can be taken in different directions or wound down.

- Working with local (poor) communities in this way can be effective in producing local improvements, but it also requires engagement with, and commitment from, the municipality and possibly also relevant national agencies.

- One programme that has attempted to create a model for urban intervention is the World Bank Metropolitan Environmental Improvement Programme (MEIP). This suggested a three-stage process: (i) starting simultaneously with local community projects, building confidence and working relationships, and at the same time undertaking strategic studies at the level of the city as a whole; (ii) followed by pilot projects on various issues, as determined by selected local communities and municipal decision-making processes developed in the first stage; and (iii) the development of larger-scale projects, possibly scaling up successful pilot projects or providing the larger-scale infrastructure necessary for local infrastructure to operate effectively.

- So, urban projects should ideally be projects for whole towns or cities. But what should be taken as the extent of the city? Given the tendency today for towns and cities to extend their influence (particularly economic and environmental) well into the surrounding countryside, and given the insuperable difficulty of organising suburban (peri-urban) projects without engaging the core urban areas, urban projects should ideally include a significant subregion beyond the immediate city boundaries.

- How should the cities be chosen? All too easily, urban projects are established through political exigencies so that it only later emerges that these did not correspond to the optimal choice. A set of criteria needs to be established and a longer process engaged in with national and local actors before decisions are taken on where to initiate urban projects. This suggests the need for a national urban programme with one or more city projects.

- Within a national programme, other activities that need to be undertaken include providing support for the development of national urbanisation policy and information systems, support for urban training programmes, support for research programmes, and so on.

- Of course, only the largest ESAs will become involved in all aspects of urban programmes in all countries. Just as many agencies choose a limited number of countries in which to work, so also with urban projects. In fact it is imperative that agencies develop mechanisms to exchange experiences with one another regularly, and also decide upon a division of labour and possibly also of territory. For instance, several agencies might co-operate at the level of global regions, each specialising in what they do best and co-operating as necessary in national programmes and even in urban projects (e.g. through decentralised co-operation). Obviously, such collaboration needs to include relevant actors and stakeholders from the countries and cities in question, including in strategic planning decisions.

Some detailed considerations

There is a learning curve to all new kinds of initiative and many mistakes are made in the process of starting up what would appear to be excellent new approaches. It is to be hoped that lessons will be learned regarding how to go about these new approaches, and that they do not end in a retreat just because it seems too difficult to get it right. Here are a few thoughts regarding the new approaches discussed in the second part of this paper:

- It might be expected from the quantity of resources going into research on urbanisation and urban issues in the South, that useful information will become more available. This will not happen, however, unless there is a marked improvement in disseminating research findings among all involved actors, North and South, be they individuals, institutions, or agencies. There is an increasingly urgent need for networking between research institutions. But, above all, there is a need for the research to be oriented towards the needs of practitioners. This might mean more action-research in particular locations involving local stakeholders, and with researchers engaging more directly with agency staff responsible for developing and managing projects. Unfortunately, on the whole, agency staff 'have too little time' to indulge in reading either theory that might help them better organise their thought processes regarding what makes an effective project, or the outputs of practical research that provide information on the details necessary to understand what projects should be trying to achieve and how to go about reaching those ends effectively.

  Because agency staff are assumed to have little time to read, it is assumed that they need to be spoon-fed with 'show-and-tell' guidelines on how to put together programmes and projects. In fact, it is questionable whether such guidelines are any more useful to agency staff than more sophisticated research outputs. The real issue is that agencies need to be convinced of the importance of good research to good programme and project formulation and administration, and that agency staff are allowed the necessary time to absorb the findings from such research before coming to conclusions on programme and project design. Researchers need to convince agency staff of the usefulness of research outputs to the efficiency and effectiveness of their work.

- It has been argued above that 'good governance' is a cover for a multiplicity of development objectives. On the one hand, a grand word to elevate otherwise low-profile activities that were underway even before the term 'governance' came into currency in development circles. On the other hand, a code for efforts to combat corruption. In the case of privatisation as a means to improve governance, it is now clear that promoting the interests of the private sector has to be rethought in terms of the difficulties of obtaining the resources necessary to improve the level of services among the poor. Indeed, efforts to work laterally to develop the capacities of the 'informal economy' and to include in this methods, for instance, of promoting community-based infrastructure construction and maintenance programmes, seem more appropriate for much of the urban South than any conventionally inspired privatisation programme – and this is increasingly recognised by ESAs working on urban issues (Haan *et al.* 1998).

Regarding the combating of corruption more directly, it may help to involve sociologists and anthropologists in generating a better understanding of how the relevant societies and political systems work in practice. Such research may be contentious, but it is necessary to be more honest about the meaning of 'good governance' in order to address the problems more effectively. If the aim is to improve the quality of life of the majority of urban citizens in the South – therefore including the poor and hence aiming directly at alleviating or eliminating poverty – then work will have to go into bringing more accountable governments into being. This will mean encouraging efforts to create transparency and to undermine existing incentives that keep corrupt practices alive. But this will take more imagination and commitment on the part of the ESAs than they have shown to date.

- Decentralised co-operation holds much promise. A major problem with conventional development co-operation is that it is carried out by national governments on behalf of an electorate who – as with so much that governments do – are therefore deprived of the direct experience of what is done in their name. Further (and this is the author's personal feeling from many years working in this field), it often seems that there is a rather large accountability gap between the ostensible political reasons for development co-operation and the way it is actually put into practice. North–South town twinning provides opportunities for the electorate to participate directly in development co-operation. There has, for sure, been much to criticise about 'town twinning' where councillors have used it to enjoy themselves at the expense of local citizens. But there has also been a mass of good experience where ordinary citizens have been able to meet and collaborate with people in culturally diverse places, to their mutual enrichment.

Until now, most twinning has been between Northern towns and cities. Now that there is a significant growth of city-to-city development co-operation between Northern and Southern cities (and local institutions such as schools and hospitals), a new set of problems arises. Here also the potential is great for personal cultural exchange of citizen groups, of professionals from different sectors, and so on. However, in the first instance, the cultural gap is great and the assumptions about what people will find when they come into contact are often quite problematic. In particular, local government personnel from the North can easily come with ideas about the superiority of what they have to offer ('we are going to give them the benefit of our superior knowledge and abilities'). Or they are faced with situations where their knowledge of how to deal with problems is irrelevant in one or more ways – too expensive, or assuming different legal competences, or insensitive to cultural differences, or simply a major language barrier.

What is required is that Northern municipalities—and any other institutions with a significant reason to engage in decentralised co-operation – develop relevant training programmes for individuals or groups who are to participate in development co-operation. In practice, the municipal associations of some European countries are already providing a service to help municipalities wishing to engage in decentralised co-operation. In this context, bilateral ESAs should provide assistance not only to individual co-operation projects but also to building up the necessary support infrastructure. In the long run, one could envisage a significant decanting of national development assistance out of the centralised agencies and into decentralised channels.

There is also space for South–South twinning or for consortia of Southern municipalities to study problems and their solutions among themselves and then to disseminate the results through municipal networks and associations. Some ESA support has been given to Southern associations (such as CityNet in Asia), and this has yielded exchanges that have had positive results (CityNet 1994, 1996). The URBS programmes, already mentioned, are concerned with establishing consortia of municipalities (Northern and Southern together) in order to improve their performance around particular themes and activities.

One more, perhaps tangential but nevertheless related, dimension of decentralisation of the development co-operation process concerns the decision-making processes of the ESAs. In recent years, some Northern governments have made discretionary funds available to their embassies, thereby shortening the bureaucratic chain that so often stymies small projects that need financial assistance at relatively short notice. ESAs are also tending to listen more carefully to local voices in formulating programmes and projects by decentralising more of the programme formulation to their own local offices.

- The need to apply participatory approaches to urban projects is now largely accepted, at least at the level of rhetoric. Getting it right, however, is not so straightforward. The first problem is that popular methods such as rapid appraisal can easily be used in a superficial way to obtain rough (and possibly erroneous) information that is then used in a very *un*-participatory way to determine what should be done and how. Such perfunctory approaches should clearly be avoided, but are, in practice, rather common.

A related problem concerns how representative these participatory planning activities really are. This is actually a very difficult matter to get right. Generally, there are political constraints on projects that easily trap such exercises into creating participatory forums that continue to exclude important groups because of schisms within the community. These divisions may be religious, ethnic, along gender or class or caste lines, or simply personal in nature.

Genuinely participatory planning exercises almost inevitably challenge existing social and political relations, and using the concept and mechanisms in an honest fashion requires practitioners to face up to this fact. They therefore need to be done over a longer period, working with communities and using an increasing number of tools available to the practitioner for accessing and incorporating otherwise 'silent voices'. This should help to ensure that the processes are at least more representative than is the case where participation is restricted only to 'official' and other vocal groups and individuals.

- A logical extension of the interest in promoting participation of beneficiaries in Northern-funded development projects would be to see more cases where boards including, or made up of, representatives from Southern countries oversee the disbursement of funds or the implementation of development assistance programmes. There is, however, little sign of any significant growth in such an approach.

  Certainly, a general move in this direction would be politically unacceptable: in the end, much co-operation will remain a matter of steering political relations at least as much as solving developmental problems. It therefore needs to be argued how participation at the basic decision-making level in terms of projects should be done in a way that is relevant to particular programmes. No doubt there is scope for considering how participation can be brought further up the line, so that it does not merely remain a harmless sop to self-help initiatives. Of course, there is a real problem at every level that 'participation' may be there solely for ideological convenience, and that committees, councils, and boards are created that are denied access to real decisions or control over finances in practice, while the appearance of participation is maintained.

- Sustainable urban development is another heading whose intellectual content must be questioned. The sustainability of many initiatives is highly questionable by any definition of the term. 'Sustainable for whom?' is a very good question. As in the case of participatory planning exercises, the political context of many projects makes it difficult to raise the issue of sustainability in any serious way: immediate problems seem so urgent that it appears a luxury to spend resources in thinking about the more distant future, and about social and environmental problems beyond the immediate context of local actions.

But ill-considered actions that seem to solve local problems are likely to have longer-term consequences that make things a good deal worse than they were originally. Examples of this run the full gamut of self-help initiatives which serve to trap poor communities into a permanent state of subservient economic and environmental conditions, through to solid waste management systems that improve on the disposal of waste but do nothing to conserve resources, to solutions of transport problems that reduce air pollution while increasing the need for non-renewable fossil-fuel resources.

Sadly, while the literature on sustainable development, and specifically sustainable cities, is burgeoning (Satterthwaite 2000), there is as yet very little sign of any coherent approach emerging within the framework of urban co-operation programmes. Perhaps this requires more time, given the extent of the challenge posed by the concept of sustainability to almost all aspects of development. Certainly, attempts are being made, such as in the development of sustainable development indicators and in occasional sectoral approaches (e.g. ICLEI's CO_2 reduction programme). However, anyone using the term 'sustainable (urban) development' should be honest about the extent to which any project thus described is in reality taking any concerted or consistent approach to the issue.

- Regarding the changing international context within which urban programmes and projects are being formulated and implemented, there is certainly room for increased analysis of potential impacts on people at the local level within development projects. Unfortunately, there is little debate among staff of development agencies, and even less among consultants carrying out projects on behalf of these agencies, regarding the basic reasons why they are being employed to do this work. Needless to say, this is on the whole rather sensitive, as it potentially has an impact on promotion prospects and even on job security. And yet it would seem a labour of Sisyphus – not to say rather hypocritical – to be involved, for instance, in local poverty-reduction programmes where the very ideological and political context within which these are being implemented tends to create the poverty in the first place!

Of course, there has been much academic debate about these issues in the past: one merely has to think of the debates in the 1970s about 'centre–periphery' theories (which were too contentious to be admitted and hence studiously ignored by the development agencies).[13] All that needs to be added here is that there is an urgent need to renew these debates and not let the machinery carry on without critical insight.

Concluding remarks

We would reiterate the need to find whatever means to reorient ESAs towards the urban realities of today; and their responsibility, if they wish to remain relevant, to address urgent problems in urban development. In the author's experience, there is a far stronger desire on the part of Southern governments for bilateral resources to be directed to solving urban problems than is reflected in the resources allocated by the agencies.

But if greater attention is to be focused on urban development, then the way in which programmes and projects are constructed and managed needs to change. As noted, there are pioneering programmes that show the way towards flexible and open-ended ways of co-operating. But, in spite of moves by a few ESAs to acknowledge the problem and to reorganise their activities along programme lines, the 'project approach' remains dominant. In the way that ESA bureaucracies work, it appears to be more convenient to run projects over relatively short timeframes, and close the books within discrete funding periods. It is also easier to demonstrate project 'successes' not only in 'commodifying' them within short time periods, but also in producing hard 'deliverables' that can be shown – physically, if possible – to anyone who might be sceptical of project benefits. It is against this background that the new approaches have to be launched, if necessary by changing the internal goals and structures of the agencies themselves.

A further underlying factor is the complexity of the very reasons for development co-operation. While it is generally presented as a more or less philanthropic gesture on the part of the more fortunate North, where the electorate might feel some moral duty to assist the less fortunate, this is clearly naïve. There are many reasons for development co-operation (Atkinson 1995) ranging from national political aims to forge good relations between governments and with particular interests, through pressure from private industry to sell their goods, and also including public sentiment concerning the desire to alleviate poverty in the South. There is also opposition to, and sometimes public scrutiny of, the content of co-operation programmes, to which governments must be sensitive.

The outcome is a complex compromise that cannot be dealt with through simple assumptions on the part of 'concerned citizens' with regard to what should be taking place. That does not, however, mean that concerned citizens (and development researchers and workers) should not continue to push for changes in the way that development assistance programmes (urban or otherwise) are identified, developed, and executed. Indeed, everyone concerned should be urged to spend some of their time distancing themselves from the immediate development tasks and making whatever contribution they can towards improving the way that things are done.

One more suggestion thus returns to the outline of a new paradigm for urban programmes and projects presented in the third part of this paper. The case needs to be put loudly, clearly, and frequently to the ESAs that urban projects should not be defined in terms of short-term sectoral inputs but that the typical urban project should be flexible, open-ended, and integrative of many aspects and many interests within those urban areas where they are located.

The second point here is that urban projects need participants who are socially (possibly anthropologically) and politically aware of the situation in which projects are developing. The pure administrators and technicians, while having a place, should seek good advice (and be prepared to take it) on the nuances of the situation in which the project finds itself. Finally, we can only hope that neo-liberalism will soon have run its course and that more attention can be given to the creation of more regional and subregional frameworks for development that protect local gains against the 'backwash' (the predatory nature) of the global economy.[14]

A closing plea (one that has often been made before and will continue to be made well into the future) is for greater collaboration between ESAs working in the urban field. While there are, unfortunately, strong political reasons for non-co-operation that stem from the competition between 'donor governments' and, with regard to international agencies, between agencies and even internally between departments, constant efforts need to be made to overcome these. In some fields and some countries, better co-operation has been forged and there are thus models that need to be promoted.

One model is of collaboration between agencies on a regional basis where each agency or type of agency contributes what it does best.

The METAP programme on the Mediterranean environment, co-ordinated by the World Bank but with the active participation of half a dozen other international and bilateral agencies, has succeeded in implementing some innovative projects. Some governments have forced co-operation between agencies or, in other cases where there were embarrassing consequences arising from lack of co-operation, forums have been convened by the ESAs themselves to minimise conflict and overlap. Such forums seem to have arisen only in areas where development co-operation has become crowded.

One such situation has arisen in Indonesia, noted in the second section of this paper, where ESA support of urban development programmes has indeed become crowded. The result has been a call on the part of the national planning agency, BAPPENAS, for all agencies involved or interested in supporting such programmes to meet regularly, to exchange information, and to co-ordinate their efforts. We would argue that some mechanisms for collaboration in urban development should become a standard part of the new approach to ESA involvement in urban development as and when resources are redirected in a more definite way into this field.

Notes

1 ESA is used here to cover UN agencies, multilateral development banks, bilateral development assistance agencies, and various foundations and NGOs.

2 Estimates in the mid-1990s put the average proportion of development assistance disbursed by European development agencies for urban programmes and projects at around 6 per cent, with the World Bank, investing in heavy urban infra-structure, spending about 18 per cent of its funds on projects in urban areas (Atkinson and Allen 1998).

3 The first *Global Report on Human Settlements* was produced by UNCHS in 1986 and regional reports were produced subsequently. But the 1996 report was altogether more substantial and, arguably, more influential.

4 In 1992 the Dutch Directorate-General of Development Co-operation

issued a policy paper on research with one of the priority themes being research into how to combat urban poverty (DGIS 1992).

5 A significant amount of innovative urban research has been carried out by research institutions in the South, particularly in Latin America, without direct reference to, or connection with, Northern institutions.

6 Over the past three decades substantial amounts of information-gathering have been commissioned by ESAs. This has often been in support of the development of national urban policies and programmes, commissioned mainly from consultants, with few copies being produced, disseminated, or made available to other researchers within ESAs responsible for developing urban programmes and projects.

For a review of the French case, see Milbert (1992).

7 However, 'decentralised co-operation' is used in different ways by different sectors of the development fraternity.

8 The following paragraphs are from Atkinson (1998; 2000).

9 There has, however, been a growing critique of development programmes, which has included some attempts to construct a new paradigm. See Atkinson (1992), Korten (1990), and Schuurman (1993)

10 This is the problem which Chairman Mao, coming from a peasant background, had: fear of moving into those dens of vice, the cities!

11 Although it might seem incredible that this romantic notion should still be found among sensible people involved in development, it nevertheless appeared as a significant argument against support for urban projects that was put forward to researchers recently investigating the priorities of ESAs with regard to urban development, particularly in the cases of Belgium and Norway (Both ENDS/ENDA Tiers Monde 1997).

12 By 'main aims' is meant the intended benefits to those in receipt of stated project benefits. Unfortunately, there are always non-stated benefits to projects that in practice contribute to bringing them into existence. These include overt and covert political gains by individual politicians and government departments and also the incentives provided by the possibilities for graft.

13 With the notable exception of the UN Economic Commission for Latin America and the Caribbean (CEPAL).

14 It is unfortunate that the rich debates about regional development that arose in the late 1970s and early 1980s (Stöhr and Taylor 1981) have gone into abeyance, and we can only hope that a debate in this general area will soon be revived.

References

Atkinson, A. (1992) 'The urban bioregion as "sustainable development" paradigm', Third World Planning Review 4(4)

Atkinson, A. (1995) 'Urban environmental management in Thailand', Trialog 45

Atkinson, A. (ed.) (1998) Sustainability Through People's Participation in Urban Development in Selected Asian Cities: The Indonesian Experience, Dresden: Büro für Stadtentwicklung und Umweltplanung

Atkinson, A. (2000) Promoting Sustainable Human Development in Cities of the South: A South-East Asian Perspective, Occasional Paper No. 6, Geneva: UNRISD

Atkinson, A. and A. Allen (1998) The Urban Environment in Development Co-operation, Luxembourg: Office for Official Publications of the European Communities

BAPPENAS/UNDP (1998) International Emergency Assistance to Indonesia's Recovery, Jakarta: National Development Planning Agency and UNDP

Bundesministerium für wirtschaftliche Zusammenarbeit und Entwicklung (BMZ) (1995) Sektorkonzept Umweltgerechte Kommunal- und Stadtentwicklung, Bonn: BMZ

Both ENDS/ENDA Tiers Monde (1997) Big Cities Small Means: European Funding for Environment and Urban Development. An Orientation Guide for Southern NGOs, Amsterdam: Both ENDS

CityNet (1994) Report of the CITYNET/ UNCRD/City of Makati Seminar on Recycling in Asia, Yokohama: CityNet

CityNet (1996) Waste Water Management in Asia, Yokohama: CityNet

Court, J.-M. (1998) *West Africa: Urbanisation and Transition to a Full Market Economy*, Club de Sahel, Paris: OECD

DGIS (1992) *Research and Development, Policy Document of the Government of The Netherlands*, Ministry of Foreign Affairs, Directorate-General of Development Co-operation, The Hague: DGIS

Douxchamps, F. (ed.) (1997) *Decentralised Co-operation: A New European Approach at the Service of Participatory Development, Methodological Study*, Brussels: COTA asbl. (for DG VIII of the European Commission)

DPU (1999) Various research papers posted by the Development Planning Unit, University College London, www.ucl.ac.uk/dpu/pui/

Haan, H.C., A. Coad, and I. Lardinois (1998) *Municipal Solid Waste Management: Involving Micro- and Small Enterprises. Guidelines for Municipal Managers*, Turin: International Training Centre of the ILO, SKAT, WASTE

Korten, D. (1990) *Getting to the Twenty-first Century: Voluntary Action and the Global Agenda*, West Hartford, CT: Kumarian Press

Lee, E. (1999) *The Asian Financial Crisis: The Challenge for Social Policy*, Geneva: ILO

Manning, N. (1999) *World Bank Indonesia Civil Service Review*, Washington, DC: World Bank

Milbert, I. (1992) *Diffusion et valorisation de la recherche urbaine française sur les pays en voie de développement dans les années quatre-vingt*, Paris: Ministère de l'équipement, du logement, des transports et de l'espace

Ringrose, N. (1999) *The Challenge of Linking*, New York: UNDP

Samol, F. (1999) *Nachhaltigkeit durch Partizipation bei der Stadtentwicklung in ausgewählten Städten Asiens: Empfehlungen für die Deutsche Entwicklungszusammenarbeit*, Forschungsberichte des BMZ Band 125, Bonn: Weltforum Verlag

Satterthwaite, D. (2000) *Earthscan Reader on Sustainable Cities*, London: Earthscan

Schuurman, F.J. (1993) *Beyond the Impasse: New Directions in Development Theory*, London: Zed Books

Swiss Development Co-operation (SDC) (1995) *Urban Development Policy*, SDC Sector Policy Series, Berne: SDC

SIDA (1996) *Towards an Urban World, Urbanisation and Development Assistance*, Stockholm: SIDA

Stöhr, W.B. and Taylor, D.R.F. (eds) (1981) *Development from Above or Below? The Dialectics of Regional Planning in Developing Countries*, Chichester: John Wiley

Stren, R. (ed.) (1995) *Urban Research in the Developing World*, 4 volumes, Centre for Urban and Community Studies, Toronto: University of Toronto

UNCHS (1996) *An Urbanising World: Global Report on Human Settlements 1996*, Oxford: Oxford University Press

UNDP (1991) *Cities, People and Poverty: Urban Development Co-operation for the 1990s*, New York: UNDP

UNRISD (1995) *States of Disarray: The Social Effects of Globalisation*, Geneva: UNRISD

World Bank (1991) *Urban Policy and Economic Development: An Agenda for the 1990s*, Washington, DC: World Bank

World Bank (1999) *World Development Report 1999–2000*, Washington, DC: World Bank

Mainstreaming the urban poor in Andhra Pradesh

Banashree Banerjee

This paper is about the Andhra Pradesh Urban Services for the Poor project (APUSP) currently being implemented in Andhra Pradesh state in southern India by the Government of Andhra Pradesh in partnership with the UK government's Department for International Development (DFID). The project covers 32 Class 1 towns, which in 1991 had a combined population of 5.5 million.[1] The project goal is to achieve 'sustained reduction in poverty and vulnerability of the urban poor in Andhra Pradesh'. The purpose is that 'the poor in Class 1 towns of Andhra Pradesh benefit from improved access to more appropriate and sustainable services' (DFID 1999).

Over a seven-year period, the project is expected directly to benefit more than 2.2 million slum dwellers in the 32 towns.[2] However, in a large country such as India, which has experienced many government- and donor-funded poverty reduction programmes over the last three decades, it is neither the scale nor the goal of APUSP that deserves attention. Rather, the merit of APUSP lies in its approach to poverty reduction.

The concept of poverty reduction in APUSP is based on three premises. First, reforms are required within municipalities in order to improve their performance in poverty reduction activities. Second, improvements in environmental infrastructure in slums have multiple impacts on improving the conditions of poor people, but need to be based on the demands of poor people and on the capacity of the municipality to operate and maintain this infrastructure. Third, civil society should be strengthened as a way to invigorate the interaction between poor people and the municipality and to stimulate policies in favour of the poor. This reflects the notion that poverty reduction requires the building of partnerships in both government and community or civil society, and that it needs to be based on the actual needs of poor people.

This concept has been translated into a three-pronged approach, consisting of funding for three inter-linked components: municipal reform (£15.7 million); environmental infrastructure improvement (£66.1 million); and working with civil society (£12.6 million). The three components are expected to be mutually reinforcing in a number of ways (DFID 1999).

The first two components are being undertaken by government and are brought together in a medium-term rolling plan, the Municipal Action Plan for Poverty Reduction (MAPP), articulated by each of the 32 municipalities with the participation of local stakeholders. Over time, the parallel civil society initiative is expected to improve the quality of participation and the poverty and vulnerability focus of the MAPP. It is also expected to influence state policy.

The first year of project implementation (2000-2001) has demonstrated the validity of the approach and the commitment of both partners (the Government of Andhra Pradesh and DFID) to the project principles. It has also brought into sharp focus the complexity of implementing some of the key principles of APUSP. In the following sections we will look into the practical implications, but first we will review the project components and the MAPP process in order to gain a better understanding of their contribution to mainstreaming the urban poor.

Contribution of project components to sustainable poverty reduction

Municipal reforms

Municipal reforms in APUSP aim to improve the way municipalities undertake responsibility for poverty reduction, which involves a wide range of improvement measures. With respect to infrastructure provision, municipalities need to set up mechanisms for consultation in order to determine and respond to the priorities of poor people. The municipalities need to mobilise adequate skills and finances to provide services as well as to operate and maintain them on a long-term basis. Even though APUSP does not provide funding to municipalities for non-infrastructure needs, the project expects them to co-ordinate poverty reduction activities in such a way that these needs are not overlooked.

Municipalities have the legal obligation to undertake poverty alleviation. As elsewhere in India, this duty has gained importance because of the decentralisation of responsibilities to municipalities for several activities, including poverty alleviation, brought about through the

74th Constitutional Amendment Act (Ministry of Urban Development 1992). So far, however, decentralisation has meant additional responsibility without additional powers or resources and with weak systems. Municipalities depend largely on central or state government funds for carrying out their activities but these funds are not always assured, lending a high degree of uncertainty to municipal functioning. Planning of any sort becomes difficult or even redundant and is therefore neglected.

However, there has been some change in the situation because of initiatives of the Government of Andhra Pradesh in the last five years, which place an emphasis on good governance and financial discipline for greater autonomy of local bodies. Measures such as incentives for higher revenue collection, support for the computerisation of certain functions, and technical assistance for updating accounts have resulted in improvement of the revenue position of most municipalities. User-charges and private sector participation in service delivery have been introduced on a small scale in a few municipalities. Greater accountability in routine municipal functions has been introduced and Citizens' Service Centres have been established for the convenience of citizens.

Parallel to this decentralisation has been a process of democratisation and increasing grassroots representation. The 74th Constitutional Amendment recognises local government as the third tier of government and Municipal Councils are democratically elected. One third of the council seats are reserved for women. The recasting of the central government's poverty alleviation schemes has meant that municipalities are responsible for facilitating the formation of a structure of representative women-only community-based organisations in slums. Resident Community Volunteers (RCVs) are elected for a neighbourhood group (NHG) of 20-40 households; RCVs in a slum or ward[3] form a Neighbourhood Committee (NHC) with one of the RCVs elected as a Convenor. NHC Convenors form the Community Development Society (CDS) at the town level and elect their own office bearers (Ministry of Urban Affairs and Employment 1998a). Programmes for the economic, social, and physical development of poor areas are expected to be implemented with the active involvement of the CDS structure. This has institutionalised the representation of poor women and given municipalities some experience of working with them.

The decentralisation and democratisation initiatives of government provide a good starting point for reforms to sustain poverty reduction.

The strategy adopted by APUSP is to build on existing initiatives of good governance and financial management and also on the participatory structures of slum dwellers. The basic tasks are to support municipalities to bring about specified improvements in financial management, planning, capacity for implementation, and mechanisms for consultations with citizens, particularly with poor people. Broad indicative areas of reform are: revenue improvement, institutional development, participatory planning approaches, service delivery improvement, operation and maintenance, training or skills upgrading, and other matters as appropriate.

The premises of this targeted approach to reform are that better ways of interfacing with citizens and their involvement in making decisions that affect them will improve targeting. Similarly, improved revenue assessment and collection will result in the generation of more resources, and improved management of funds through transparent accounting and budgeting systems will lead to better allocation of resources for provision of services and for their operation and maintenance. This, in turn, will provide more satisfaction to the users of these services and give municipalities an incentive to take measures such as cost recovery and tax increases which may otherwise be politically difficult. The process will be further stimulated by a more vocal and informed civil society which can impress on municipalities the need to improve services for poor communities and involve them in decision-making processes.

The central issue is that improvement in performance requires the municipalities to be willing to change. Reforms that are driven by government policy and state-government directives are one way to bring about such change. In the long term, the pressure created by a strengthened civil society may also induce change in the ways municipalities work. However, if reforms are to benefit poor people in any substantial way, the incentives have to be different.

In APUSP, funding for improvements in infrastructure for poor people is expected to provide the incentive to reform. Measurable improvements in performance are the trigger for gaining access to APUSP project funds for infrastructure improvement. There are '... no automatic entitlements for those municipalities who do not demonstrate a commitment to change, to address the needs of poor people, and the ability to operate and maintain the infrastructure provided' (DFID 1999).

It is worth mentioning that the incentive system for pro-poor planning is breaking new ground in Andhra Pradesh and in India. Such a system is very different from the present policy and practice of equal shares for different administrative units (district, town, ward) based on per capita allocations. Allocations may currently be topped up for particularly vulnerable groups, but they are never based on performance.

Environmental infrastructure

The focus of APUSP on improvements in environmental infrastructure is in response to the current deficiency and inability of local government to deal with the situation. Such improvements are urgently needed in most of the 32 towns covered by APUSP. This is well illustrated by studies carried out during the design of the project (see Table 1).

It is well known that municipalities do not generate sufficient revenues to cater to the service needs of the growing population of poor people. This has been taken care of to some extent by several central and state government schemes undertaken during the last three decades. However, their impact has not been significant. The allocations have been meagre compared with the large and growing need, and thinly spread in order to share the benefits across political constituencies. Invariably the quality of services has been poor, and deteriorated rapidly since there was no attention paid to allocations for operation and maintenance. The schemes were top-down, with no scope for municipalities or poor communities to comment on the way they would be run. A significant change in the programmes being implemented since 1998 is the involvement of women-only

Table 1: Environmental infrastructure deficiency in slums in Class 1 towns of Andhra Pradesh	
Infrastructure deficiency	Percentage of slum households
No municipal water supply	46%
No latrines (open defecation)	29%
No all-weather roads	41%
No drainage	45%
No street lighting	20%

Source: APUSP project design studies, 1998

representatives of community-based organisations in prioritising infrastructure needs in slums and in implementing some of these through community contracting (Ministry of Urban Affairs and Employment 1998a and 1998b; Rao 2000).

APUSP project funds are primarily intended for in-settlement upgrading of water supply, drains, latrines, roads, street lighting, and garbage disposal within slum areas, and also for infrastructure necessary to link these services to town networks. The adverse effects of environmental problems such as area-wide flooding are also taken into consideration. This is different from previous slum improvement programmes, which did not consider linking arrangements and wider environmental problems, often leading to drains without out-falls, taps without water, and persistent flooding. Hygiene promotion is included in APUSP as an adjunct to improvements in infrastructure in order to enhance the health benefits of improved services.

This emphasis on infrastructure does not mean that the lack of it is the only deprivation faced by poor people in Class 1 towns. Focusing on infrastructure as a means to poverty reduction is justified by two arguments. The first is that improvements in infrastructure have multiple impacts on poverty. This has been amply demonstrated in an impact assessment study of DFID-supported slum improvement projects in India. It was shown that although infrastructure contributes primarily to improving the quality of life, it also has positive impacts on the survival and security dimensions of poverty by reducing vulnerability to disease and improving conditions for income enhancement (Amis 2001). The lessons from that study have informed the design of APUSP. These findings are also supported by the perceptions of poor communities in the Class 1 towns of AP. People living in slums who participated in appraisal exercises during the design of APUSP, identified multiple and wide-ranging benefits arising from improved water supply, drains, latrines, roads, and electricity.

For example, people leaving in slums in Warangal (Tumulakunta slum) commented that the provision of clean drinking water, latrines, and drains meant less diarrhoea, less disease, fewer mosquitoes, and less malaria. Fewer pigs grazing on the streets also meant improved safety. Because people felt healthier, they would be able to undertake more work, they would spend less on medicines, and their incomes would rise. Access to a nearby clean water supply meant that women would have more time free for both income generating and leisure activities.

Better roads and street lighting meant that rickshaw carts would be able enter the area, that people would be less likely to trip and fall, that the risk of snake bites would decrease, and that women and children would experience increased safety. Street lighting would enabe people to undertake adult literacy and other study programmes, which would then have benefits in terms of increased income (DHU Consortium 1998).

Overall, people identified improvements to their environment and housing as improving their health, increasing their incomes, building a sense of pride in their surroundings, and increasing their contentment.

The second argument for the focus on infrastructure is that municipalities have some capacity to address the infrastructure needs of poor people, but next to no capacity to address the more difficult problems related to social deprivation, employment, and entitlements. Even the better-equipped municipal corporations in the large cities where DFID slum improvement programmes were carried out, could not do justice to the social and economic components of those projects (Amis 2001). The alternative strategy contained within APUSP is to address non-infrastructure needs through the civil society component.

Strengthening civil society

The implication from the previous sections is that strengthening civil society represents an attempt to strengthen the capacity of citizens, particularly poor communities, to make demands of the municipality, and this is an important part of the project's civil society component. The other part is related to an attempt to find alternative channels, through civil society organisations (CSOs),[4] to address wider survival, security, and livelihood problems faced by poor people.

The third component of APUSP runs as a parallel project because the partners, channels of assistance, and types of activities are different from the governance and service provision focus of the other two components. Independent funding and technical assistance are expected to provide an incentive for links with other non-governmental networks and funding sources, thus widening the ambit of poverty reduction activities.

The civil society initiative in a town starts with a participatory planning appraisal (PPA), which is carried out by an experienced NGO and involves different stakeholders in the town. The PPA explores local concepts of poverty and vulnerability, livelihood strategies, poor people's perceived priorities, local views on programme and policy implementation, etc.. Issues highlighted in the five PPAs carried out to date include aspects such as insecurity of tenure and employment, alcoholism, violence, caste discrimination, difficulties in accessing institutions and entitlements, poor services, poor health, vulnerable population groups such as deserted women, elderly, unemployed youth, etc.. The issues are not the same between different towns or even between neighbourhoods in the same town.

The purpose of the PPA is to build a shared understanding of the local dimensions of poverty and to form a town level working group (TLWG) of CSOs and municipal representatives. The tasks of the TLWG are to prepare a Town Level Framework Plan, to monitor projects under the plan, and to support the building of local partnerships for poverty reduction. Both the PPA and TLWG may have representation from the municipality, but they are not driven by it.

A Management and Support Team (MAST) has been set up to manage the Urban Initiative Fund (UIF) which can be accessed in three different ways. First, contracts for programmes of three years or more will be given to large NGOs or institutions for work in one or more towns related to issues such as legal literacy, working children, etc.. Second, shorter-term more inclusive contracts with measurable outcomes are issued for services in areas such as needs assessments, consultancy services for poor people, capacity-building activities, operational and action research, and communications material development. The third window of access is through a Rapid Response Fund, which aims to provide a large number of CBOs with direct access to the UIF for capital expenditure related to the expressed needs of the community. Projects will be prioritised in Town Level Framework Plans and monitored by the TLWG. The CDS women's groups are expected to be the main channels for this funding.

The UIF is expected to start operating in early 2002, once procedures have been defined and possible CSO partners identified. The UIF will provide windows of opportunity to those stakeholders who are best-suited for specific poverty-reduction activities to undertake the activities. Further, these activities will be defined in a transparent manner, based on a shared understanding of local poverty. This approach is expected to overcome the limitations of earlier DFID slum improvement programmes where social, health, and economic support programmes were implemented uniformly across slums by municipalities with indifferent results (Amis 2001).

The PPA and accompanying research on its findings will also inform social policy and, through MAST, may affect the way poverty programmes are structured in future. The immediate impact will be on improving the poverty focus of the MAPP.

The Municipal Action Plan for Poverty Reduction as a framework for mainstreaming the poor

MAPP objectives and concept

Each of the 32 municipalities is required to prepare a MAPP to enable it to gain access to APSUP funds. The MAPP enables a municipality to define how it will achieve three linked objectives in its own context. These objectives derive from the principles of APUSP and are:

- to improve municipal governance and management so that municipalities become more efficient and responsive to the needs of the people, especially poor people;
- to improve environmental infrastructure for poor people in a sustainable way;
- to identify and undertake poverty reduction measures with the active participation of poor people and civil society.

The MAPP is a rolling plan, updated periodically. It begins with a Basic MAPP, in keeping with the current capacity of municipalities, and later evolves to a Full MAPP (see Table 2). The MAPP contains the municipality's strategy, proposals, and implementation plan with measurable outcomes for municipal reform and environmental infrastructure and its approach to convergence[5] with other poverty alleviation programmes in other sectors, e.g. education, health, employment, income generation, etc..

In the first year of project implementation, the *Basic MAPP Guidelines* were drafted and piloted through a closely guided process in three towns (Chittoor, Qutbullapur, and Rajahmundry), and finalised after extensive consultation with municipalities. Guidelines were prepared by the APUSP Team (Municipal Strengthening Unit and Appraisal and Monitoring Unit) and consultants.[6]

The APUSP Team conducts interactive regional workshops for five or six municipalities at a time. The main objectives are to familiarise senior elected and executive municipal functionaries with the guidelines and process, and to build their capacity to undertake the preparation of their MAPPs. They may do so on their own or request assistance from the APUSP Team. Ten municipalities are currently in various stages of MAPP preparation.

Elements	Basic MAPP	Full MAPP
Timeframe	1-2 years	3-5 years rolling plan
Database	Uses existing data	Develops database
Municipal reform and performance improvement	- Simple and few reforms - Essential training for MAPP	- More complex reforms and improvement measures - Training for performance improvement also
Environmental infrastructure	In a few wards on the basis of selection criteria	Phased yearly programme including a large number of wards
Convergence	Only of urban poverty programmes implemented through the municipality	Includes programmes of other agencies and UIF under C3
Resource mobilisation	Planned within DFID and available resources	Proposes to mobilise additional funding

Source: APUSP Project Document, 1999

According to the guidelines, MAPP preparation follows a nine-stage process in a municipality (APUSP 2001). It is worth summarising this process as it contributes to setting up a participatory, inclusive, and transparent approach to poverty reduction in a town-wide context and within the framework of municipal planning and budgeting. The process has the potential to contribute significantly to mainstreaming the poor.[7]

Stages in MAPP preparation

Preparatory steps

Municipalities are required to form two local committees before embarking on the MAPP process. The Municipal Reforms Committee (MRC) is constituted to give strategic guidance to the MAPP process. It is headed by the Mayor or Municipal Chairperson and includes the local MLA/MP, the floor leader of the opposition party and other members of the municipal council, the Municipal Commissioner,[8] two persons from outside the council, and the CDS President. The Municipal Task Force (MTF) takes day-to-day responsibility for preparing a MAPP. It is headed by the Commissioner and is a multi-disciplinary team consisting of heads of the functional sections of the municipality.

Stage 1: Getting started

The APUSP project and the purpose and process of the MAPP are introduced by the municipality at a large meeting to which representatives of a wide range of stakeholders are invited. The members of the MRC and MTF are also introduced.

Stage 2: Problem identification

This starts with a workshop co-ordinated by the municipality with representatives of stakeholder groups (elected municipal councillors, municipal staff, CDS and other CBOs, NGOs, and other organisations working with poor people). One third of the participants are women. The participants work in groups to articulate a vision statement for the town and identify problems with respect to poverty, infrastructure, and municipal performance. The workshop identifies two working groups from among the participants to provide a more detailed analysis of the problems over a period of three to four weeks.

Working Group 1 on municipal performance improvement carries out a municipal SWOT analysis (strengths, weaknesses, opportunities, and threats) in relation to financial status, staffing, service delivery, and interfacing with citizens. The problems and their causes are analysed with the involvement of the entire cross-section of municipal staff and elected representatives and strategic objectives for improving municipal performance are identified and ratified by the MRC. Proposals are prepared to address these objectives and assessed against criteria such as benefits, political and social acceptability, technical and managerial feasibility, cost, and measurable outcomes within the MAPP period.

Working Group 2 on poverty and infrastructure deficiency identifies different kinds of poor settlements, uses existing data to rank them in terms of poverty and infrastructure deficiency, and shows the ranking on a matrix. It also places poor settlements in a city-wide perspective of ward boundaries, service networks, and environmental problems such as flooding, sea and river erosion, and pollution. This analysis is shown on maps and charts. The poorest and most deficient settlements are visited by a technical screening group to check site conditions and the need for off-site infrastructure.

The two working groups meet to ensure co-ordination and compatibility of outputs. The findings of Group 2 which are related to need for better data, network design, staff capacity building, equipment, etc. are incorporated into the municipal improvement proposals of Group 1.

Stage 3: Strategy formulation

A two-day workshop is convened with the participants of the problem analysis workshop. The findings of the two working groups are presented and the workshop recommends which poor settlements should be a priority to be included, which strategy is to be followed for infrastructure investments, and which reform proposals are to be taken up in that MAPP. The MRC deliberates on the recommendations and endorses them, with or without changes. The decision of the MRC and the next steps in MAPP preparation are shared with the workshop participants.

Stage 4: Preparation of reform proposals

The MTF reviews the reform proposals recommended by the strategy formulation workshop and consolidates them into a set of proposals to meet the strategic objectives for improving municipal performance. The expected outcomes of each proposal are considered and an implementation plan is prepared for the proposals.

Stage 5: Preparation of environmental infrastructure proposals

The first step at this stage is micro-planning with community groups in the priority settlements. The process is undertaken by a community micro-planning group, co-ordinated by the NHC Convenor and consisting of all RCVs in the settlement, representatives of other women's and youth groups, fieldworkers of programmes in the area (literacy, health, woman and child development, etc.), and municipal sanitary workers. The exercise is facilitated by a multi-disciplinary municipal micro-planning team and takes four to five weeks. The broad steps in the process are:

- inventory of existing infrastructure and needs identification by the Group, using participatory mapping techniques;
- preparation of a draft Settlement Plan for Infrastructure;
- technical assessment by municipal engineering staff;
- community feedback and agreement on a final Settlement Plan for Infrastructure showing rehabilitation proposals for existing infrastructure and proposals for additional infrastructure;
- discussion of different implementation and operation and maintenance responsibilities.

The second step is the preparation of environmental infrastructure proposals based on the Settlement Plans for Infrastructure and off-site infrastructure needs. The engineering section of the municipality prepares these with assistance, if required, from the local office of the Andhra Pradesh State Public Health Engineering Department (PHED). The process is overseen by the MTF. An implementation plan is prepared for the proposals.

Stage 6: Finalising the MAPP document

The MTF is responsible for this task. The document outlines the process of MAPP preparation and gives proposals for reform and infrastructure improvement as detailed in Stages 4 and 5. The MTF cross-checks the document against APUSP appraisal criteria. The document is presented to the Municipal Council for adoption.

Stage 7: Appraisal and approval

The AMU carries out concurrent field appraisal of the MAPP process and final desk appraisal according to agreed criteria. These criteria include poverty and gender focus, participation, and municipal capacity to engage in these aspects. The Empowered Committee approves the proposals on the basis of the appraisal report.

Stage 8: Preparation of detailed proposals

Detailed proposals are prepared after the MAPP is approved. The proposals are expected to indicate clearly measurable outputs at milestones, procurement and operation arrangements, and detailed costings including for operation and maintenance. The infrastructure proposals are broken up into sub-projects for appropriate contract packaging. Small sub-projects for roads and drains may be contracted to willing community groups. In any case, community groups are expected to monitor contracts in their area.

Stage 9: Sub-project review

The sub-projects are reviewed for technical and managerial feasibility by the AMU, after which funds are released.

The Basic MAPP process in practice

Experience from managing the MAPP process in the three pilot municipalities shows that the process is valued by the municipalities for its clarity, transparency, and acceptability. There is representation of civil society, including poor communities, at all stages where problems and needs are assessed and decisions made about solutions. The guidelines represent a highly participatory process, both within and beyond the municipality, which is completely different from previous practice. For this reason most municipalities will require guidance for preparing the first MAPP. In the following section we review how some critical issues related to poverty reduction are dealt with in practice.

Critical poverty reduction issues in the Basic MAPP

Availability of funds

Funding for infrastructure improvement for the poor is assured for seven years, as long as the municipalities show adequate progress on reforms and prepare MAPPs. Judging from the present enthusiasm, these conditions will be fulfilled. The bulk of DFID infrastructure funding is designated for in-settlement improvements. The selection of priority settlements through the transparent process of analysis and decision-making in the MAPP ensures that this funding will necessarily benefit the poorest communities in the analysis. Off-site infrastructure funds may lead to benefits accruing to the non-poor. However, guidelines specify that only up to 35 per cent of the infrastructure funds are to be used for off-site infrastructure, and that at least 50 per cent of the beneficiaries should be poor. This implies that, at the most, 17.5 per cent of the infrastructure funds may benefit communities that are not poor.

If the convergence principle works, additional funds from other programmes may be brought in, in addition to which funding for poverty programmes such as Swarna Jayanti Shahari Rojgar Yojna (SJSRY, the Silver Jubilee Urban Employment Programme) and the National Slum Development Programme (NSDP) will be available to the municipalities. At present there is a reluctance to bring these into the ambit of the Basic MAPP for fear of complicating the process, although this may be possible in subsequent cycles once the approach has proved itself. The feasibility of converging programmes and projects funded through the UIF will become clearer once the fund starts operating.

The more ambitious and high-performance municipalities are expected to generate local resources, some of which may fund poverty reduction initiatives. They may also use the Full MAPP to mobilise additional resources from national and international funding agencies, some of which have already shown interest.

Targeting poor people for infrastructure improvement

The targeting of poor settlements in the MAPP is determined by two interrelated parameters: poverty and vulnerability is one, and infrastructure deficiency is the other. Shortcomings in quantitative and qualitative terms for water supply, sanitation, drains, flooding or erosion, roads, street lighting, and garbage disposal are used as indicators. The *Basic MAPP Guidelines* give guidance on selection of the indicators and allow the municipalities to give appropriate weightings, depending on local conditions, to each of the indicators in order to arrive at a composite index of environmental infrastructure deficiency.

Poverty and vulnerability indicators are grouped into three broad categories: economic, social, and entitlements. Initially a wide range of indicators was listed, based on earlier poverty data for the 32 towns,[9] participatory poverty studies elsewhere in the country, and findings of the first participatory planning appraisal. The poverty and vulnerability indicators chosen at first were: below the poverty line (BPL), dependence on daily wages, working women, and working children (for the economic-income and employment-grouping of indicators); scheduled caste or scheduled tribe (SC/ST) and illiteracy (for the social indicators); and insecure land tenure or no ration cards (for the entitlements indicator).

The list of indicators was given for guidance to the three municipalities undertaking the pilot MAPPs but the list eventually had to be cut down to two indicators: below the poverty line (BPL) and scheduled caste or scheduled tribe (SC/ST), since the information on other economic and social indicators was incomplete. The inclusion of entitlements as an indicator was considered controversial, since the state government is currently reviewing its welfare programmes as part of the World Bank-supported Andhra Pradesh Economic Reforms Programme, and it had to be omitted for the time being. There seems to be a political concern at state government level about raising expectations which it may not be possible to meet because of policy changes. So the composite indicator for poverty and vulnerability is made up of BPL and SC/ST households, which are the conventional indicators used for targeting poverty programmes in India.

Settlements are given scores for each of the indicators. The average scores for poverty and infrastructure deficiency are then determined separately and clustered into three ranges representing the worst, not so bad, and best settlements. These ranges of one to three are used to rank poor settlements according to poverty and infrastructure deficiency and represent them on a simple matrix format (see Figure 1). The settlements that are poorest and most deficient in infrastructure are in the cell in the bottom right-hand corner (p3/i3).

The 3x3 matrix, as it is now called, has emerged as an appropriate tool for targeting poor settlements for infrastructure improvement in

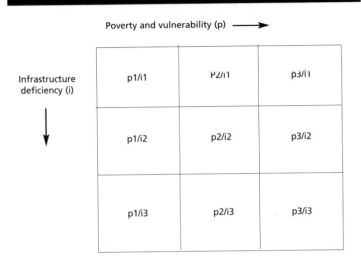

Figure 1: Poverty and infrastructure deficiency matrix

Poverty and vulnerability (p) ⟶

Infrastructure deficiency (i)

p1/i1	p2/i1	p3/i1
p1/i2	p2/i2	p3/i2
p1/i3	p2/i3	p3/i3

Source: Based on Basic MAPP Guidelines, 2001

the MAPP. It gives a comparative picture of poor settlements in a town. It is simple enough to be understood and used as a working tool by a diverse group of stakeholders, including representatives of poor communities. It is transparent and non-controversial and acceptable to local politicians, poor communities, and municipal officials. The analysis is carried out by the working group on poverty and infrastructure which includes representatives from the major stakeholder groups. In all three pilot MAPPs, the poorest and most deficient settlements were selected at the strategy formulation workshop.

The matrix can be considered as a major breakthrough, considering conventional and accepted practices of either evenly spreading resources across all slums, or selecting slums on the basis of slum notification and political constituencies. However, it has been criticised by academics for presenting an oversimplified picture of complex realities. It is argued that it is not the matrix but the data and indicators which need to be more robust. The accepted approach of using existing data for the Basic MAPP has its limitations, which are recognised by the municipalities and the MSU. Consequently, pilot MAPPs for Rajahmundry and Qutbullapur have included the need to improve information on poor settlements in their reform agenda.

The participatory planning appraisals are expected to demonstrate the importance of certain indicators and help resolve certain issues such as whether or not entitlements are critical as indicators of poverty and vulnerability. The sharing of findings from the PPAs is an important step in understanding poverty in the Class 1 towns, and therefore, towards better targeting of poor people.

The other weakness related to targeting in the Basic MAPP is also related to inadequate data: only notified slums have been included, even though they form only a part of all poor settlements in a town. The practice is to carry out detailed surveys only in slums notified under the Andhra Pradesh Slum Improvement Act of 1956 (Government of Andhra Pradesh). Government infrastructure programmes are implemented in notified slums, unlike APUSP, which includes all poor settlements (slums not yet notified, relocation areas, and housing layouts for economically weaker sections, EWSs). Local knowledge confirms that often the un-notified slums are much worse than notified slums, both in terms of poverty and infrastructure deficiency. However, it is the lack of data that prevents such settlements from being included in the Basic MAPP, even though there is local political pressure to do so.

In this instance, advantage can be taken of MAPP's design as a rolling plan and the opportunity to include critical inputs during the seven-year life of the project. Better understanding of poverty, resolution of welfare policy issues, and improved data may ultimately lead to better targeting of poor people in subsequent cycles of MAPP.

Participation of poor communities

Micro-planning is now the accepted tool in India for eliciting the participation of poor communities in determining their needs and priorities and planning for improvement of their settlements. The difference here is that micro-planning is nested within a wider town-wide framework of participatory analysis and decision making, unlike the usual slum-by-slum approach to participation, facilitated by municipal or NGO field staff.

The MAPP uses to advantage the federated structure of women's groups already existing in the towns. The functionaries of the apex level CDS participate in the MAPP formulation workshops side by side with the Mayor or Chairperson, councillors, Commissioner, and officials of the municipality, MLA, MP, and other institutions. They are also members of the working group on poverty and infrastructure deficiency. In addition, the CDS President is a member of the MRC. This way the MAPP process gives participation of poor communities a high priority in decision making.

Experience so far has shown CDS members to be equal to the challenge of participating effectively with other stakeholders. This can be attributed to the fact that they represent the primary stakeholders and have been selected for their leadership qualities and ability to negotiate and manage activities on behalf of poor people. They have also attended capacity-building workshops conducted as part of the SJSRY programme and by MAST. The MAPP process itself is a capacity-building measure and gives all stakeholders equal opportunity to participate.

Micro-planning is the first step in articulating funding proposals for infrastructure improvement and is therefore given importance by municipalities. It has been designed as an interactive process between community groups and municipal field staff. RCVs and NHC Convenors, who constitute the base and middle levels of the CDS structure, lead problem identification and demand assessment, while the municipality responds with technical solutions for infrastructure. Finally a joint decision is made. This implies that both sides have to have the capacity to deliver their part of the results and work together.

Experience from the pilot programmes shows that working with the community is a new experience for many of the RCVs. They are not even fully aware of their general roles and responsibilities. The brief training on micro-planning is not enough of a basis for effective participation. This is expected to change once the capacity-building programmes of Component 3 reach the towns. However, that is unlikely to happen before the first cycle of Basic MAPPs is completed in the 32 towns.

Similarly, the Municipal Micro-Planning Teams have their weakness. They consist of engineering, sanitation, and revenue staff, who are not used to working with communities, and the brief orientation to micro-planning is not sufficient to promote the skills and attitudes required for such work. Only eight of the 32 municipalities have community development staff. The APUSP project provides for recruitment of core community development staff. However, so far the state government has not been able to finalise the recruitment modalities. Project funds will support community development staff as and when they are in place. It is assumed that they will continue to be employed after the project period as higher revenues generated by financial reform will mean that their salaries can be met, although of course this may not happen in all towns.

In any case, it makes sense to develop skills and attitudes of other staff, particularly engineers, for working with poor people. Micro-planning, contract management, operation and maintenance of infrastructure all require engineers to work with community groups. This is seen as an important part of the municipal performance improvement activity along with the training of elected representatives to be more responsive to poor communities.

In addition to training and placement of community development staff, the capacity of municipalities to work with poor people is expected to be strengthened through appropriate communication and information tools and expansion of activities of the present Citizens' Service Centres to include information services.

Meeting non-infrastructure needs

The Basic MAPP design relies on the principle of convergence for meeting the non-infrastructure needs of poor people. The idea is to co-ordinate and converge inputs from different sources, including government and NGO programmes and initiatives under Component 3 of APUSP. This is not likely to be put into practice in the first cycle of Basic MAPP.

Component 3 programmes have yet to be initiated. Even when they are, it is difficult to see how the MAPP can serve as a co-ordinating mechanism. Their success lies in linking up with the Town Level Framework Plan, which may have very different timeframes and processes. Addressing non-infrastructure needs through this channel is more likely to be a parallel process.

Other programmes have their own norms for targeting and fund allocation, which are difficult to match with the MAPP process and timeframe. The levers for change do not rest with the municipality but with the concerned funding institutions, with whom a policy dialogue may have to be initiated.

Conclusion: sustaining poverty reduction and main-streaming poor people

The MAPP is a good basis for sowing the seeds of sustainable poverty reduction with the institutional focus of the municipality. The investment in infrastructure improvement forms the starting point for immediate improvements in municipal performance in terms of working with poor people, improved analysis of problems and targeting, multi-disciplinary working, and allocation for operation and maintenance of improved services. It remains to be seen whether or not revenues will increase as a result of reform and, if so, whether they are eventually used for improving the conditions of poor people and for supporting institutional arrangements for working with poor communities. A better-informed and vibrant civil society and transparent processes may actually make that happen.

The MAPP also institutionalises and legitimises the participation of women representatives of poor communities at strategic and grassroots-level decision-making processes, and establishes a link between the different levels. Transparent processes and the opening up of opportunities for the participation of a wide range of stakeholders is already beginning to have spin-off effects in terms of creating a town-wide constituency for poor people. This will be taken further through civil society partnerships and networks.

The functional and purposeful approach to participation in the MAPP has its limitations and needs to be supported by an awareness of rights and responsibilities and empowerment strategies of Component 3 for medium- and long-term benefits.

The analytical and rolling nature of the MAPP allows weaknesses in the areas of service delivery and working with poor people to either be addressed as part of the reforms component or to be taken up in the next MAPP cycle (e.g. data on poor settlements). APUSP places the municipality almost in the position of a 'mother institution' for poverty reduction. Not only is it expected to adopt responsive procedures towards delivery of services for poor people and their sustenance, but also to be involved in the parallel civil society initiatives through the PPA and membership of the Town Level Working Group. This brings into focus the importance of municipal reform and performance improvement and links up directly with the government policy of decentralisation and municipal responsibility for poverty alleviation. It is for this reason that municipal capacity building is high on the APUSP agenda.

Together the APUSP project principles, its multi-pronged approach, and the down-to-earth mechanism of the MAPP to translate these in the context of each municipality create a highly conducive environment for mainstreaming the concerns of poor people. The first year of project implementation has shown that this is not an assumption but a reality. The implication is that the sustainability of the MAPP process is, in itself, central to mainstreaming poor people's concerns. The question is whether the municipalities and state government will continue to apply the process beyond the project period and whether it will be applied in the other towns as well. It must also be understood that mainstreaming poor people can only happen over a longer timeframe and within a policy framework. APUSP can certainly demonstrate a way forward and the ultimate test of the project will be in its influence at a wider level: on social policy through the participatory planning appraisals, on state and national programmes for pro-poor municipal reform, on allocations for urban poverty reduction, and in expanding the role of CSOs in empowerment and urban poverty reduction.

Notes

1 A nationwide classification based on population. Class 1 towns have a population of between 100,000 and 1 million.

2 The slum population is often used as a proxy for the poor population, even though it is well established that not all people living in slums are poor.

3 A ward is the lowest administrative and electoral unit in a municipality.

4 Civil society organisations (CSOs), for the purpose of APUSP, include development NGOs, voluntary organisations, academic and research institutions, local media, community-based organisations, private sector companies, and professional and business bodies.

5 The term 'convergence' is often used in India in relation to planned co-ordination of development programmes, which address different aspects of a broader problem. The idea is to build synergies between interventions that may otherwise be separate and distinct. The term is also used for pooling resources from different sources. The MAPP and micro-planning provide the framework at town and settlement level for converging programmes

(social, health, income generation, etc.) and resources (from donors, government, the private sector, poor people) for addressing the felt needs and priorities of the poor.

6 The Government of Andhra Pradesh has appointed a Project Co-ordinator and set up a Municipal Strengthening Unit (MSU) and an Appraisal and Monitoring Unit (AMU) under the Commissioner and Director of Municipal Administration to manage the first two components of APUSP. Component 3 is managed separately by a Management and Support Team (MAST). An Empowered Committee with state government and DFID representatives makes policy decisions.

7 Although APUSP does not use the term 'mainstreaming the poor', it does make an attempt to not leave poor people in the margins by institutionalising the planning, financial and participatory mechanisms for sustainable poverty reduction.

8 Municipal Corporations are headed by elected Mayors and Municipalities by elected Chairpersons. Four of the 32 towns are corporations. Each Municipal Ward is represented by a

Councillor or Corporator in the Municipal Council or Corporation. The MLA (Member of the Legislative Assembly) is the local elected representative in the state government Legislative Assembly. The MP (Member of Parliament) is the local representative in the National Parliament. The Municipal Commissioner is the executive head of a municipality and is appointed by the state government for a term of about three years.

9 Recent surveys of slums and poor people living in the 32 towns are: the Andhra Pradesh slum survey (1994), the Below the Poverty Line (BPL) survey carried out as part of the Swarna Jayanti Shahari Rojgar Yojna (SJSRY) programme (1998), and multipurpose slum survey as part of the Janmabhoomi programme of the Andhra Pradesh government (2000).

References

Amis, Philip (2001) 'Rethinking UK aid in urban India: reflections on an impact assessment study of slum improvement projects', *Environment and Urbanization* 13(1)

APUSP (2001) *Basic MAPP Guidelines*, Hyderabad: Government of Andhra Pradesh, Department of Municipal Administration and Urban Development, available at http://www.apusp.org/

DFID (1999) 'Andhra Pradesh Urban Services for the Poor (APUSP)', unpublished project document

DHV Consortium (1998) 'APUSP: Draft Design of Institutional Reform and Urban Services Components', unpublished report

Government of Andhra Pradesh (1956) Andhra Pradesh Slum Improvement (Acquisition of Land) Act, *Andhra Pradesh Gazette Part IV-B Extraordinary*, 15 November

Ministry of Urban Affairs and Employment (1998a) *Guidelines for Swarna Jayanti Shahari Rojgar Yojna*, New Delhi: Government of India

Ministry of Urban Affairs and Employment (1998b) *Guidelines for National Slum Development Scheme*, New Delhi: Government of India

Ministry of Urban Development (1992) *The Constitution Seventy-fourth Amendment Act 1992 on Municipalities*, New Delhi: Government of India

Rao, K. Rajeswara (2000) 'Clean and green cities: participation of communities and neighbourhood groups', *Shelter* 3(1)

Learning from informal markets:
innovative approaches to land and housing provision

Erhard Berner

> *Rapid growth of illegal settlements in and around cities can be viewed not as the growth of slums but, in a very real sense, as the development of cities which are more appropriate to the local culture, climate and conditions than the plans produced by the governments of these same cities.*
> (Hardoy and Satterthwaite 1989: 8)

Introduction: the urbanisation of poverty

The 1980s and 1990s witnessed an unprecedented acceleration of urbanisation processes worldwide. City dwellers will soon outnumber those in rural areas, and virtually all of this growth is taking place in developing countries. While this trend is nearly complete in most of Latin America, latecomers like the countries of sub-Saharan Africa are rapidly catching up. In the past, urbanisation was seen as a positive process, linked to modernisation, industrialisation, and global integration. In recent years, however, it has become obvious that relatively well-paid and secure employment in the public and formal sector is available only for a shrinking minority of the urban population. Economic restructuring, driven by global competition and often accompanied by structural adjustment programmes (SAPs), is destroying many of these jobs and forces an increasing number of people to eke out a living in the informal sector. Urban poverty poses a daunting challenge to international, national, and local development policies: 'More than 600 million people in cities and towns throughout the world are homeless or live in life- or health-threatening situations. Unless a revolution in urban problem solving takes place, this numbing statistic will triple by the time the next century passes its first quarter.' (N'Dow 1996: xxi)

In only very few countries has migration from the countryside been curbed by the urban crisis and worsening living conditions. Cities still serve as safety valves for rural economies which are doing even worse: 'Most people flee to the cities because no matter how life there may be, it is generally better than the rural one they are leaving behind. Their new homes may be squalid shanties without plumbing or heat. But at least in the cities they have opportunity.' (*Newsweek: Megacities* 10 June 1996) The fundamental precondition of grasping opportunity is precarious though: it is access to urban space, which means access to the city itself. Kolstee *et al.* (1994: 27) describe the policies of the 'closed city':

> The urban authorities have tried to discourage new migrants in
> various ways. The harshest measures include levelling illegal
> settlements, expelling migrants without residence permits,
> arresting illegal workers, campaigns against street trading,
> prohibiting certain occupations and mass deportation. [...]
> Such measures have seldom had the desired effect and certainly
> not permanently.

In most developing countries, the formal market mechanism has systematically failed to satisfy the rapidly increasing housing needs of the population. It is estimated that between 30 and 70 per cent live in 'irregular' settlements, and this is a growing tendency (Durand-Lasserve 1997: 11). According to the United Nations Centre for Human Settlements (UNCHS), 64 per cent of the housing stock in low-income countries, and up to 85 per cent of new housing, is unauthorised (UNCHS 1996: 200). Self-help housing, *vulgo* squatting, has long been seen as detrimental to sound urban development and orderly planning. In the last two decades, however, it has been increasingly recognised as the only means available to fulfil the immense demand for mass housing in the cities, and thus as a solution rather than a problem. John Turner's influential book *Housing by People* (1976)[1] and the first Habitat conference in 1976 marked this paradigm shift towards an 'enabling approach' (UNCHS 1996: 337ff.; Pugh 1997). 'Getting the incentives right' for the formal private sector to move downmarket, the strategy favoured by the World Bank, has largely failed to produce a significant increase of low-cost housing supply (Baken and van der Linden 1993; Jones 1996: 248). Recent literature on urban housing (for instance the contributions in *Habitat International* 24(2)) widely agrees that self-help housing is still the only 'architecture that works' (Turner 1968) in sheltering the poor.

Sprawling informal settlements in and around most of the world's cities demonstrate the capacity of self-help housing. Of course they are substandard, often even squalid, by conventional judgement, and by that of most governments. Their image as 'slums', however, belies the tremendous economic value they represent[2] as well as the indispensable role they play in the urban economy. Not only are they the major base of informal-sector enterprises which, as Sassen (1991; 1994) argues, are gaining importance in the process of globalisation; in many cities worldwide, the majority of the formal labour force and even civil servants have no access to legal and adequate housing. The role of squatter colonies is thus fundamental rather than marginal: the urban economy is heavily subsidised by their existence, and cannot function – much less be competitive – without this subsidy (Berner 1997b: 169; Aldrich and Sandhu 1995: 20).

In the urban context, poverty exists in stark and direct contrast to wealth, modernity, and progress. Urban poverty is closely related to physical segregation; while it is not restricted to the enclaves of slums and 'depressed areas' it is heavily concentrated in these places. This is reflected in the views of analysts, policy makers, and activists. The Philippine NGO newsletter *Anawim* highlights the environmental implications: 'The urban poor have been commonly associated with unemployment, shanties, overcrowding, filth, stink of uncollected garbage, lack or total absence of social services, malnutrition and just about everything that makes life miserable.' (*Anawim* No. 3, 1987: 4) For Cedric Pugh, 'this visual imagery expresses part of the reality, and it is so plain and obvious that the nature of the relationship between housing and poverty is seldom explored in-depth' (1995: 34).

The fundamental importance of land and housing for understanding urban poverty is increasingly recognised: 'Housing which meets adequate standards as well as cultural definitions of security of tenure is an essential part of a decent standard of living.' (Aldrich and Sandhu 1995: 31) UNCHS (1996: 109) prefers 'housing poverty' over other definitions, notably income-based ones, though also deploring the lack of reliable and comparable data. Table 1 presents the 'nature of the relationship between housing and poverty' as a multidimensional one. Substandard informal housing has two major dimensions, namely (a) lack of quality or infrastructure or space, and (b) insecurity. Both are *factors, indicators*, and *causes* of poverty.

Table 1: Dimensions of housing poverty		
Housing as a *factor* of poverty	Lack of quality, infrastructure, and services	• Quality of life affected by crowding, noise, dirt, pollution, garbage, inadequate facilities
		• Health affected by lack of sanitation, unsafe water supply
		• Future prospects affected by restricted access to education
	Insecurity	• Even households capable of coping at present may be thrown into emergency by evictions (loss of assets, inaccessibility of income sources): *vulnerability*
Housing as an *indicator* of poverty	Lack of quality, infrastructure, and services	• Reliability: only poor households can be expected to accept the above conditions
	Insecurity	• *But*: research reveals that not all residents of informal settlements are poor
Housing as a *cause* of poverty	Lack of quality, infrastructure, and services	• Lack of infrastructure (electricity, water, accessibility) is a liability for enterprises
		• Bad reputation may put off potential customers
	Insecurity	• Investments, particularly in immobile assets and environmental upgrading, are prevented by the risk of demolition

To clarify the argument still further, we state that housing poverty is largely determined by land supply and allocation. Hardoy and Satterthwaite's (1989: 113) insight that there is no 'housing gap' but rather a dearth of suitable and affordable land for self-help housing is meanwhile accepted among experts and officials who agree that urban land is the 'essential ingredient' (Murphy 1993: 42). Although Turner's scepticism of governmental activities was well founded, his plea for a minimalist state has not stood the test of time (Werlin 1999). There is overwhelming evidence that active policies are required in the provision and distribution of this vital ingredient:

Land, because of its unique nature and the crucial role it plays in human settlements, cannot be treated as an ordinary asset, controlled by individuals and subject to the pressures and insufficiencies of the market. Private landownership is also a principal instrument of accumulation and concentration of wealth and therefore contributes to social injustice; if unchecked, it may become a major obstacle in the planning and implementation of development schemes.
(UN 1976: 61)

However, very few national and local governments have proved that they can rise to the challenge.

Conventional policies: why do they fail?

With the cornerstones of the debate firmly in place, one would expect effective policies of self-help housing promotion, and of allocation of urban land in particular, to have emerged during the last 30 years. However, very few of the 'slum upgrading' and 'sites and services' schemes of the 1970s and 1980s, many sponsored by the World Bank, took the land issue into consideration: 'While land tenure was recognised as important, it was not seen as an essential precondition of successful slum upgrading policies.' (Werlin 1999: 1524) Even today, UNCHS's 'Best practices' database (www.bestpractices.org) reveals a remarkable lack of land provision policies, a lack that itself needs explanation. We will return to this question at the end of this paper. Governments' approaches to land and housing have oscillated between two extremes, viewing housing either as a human right, or as a commodity like any other. The latter position gained popularity in the course of structural adjustment; the former has consequently 'gone out of fashion' (Gilbert 1999: 1073), but is currently being revived in South Africa where the ANC administration feels duty-bound to provide millions of houses to the suffering non-white population. Not surprisingly, implementation is virtually non-existent.

If illegal settlements are merely seen as a violation of private or public property rights, then the forceful and, if necessary, violent restoration of these rights is the obvious solution. To date, states have been far more effective in the destruction of mass housing than in its construction. Apart from the legal aspect, massive *demolitions* and *evictions* are justified on the grounds of improvement and beautification of the city, removal of centres of crime and health hazards, and more intensive and lucrative use of land in strategic locations (UNCHS 1996:

245f.). Apart from human suffering and trauma, and the large-scale destruction of assets, this policy is almost always unsustainable. As relocation sites are rarely provided, and when they are they are in most cases unattractive in terms of location and infrastructure, evicted people find no alternative but to return to informal settlements in the city. In not a few cases they actually reoccupy their old area. A case in point is the Tondo area in Manila where more than 25 years after a large-scale, World-Bank-sponsored resettlement project (Rüland 1982), huge squatter settlements still persist.

Social housing produced by the state is the other extreme. With the notable exception of Singapore,[3] however, governments in developing countries have proved neither effective nor efficient as housing providers. Typically, immense expenditures for land and production yield negligible output, with the profit pocketed by speculators and poorly monitored contractors. To make things worse, most of the programmes suffer from huge targeting errors. Despite the subsidies, the land costs and adherence to inappropriate building regulations (often derived from colonial models; see Hardoy and Satterthwaite 1989: 38ff.) make the resulting products unaffordable for the poor, so they tend to end up in the hands of the régime's cronies and other privileged groups.

Since the 1970s, participation and self-help have become the buzzwords of the low-cost housing debate. *Slum upgrading* and *sites and services* are the major approaches to introduce these elements into practical policies. Both are steps in the right direction. Obviously, it is more efficient to improve existing settlements and provide them with infrastructure than to produce new ones from scratch, and to supply serviced land for self-help housing than merely to watch uncontrolled slum proliferation. Yet the overall performance of upgrading and sites and services schemes is disappointing (UNCHS 1996: 344ff.). Werlin (1999) goes as far as to call slum upgrading a 'myth'.

Again, planning standards for upgrading are often unrealistically high. This leads in turn to rising living costs and the uprooting of considerable parts of the population, of course usually the poorest (Hasan 1992). Their resettlement, sometimes welcomed as 'decongestion', entails social, political, and financial costs. Inappropriate standards also increase the necessary public investment which either leads to narrow single interventions (e.g. paved pathways) or severely limits the outreach of the programmes. In most Third World cities, newly emerging slums by far outnumber upgraded old ones in any given period. Even Indonesia's Kampung Improvement Programme (KIP), widely considered as one of the most successful large-scale upgrading schemes, suffers from a fundamental flaw: the question of land tenure is not addressed. Many of the improved settlements are still technically illegal. The resulting insecurity has limited participation and led to considerable maintenance problems (Silas and Indrayana 1988).

The market price for urban land in (more or less) attractive locations has also hampered sites and services schemes. Prime land is of course not available for this purpose. Private owners would expect adequate compensation, and governments will be hesitant to 'squander' their own property. In effect, most sites and services projects are carried out in remote peripheral locations, often 30–40km away from the city centres. Only people without any choice will accept these conditions. In a rather typical case from Pakistan, 'out of the 15,000 plots developed, by 1985 only 35 plots were found to be inhabited; the rest remained vacant' (Siddiqui and Khan 1994: 279). In more central locations, serviced sites ended up in the hands of affluent groups, often after being subjected to various forms of speculation (van der Linden 1986).

This discussion should not create the image that many governments come up with consistent policies. By far the most common approach is that of 'muddling through' (Durand-Lasserve 1997) and consists of long periods of negligent tolerance and inactivity, interrupted either by violent campaigns against squatters or by populist distribution of benefits among some of them. The latter includes, particularly in Latin America, the legalisation of certain settlements while at the same time carefully avoiding setting the basis for legal claims by others.

Baross (1990) provides a systematic account of the reasons why conventional policies inevitably end up in the 'too little, too expensive' trap, arguing that formal housing development – be it private or public – is characterised by the sequence of Planning–Servicing–Building–Occupation. At each step a steep price increase occurs, usually further fuelled by speculation. In Rio de Janeiro, for instance, the land conversion multiplier (price increase through planning) is estimated at 40, and the land development multiplier (price increase through servicing) at a further 11 (UNCHS 1996: 250f.). It is principally this process that makes formal urban housing an extremely scarce and expensive commodity, an 'architecture that does not work' for a large proportion of the population.

Informal land markets: why do they work?

Faced with market and state failures, most urban dwellers in the developing world have to rely on their own initiative in order to find shelter. The crucial question is how, or more precisely where, informal settlements emerge. The terms 'spontaneous settlements' and 'clandestine subdivision' suggest that urban land is just there for the taking by enterprising individuals and families. This picture is misleading. Even for the most modest demands, a parcel of land has to fulfil two minimal conditions to be suitable: accessibility (some public transport) and a source of water. To be attractive, it has to be located not too far from the places of employment, i.e. industrial and commercial centres. If such idle land does exist, it is as a rule *hazardous*. Places like mountain slopes and riverbanks put their inhabitants at physical risk, especially in the tropics, which experience rainy seasons. Residents of dumping grounds and heavily polluted industrial areas are not much better off. If a suitable site is vacant because it is being held back for speculation purposes, the owner will use all means available to evict unwanted occupants.

Less marginal locations in the city usually have a price tag attached to them. Even sidewalk dwellers in India or the Philippines have to pay regular fees to policemen or syndicates. Denis Murphy, one of the most experienced practitioners in the area of housing problems in Asia, comes to the sobering conclusion that 'there is no free squatting' (1993: vii; cf. Berner 1997a: 69f.). Pal Baross's (1983) distinction between non-commercial and commercial articulation of illegal land supply thus becomes questionable. Where traditional systems of land allocation exist they are often losing significance or becoming commercialised themselves (see, for instance, Payne 1997: 6ff.; van Lindert and van Westen 1991).

Although the extent and characteristics of extra-legal development vary from country to country (as well as between cities and even between settlements), it is safe to say that it serves a large share of the low-income population, and of incoming migrants in particular: 'Illegal or informal land markets ... have provided the land sites for most additions to the housing stock in most cities of the South over the last 30 or 40 years.' (UNCHS 1996: 239) Among the major influencing factors, all of them interrelated, are (a) economic development and political system of a country; (b) size and growth of a city; (c) availability, quality, and ownership status of unsettled land in and around the city;

and (d) governments' ability and willingness to enforce the law and implement its policies. Of course, this constellation also varies over time. The recent economic crisis in South-East Asia, for instance, at least temporarily altered the situation in the affected countries by reducing competition for urban land. Commercial development was reduced as even ongoing building activities became unviable, and many speculators had to sell at almost any price to prevent going bankrupt. At the same time, governments tended to show more tolerance of illegal settlements in order to regain some of the popularity formerly based on continuous economic growth. At the time of writing, however, the pressure on informal settlements had largely returned to the pre-crisis level.

As in the case of the informal sector, definition of extra-legal subdivision is basically residual as transactions in the informal land market are not controlled and registered by the authorities. This implies that houses are built without permits and that their quality as well as the provision of infrastructure may be substandard, which is precisely what makes them affordable for low-income groups: 'It is their ability to cut corners – and costs – which has helped the commercial subdividers to expand their operations and to provide plots which are more appropriate, affordable and easily available than any other housing option.' (Payne 1989: 2) The land subject to extra-legal subdivision is often destined for other purposes, e.g. agricultural, recreational, or as natural reserves. Obviously, most of the land suitable for such purposes is located on the urban fringe. It cannot be too remote, however, because, unlike middle-class suburbanites, the prospective buyers do not have private vehicles and can ill afford high transport costs in terms of money and time.

Apart from these common characteristics, there are notable differences in the legal status of settlements. Baken and van der Linden observe a 'continuum of subdivisions, ranging from almost, or partly, legal to completely clandestine' (1992: 29). Private landowners may themselves act as developers and sell or rent out parcels. This procedure can be seen as semi-legal, as property rights are not violated. Moreover, this type of 'tolerated invasion' is beneficial for all parties involved. The settlers find shelter and relative security of tenure at a modest rate (at least initially); they accept in turn that infrastructure is at best minimal, at worst non-existent, and they have to develop the place through their own efforts. The owners not only derive a short-term profit from rent or sales; the settlers convert barren hillsides, marginal fields, or swampy marshes into housing land, thereby increasing their value and creating a *fait accompli* for future use. As the landowners usually keep the formal title, they can later capitalise on the value-added. As noted elsewhere, they may either continuously raise the rent or declare their tenants to be outright squatters when the city closes in on the formerly marginal locations (Berner 1997a: 143ff.).

As urban land markets are commercialised, the conversion business is increasingly being taken over by professional, tightly organised syndicates which make huge profits out of the housing needs of low-income groups (Amis 1984; Payne 1989). In order to do so they have to be capable of establishing effective control over a suitable piece of land. Like the whole phenomenon of extra-legal subdivision, the strategies of squatter syndicates vary between places and over time. Outright land-grabbing against the expressed will of the legal owner appears to be rare, except in cases where the syndicates have political backing (Baken and van der Linden 1992: 23; Turkstra 1998: 20). In the case of public land, local administrators, police officers, or military personnel almost invariably have a hand in the syndicates – either actively or as recipients of bribes. 'In the extreme, politicians and officials manipulate the regulations to create artificial shortages and drive people towards the informal sector, which may then be supplied by the public officials acting as private developers but using public land.' (Jones 1996: 250)[4] Depending on culture and legal system, local strongmen like chiefs (who in parts of Africa have the traditional right to decide on land use) or party officials (who play the same role in some former socialist countries) may also be powerful stakeholders.

Developers' initial investment in infrastructure is restricted to the most basic needs. As noted above, one such necessity is accessibility as people have to get to and from their place of work. A basic access road will attract suppliers of public transport, e.g. communal taxis, tricycles, or trishaws (often unregistered themselves); in some countries people are willing to walk long distances, in which case a pathway may be sufficient. The second precondition is a source of water, for which some faucets are set up, a deep well is drilled or at least a delivery service organised. Illegal electricity tapping is not uncommon. Environmental concerns, with sanitation and garbage removal, for instance, are obviously not high on the list of priorities.

The 'serviced' land can then be subdivided and sold – though what is actually sold is the 'right to squat' on a certain plot, and no one mistakes this for a legal title (Payne 1997: 7). It is not uncommon for part of the land to be set aside for speculation purposes (UNCHS 1996: 243). Another pattern is 'slumlordism', i.e. acquisition of several plots by a single person who rents them out with or without a house. The first wave of occupants is commonly organised in a larger group to reduce the vulnerability of the settlement in the critical initial period; this procedure can easily be mistaken for a non-commercial invasion.⁵ The going prices within a city depend on location or centrality, security of tenure, and quality of infrastructure. Although empirical evidence is scattered, it is safe to assume that the informal land market functions pretty much like its formal counterpart, so that comparable plots will yield similar prices. Customers are often renters from other low-cost settlements who have saved enough (or have access to sufficient credit) to pay a considerable down-payment and save on regular rent payments in future (van der Linden 1990).

Saving on rent is, however, not the only rationale of low-income groups that are striving for home ownership. A house, even if it is just a shanty in an informal settlement, is after all an *asset*—one that is likely to grow in value in the course of urban development. In newer debates about poverty, lack of assets is identified as a major aspect of the poor's vulnerability (e.g. Chambers 1995; Moser 1998). Incremental improvements to the house, in this view, are a form of savings as labour and capital are invested to make the asset more valuable. Hardoy and Satterthwaite, quoting a Brazilian squatter, underline that not only material input is involved: 'The value of my house – 26 years of struggle.' (1989: 62) Increased security, however, is precarious. First, in the case of an eviction, the whole property may be lost in an instant (which is just another form of vulnerability); second, even in emergencies people will think twice about selling their house as this may jeopardise their access to their sources of income. Improving security of tenure is thus a major goal for residents of informal settlements.

To sum up, squatting and renting from squatters (cf. Rakodi 1995) is not a cheap way to live in the city. On top of the price of land 'rights' and other illicit payments, costs of water, electricity, and other services are normally much higher than those regular customers pay. Taking into consideration the often congested living conditions and the lack of open space, residents of extra-legal subdivisions may pay just as much money per square metre as those in legal ones, sometimes even more. The major benefit lies in the possibility of incremental development and building improvement which leads to a spreading of the costs: 'Ultimately, the difference between the two systems is probably not the price limit *per se* but the way low-income families phase their expenses for housing.' (Baross 1990: 7)

Facilitating self-help housing: innovative approaches

The Philippine 'Community Mortgage Programme' (CMP)[6]

The housing situation in Metro Manila and other urban centres in the Philippines is typical for a developing country. To date, neither the market nor the state have accomplished much in terms of mass housing. Housing policies under the Marcos régime were fragmented and largely ineffective (see Berner 1997a: 28ff. for a comprehensive discussion). Ambitious programmes of public housing turned out to be far too expensive for the alleged target group of the urban poor and served mainly the régime's vassals. Relocation to mostly unserviced sites outside the cities and, even more frequently, large-scale demolition remained the favoured 'solution' to the housing problem. As a result, roughly half of the Philippines' urban population is living in illegal settlements on public or private land.

The Community Mortgage Programme (CMP) was the first result of the paradigm shift towards enabling government in the field of housing, aimed at a more equitable *and* more rational use of urban land. The programme was passed in 1988 and launched in 1989, but significant implementation was started only under the Ramos administration after 1992. In 1992 it was integrated into the framework of the Urban Development and Housing Act (UDHA), which is, at least in principle, a comprehensive approach to the problems in question. Both CMP and UDHA came into being as a reaction to intensive lobbying by NGOs and grassroots groups.

In a nutshell, CMP offers squatters the opportunity to buy the land they occupy (or comparable land if that is not possible, e.g. in the case of priority projects) without compulsory and costly upgrading measures. Like other recent credit programmes (such as the Grameen Bank's schemes), the CMP requires beneficiaries to be organised, as the land titles are transferred to associations rather than individuals. After the residents and the respective landowner have agreed on a price, the land is paid for through a state credit which is to be repaid over a period of 25 years. NGOs are involved in all stages of the process. They inform the squatters about the legal requirements (e.g. official registration of the association), assist them during the negotiations with the owner, offer services like surveying and legal consultations, and serve as 'originators' (guarantors) of the loan.[7] The crucial problem for all credit programmes aimed at poverty alleviation – the target group's lack of collateral, which results in poor recovery rates – is thereby avoided. First, there *is* a collateral as defaulters will lose their land titles after a period of grace; and, second, NGO originators will put pressure on the residents' associations, which transmit this to their tardy members. Another advantage of the CMP is its cost efficiency. A maximum output can be realised on limited fiscal burdens by capitalising unproductive public property. Much of the land in question is owned by government, and private owners can be compensated in kind through land-swapping schemes.[8]

The question remains, however, that of how and why the CMP works. On the surface it is a conventional consolidation scheme, market-oriented in an almost neo-liberal way, and fully committed to the goal of cost recovery. Despite supposedly being aimed at the poorest 30 per cent of the urban population, there is no regulated price discount. Subsidised interest rates have a limited effect on beneficiaries' burdens – the subsidy is in fact criticised as jeopardising the programme's sustainability (Lee 1995). As compulsory expropriations are not provided for, the owners can expect to get the full value of their land. In short, the CMP alone cannot solve the sharpening contra-diction of high land prices and the low incomes of the large majority of the population. Under market rules, it would at best produce middle-class settlements on the city's outskirts.

Access to urban land – or the 'right to the city', as Lefebvre (1974) puts it – is, however, not exclusively regulated by the market mechanism but is an eminently *political* issue. The distribution of space in the city cannot be grasped without the added dimension of conflict and struggle (Berner 1997a: 38f.; Castells 1983: 3). The existence of potential and actual resistance to displacement is a precondition for the meaningful implementation of the CMP. Urban land is significantly depreciated by squatter occupation as it is not immediately available for the market. The market value of land is thus fictitious in considerable parts of the city: owners can dictate the price only if they can establish actual control of their land. This process is tedious, costly, and risky. As the residents are often capable of organising themselves and find allies among NGOs, media, church people, and local politicians (Berner and Korff 1995), the outcome of an eviction attempt can hardly be predicted by the landowner. Against such a background, landowners are willing to offer substantial discounts. In the cases we observed, residents paid only about 15–20 per cent of the market price of comparable idle land in the vicinity. The resulting expenses are in most cases considerably lower than the rent for a single room at the same place.

The CMP has been quite successful in Manila and elsewhere because it offers the chance for a compromise between contradictory motivations: the owners can sell their land and 'revive' dead capital, albeit at reduced prices, without the incalculable costs and risks of a demolition; the squatters can 'buy security' and preserve their settlement from the permanent threat of eradication that has never been quantifiable.

One of the unintended consequences of the CMP is its divisive impact on the participating communities:

> *Ironically, the ultimate success of one local organisation – the legal*
> *purchase of the locality land through the Community Mortgage*
> *Programme – had a deeply disruptive impact on the community.*
> *For about one third of the population, mainly the poorer ones,*
> *it meant that they had to pay for the land they used to live on for free,*
> *and pay more than they could afford.* (Berner and Korff 1995: 217)

The more specific the figures of future payments, the more people decide that they cannot accept the necessary cutbacks on consumption or they are altogether unable to shoulder the financial burden. A family with sufficient income sources in the settlement or its vicinity will be willing to pay much more than those who commute long distances or have no regular job. What starts as a process of internal division almost inevitably turns into open and violent conflict. After the transfer of property rights, the association has to pay for the land – more precisely, for *all* of the land; the owners are not interested in selling scattered plots, so that those whose occupants wish to stay remain as squatters. The beneficiaries, thus, not only have to pay for their own land but also for that of non-members. On the other hand, there is plenty of demand for the land in question from within and without the settlement. Many residents would like to enhance their congested living conditions, build rooms to let, or invite relatives to move to Manila; for others, the former squatter land is simply an outstanding bargain. While the marginalised sectors of the population are expelled by their neighbours and forced to find shelter in other squatter settlements, the former slums become middle-class areas.[9] This change is very visible: no longer forced to keep their property mobile, the new landowners invest heavily in upgrading and extending their houses and enhancing the environment.

Hyderabad's incremental development scheme 'Khuda ki Basti' (KKB)[10]

Unlike the CMP, and for reasons to be discussed below, the incremental development scheme in the Pakistani city of Hyderabad has remained an isolated intervention (notwithstanding a small-scale replication in Gharo which was initiated by an NGO without clear authorisation from the government). However, Khuda ki Basti (meaning 'settlement of God') went farthest in terms of 'learning from informal markets' by actually imitating illegal developers' strategies. It is thus exemplary for the argument of this paper. KKB came into being in 1986 as the reaction of the Hyderabad Development Authority (HDA) to a familiar situation: government-produced townships occupied by the middle classes, a gaping void in sites and services projects, and rampant illegal subdivision and squatting.

Based on Jan van der Linden's groundbreaking ideas, the HDA set aside 100ha of a large sites and services scheme some 12km outside the city centre, but only 1km away from a rapidly growing cluster of squatter settlements. The land was subdivided into 70m² plots and serviced only by the two essentials, namely a feeder road and communal water supply. The costs for this initial infrastructure were covered by a modest 'entry fee' of US$33, thereby undercutting the going rates on the informal market by as much as two thirds (Siddiqui and Khan 1994: 283). However, there was no attempt to exclude the informal sector completely; suppliers of simple building materials, credit, and advice were allowed in the area.

A simple one-window procedure and non-implementation of building regulations except for the layout, were the fundamental preconditions for the success of the scheme. Both the HDA and the support NGO Saipan maintained offices at the site to provide advisory services and monitor the implementation. Beneficiaries could improve their houses over time according to their individual financial capacities, and additional infrastructure was provided if and when certain amounts of savings – not instalments, note – could be collected. If the target of US$1.75 per month was met, full ownership of a fully serviced plot could be obtained in a period of 15 years. While there were some defaulters, others accumulated funds far in excess of the targets in order to get facilities quickly.

To achieve targeting and discourage speculators, a unique system of 'reception camps' was applied for a certain period of time. Only families who came to these camps with all their belongings and stayed for a number of days were eligible for a plot.[11] Beneficiaries had to start construction immediately, and land titles (or rather entitlements called 'dwelling permits') were given only after completion of a house and could be cancelled if the plot was vacant or the house abandoned. This method of self-targeting made the scheme unattractive for non-poor, to the extent that one can actually speak of over-targeting. The presence of some better-off people with higher education in 'real' informal settlements is beneficial to the communities as they provide employment as well as leadership (Berner 1997b: 175). KKB's marked social homogeneity led to a low level of local economic activities (and may have contributed to difficulties in community organising, as we shall see below). This became obvious when during ethnic turmoil between 1989 and 1992, transport to Hyderabad was difficult and nearly half of the residents left the area.

Not surprisingly, informal developers put up the fiercest resistance to the scheme. It is quite obvious (but often overlooked) that syndicates and middlemen will not easily accept being 'eliminated'. In the KKB case, land-grabbers connected with the Board of Revenues (the supposed custodian of public land) invaded the scheme by extorting 'fees' from *bona fide* residents, encroaching on parts of the land, and threatening HDA personnel with violence and abduction. Establishing a police post worsened the situation as the police took the side of the syndicate and began to harass the residents themselves (Siddiqui and Khan 1994: 288). Even more threatening was the land-grabbers' influence in the political and administrative system. Several serious attempts to sabotage or abolish the scheme outright were frustrated only because it had gained some national and international recognition (interview with Monique Peltenburg, a co-worker of van der Linden). Non-replication, despite clear advantages over the conventional sites and services approach, however, seems to indicate that vested interests in informal housing eventually prevailed.

More generally, KKB reveals the limitations of innovative schemes 'without basic changes in society's power structure ... and even without any definite political programme in favour of the poor' (Siddiqui and Khan 1994: 289). Community participation in the KKB case was merely technical. Residents were unable to organise themselves effectively and remained caught in the dependency of traditional patron–client relations (van der Linden 1997a). Instead of getting legitimate demands fulfilled, they received *favours* that could be withdrawn, and easily withheld from others in need.

Conclusions

A number of lessons for sustainable housing and land-use policies can be drawn from the above discussion. In Jan van der Linden's words, 'what is needed in brief is a bridging of the gap between the legal and the illegal systems, starting with the recognition that illegal systems have in the past achieved far more than any official initiative' (van der Linden 1994: 225; see also Fekade 2000; Kombe and Kreibich 2000).

- There is always a need for active policy in urban environments. To expect market forces to generate a rational distribution of urban land has proved a mistake, to say nothing of being inequitable. Industrial and commercial ventures are able to bid much more for the use of limited urban space than all but the wealthiest groups. Even in the industrialised countries, governments take this into consideration by applying a certain policy mix of zoning, land price control and taxation, rent ceilings, provision of or support for low-cost housing, or rent subsidies.

- Given governments' limited resources and capacity they should simply abandon the role of housing provider and turn towards a truly enabling approach. In other words, they should contribute the 'essential ingredient', namely land, and leave housing production to people's initiative. Effective co-operation between government and other actors, NGOs and the private sector in particular, is an essential element of the enabling approach.

- The conventional sequence of planning–servicing–building–occupation turns raw land into a scarce and expensive commodity, especially if cumbersome administrative procedures and transaction costs are considered. The lesson to be learned from illegal subdividers is to reverse this sequence: start with absolutely minimal infrastructure and services and allow for *incremental* development of individual houses and settlements. This strategy implies the need for a thorough revision of regulated standards, and an annulment of most of them.

- The fundamental importance and tremendous economic value of the existing housing stock – whether or not is was produced legally – should be recognised. This suggests the need for large-scale consolidation and legalisation of squatter settlements. Insecurity of tenure, apart from increasing people's vulnerability and putting their assets in jeopardy, is a major obstacle to investment: as squatters are forced to keep their property mobile they are reluctant to put money into productive ventures.

- Insecurity is also a fundamental cause of the persistence of unsanitary conditions. Environmental upgrading requires considerable investment and the long-term commitment of the residents, e.g. in non-pollutive sanitation and waste disposal management (Lee 1998). Such contributions are unlikely if people are unsure whether they will enjoy the benefits.
- If demolitions are unavoidable, it is crucial to have an adequate relocation site. Relocation to places far away from the cities is unacceptable to the 'beneficiaries' and has to be forced on them at high economic, social, and political cost. Moreover, it is not sustainable as many of the affected families return to the city, frequently to their original site.

Strategies aiming at equitable and sustainable urban development have to be two-pronged: they have to preserve as much as possible of the existing housing stock and facilitate its upgrading without making it unaffordable for the original residents (or at least most of them); and they have to provide sufficient space for new low-cost settlements, be it through the use of public land or through expropriations. The examples discussed demonstrate how this strategic orientation translates into practical policies. They are certainly not without flaws, and the scale and consistency of implementation leave much to be desired. A comprehensive approach towards urban poverty alleviation will require elements of several programmes, integrated with measures of income and employment generation and human resource development (cf. UNCHS/ILO 1995). There can be little doubt, however, that both the CMP and KKB are (or were) steps in the right direction. Both programmes have effectively enhanced the supply of land and housing for low-income groups, albeit on very different scales.

Their replicability is a question of political will rather than a technical matter. The Hyderabad case exemplifies that vested interests in both formal and informal land markets are likely to mount stiff resistance to serious reforms in this sector. Huge sums of money are made in informal housing. The profiteers, if not holding public office themselves, can be expected to be well-connected politically. Only continuing pressure from below, as illustrated in the Philippine case by the alliance of NGOs and local organisations, can ensure that solutions will be sustainable.

Notes

1 Harris (1998) points out that many of Turner's ideas had already been formulated by Jacob Crane in the 1940s and 1950s.

2 These values are still rather indiscriminately destroyed in demolitions. Administrators and planners do not seem to take their commitment to self-help housing promotion all that seriously; see next section.

3 Apart from the advanced degree of economic development combined with high public revenues, a number of unique factors contributed to Singapore's successful housing policy. Government inherited 40 per cent of the land area and acquired another half of the remainder through a draconian expropriation. Moreover, as a city-state Singapore is able to control migration and, thus, demand for housing. Much of the problem is thereby exported to Johor Baru.

4 These vested interests help explain the persistence of informal practices and are crucial obstacles for innovative policies; see concluding section.

5 Non-commercial invasions do occur, but probably far less often than some of the literature suggests. Moreover, there is evidence that they require specific conditions, e.g. the abundance of low-quality public land (Baken and van der Linden 1992: 23) or particular political circumstances (UNCHS 1996: 244).

6 Parts of this section are based on Berner (2000).

7 NGO involvement is not, however, a necessary condition. We have documented the case of a squatter association which went through the whole process without any outside assistance. The mastermind of this success was a Philippine army commander, himself a resident, who had studied law before his military career (Berner 1997a: 151f.).

8 This advantage has proved to be rather theoretical. In practice, cash-strapped state agencies, just like private owners, tend to sell public property to the highest bidder. The conversion of Fort Bonifacio in Makati into a high-class commercial-cum-residential area is a case in point.

9 This process is merely an acceleration of what goes on in informal markets anyway. Informal brokers are quite ready to go up-market: the more attractive a settlement is in terms of location, security, infrastructure, and services, the higher the prices charged by them, and the more families are evicted with or without some compensation (Gilbert 1990).

10 This section is based largely on Aliani and Sheng (1990), Siddiqui and Khan (1994), and van der Linden (1997b). Thanks go to Monique Peltenburg who provided first-hand knowledge.

11 As it turned out, the system was prone to misuse and has 'not performed very well as a sieve to select genuine applicants' (van der Linden 1997b: 40). Both HDA personnel and middlemen collected bribes for allowing families to leave early or altogether by-pass the procedure.

References

Aldrich, Brian C. and Ravinder Sandhu (1995) 'The global context of housing poverty', in Brian C. Aldrich and Ravinder Sandhu (eds) *Housing the Urban Poor: Policy and Practice in Developing Countries*, London: Zed Books

Aliani, Adnan Hameed and Yap Kioe
Sheng (1990) 'The incremental
development scheme in Hyderabad:
an innovative approach to low-income
housing', *Cities* 7(2): 133–48

Amis, Philip (1984) 'Squatters or tenants:
the commercialisation of unauthorised housing in Nairobi', *World
Development* 12(4): 87–96

Baken, Robert-Jan and Jan van der Linden
(1992) *Land Delivery for Low Income
Groups in Third World Cities*,
Aldershot: Avebury

Baken, Robert-Jan and Jan van der Linden
(1993) 'Getting the incentives right:
banking on the formal private sector',
Third World Planning Review 15(1):
1–22

Baross, Pal (1983) 'The articulation of
land supply for popular settlements
in Third World cities', in Shlomo
Angel, Raymon W. Archer, Sidhijai
Tanphiphat, and Emiel A. Wegelin
(eds) *Land for Housing the Poor*,
Singapore: Select

Baross, Pal (1990) 'Sequencing land
development: the price implications
of legal and illegal settlement growth',
in Baross and van der Linden (1990)

Baross, Pal and Jan van der Linden (eds.)
(1990) *The Transformation of Land
Supply Systems in Third World Cities*,
Aldershot: Gower

Berner, Erhard (1997a) *Defending a Place
in the City: Localities and the Struggle
for Urban Land in Metro Manila*,
Quezon City: Ateneo de Manila
University Press

Berner, Erhard (1997b) 'Opportunities
and insecurities: globalisation,
localities and the struggle for urban
land in Manila', *European Journal of
Development Research* 9(1): 167–82

Berner, Erhard (2000) 'Poverty alleviation
and the eviction of the poorest:
towards urban land reform in the
Philippines', *International Journal of*

Urban and Regional Research 24(3)

Berner, Erhard and Rüdiger Korff (1995)
'Globalisation and local resistance:
the creation of localities in Manila
and Bangkok', *International Journal
of Urban and Regional Research* 19(2):
208–22

Castells, Manuel (1983) *The City and the
Grassroots*, London: Arnold

Chambers, Robert (1995) 'Poverty and
livelihoods: whose reality counts?',
Environment and Urbanization 7(1):
173–204

Durand-Lasserve, Alain (1997)
'Regularising land markets', *Habitat
Debate* 3(2): 11–12

Fekade, Wubalem (2000) 'Deficits of
formal urban land management and
informal responses under rapid urban
growth, an international perspective',
Habitat International 24(2): 127–50

Gilbert, Alan (1990) 'The costs and
benefits of illegality and irregularity
in the supply of land', in Pal Baross
and Jan van der Linden (eds) (1990)

Gilbert, Alan (1999) 'A home is for ever?
Residential mobility and home-
ownership in self-help settlements',
Environment and Planning A 31(6):
1073–92

Hardoy, Jorge E. and David Satterthwaite
(1989) *Squatter Citizen: Life in the
Urban Third World*, London: Earthscan

Harris, Richard (1998) 'A crank's fate
and the feting of a visionary:
reflections on the history of aided
self-help housing', *Third World
Planning Review* 20(3): iii–viii

Hasan, Arif (1992) 'Housing Policies
and Approaches in Changing Urban
Context', paper prepared for UNCHS
and PGCHS, Leuven: Catholic
University

Jones, Gareth A. (1996) 'The difference
between truth and adequacy:
(re)joining Baken, van der Linden
and Malpezzi', *Third World Planning*

Review 18(2): 243–56

Kolstee, Theo, Joep Bijlmer and Fon van Oosterhout (1994) *Urban Poverty Alleviation*, The Hague: Ministry of Foreign Affairs

Kombe, Wilbard J. and Volker Kreibich (2000) 'Reconciling informal and formal land management: an agenda for improving tenure security and urban governance in poor countries', *Habitat International* 24(2): 231–40

Lee, Michael (1995) 'The Community Mortgage Programme: an almost-successful alternative for some urban poor', *Habitat International* 19(4): 529–46

Lee, Yok-Shiu F. (1998) 'Intermediary institutions, community organisations and urban environmental management: the case of three Bangkok slums', *World Development* 26(6): 993–1011

Lefebvre, Henri (1974) *Le Droit à la Ville* followed by *Espace et Politique*, Paris: Anthropos

Linden, Jan van der (1986) *The Sites and Services Approach Reviewed*, Aldershot: Glover

Linden, Jan van der (1990) 'Rental housing of the urban poor in Pakistan: characteristics and some trends', in UNCHS (ed.) *Rental Housing: Proceedings of an Expert Group Meeting*, Nairobi: UNCHS

Linden, Jan van der (1994) 'Where do we go from here?', *Third World Planning Review* 16(3): 223–9

Linden, Jan van der (1997a) 'On popular participation in a culture of patronage: patrons and grassroots organisations in a sites and services project in Hyderabad, Pakistan', *Environment and Urbanization* 9(1): 81–90

Linden, Jan van der (1997b) 'Policies Put into Practice', consultant's report, Amsterdam: Free University

Lindert, Paul van and August van Westen

(1991) 'Household shelter strategies in comparative perspective: evidence from low-income groups in Bamako and La Paz', *World Development* 19(8): 1007–28

Moser, Caroline O. N. (1998) 'The Asset Vulnerability Framework: reassessing urban poverty reduction strategies', *World Development* 26(1): 1–19

Murphy, Denis (1993) *The Urban Poor: Land and Housing*, Bangkok: Asian Coalition for Housing Rights

N'Dow, Wally (1996) 'Introduction', in UNCHS (ed.) *An Urbanising World: Global Report on Human Settlements 1996*, Oxford: Oxford University Press

Payne, Geoffrey (1989) *Informal Housing and Subdivisions in Third World Cities: A Review of the Literature*, Oxford: CENDEP

Payne, Geoffrey (1997) *Urban Land Tenure and Property Rights in Developing Countries: A Review*, London: IT Publications

Pugh, Cedric (1995) 'The role of the World Bank in housing', in Brian C. Aldrich and Ravinder Sandhu (eds) (1995)

Pugh, Cedric (1997) 'The changing roles of self-help in housing and urban policies, 1950–1996', *Third World Planning Review* 19(1): 91–109

Rakodi, Carole (1995) 'Rental tenure in the cities of developing countries', *Urban Studies* 32(4–5): 791–811

Rüland, Jürgen (1982) 'Squatter Relocation in the Philippines: The Case of Metro Manila', Research Paper No. 5, Lehrstühle Geowissenschaften, Bayreuth: Universität Bayreuth

Sassen, Saskia (1991) *The Global City: New York, London, Tokyo*, New York: Princeton University Press

Sassen, Saskia (1994) *Cities in a World Economy*, Thousand Oaks, CA: Pine Forge Press.

Siddiqui, Tasneem A. and M. Azhar Khan (1994) 'The incremental development scheme', *Third World Planning Review* 16(3): 277–91

Silas, Johan and Eddy Indrayana (1988) 'Kampung Banyu Urip', in B. Turner (ed.) Building Community: *A Third World Case Book*, London: Habitat International Coalition

Turkstra, Jan (1998) 'Urban Development and Geographical Information: Spatial and Temporal Patterns of Urban Development and Land Values Using Integrated Geo-data. Villavicencio, Colombia', PhD thesis, Utrecht: University of Utrecht

Turner, John F.C. (1968) 'The squatter settlement: an architecture that works', *Architectural Design* 38(4): 357–60

Turner, John F.C. (1976) *Housing by People: Towards Autonomy in Building Environments*, London: Boyars

United Nations (ed.) (1976) *Report of Habitat: United Nations Conference on Human Settlements*, Preamble, Section D, New York: United Nations

UNCHS (ed.) (1996) *An Urbanising World: Global Report on Human Settlements 1996*, Oxford: Oxford University Press

UNCHS/ILO (eds) (1995) *Shelter Provision and Employment Generation*, Nairobi and Geneva: UNCHS/ILO

Werlin, Herbert (1999) 'The slum upgrading myth', *Urban Studies* 36(9): 1523–34

Lowering the ladder: regulatory
frameworks for sustainable development

Geoffrey Payne

Why do so many people in the cities of developing countries live in housing and urban settlements which ignore official planning regulations, standards, and administrative procedures? Clearly, there are many factors to consider in attempting to answer this question. However, opportunities for access to legal shelter are significantly influenced by the social and economic costs of conforming to official requirements. Where these costs are greater than households can afford, they have little alternative but to seek other options. An extreme example of this is squatting, although there are now many other processes of varying degrees of legality, or illegality, operating in most cities. For example, households may construct a house on land they own, in an area officially designated for residential development and in conformity with building regulations, but not in conformity with administrative regulations. Since such developments will not qualify for the essential documentation required by the authorities, they may be regarded in the same category as other unauthorised housing.

Under such conditions, the ability of urban authorities to impose official norms is restricted to developments under their direct control. Elsewhere, the proportion of people unable to conform has reached a critical mass that enables people to act with relative impunity in undertaking further illegal actions. Such processes not only challenge the authority of the urban agencies responsible for managing urban development, they also threaten public respect for all other laws and official regulations. Increasing access to legal shelter for the urban poor and improving urban governance for all sections of the increasing urban population therefore require that this issue be addressed by researchers, policy makers, and administrators alike.

Although unauthorised housing and urban development has become so widespread in many places as to represent the norm, households may still be exposed to insecurity and limited access to credit, services, and public facilities. They may also suffer from social and environmental costs, isolating them from civil society.

Many of the planning regulations, standards, and administrative procedures operating in developing countries have been inherited or imported from countries where the economic, social, institutional, and climatic conditions are significantly different from those in the South. For example, building regulations in the southern African kingdom of Lesotho are based on those of Sweden, and those of the highlands of Papua New Guinea on Australian category 'A' regulations derived from coastal conditions.

Initial intervention by many international agencies to improve urban housing conditions in the South focused on designing and implementing pilot projects. Sites and services projects were undertaken in the hope that the experience gained would filter through to the mainstream activities of urban development agencies and gain acceptance for the principle of incremental development. In some cases, as in the Nairobi Dandora projects funded by the World Bank in the early 1970s, reviews were commissioned of existing planning and building regulations, standards, and administrative procedures with a view to making them more appropriate to local conditions. Perhaps inevitably, these indicated that existing standards were too high for many people to be able to conform with them and it was recommended that some be reduced. However, the subject was particularly sensitive and it was more than 20 years before any of the recommendations were accepted, and even then only in a partial form.

It is understandable that central or local governments are reluctant to adopt planning and building standards that were once imposed on them by colonial powers, or which are routinely applied in countries reflecting standards to which they aspire. However, inappropriate regulatory frameworks raise the cost of getting onto the legal housing ladder to such a level that the urban poor cannot do so, inhibiting the rate at which long-term improvements can be made in housing and environmental living conditions. In particular, they inhibit social cohesion and economic activity, waste land, discourage private sector participation in housing markets, encourage corruption, and even accelerate the growth of the unauthorised settlements they were intended to prevent. For all these reasons, it is important to assess the social and economic costs of each component in order to identify options for reform. Once this is done, it will then be possible to identify the institutional, technical, and other constraints to more appropriate frameworks.

Among early studies of regulatory frameworks, attention focused on the administrative procedures by which urban development proposals are processed. Kitay (1985: 20) claims that in many developing countries it can take many years to record a land transaction on official title registers, and delays are a major impediment to the involvement of private sector developers in low-income housing. In a similar vein, Struyk *et al.* (1990) record that in West Java, land transfers take an average of 32.5 months for a title to be issued and estimate that this adds between 10 and 29 per cent to the cost of land acquisition. In an influential analysis of urban administration in Peru, de Soto (1989) calculated that administrative procedures were so cumbersome that development could not take place unless people ignored the rules, or secured preferential treatment through political or bureaucratic patronage. Similarly, in Tanzania, applicants for building permits have to go through 28 different steps, taking time off work to visit different agencies, which may more than a year (Payne 1997).

Other studies, such as Durand-Lasserve (1987), Dowall and Clarke (1991), and Farvacque and McAuslan (1992), have also stressed the need to review regulatory frameworks. However, empirical evidence of the extent to which particular planning regulations, standards, or administrative procedures constitute the most significant barriers to improving access by the urban poor is not easily available. In recent research on public–private partnerships (Payne 1999), it was found that planning standards impede the growth of innovative approaches to shelter provision for the poor. This finding is consistent with other research by ITDG (2000) on building standards, which has demonstrated that they are invariably inappropriate to the needs of the urban poor and that their impact has been to marginalise people, rather than uplift them.

Planning regulations

Planning regulations are generally intended to prevent incompatible land uses or development considered to be against the public interest. Few would object to regulations which separate polluting industries from residential neighbourhoods. However, regulations which inhibit residents from using their dwellings for income-generating activities such as petty manufacturing, commerce, or rental subdivisions, deny them a major opportunity to supplement low and often irregular cash incomes and work their way out of poverty. They also reduce the amount of housing available for the poorest households and inhibit house and environmental improvements.

Few planners responsible for formulating or enforcing planning regulations would consider these outcomes desirable. However, it has proved immensely difficult to waive or even relax them. As McAuslan (1989: 30) states in relation to Madras:

> ... so concerned have the authorities been to close every loophole against illegal development, corruption, exploitation of scarce resources, the exercise, and therefore the possible wrongful or non-exercise, of discretion, that the principal aim of the Madras Metropolitan Development Authority – to get orderly and equitable development underway in Madras and its environs – has been lost sight of.

As a result, 'laws were not being observed or enforced, illegal and unauthorised development was widespread and plans were not being followed'.

McAuslan goes on to claim that the legal regulations in Madras also lack consistency, and the more complex they become the more likely this is to happen. By attempting to control all aspects of land development, particularly land use, planning regulations have therefore restricted both access to land and the options for those who do gain access. Such approaches are the reverse of the approaches adopted in most unauthorised settlements, where a significant proportion of the population may be employed locally and in ways which benefit the wider urban economy. For example, in China and even in Japan, many of the components required in hi-tech manufacturing are produced in home-based units.

Such restrictive regulations also have a more pernicious aspect. Their obtuse language, complexity, and comprehensiveness load the dice in favour of professionals, their affluent clients, and the political elite, and against the uninitiated majority.

Among the regulatory factors restricting investment in urban land development, particularly for commercial and industrial uses, few have greater impact than zoning regulations. By insisting on the complete segregation of residential, commercial, industrial, and recreational activities, these negate the very qualities that make cities dynamic and attractive places in which to live and work. Most thriving cities, including popular destinations for tourism, embody mixed land uses, low- to medium-rise development, and medium to high densities. Yet these qualities are often impossible to achieve within current zoning and other planning regulations.

Planning standards

Concern over unplanned development of squatter settlements has often been used as the justification for establishing what are regarded as minimum acceptable standards of development. As with planning methods and regulations, these are often based on inherited or imported standards, or reflect aspirations for national development based on some notional assessment of what is accepted in Europe or North America.

Consideration of what constitutes acceptable standards has invariably been examined at the individual rather than city level. Thus, standards on road widths and standards of construction, plot size, utilities provision, or building design are considered in terms of what a notional household should regard as adequate and not on what this implies at the scale of the city. If it is considered important for households to have space to grow food on their plots, and enjoy private open space, standards may require minimum plot sizes in excess of 300m². However, the low densities that result may make it prohibitively expensive to install basic utilities or operate an efficient public transport system, thereby isolating people from employment centres and community facilities which may be even more important than the option of growing crops.

The imposition of official standards on private sector projects increases costs, which are passed on to purchasers, reducing the ability of the private sector to serve the needs of lower-income groups. In developments designed and implemented by public sector agencies, the gap between the cost of meeting official standards and the ability of residents to afford them was either not quantified or was covered by various subsidies and has proved to be unsustainable on a large scale.

As competition for urban land increases, so does the need to put it to more intensive and effective use. Studies of squatter and other unauthorised settlements in which the planning standards are based on local perceptions and not on official ordinances, all suggest that people are willing to accept higher densities, mixed land use, and less space for roads than are required by official standards. This is largely because official standards do not normally take into account the capital and recurring costs involved in their implementation or the implications for urban development and management.

An equally important consideration is that standards rarely distinguish between initial and consolidated standards of development.

Yet almost all locally controlled development is incremental in nature, with people building a modest house initially, which they expand and improve as resources become available. In many cases, such housing reaches official standards eventually, though attempts to impose such standards at the outset raise the bottom rung of the housing ladder too high and exclude people from participating in the legal housing market. Ironically, therefore, standards designed to ensure good-quality urban development are partly responsible for the growth of unauthorised and substandard development.

A major consideration in this respect is the cost of roads. In any large urban development project, the area occupied by roads will be considerable. This land has to be acquired, developed, and maintained permanently, yet generates no direct return on the investment. Despite this, it is common to find standards for road reservations higher than those found in Europe. Clearly, such standards cannot be justified on objective grounds.

Similar concerns can be cited in the case of utilities provision. By insisting on individual connections to a public water supply, consumption levels will be substantially higher than if initial provision is off-plot. Individual connections require a higher (and more expensive) standard of waste disposal and drainage that may be impossible to provide to all those in need, or may prove too expensive for many households to afford, even with subsidies.

Finally, the imposition of high standards on house design and construction, with maximum floor area ratios, required setbacks, and minimum gaps between buildings, also raises costs and lowers densities, with adverse consequences for the urban poor.

Administrative procedures

In a major review of urban policy within the World Bank, Cohen (1992: 13) cited regulatory frameworks as the second major constraint to improving urban productivity in countries receiving Bank support. He suggested that a key question should be what the costs and benefits of all these regulations are, and proposed that the Bank would introduce regulatory audits, or cost–benefit balance sheets of the regulatory systems operating in specific cities, to eliminate elements which constrain economic activity. While accepting that some regulations are undoubtedly necessary, he suggested that others, such as the common requirement that the distance between two buildings should be equal to their height, did not appear to have a rational justification.

This concern with regulatory frameworks was reinforced in the Bank's subsequent Housing Sector Policy Paper (1993: 11) which stated that 'nothing influences the efficiency and responsiveness of housing supply more than the legal and regulatory framework within which housing suppliers operate'. The paper contrasts the simple and efficient regulations of Thailand with the cumbersome approach adopted in Peru, where it was estimated to take almost seven years from project inception to occupation of units in new developments. Not only do these delays increase costs, but regulations also eliminate cheap housing and force the poor to spend a larger proportion of their incomes on housing.

The extent to which administrative procedures affect the urban poor in the case of Peru was quantified extensively by de Soto (1989). This indicated that it took 289 days to establish a factory legally, while procedures for legally obtaining a plot of land were estimated to take six years and eleven months, or 56 times the official minimum wage at the time! He concluded that this forced people out of the legal market, even if they were otherwise willing and able to obtain legal shelter. Consequently, the informal sector in Peru accounted for about 70 per cent of all new construction, employed 439,000 people, and provided 90 per cent of the city's transportation. Following recommendations resulting from this study, the situation in Peru has improved considerably, though this is the exception rather than the rule.

In many countries, it is even difficult for people to obtain information on administrative procedures which they are expected to follow. In Lesotho, for example, all forms relating to registering land titles or to developing plots are written in English, although many people cannot even read the local language.

Procedures tend by their nature to become more, not less, complex over time. In some cases, they may also become contradictory. In Tanzania during the 1980s, recipients of plots in sites and services were required to build and occupy a house within 12 months or forfeit their plots. However, it took considerably longer than this to complete all the steps required to obtain official permission to build a house, though failure do so could also lead to the forfeiture of their plot!

However, the full impact of complex administrative procedures is rarely even recognised. This consists of the financial cost imposed by delays in the time taken to conform to, or obtain unofficial exemption from, official permissions. This is particularly serious in countries experiencing high rates of domestic inflation and even higher real rates of interest. Clearly, where interest rates are in the region of 20 per cent a year or more, a delay of a year in obtaining permission to build on recently acquired land dramatically adds to total costs. During many years of organising planning simulation exercises for professionals in urban development agencies, this writer has found that participants rarely consider the cost of money in discussions on urban project costs. When the cost of borrowing funds to undertake projects is included, it becomes abundantly clear how expensive lengthy procedures can be and how much could be saved by simplifying them.

However, the greater the number of desks which applicants have to visit in order to obtain planning permission, the greater the opportunities for staff to exact personal benefits. As long as public sector salaries remain low, such tendencies become difficult to resist and vested interests, especially bureaucrats who extract bribes from people seeking permissions, become entrenched. While it is relatively easy to propose that the administrative system should be reformed, ensuring that such reforms are implemented requires that these interests be taken into account.

Recent trends

It is clear from the above that the underlying rationale for regulatory frameworks has traditionally been to assert control over processes of urban development. Methods have tended to be reactive rather than proactive and rigid rather than flexible. The evident failure of such approaches makes the concerns expressed by various observers and the World Bank, to change this approach to more market-sensitive approaches, both justified and urgent.

However, in view of the current impact of globalisation and privatisation, it is important to consider what an appropriate basis should be for more relevant regulatory regimes. For example, deregulation is unlikely in itself to improve significantly the efficiency of urban management of land and housing markets, or access to these by the poor. This has been recognised by Cohen (1992) and the World Bank in its Housing Sector Policy Paper, which claimed that 'nothing influences the efficiency and responsiveness of housing supply more than the legal and regulatory framework within which housing suppliers operate' (World Bank 1993: 11). The Bank recommended the introduction of regulatory audits listing the costs and benefits of selected regulations as a basis for reform and introduced such audits in Mexico in the early 1990s, to identify bottlenecks at the local level and design reforms to remove them. Initial work identified unnecessarily high building standards, large plot sizes, oversized roads, and complex titling procedures. It estimated that 25 per cent of housing costs in Mexico were attributable to clearly excessive local regulation. However, it appears that further more detailed audits have not yet been undertaken.

The Bank links these measures to the strategic objective of increasing urban productivity and emphasises the linkage between sectoral policies, such as housing, and the macro-economy. Its approach to regulatory reform has been questioned by Jones and Ward (1994: 42) who suggest that the Bank has restricted its attention to the formal segment of the land market. They express doubts about the application of deregulation to the informal segment of the market, since this is already unregulated. While they acknowledge that removing selected planning and land-use regulations may decriminalise certain activities, hinder corrupt officials, and allow some capital to be invested, they claim that it will do little for the conditions under which the occupants or providers of land or housing compete for resources, and may also expose them to taxes and other costs from which they had previously been exempt. They indicate that the effect of the Bank's policy would be to formalise informal processes rather than deregulate land and housing markets, which they consider 'a curious form of radicalism in societies where 80 per cent of households already fend for themselves in an unregulated manner'. However, this overlooks the fact that existing regulatory frameworks impose costs and conditions which discriminate against the poor and render them vulnerable to exploitation by unscrupulous developers and other providers of commercial shelter in the informal sector. While access to formal shelter undoubtedly involves costs in the form of taxes, these may also confer benefits if the costs are affordable and residents receive benefits in the form of services and facilities in return.

Future prospects

The real questions should perhaps be: what aspects of the land and housing development process should be regulated and how should this be achieved? This in turn poses the question of what objectives regulations are intended to fulfil. Two possibly conflicting elements appear necessary in that new regulatory regimes will be required to stimulate domestic and external investment and also provide transparent and equitable guidelines for development led by others. In this context, the World Bank has a strong case for proposing that it should concentrate on identifying those regulations which create the most severe distortions in sector performance (World Bank 1993: 35), though the final objective should perhaps be broader than this.

Such changes will require a fundamental change in working practices, attitudes, and value systems and will take time to take root. Addressing powerful vested interests will also be more challenging than preparing objective recommendations based on costs, since they represent the greatest constraint to change. One option in addressing this issue will be to reduce the number of steps required to obtain planning permission, as in Peru, and to make the processing of applications more transparent. Another way is to require the relevant authorities to process proposals within a specific timespan, failure to achieve which entitles the applicant to proceed. This approach has been adopted with great success in Mali.

Before changes can even begin, however, it will be important for policy makers and administrators to obtain accurate assessments of which components of the regulatory framework represent the greatest bottlenecks to the creation of more focused and appropriate frameworks. This, in turn, requires research into the various social and economic costs of existing planning regulations, standards, and administrative procedures. The regulatory audits proposed by the World Bank in Mexico represent an important step in this process and other recent research into building standards in Kenya and Zimbabwe has provided valuable findings (ITDG 2000). In particular, it appears that relatively few countries have undertaken reviews of regulatory frameworks and, of those that have, information on their adoption and implementation is difficult to obtain.

The ITDG research emphasised the need to obtain the views of residents on housing standards and found that many people were not aware of existing standards and, of those who were, many found them socially or financially inappropriate. For research focusing on planning standards, it is essential to include a wide range of stakeholders, since residents may be less able to appreciate the wider urban implications of personal preferences and it will be necessary to obtain agreement on the options for reform. However, present arrangements have created strong vested interests based on professional and personal considerations. Changing practices will therefore require that these interests be addressed and that proposals be formulated which can generate sufficient support to be implemented.

These issues will be addressed in two major research projects that are about to start with support from the UK Department for International Development (DFID). These will examine regulatory frameworks for upgrading of existing settlements and for affordable new settlements in India, Kenya, Lesotho, South Africa, Tanzania, and Turkey. Examples from other countries will be included as appropriate.

While economic factors will play a critical part in both studies, cultural, gender, and public health aspects will also be given prominence. In many countries, particularly in sub-Saharan Africa, plot sizes, for example, are traditionally much larger than in Asia. Equally important will be the need to distinguish between initial and full standards, and attention will be given to determining the minimum level sufficient to permit permanent occupation of a plot. This should be at standards affordable to the majority of people – using market costs as the yardstick – since standards which are significantly higher than this will be dependent upon subsidies.

A key consideration will be that both utilities and building standards can and should be designed to minimise initial entry costs to legal shelter – to lower the bottom rung of the housing ladder. This will need to be designed in ways which can facilitate subsequent upgrading and consolidation, using approaches such as that proposed in Davidson and Payne (2000).

The research will build on recent and current practice in several countries. India has regularly revised its planning standards in line with changing needs and circumstances, which are based on excellent research by the Housing and Urban Development Corporation. Peru has incorporated many of the recommendations of de Soto's research and introduced 'one-stop shops' to streamline the procedures for processing development proposals. Chile has also made considerable changes in its regulatory framework for urban development, though Smolka and Sabatini (2000) suggest that the way in which these changes are assessed varies greatly according to one's ideological position. While they have undoubtedly improved the supply of housing and the efficiency of the housing market, many poor communities have been evicted from well-to-do areas, a result which the authors note would meet strong resistance in less autocratic societies where the rights of poor occupants are recognised as legitimate. The ultimate assessment of progress in regulatory reform will be by the poor themselves, since they are most directly affected by the conditions influencing access to officially sanctioned shelter.

Care will also be taken to distinguish between those elements on which relaxation would be desirable and those on which enforcement should concentrate. For example, relaxed attitudes to planning regulations and standards has enabled the urban poor in Turkey to obtain relatively easy access to land and services for many decades, yet a similar attitude to the enforcement of building regulations led to a heavy death toll and massive destruction when earthquakes struck in 1999.

Finally, the research will identify the public sector agencies at central, provincial, and municipal levels which are responsible for formulating and implementing regulatory frameworks and any changes necessary to meet basic needs and provide local flexibility. It is hoped that the projects will provide a series of matrices that can identify the specific bottlenecks which impose the highest social and economic costs. By addressing the constraints opposed to relaxing or replacing these, it is hoped that the costs of access to affordable and legal shelter for the urban poor can be significantly reduced and opportunities for them to use shelter as a vehicle for development increased.

Preliminary recommendations

It is perhaps inadvisable to propose recommendations on the strength of research which has not even started. However, the research team will need to arrive at conclusions and recommendations on several key questions. The following ideas are therefore offered in the interests of exposing initial prejudices and encouraging feedback to help inform the research.

The first question concerns how decisions should be made regarding regulatory frameworks in fast-growing settlements in developing countries. The broad answer to this is that decisions should be made at the lowest administrative levels which have sufficient competence to formulate and enforce the various regulations, standards, and procedures. However, such decisions should not be the sole preserve of public officials, most of whom have been educated to require inappropriate standards, but should include community groups, NGOs, and private sector developers. This will ensure that regulatory frameworks are closely related to what can be achieved for all sections of society on a long-term, sustainable, basis. It is also vital that regular audits be undertaken of the impact of specific regulations, standards, and procedures to see what changes are needed to reflect changing needs and resources.

Second, how will revised regulations, standards, and procedures lead to sustainable development? It is clear from experience that the urban poor have not benefited equally from the development of towns and cities in developing countries, despite their substantial contribution to them. Relaxing or abandoning many rules and regulations is unlikely, therefore, to cause additional suffering since the poor do not follow existing requirements. However, developing and enforcing regulatory frameworks which the poor themselves consider appropriate could reduce the need for unplanned development and the vulnerability of the poor to exploitation. This will require professionals to listen to and learn from what the poor want and can afford, rather than making arbitrary decisions on their behalf.

Third, what kinds of regulatory frameworks are necessary and what kinds are not? The most relevant principle here is that regulation should be appropriate to the scale of the activity involved and its social, economic, and environmental impact. While a heavily polluting factory should, therefore, be subject to intense scrutiny from municipal and possibly even central government agencies, the opening of a micro-enterprise in a domestic dwelling is a matter primarily for the residents and their immediate neighbours. In the 1970s and 1980s, when the *gecekondus*, or unauthorised settlements, of Ankara were developed by the people who lived in them, it was common for a range of non-residential activities, such as shops and workshops, to operate within the neighbourhood, provided neighbours did not object. Municipal inspectors would intervene only if a number of people living near a particular activity made an official complaint, at which point the planning regulations would then be applied. The more formal subdivisions created by commercial developers since that period have weakened this self-regulating system, although it would seem to represent a reasonable approach in principle. The most important aspects for the development of new urban areas relate to the standards, regulations, and procedures by which the public realm is defined. Emphasis here should be on creating developments in which the maximum proportion of available land is allocated to private, revenue-generating uses, and the minimum area allocated to roads. Second, standards for the initial provision of public utilities should be based on the minimum level essential for permanent occupation of the land or dwelling. These should be designed with a view to the efficient and economic upgrading of utilities as resources become available. Standards and regulations for the development of individual plots should be restricted to aspects concerned with structural safety, such as earthquake resistance; all others should be advisory rather than mandatory, and presented in a form which is easily understood by all social groups. Lastly, procedures should be kept to the absolute minimum and focus on aspects of public concern.

Finally, if formal regulatory regimes are largely ineffective in informal urban communities, what kind of regulation is needed to protect people's well-being? For many situations, it is likely that community management will be the most appropriate level to resolve disputes, assuming that the public realm has been developed in accordance with the criteria outlined above. Recourse to outside agencies or authorities should be regarded as the exception and not the rule.

The above suggestions are based on experience rather than evidence. However, they seek to encourage regulatory frameworks that will enable the urban poor to obtain access to legal shelter and participate actively in the key decisions which affect their lives. Such an inclusive approach will be necessary if cities are to be socially, as well as economically and environmentally, sustainable.

References

Cohen, M. (1992) 'Urban policy and economic development: the agenda', in N. Harris (ed.) *Cities in the 1990s: The Challenge for Developing Countries*, London: UCL Press

Davidson, F. and G. Payne (2000) *Urban Projects Manual* (2nd edn), Liverpool: Liverpool University Press

de Soto, H. (1989) *The Other Path: The Invisible Revolution in the Third World*, London: I.B. Tauris

Dowall, D. and G. Clarke (1991) 'A Framework for Reforming Urban Land Policies in Developing Countries', Urban Management Programme Policy Paper No. 1, Washington, DC: World Bank

Durand-Lasserve, A. (1987) 'Articulation Between Formal and Informal Land Markets in Cities in Developing Countries: Issues and Trends', mimeo.

Farvacque, C. and P. McAuslan (1992)

'Reforming Urban Land Policies and Institutions in Developing Countries', Urban Management Programme Policy Paper No. 5, Washington, DC: World Bank

Intermediate Technology Development Group (ITDG) (2000) *Enabling Housing Standards and Procedures Project: Final Report*, London: Department for International Development (DFID)

Kitay, M.G. (1985) *Land Acquisition in Developing Countries*, Cambridge, MA: Lincoln Institute of Land Policy Studies

Jones, G. and Ward, P.M. (eds)(1994) *Methodology for Land and Housing Market Analysis*, London: UCL Press

McAuslan, P. (1989) 'Land Law, Tenure and Registration Issues and Options', paper presented at Urban Land Development Seminar, Washington, DC: World Bank

Payne, G.K. (1997) *Urban Land Tenure and Property Rights in Developing Countries: A Review,* London: IT Publications

Payne, G.K. (1999) *Making Common Ground: Public–Private Partnerships in Land for Housing,* London: IT Publications

Smolka, M. and F. Sabatini (2000) 'The land market deregulation debate in Chile', *Land Lines* 12 (1): 1–3

Struyk, R., M. Hoffman, and H. Katsura (1990) *The Market for Housing in Indonesian Cities,* Washington, DC: The Urban Institute Press

World Bank (1993) 'Housing: Enabling Markets to Work', World Bank Policy Paper, Washington, DC: World Bank

Cities for the urban poor in Zimbabwe: urban space as a resource for sustainable development

Alison Brown

This paper explores the political, economic, and social processes that influence the development of urban form in cities of the developing world. It argues that urban space in fast-growing cities is undervalued by city officials and, as a result, fails to support the livelihood needs of the urban poor. The lack of recognition of urban space as a critical urban resource, and its potential contribution towards improving the quality of life for the urban poor, is a major constraint on the achievement of sustainable development. The paper draws conclusions from a case study of Harare.

The focus of recent land development in Harare has been on meeting the needs of low-income households for shelter and services. This has led to a quantitative approach to housing provision that focuses on individual housing units. It ignores broader questions of urban environmental quality and performance (Awotona *et al.* 1995), and creates sterile environments, de-emphasising the city's role as a centre for collective life and as a source of livelihood for the urban poor (Dewar 1993; Behrens and Watson 1997). Cities such as Harare must therefore understand their important role in finding and implementing appropriate measures to influence and control the use of public space for these purposes.

The paper first explores the concept of urban space as a framework for the analysis. Using the illustration of Harare, it then examines how the political context has shaped the city, in the pre- and post-independence era. The effects of economic structural change are then considered, including the dramatic increase in urban poverty. The social demands on urban space resulting from economic upheaval, and people's different perceptions of these, are then considered. The last section argues that urban space should be treated as a critical resource, as reflected in significant policy shifts.

Urban space in the context of sustainable development

The physical space of cities is delineated by a complex system of social conventions. Among these are conventions that define different spaces in urban areas as either private or public. Private space is marked by a system of barriers or signs to deter strangers from entering. Public space is the area outside individual or small group control and is usually multi-purpose in function, although the division is not always clear (Madanipour 1999). In this paper, the term 'urban space' is used to encompass all those areas of the urban environment that are not exclusively private, but are in some way shared with others in the community. This may include areas of land in government ownership, such as roads or stream reserves, but may also include other undeveloped or ill-defined spaces.

In densely populated urban areas, many poor households have very restricted access to private space, as a result of small plot sizes, multiple households on plots, and high room occupancy; urban space is an important resource for these households. The space immediately outside the house or shelter forms an extension of living space and a centre for social interaction. More critically, low-income households frequently gain part or all of their income from informal sector activities such as petty trading, manufacture, or urban agriculture, which rely on access to urban space.

In low-density areas, often on the peri-urban fringe, the problems of poor households result not from lack of space in the home, but from the relative isolation of households from urban centres which provide a choice of employment opportunities and a range of facilities for healthcare or education. In this context, urban space becomes a barrier that has to be traversed at considerable cost to the households whose income is insufficient to provide for the cost of public transport.

Two factors are central to understanding the operation of urban space. First, an analysis of the political and economic forces which influence its production and regulation, and, second, an awareness of the social functions of space and people's perceptions of it within the urban environment (Madanipour 1996). The production of urban space is largely influenced by the land and property development process and the financing mechanisms, regulations, and land tenure arrangements of the city's major institutions and groups (central and municipal government, landowners, development agencies, the construction industry, etc.).

The perception of urban space has been explored by designers such as Lynch (1979) and Bentley *et al.* (1985), and others have looked at the cultural forces which shape city form (Dandekar 1998). However, there has been relatively little consideration of the social dimensions which influence how space is perceived and used, or the different meanings attributed to space by different groups in society. Madanipour (1996) argues that environmental awareness depends on social and economic hierarchies, and that our interaction with urban space cannot be fully understood without understanding the social context of urban life. He argues for a socio-spatial approach to urban analysis which identifies the role of space in social interaction.

The adoption of goals for sustainable urban development requires an assessment of the effect of development on both the natural and human environment. This suggests integrated approaches to urban development, which combine social, economic, and environmental considerations, to give equitable access to resources both within and between generations (Haughton and Hunter 1994). In low- and middle-income countries, an important component of sustainable development strategies has been to find ways of increasing the access of low-income groups to land for shelter, by seeking more efficient use of land, or forms of tenure which improve the security of households (UNCHS 1996). It is argued here, however, that land for shelter is only one facet of the land resource so crucial to low-income households, and that land for livelihoods or social interaction is equally necessary in contributing to quality of life.

Political influences on urban space in Harare

The political context in Harare has profoundly influenced the city's physical form and urban space, and the policies of segregation pursued by the settler community are imprinted on the urban fabric. Modern planning has reinforced this historic polarisation, and the former racial divide has become an income divide in the post-independence city. Government housing policies have concentrated on the provision of single-use, low-income housing projects, and have reinforced segregation and created new low-income communities which are isolated on the outskirts of the city.

Harare was established as a settler colony in 1890. The colonial government was concerned to establish a pleasant environment for the settler population, to support the manufacturing base of the new city, and to control the African labour force (Rakodi 1995). The new settlement was built around a small fort and administrative offices for the British South Africa Company, and a cadastral plan was prepared with generous streets laid out on two intersecting grids. The first settlement for African workers was established in 1892, and legislation in 1906 allowed the designation of separate black residential areas, and made it compulsory for all African workers not living at their place of work to live in these locations. In 1907, some 20 ha was allocated for the first African township at Harari (now Mbare), 3 km south of the city centre (Zinyama et al. 1993).

From this time, the city developed along strictly segregated lines. The municipality area, or townlands, was gradually developed for the settler community, and outlying private farms were subdivided into large residential properties, which were attractive because of cheap land, a rural environment, and freedom from municipality rates and controls (Zinyama et al. 1993). The first major subdivision outside the municipal area was at Avondale, 6 km north of the city centre, which was incorporated into the municipality in 1934. Meanwhile the shortage of African housing was becoming acute and, by 1935, an increase in squatters living just outside the city led the government to identify a second township for 2500 people on the state-owned Highfield Farm, about 8 km south-west of the city centre.

The pace of development increased after the Second World War with an influx of new settlers from Europe. Each new suburb was designed according to imported planning fashions of the time, illustrating the 'garden city', 'neighbourhood', and Radburn design concepts (Davison 2000). During the 1950s and 1960s, eight Town Management Boards (later Town Councils), and one Rural Council were set up to administer the outlying areas. During the post-war years, expansion of the urban economy resulted in critical housing shortages for the African population, and employers were required to provide accommodation for workers, while the local authorities built hostels and small family houses for rent in Mbare and Highfield. Where possible, African housing was exported beyond the city limits, and new areas were developed to the south and west of the city including Dzivarasekwa and Kambudzuma in the 1960s, and Glen Norah and Glen View in the 1970s.

Low-income housing

As a result of the struggle for independence in the 1970s, an influx of refugees led to further pressure for housing and the growth of squatter areas to the south of Harare. In 1974 a decision was taken to establish a new town at Chitungwiza some 25 km south of the city beside two established settlements for airport workers. By 1982 the new town had grown to a population of 170,000 (Zinyama 1993), and is now the third largest urban complex in the country.

In Zimbabwe, the supply of land for low-income housing has always been considered as a public sector responsibility and, since independence in 1980, housing policy has aimed to redress the shortage of such through state initiatives, mainly through the provision of serviced plots for home ownership. In the early 1980s work started on several sites and services schemes in Harare, for example Warren Park, Kuwadzana, Hatcliffe, and Budiriro. A decision taken in the late 1970s to sell off the municipal rental stock to sitting tenants was implemented during the first half of the 1980s, when nearly two-thirds was sold (Rakodi 1995).

Unusually for a fast-growing city, Harare's authorities have remained intolerant of informal sector housing. The extensive squatter areas of the late 1970s were all cleared, with little public outcry (Rakodi 1995). New informal settlements are quickly removed and their populations exported to various holding camps, for example Porta Farm, 40 km to the west of the city centre near Lake Chivero. The exception is Epworth, a large settlement on Mission land located 10 km southeast of the city centre, beyond the Harare Municipality boundary, which now accommodates about 50,000 people and is the only regularised squatter area in Harare.

The pressures of rapid urban growth are, however, manifest in high plot occupancy and considerable overcrowding, particularly in low-income areas near the city centre, where the increase of backyard shacks for rent causes considerable social pressures. The social cost of inadequate housing is high. Average occupancy rates in the low-income areas are estimated at about 12 people per unit (Harare City Council Social Survey 1996), but occupancies as high as 27 people living on one stand have been found (unpublished study). Auret (1995) cites problems of family breakdown, increases in crime, threats of assault to and abuse of women, an increase in the number of street children, malnutrition, and high incidences of communicable diseases, which she found to be associated with overcrowding and poor housing.

The population of Harare is now estimated to be about 1.2 million with around 0.7 million in Chitungwiza and a growth rate of around 6 per cent a year. There are about 120,000 low-income households on the City Council's waiting list, and there is a significant shortage of middle-income housing, for which no provision has been made in recent years. Poor households are concentrated in a relatively small sector of the city. At the end of 1997 it was estimated that about 64 per cent of the municipality's total housing stock was in the low-income areas. These house about 75 per cent of the urban population but occupy perhaps a quarter of the municipality area. Some 48 per cent of the population in low-income areas was found to be lodgers, with just over 1000 squatters, although some 12,000 squatters have been relocated to Hatcliffe and others to Porta Farm (Mubvami and Hall 1998).

The land development process

Planning legislation was introduced in 1933 and 1945, ostensibly modelled on the British planning system, but essentially a zoning system operating in the settler areas as a Town Planning Scheme. The standards adopted reflected imported engineering standards for road and infrastructure design, but served to reinforce the cultural divide between the settler minority and the African majority. A regulation that any plot where sewage disposal was by septic tank should be a minimum of 4000 m², reinforced the low-density pattern of settlement, and the subdivision of plots was prohibited. A new planning act in 1976 (amended in 1996) introduced a system of master and local plans, which were extended after independence to cover the township areas.

Designs for African housing were intended to ensure the provision of adequate infrastructure at minimum cost. Research initiated at the end of the 1970s led to the publication in the early 1980s of a series of design manuals, relating to planning standards, building regulations, and water and sewerage designs for the Ministry of Local Government and Housing (Musekiwa 1993; Musandu-Nyamayaro 1993). These documents have had a profound impact on the geometric design and appearance of low-income housing areas and, although now updated, the least-cost philosophy still holds (Davison 2000). Ironically, these manuals perpetuated the separation of low-income housing areas from other sectors of the city, as there is no mixing of plot sizes within the low-income housing schemes.

Urban space in Harare is thus a by-product of the polarised city and its dual planning processes. The overall density of development is extremely low, estimated at 24.7 persons per hectare (about four households per hectare) in the Harare Combination Master Plan in 1989, although this has undoubtedly increased. Wide drainage reserves, or *vleis*, along the streambeds enhance the dislocated character of the settlement and there is almost complete separation of high- and middle-income areas from the low-income communities, which are found mainly in the south-western segment of the city. A study (Swedeplan 1989) estimated that a population of between 141,000 and 354,000 could be accommodated on infill plots in four suburbs alone.

This type of urban layout is completely contrary to the philosophy of sustainable development, which tends to advocate compact cities, mixed-use development and to minimise the use of non-renewable transport resources through high-density construction. In Harare, the segregation of low-income areas from richer suburbs and employment areas, and extremely low densities, severely limits the choice of employment strategies for poor families. The adoption of a philosophy of sustainable development would necessitate a complete rethink of the approach to urban planning and the management of urban space in Harare.

Economic influences on urban space in Harare

Many post-colonial governments inherited economies that were structurally weak, and introduced very little radical change. Trade patterns determined in the colonial period relied on the production and export of raw materials and agricultural produce, which experienced a decline in world market share during the 1970s and 1980s (Rakodi 1995).

Zimbabwe's economy is based on primary production of agricultural produce, and manufacturing. At independence in 1980, the government inherited a controlled economy that had suffered from years of isolation and under-investment during the period of UDI (Unilateral Declaration of Independence) and international sanctions, and a GDP heavily dependent on agricultural production. In addition to foreign exchange and import restrictions, new controls introduced after 1980 included protection of staple foods and wages. In subsequent years, government expenditure rose to over 50 per cent of GDP, mainly as a result of increased spending on health, social services, and infrastructure, partly funded by increased taxation which further undermined the capacity of the private sector to make new investment (Munjoma 1999).

Unusually for Southern Africa, in 1980 the majority of Zimbabwe's urban workforce was employed in the formal economy, partly because a formal sector job had been a condition of urban residence, and partly because planning controls restricted commercial activities on residential plots (Rakodi 1995). By the end of 1980s, rising unemployment, increasing inflation, and difficulties in financing the spiralling budget deficit, led to the recognition of the need for major structural change.

By 1989, the workforce was increasing by about 200,000 school-leavers a year, but the economy was capable of creating only 20–30,000 new jobs annually, mostly in health or education. Unemployment had increased from about 8 per cent at independence to around 26 per cent by the end of the decade. Inflation was running at 11 per cent during most of the 1980s and later increased to 17 per cent, meaning that, with nominal interest rates at about 12 per cent, the real interest rate was negative. Central government debt had reached 71 per cent of GDP in 1989, of which 36 per cent was external. The situation was exacerbated by successive devaluations of the Zimbabwe dollar, and a failure to attract significant foreign investment during the 1980s (Munjoma 1999).

From 1991 to the end of 1995 the government introduced an Economic Structural Adjustment Programme (ESAP) which signalled an end to its 12-year socialist economic policies. The move was broadly supported by the World Bank and the IMF, and the first step in October 1990 was a partial relaxation of import licences, with the full programme introduced in January 1991. The government's objectives were to reduce the budget deficit through: the removal of subsidies; the adoption of appropriate fiscal and monetary policies; the liberalisation of trade to increase exports and imports of manufacturing components; and the removal of controls on prices, labour, and wages. The Zimbabwean approach to structural adjustment also included a focus on employment creation and social welfare, with a programme of cost recovery for social services (Robinson 1991; Nyangulu 1991).

Despite a promising start during 1991, severe drought in 1992 led to an 8 per cent drop in GDP that year, and triggered the country's worst recession since independence. The private sector was unprepared for foreign competition and manufacturing output declined by 20 per cent between 1991 and 1996. Per capita GDP dropped sharply in 1991 to below the 1980 level, and inflation escalated to a staggering 42 per cent in 1992, fuelled by a shortage of agricultural commodities and the phasing out of consumer subsidies. Foreign exchange rates were controlled until 1993, and were regularly adjusted downward to compensate for the gap between Zimbabwe's inflation rate and those of its major trading partners. Exports increased but the cost of imports also rose, further stoking inflation. By 1995–96 the debt burden had risen to 80 per cent of GDP, and debt repayment constituted over 30 per cent of government expenditure.

By the end of ESAP in 1995, per capita GDP and consumption and expenditure on health and education were lower than in 1990. Formal sector employment had grown by only 12,000 new jobs per annum, and virtually none of the ESAP macro-economic targets had been met (Munjoma 1999). In 1996, the government introduced a second round of economic reform, the Zimbabwe Programme for Economic and Social Transformation (ZIMPREST). By 1997, agriculture and forestry still accounted for 19 per cent of GDP and mining and quarrying 2 per cent, while manufacturing had fallen to 18 per cent. Distribution, hotels, and restaurants accounted for 20 per cent. The largest manufacturing sectors are food and drink, metals and metal products, and chemicals and plastics (CSO 1998).

The economy of Harare is very similar to that of the country as a whole. There are two main employment centres in the city, the central area and the large industrial area of Wokington/Southerton in the south-west. Efforts to decentralise industrial production in the 1970s and 1980s to the outlying settlements of Chitungwiza and Norton were not successful.

One of the more surprising results of the ESAP era was a property boom in the city centre between 1991 and 1997, with the development of more than 30 high-quality new office blocks, and an increase of 60 per cent in the amount of office floor space for rent, totalling about 275,000 m^2. Several factors contributed to this growth. First, there was a belief in the long-term improvements in the economy as a result of ESAP, and soaring inflation and negative real interest rates made the money markets unattractive for investment. There were still restrictions on international investment, and tight controls on the remittance of dividends by foreign companies, with the result that cash-rich companies were looking to protect their portfolios through safe investments in the local economy.

Pension and insurance funds were leaders in the investment boom, as a result of progressive relaxation in the amount of discretionary funds they could invest, and about two thirds of the new floor space was built by these institutional investors. By 1996, investment in the commercial office sector had slowed, partly because high interest rates had meant investment returns on the money market reached up to 25 per cent, and were more attractive than the 10 per cent yield from property investment, and partly because of high building costs resulting from high inflation (Munjoma 1999; Matisma 1996; Mugiyo 1996).

The property boom transformed Harare city centre into a modern high-rise city with a dramatic skyline. It also created a powerful lobby among vested interests in promoting continuing control of the urban space of the city centre, retention of high levels of parking, and restriction of informal activities. In 1998, commuter bus services – the minibuses providing low-cost transport – were restricted from stopping on the roadside in the city centre and were relegated to outlying termini, and a one-way system of traffic management was introduced to ease traffic congestion, but did nothing to make it easier for pedestrians to get around.

Social influences on urban space in Harare

ESAP also led to a dramatic and sudden increase in poverty in Harare, and throughout the country. Structural adjustment policies have severe consequences for the urban poor, as removal of consumer subsidies, cuts in government expenditure, and opening the private sector to competition result in a decline in real wages and an increase in unemployment which disproportionately affect poor households. The Zimbabwean experience was no exception.

Faced by the growing poverty crisis, in 1993, the government set up a Poverty Alleviation Action Plan (PAAP). A poverty assessment study carried out in 1996 as part of the programme found that 41 per cent of Harare's population could be classified as 'poor', with incomes below the consumption poverty line (Z$2500 a month, equivalent to US$250),[1] and of these over half were 'very poor' with incomes below the food poverty line (Z$1500 a month, US$150) (Mubvami and Hall 1998). Although urban poverty in Harare is slightly below the national level of 44 per cent, this represents a very significant proportion of the urban population.

A Poverty Action Plan, launched in 1995, led to the Harare City Consultation, a joint initiative between the City Council and the Municipal Development Programme, with technical assistance from the Urban Management Programme of UNCHS (Habitat) in Nairobi. This included community development and social safety nets providing free education and healthcare for the poorest households. The City Council is providing new sites for the informal sector, and the Department of Housing continues to provide serviced plots for allocation to individuals and housing cooperatives.

However, political and economic factors make implementation of any coordinated poverty reduction programme extremely difficult. Harare City Council has operated at a deficit budget for some years – it was Z$732.6 million (US$30.7 million) in 1998 – and has now adopted a financial recovery programme (Mubvami and Hall 1998). In 1999 the council was suspended for corruption, and the city is being run directly by a government minister. The national economy is being crippled by war and disputes over land reform, and political unrest prior to and in the aftermath of the June 2000 election has caused a drastic loss of confidence in the national economy, and led to further devaluation of the Zimbabwe dollar.

Increased poverty creates new and competing pressures on urban space, largely because of the increase in informal sector business and trading, much of which takes place in the street or on undeveloped land. It is difficult to estimate the level of informal sector activity in Harare, as the available figures are conflicting, but there has undoubtedly been a significant increase since 1991. Census figures in 1992 indicated that only 8 per cent of the 500,000 economically active people in Harare Urban Area were working in the informal sector, with 70 per cent formally employed and 20 per cent unemployed, but this is likely to be an underestimate (GoZ 1992). By the mid-1990s, the City Council's research section estimated that the proportion of people in formal sector employment in the city had dropped to 35 per cent, largely as a result of ESAP (Mubvami and Hall 1998). A study in the low-income areas of Dzivarasekwa and Tafara found that the majority of residents employed in the formal sector earned wages below the food poverty line, that unemployment, redundancies, and low pay were seen as the main causes of poverty, and that some 94 per cent of households in the study were engaged in vending, and 50 per cent in urban agriculture (Matshalaga 1997).

Various recent studies highlight the characteristics of the informal sector in Harare. There is a sharp gender division of labour with women predominating in the petty retail trade, particularly in the least profitable sector of fruit and vegetables (Nachudwa 1995; Matemba 1996). There are various specialist retail sectors such as the sale of building materials (Brown 2000) or metal construction materials

(Nangati 1995). Within the production sector there is a preponderance of operators in activities such as carpentry and basketwork, but products also include clothing, shoes, tinsmithing, and mattress-making (Mupedziswa 1994). Services include activities such as hair-cutting, mending watches, electrical repairs, welding, and auto repairs.

City centre operators tend to focus on consumer goods and earn rather higher incomes than elsewhere in the city. In 1998, the City Council estimated that about 1000 informal traders operated in the city centre (Mubvami and Hall 1998), most in designated flea market locations. A survey in 1997 of 40 traders in six flea markets in the city centre found that 70 per cent had joined this business between 1995 and 1997 (Chikaya 1997). These regulated city centre markets are not allowed to sell food, and concentrate on clothing, cassettes, tapes, and kitchenware, with considerable numbers importing goods from South Africa, Botswana, or Zambia, and second-hand clothes from Zambia or Mozambique. Daily rents varied between Z$10 (US$0.8) in peripheral locations to Z$150 (US$12) in prime locations, but earnings were comparatively high, ranging from Z$500 (US$41) to Z$2000 (US$166) a week.

While the difficulty of raising capital is the single most pressing problem facing informal sector businesses, lack of reliable and secure premises from which to operate is also a serious constraint, particularly for those conducting their business in the open. The problems of trading in the sun or rain, with consequent damage to goods, are compounded by lack of security for capital equipment (such as welding machines), goods or takings, and harassment by the police and municipal authorities. Even in the city centre, markets are overcrowded, with a lack of toilets, water taps, and lock-up facilities (Mupedziswa 1994; Chikaya 1997). Most traders have to pack up their goods at the end of the day, but the small minibuses – the cheapest form of urban transport – will not transport them and their goods, thus forcing them to hire expensive taxis (Auret 1995).

Perceptions of urban space in Zimbabwe

Preliminary views on people's perceptions of the urban environment were obtained from two pilot studies using street interviews carried out in the late 1990s in the city centre, and in Machipisa, the main shopping centre at Highfield, a low-income housing area about 8 km south-west of the centre (Brown 2000). The studies found considerable concern about the deteriorating street environment and increasing pressures on urban space, particularly the increase in informal trading, poor street environment for pedestrians, and escalating street crime.

In the centre, attitudes are polarised between those who want to see an orderly, managed environment symbolic of a city centre, and those trying to make a livelihood. People's perceptions of urban space differed significantly depending on their employment status, reasons for being in the city centre, and where the interview took place. Some valued the smart, more upmarket character of the eastern part of the city centre, while others were concerned about the difficulty of negotiating the western area as a pedestrian, and environmental factors such as traffic, noise, dirt, and the problems of pickpockets and street kids.

Attitudes surrounding the informal sector were conflicting. Hawkers themselves resented police harassment, and petty pilfering of goods. They would prefer locations near the main tide of pedestrian flow, and shelter for the rainy season. Some people saw hawkers as part of the wider problem of poverty, and considered that the locations of stalls should continue to be strictly controlled. In the city centre, an interesting example of informal management of urban space can be seen in the management of parking meters by street children. This occurs in several locations and improved management of this system has been proposed as a way of both improving the income of the street children and improving the management of parking facilities (Nyamvura 2000).

The suburban shopping area of Machipisa has a very different function from the city centre and perceptions differed significantly. The area was laid out, probably in the 1970s, according to planning principles of the time. It covers approximately 15 ha and includes 96 designated commercial plots, many of which are subdivided, selling a mixture of food, clothing, electrical and other goods (Ndhlovu 1999). The local plan (City of Harare 1990) allows for expansion of the shopping centre by relocating the bus terminus to the other side of the road, a policy implemented in 1999. The plan also estimates that the surrounding area of Highfield had a population of 98,500, living in 15,200 residential units, half of which had been constructed without planning permission. Of the total population, 38,500 people (39 per cent) were found to be renting, many of those (26,200 people) living in illegal outbuildings.

Preliminary conclusions from the Machipisa study indicate that it caters for a local catchment, with 39 per cent of those interviewed walking to the centre and 42 per cent travelling by commuter bus.

The proportion of people walking to the centre is extremely high, probably because lower-income groups cannot afford public transport fares. It is perceived as a modern employment, leisure, and service centre, with a good range of shops. Several people described its character as 'beautiful', although others felt that it had 'nothing' to commend it, citing problems of dilapidated buildings or crime. Good transport services and its accessibility play a significant role in its attraction. Leisure activities were also an attraction – including the beer halls, turf club, sports facilities, and library.

As in the city centre, hawkers were the subject of conflicting opinions. There was a division between those who do not like the proliferation of the informal sector because the traders are thought to exacerbate pavement congestion and crime, and those who consider the main problem to be the lack of organisation of, and facilities for, informal traders. Traders themselves are concerned about the lack of toilets, water taps, and shade. There are degrees of informality within the area, and in one market stallholders with municipality licences sublet to about eight or nine tenants, making profits of ten times the licence fee. Even on the pavements there are those who consider themselves 'established' – regular traders who trade from tables at the same pitch each day – and 'newcomers' – resented by the more established group, many of whom sell vegetables from plastic sheets on the ground. There are periodic confiscations of goods by the City Council and the police, particularly of fruit or vegetables, a phenomenon that was reported to be worse when foreign dignitaries arrive.

Thieves and petty pilfering are serious problems. There seem to be two facets to this: first, pickpockets who target shoppers and, second, stealing from the informal traders, who lose either goods or money if their attention is distracted. This is a particular problem for informal traders who are operating on their own. Interestingly, a specialist plumbing and electrical market located in an enclosed compound north of the main centre has very little petty crime. Set around four sides of a rectangle, it has only two entrances and forms a safe enclave where stallholders watch out for each other's goods. Customers may park their vehicles unlocked in the compound, and traders leave their wares in the stall at night, supervised by a private night watchman. Pilfering, however, occurs outside the compound, although the presence of a police post in the vicinity is thought to improve security.

Dirt and noise were also major issues of concern. Poor refuse collection in the shopping area, and a broken sewer in one of the unpaved service streets, were mentioned. People are also concerned about environmental problems, mentioning the lack of drinking fountains, toilets, shade, shelter, and need for places to sit, and the dilapidated appearance of the centre.

Policy implications

Urban space is a scarce resource which cannot be ignored in the context of the debate on sustainable development. In many cities, public space occupies about 20 per cent of the urban realm – in Harare it is probably more – and has many competing functions: as a channel for communications, source of livelihood, or place for social interaction. It is a crucial resource for poor households, particularly those engaged in informal sector employment who suffer from harassment, crime, insecurity of trading location, lack of shelter, and lack of facilities. Yet planning regulations, economic development decisions, and highway improvements create physical spaces that take no account of the needs of the poor, while municipal policing and control inhibit the legitimate attempts of poor households to support themselves.

This paper has shown how the political influences which shaped the development of Harare, compounded by modern-day planning policies, have resulted in a polarised city, where the urban poor are segregated in low-income, single-use ghettos, without the employment opportunities that mixed neighbourhoods have. Many of these suburbs are located so far from centres of employment that travel costs make access to all but local employment facilities prohibitive. Economic structural adjustment policies in Harare have resulted in a city centre environment where greater control of the street is espoused, and has had profound social consequences in the escalating scale of urban poverty. The breakdown in municipal management, which has occurred as a result of the economic crisis and chronic mismanagement, has left a vacuum where crime flourishes and there is little support for the legitimate self-help efforts of the urban poor.

The policy implications of viewing urban space as a crucial resource are considerable. At the city-wide scale, there is scope for allowing building at higher densities, mixed-income neighbourhoods, and more provision for informal activities. The potential for infill development on reserved land should also be explored. At the local level, administrative measures to improve the management of existing space could be explored, in particular the scope for informal arrangements such as those made by the traders in the plumbing and electrical market in

Machipisa. The idea of parking meters supervised by street children in the city centre could also be explored.

There is considerable potential for improving trading facilities for the informal sector, not least by removing the haphazard and indiscriminate confiscation of goods. The aim could be to allow those who at present operate illegally to make a small increment in security and level of formality, to a point where they are happy to pay rent, which can be used to fund further management initiatives. More detailed information would be required on informal trading, including levels of informality, specialisation of trade, sources of supply, storage of goods, and security, before any detailed proposals could be framed. The focus of future policy may be on relaxing current regulations, appropriate planning guidance, and innovative management measures to support informal trading initiatives and reduce crime.

A further policy initiative is to consider the importance of walking as a mode of transport in urban contexts. In poor cities, where a large majority of the population walks, either as the principal way of getting around or to and from public transport, the effect of insensitive traffic management or poorly located bus stations is considerable, and is borne largely by the urban poor. Mechanisms could be sought for levering private funding for local improvements of facilities, such as the supermarket in Machipisa, which funded provision of the new bus station.

This paper has shown how, in Harare, the failure of official policy and regulations which affect urban space to recognise the needs of low-income population groups inhibits these people's ability to help themselves. Planning is seen as a rigid set of standards and urban space is a by-product of the planning process, not a resource in its own right. The standards reinforce the structural segregation built into the urban system, and the process of forward planning merely seeks to reinforce the status quo. While NGOs in the cooperative movement are working closely on participatory methodologies for housing provision, this approach is not widely used elsewhere to assess the impact of planning policies on the urban poor. The scope for working with communities to respond to current development pressures is considerable, and still largely unexplored.

Acknowledgement

This article is based on findings from a UK Government Department for International Development (DFID)-funded link with the Department of Rural and Urban Planning (DRUP) at the University of Zimbabwe. Particular thanks are due to Celia Davison and Trynos Nyamvura at DRUP in compiling this information.

Note

1 Between January 1996 and November 2000 the exchange rate has plummeted, from a low in 1996 of US$1 = Z$9 to US$1 = Z$55.

References

Auret, D. (1995) *Urban Housing – A National Crisis*, Harare: Catholic Commission for Justice and Peace in Zimbabwe

Awotona, A., M. Brigss, and L. le Grange (1995) 'Approaches to human settlement development: implications for research into upgrading of South African townships', Working Paper No. 3, *The Integration and Urbanisation of Existing Townships in the Republic of South Africa*, Newcastle upon Tyne: Centre for Architectural Research and Development Overseas, University of Newcastle upon Tyne, UK; and Cape Town, South Africa: School of Architecture and Planning, University of Cape Town

Behrens, R. and V. Watson (1997) *Marking Urban Places. Principle Guidelines for Layout Planning*, Cape Town: UCT Press

Bentley I., A. Alcock, P. Murain *et al.* (1985) *Responsive Environments: A Manual for Designers*, Oxford: Butterworth Architectural

Brown, A. (2000) 'Cities for People in Zimbabwe: Working Paper on Urban Space Design in a Developing Country City', paper presented at the N-AERUS/UNRISD conference 'Cities of the South: Sustainable for Whom?', 3–5 May, Geneva

Chikaya, O. (1997) 'Flea Markets: Dynamics as a Possible Alternative in the Urban Economy', unpublished dissertation, Harare: Department of Rural and Urban Planning, University of Zimbabwe

City of Harare (1990) *Highfield Local Development Plan No. 18*, Harare: Harare City Council

CSO (1998) *Zimbabwe Facts & Figures*, Harare: Central Statistical Office

Dandekar, H. (1998) *City Space and Globalization: An International Perspective*, Ann Arbor: College of Architecture and Urban Planning, University of Michigan

Davison, C. (2000) *An Evaluation of Existing Residential Layout Designs, Approaches in Zimbabwe and Suggestions for an Alternative Approach*, Harare: Department of Rural and Urban Planning, University of Zimbabwe

Dewar, D. (1993) 'Urban Housing in Southern Africa: the Need for a Paradigm Shift', paper presented at the '2nd Symposium on Housing for the Urban Poor – Housing, Poverty and Developing Countries', Birmingham, UK

Government of Zimbabwe (GoZ) (1992) *Zimbabwe National Census Report 1992*, Harare: Central Statistical Office

Haughton, G. and C. Hunter (1994) *Sustainable Cities*, London: Jessica Kingsley

Lynch, K. (1979) *The Image of the City*, Cambridge, MA: MIT Press.

Madanipour, A. (1996) *Design of Urban Space: An Inquiry into a Social-spatial Process*, Chichester: John Wiley

Madanipour, A. (1999) 'Why are the design and development of public spaces significant for cities?', *Environment and Planning B, Planning and Design* 26: 876–91

Matemba, J. (1996) 'The Study of Informal Economic Activities in Mbare with Special Reference to Vending Activities, as a Creative Alternative to Unemployment', unpublished dissertation, Harare: Department of Rural and Urban Planning, University of Zimbabwe

Matisma, K. (1996) 'Major Trends in Commercial Office Development, 1990–1995', unpublished dissertation, Harare: Department of Rural and Urban Planning, University of Zimbabwe

Matshalaga, N. (1997) *The Gender Dimensions of Urban Poverty: The Case of Tafara*, Harare: Institute of Development Studies, University of Zimbabwe

Mubvami, T. and N. Hall (1998) *Harare City Consultation on Urban Poverty*, Harare: School of Social Work

Mugiyo, I. (1996) 'The Role of Insurance Companies and Pension Funds in the Commercial Property Market: a Case Study of Harare', unpublished dissertation, Harare: Department of Rural and Urban Planning, University of Zimbabwe

Munjoma, T. (1999) 'Property Investment Under an Economic Structural Adjustment Programme: the Case of the Harare Central Business District Office Development', unpublished PhD thesis, Aberdeen: Department of Land Economy, University of Aberdeen

Mupedziswa, R. (1994) *The Informal Sector and Employment in Zimbabwe: A Study of Small Scale Production Enterprises in the Greater Harare Area*, Harare: School of Social Work

Musandu-Nyamayaro, O. (1993) 'Housing design standards for urban low-income people in Zimbabwe', *Third World Planning Review* 15(4): 329–54

Musekiwa, A. (1993) 'Low-income house development in Harare: a historical perspective', in L. Zinyama *et al.* (eds) *Harare: The Growth and Problems of the City*, Harare: University of Zimbabwe

Nachudwa, D. (1995) 'Women in micro-enterprises: the case of Mbare, Zimbabwe', in S. Sithole-Fundire *et al.* (eds) *Gender Research on Urbanization, Planning, Housing and Everyday Life, Phase 1*, Harare: Zimbabwe Women's Resource Centre and Network

Nangati, F. (1995) 'An Assessment of the Viability of Informal Sector Enterprises: a Study of the Production and Marketing of Metal Construction Materials in Harare', unpublished dissertation, Harare: Department of Rural and Urban Planning, University of Zimbabwe

Ndhlovu, S. (1999) 'Report on Machipisa Shopping Centre', unpublished student project, Harare: Department of Rural and Urban Planning, University of Zimbabwe

Nyamvura, T. (2000) 'Study of Parking in Harare CBD', unpublished report, Harare: Department of Rural and Urban Planning, University of Zimbabwe

Nyangulu, N. (1991) 'The social cost of economic reforms and structural adjustment in Zimbabwe', in *The Social Implications of Structural Adjustment Programmes in Africa*, presentations and edited proceedings of a workshop held at University of Zimbabwe, Harare

Rakodi, C. (1995) *Harare: Inheriting a Settler-colonial City: Change or Continuity?*, Chichester: John Wiley

Robinson, P. (1991) 'What is structural adjustment?', in *The Social Implications of Structural Adjustment Programmes in Africa*, presentations and edited proceedings of a workshop held at University of Zimbabwe, Harare

Swedeplan (1989) *Harare Infilling Study*, Harare: Department of Physical Planning, Ministry of Local Government, Rural and Urban Development

United Nations Centre for Human Settlements (UNCHS) [Habitat] (1996) *An Urbanizing World: Global Report on Human Settlements*, Oxford: Oxford University Press

Zinyama, L., D. Tevera, and S. Cumming (eds) (1993) *Harare: The Growth and Problems of the City*, Harare: University of Zimbabwe

Innovations for sustainable development in cities of the South: the Habitat-Cuba approach

Carlos García Pleyán

It is well known that the Cuban Revolution has provided broad and equitable access to national systems of education, health, employment, social security, cultural, sport, recreation, and so on. After a traumatic start to the 1990s, when the country was left without commercial, financial, technological, political, or military backing or aid, Cubans nevertheless managed to survive and began to establish their own direction in a particularly adverse global context. Cuba's rapid insertion into a neo-liberal form of globalisation is now having social, cultural, and economic impacts. As was to be expected, the development of commercial relations has begun to generate inequalities in our cities, at the human level, as well as in the physical and practical sense. We need to find effective ways to neutralise this process.

However, the crisis also helped us to realise that the existing development model was unsustainable. It is becoming clearer that for social policies to be completely subsidised from the centre is, quite simply, unfeasible. We now know that technologies that are based on the excessive consumption of energy, that are not economically viable, that tend to destroy the natural environment, and lead to unsatisfactory buildings and other constructions, are totally inappropriate. In addition, they tend to generate a welfare mentality which paralyses initiative and creativity.

Housing is an area in which the technological approach has been especially inappropriate, both environmentally and culturally, because standardised production does not take local conditions into account. Architectural and urban planning solutions that might be acceptable in cold climates in countries with large reserves of energy have been singularly out of place in the Cuban context.

On the other hand, even if social programmes could achieve blanket coverage, the sheer cost of maintaining the essential housing programme forced the government to make a choice. The decision was to provide housing to workers who were involved in government job-creation programmes (agriculture, industry, tourism, science, etc.). The needs of new couples, of immigrants from the countryside to the towns, or from one province to another, of private sector employees, or workers in the informal sector, had to be deferred. In most such cases, these needs were met through the individual's own efforts. Looking back over the last 40 years, approximately half of all housing has been built by the residents themselves.

Such is the background behind the emergence of organisations like Habitat-Cuba: a group of professionals, most of whom have worked in state institutions involved with urban planning, urban design, and housing, who have come together with a view to trying to change the approach and mentality concerning the way in which the urban environment is created and transformed. Habitat-Cuba indeed aims to become a centre of technological and cultural innovation.

This innovation is founded upon three pillars: supporting the conscious participation by the residents of low-income neighbourhoods in changing their surroundings; encouraging them to think of economic, cultural, and environmental solutions that are sustainable; and stimulating greater interaction and co-operation among all the relevant social actors.

I should emphasise that Habitat-Cuba's approach is not simply a methodological approach (that is, a specific path to follow in order to reach a given end) but rather an attempt to accompany the process through means of an institutional strategy that will reveal within any given context not just *what* to do but *how* and *with whom*. Habitat-Cuba therefore seeks to serve as an intermediary that can articulate and draw together the traditional state approach to housing and residents' self-help initiatives.

The housing problem is a complex matter that involves a range of actors. The three most important of these, each of them having its own approaches and visions, are the state (represented by local government institutions which take decisions on the deployment of resources), urban professionals (who supposedly provide appropriate solutions), and the community, or the people experiencing the problem. Traditionally, the housing question in Cuba has revolved around two kinds of activity. On the one hand, people have been solving their own problems in isolation from the other two actors (i.e. often without any technical help, without legal title, and without access to credit). On the other hand, the state has had the capacity to combine material and financial resources with technical help, but without adequately involving the affected population in meeting their needs – except, that is, as part of the workforce. Habitat-Cuba seeks to facilitate the integration of these three actors in transforming the urban environment, something that demands that we work very closely with each of them.

First, we try to encourage residents of low-income neighbourhoods genuinely to 'own' whatever technical solutions are adopted. This can only be done if the community participates fully in everything, including how they conceive of the neighbourhood and how they view housing needs. It is vital that any solutions respond both to social demands but also to the natural and human environment. This implies community participation not only in the implementation phase, but also in the diagnosis of the problem and in the generation of ideas to address it. We need to find ways to ensure that people's initiatives become more sustainable while the community also becomes more autonomous. In other words, moving from social architecture to the social management of architecture.

Second, it is a question of discovering ways of achieving stable co-operation and dialogue among public institutions that permit them to 'own' their new methods of working and to do things in ways that can be replicated by the bodies responsible for deploying state resources. To do this, these institutions must not merely modify their use of technology – using local materials and technologies adapted to the problems and resources of each locality – but also facilitate local participation.

Third, professionals in the urban sector – mainly architects and engineers – need to understand that it is not just a question of putting up buildings, but that in the process of transforming the urban landscape they are also building communities in the sense of social relations, be that co-operation, representation, or exchange. Moreover, that in the process of building individual houses, we are contributing to the construction (or destruction) of much broader physical and social spaces, i.e. neighbourhoods and cities. We need to think globally but act locally, moving nimbly back and forth between urban architecture on a city-wide scale right down to the local neighbourhood.

But changing the habits and behaviours of each of the different actors is not enough. There are also various general principles that should guide our work:

- To achieve effective co-operation, it is critical to try to harmonise the distinct *timescales* in which each participant thinks and acts: technicians, aid agencies, residents, public institutions. Each one of these tends to have a distinct perception of the necessary and realistic rhythms at which the various processes can evolve, and this is something that constantly gives rise to misunderstandings. It is therefore important to make the effort to inform and explain to all parties in such a way that each can understand what may be perceived by the other as unjustified pressures either to rush ahead or to delay work. Residents are often exasperated by the slow pace of planning and project implementation processes, while technical experts also become restless with the necessarily slow pace of participatory processes.

- It is essential to understand the potential significance of these experiences from three different angles: from that of research (which permits us to reflect upon and learn from our successes and failures); from that of concrete actions (without which the local population sees no point in the process); and from the perspective of training (which allows knowledge to be passed on and so contributes to the creation of culture).

- It is equally important to have an appropriate understanding of the role of international co-operation projects. These should be situated within a programmatic framework that gives them meaning, and these same programmes must also fit into an institutional strategy. The purpose is not just to resolve the housing problem, but also to develop new ways of working. Thus, projects should not become ends in themselves, but rather serve as demonstrations of the principles mentioned above: environmental sustainability, appropriate technology, community participation, and inter-institutional co-operation.

Finally, one of the greatest challenges facing initiatives like Habitat-Cuba is to generate activities that are both replicable and sustainable. It is not enough to be innovative if this technological input has no real social impact. We therefore need, first, to confront institutional inertia directly and to engage in a process of trying to convince the state entities – which, in the case of Cuba, assume responsibilities the length and breadth of the country – by combining good arguments and concrete actions. Second, we need to build firm bridges that will allow new generations of students (as well as their teachers) to live these experiences in the flesh, as it were, and so bring new life to the closed world of academia. Finally, we must learn to discover, together with ordinary people, ways that will enable them to assume their role in these processes, without being either manipulated or abandoned.

What role for European scientific co-operation in this context? It is clear that any proposal should be jointly designed by those offering and those receiving such assistance. But it will play a significant role only if it addresses certain questions: what are we willing to give up, not so much in the material sense but in terms of culture? To what extent are we really helping others, or in fact helping ourselves? How should we approach the enormous economic and financial imbalances between the two sides of such a partnership? How can we avoid reading the South with dictionaries and grammars of the North, and vice versa? How, for instance, can a population that is not itself protected go about protecting the natural environment? Do we want just to transfer experiences or resources, or are we looking for mutual exchange? Co-operation with the South: sustainable for whom?

Experience to date suggests at least three essential concerns: first, that in order to achieve sustainable results, international co-operation needs to be willing to collaborate over the long term and to be firmly rooted in the local context. Second, technical or cultural exchange needs to be two-way, allowing for a fluid dialogue based on mutual knowledge or recognition of the scientific, social, and institutional context of each party. And third, this collaboration needs to be framed in integrated programmes based on combined actions in development, in research, and in training. There is no other way to be sustainable.

Private–public partnership, the compact city, and social housing:
best practice for whom?

Fernando Murillo

The *Casa Propia* (Own Home) programme of the Buenos Aires City Government (BACG) is an innovative if controversial case of public–private financing of social housing. The programme aims to encourage the private sector to build housing on private land for sale to low-income buyers, who receive 'soft' credits from the state. The *Casa Propia* experience suggests that, in Argentina, the absence of consolidated *redes de contención social* (social contingency networks) has resulted in a housing programme that emphasises financial viability over social and environmental concerns.[1] Negative social and environmental impacts arise from this neglect.

Buenos Aires and its social housing production

The 12 million residents of the Greater Buenos Aires metropolitan region account for 40 per cent of Argentina's population. In the densely populated city of Buenos Aires, home to three million of the metropolitan area's residents, approximately 15 per cent of the population is in need of housing. Of these, some 51 per cent are low-income households (average monthly incomes below US$1000), 34 per cent lower-middle-income households (monthly incomes between US$1000 and US$2000), and 15 per cent middle-income households (monthly incomes between US$2000 and US$3000) (Gobierno de la Ciudad de Buenos Aires 1998).

In response to a severe shortage of land available for public (social) housing, the local government decided to increase population densities in selected areas and new regulations permitting the construction of high-rise buildings have been adopted to facilitate this. The approach being applied to such zones is generating a process of rapid urban renewal, resulting in the more 'compact city' sought by planners. Public or low-income housing schemes have been developed to further this aim. Prominent among them is the *Casa Propia* programme.

Casa Propia: **the search for a sustainable housing policy**

Casa Propia was the brainchild of Fernando De la Rúa, formerly president of the Republic of Argentina, while he was Head of the Autonomous Government of Buenos Aires in 1996. At that time he established the *Casa Propia* programme with the idea of improving the levels of efficiency and transparency in the management of public funds for social housing, while promoting development in a low-density sector in the southern region of Buenos Aires where land costs had been relatively low. Although created independently of the Municipal Commission for Social Housing (*Comisión Municipal de la Vivienda*, or CMV), the traditional developer and manager of the city's social housing, *Casa Propia* has been integrated into the CMV. From a social housing perspective, however, the two programmes have yet to be integrated. This article describes why this has been difficult to achieve.

The hypothesis of *Casa Propia* is that social housing provided through the market tends to be sustainable and to enhance the conditions of the private market. Private capital and land may thus benefit efforts to implement public policy, and enhance the choices for 'buyers' in the housing market. At the same time, efforts by the BACG to increase densities within the city – which may be perceived as contributing to 'ecological sustainability' – generate a set of competitive advantages for real estate investors. Among these is the possibility of offering lower prices and attracting lower-income buyers into the market. *Casa Propia* proposes that the financial sustainability of the programme be complemented by social and environmental sustainability, by including the lower-income brackets and renewing degraded areas at the same time.

Casa Propia **as an example of 'best practice'**

As initially proposed, *Casa Propia* was designed to provide subsidised housing to low-income groups through a range of innovative mechanisms and approaches to urban development. The programme drew its inspiration for financing from the World Bank, which in a special mission to the city, urged the local government to develop *Casa Propia* as a model of public–private partnership in order to achieve financial sustainability of a social housing programme. Other principles for best practices in housing, such as those promoted by the United Nations Centre for Human Settlements (UNCHS), especially those relating to social integration, bear comparison with the overriding concern for financial sustainability and accountability of the programme listed below: [2]

- *Public–private partnership*: By combining funds from FONAVI (Fondo Nacional de la Vivienda – National Housing Fund), CMV, and private banks, *Casa Propia* would increase the overall availability of housing in the sector.

- *Impact*: *Casa Propia* was intended to stimulate development in the southern area of Buenos Aires, traditionally less privileged than more central districts.

- *Sustainability*: financial sustainability was expected to result from creating a long-term profitable market for construction companies. By limiting the number of units per building, administrative and operational costs would be kept low for the residents, also enhancing the sustainability of the project. Social sustainability was to be achieved by the use of housing designs that would avoid the stigma usually attached to public housing.

- *Transparency*: a Project Evaluation Committee comprising different organisations ensured that the project met construction regulations, fiduciary responsibility, and regulations imposed specifically by *Casa Propia*, including free selection by purchasers of apartments from among different designs and locations.

- *Leadership*: the potential for replicability of the initiative should lead to new projects and programmes locally and elsewhere.

- *Community empowerment*: the programme envisages the increase of access to housing for disabled people and vulnerable groups.

As implemented, *Casa Propia* provides housing for families in the lower end of the middle-income bracket, rather than lower-income groups *per se*: households with a monthly income of less than US$2000 are covered by Programme 001 (version a or b);[3] those with more than that amount are covered by Programme 102. Programme 001 entitles purchasers to receive loans from public sources (FONAVI and CMV) covering, respectively, 80 per cent of the purchase price at a fixed interest rate of 4 per cent over 20 years. The purchaser is responsible for the down payment of 20 per cent. But many *Casa Propia* 001 participants receive a loan equal to 5 per cent of the purchase price to use as part of the down payment. This loan also comes from FONAVI/CMV, with a 4 per cent interest rate. By contrast, *Casa Propia* 102 is financed entirely with private funds, 80 per cent from banks at an average of 13 per cent over 20 years and 20 per cent as a down payment from the buyer. Each operation targets different income groups: the upper price (for construction and plot) for option 102 is US$825/m². Option 001 offers two alternatives, US$750/m² and US$775/m².

In both cases (001 and 102) the interest rates are below the prevailing market rate of 15 per cent. But the difference in interest rate between the two is substantial (compare 4 per cent for 001 and a variable but average rate of 13 per cent for 102). Given that the difference in income of the two eligible groups is in practice only a few pesos, the lack of intermediate interest rates and loan durations is difficult to justify.

Comparative analysis of projects produced by *Casa Propia*, CMV, and the free market

To understand how *Casa Propia* compares with operations managed by the CMV and the free market, we cite four kinds of data: production costs, selling price, monthly mortgage payments, and income levels of target groups.

The selling prices, which reflect the total cost of land, planning, and construction for the different operations within *Casa Propia* are shown in Table 1, column 3. A comparison of the maximum price for 001 apartments to those of 102 reveals a difference of approximately 7 per cent between the selling prices of apartments involving official financing and those without. The difference is even smaller for similar-sized apartments available in the open market.

Columns 5–7 in Table 1 show the important impact of interest rates on finance costs and mortgage payments on apartments with roughly similar purchase prices. Total payments, the sum of the selling price plus interest costs, under *Casa Propia* 001 are some 55 per cent less than those of 102, which are in turn nearly 15 per cent less than payments made on fully open market purchases with prevailing interest rates. The impact of these are seen in column 7, which lists the monthly mortgage payments under each alternative, and column 8, which lists the income levels of which the share of mortgage payments would not exceed 30 per cent, the CMV standard for low-income housing. Thus only the one- and two-room apartments with fully subsidised interest rates are affordable to families with monthly incomes below the US$2000 barrier.

Because *Casa Propia* established no mechanisms to make more of its apartments affordable to lower-income groups, the programme as

Scheme	No. of rooms (area: m²)	Production cost/price	Interest rate (%)	Finance costs	Total (price + interest)	Monthly mortgage payment (30%)	Monthly payment ÷ income
Casa Propia 001a and 001b	1 (35)	33,750 34,875	80%: 4 15%:down payment† 5%: 4	10,800 5568 **16,368**	50,118	417	1392
	2 (42)	45,000 46,500	As above	14,400 7425 **21,825**	66,825	556	1856
	3 (60)	60,000 62,000	As above	19,200 9900 **29,100**	89,100	742	2473
102	1 (35)	37,125	11–13	40,837	77,962	649	2163
	2 (42)	49,550	11–13	54,505	104,055	867	2890
	3 (60)	66,000	11–13	72,600	138,600	1155	3850
CMV	2	–	4	–	–	251	836
	3	–	4	–	–	320	1066
Open market	1 (35)	35,000	15	52,500	87,500	729	2430
	2 (45)	48,000	15	72,000	120,000	1000	3333
	3 (65)	62,000	15	93,000	155,000	1291	4305

Table 1: Relationship between income of purchasers and cost per housing unit*

*As the Argentine peso was equivalent in value to the US dollar at the time of data collection, all sums of money apply to either currency.
†Down payments are US$1600, US$2250, and US$3000, respectively, for the three types of Casa Propia apartment.
Sources: documents and publicity brochures for the Casa Propia programme (GCBA1999); brochures, project documents, and reports of the CMV programme, *Terreno, Proyecto y Construcción*; data published in the magazine *Mundo Inmobiliario*.

a whole tends to benefit only those groups occupying the top of the lower-middle-income category, i.e. those just reaching the middle-income category. Because *Casa Propia* operations 001 and 102 were designed and constructed by the private sector on privately owned land, they responded to the incentive to recover the highest costs feasible within the target income groups, i.e. those on either side of the US$2000 per month barrier. This process effectively priced groups with less buying power – even US$1500 per month – out of these operations.

In retrospect, other perverse effects (from the programme designer's perspective, not that of the construction companies) could be seen in a number of the operations in the southern area of the city. There, private developers of *Casa Propia* projects decided not to sell to beneficiaries of FONAVI's soft credits. By excluding buyers such as these, the developers would not be subject to a cap on maximum apartment sizes and purchase prices. This regulation could be circumvented If sales were only to buyers of the fully market-led 102 category of apartments. For the developers, the additional advantage was that the city channelled buyers in sufficient quantity and facilitated their purchases by providing loan guarantees to private lenders. This actually expanded the lower end of the home-buying market, as private banks on their own rarely made loans to this income sector.

In comparison with other low-income housing programmes operated by CMV, mortgage payments under *Casa Propia* 001 are considerably higher (column 8). Yet because CMV housing is limited, *Casa Propia* opens up access to low fixed interest rate loans over a relatively long term that would not otherwise be available, and may even have helped to improve the access of low-income borrowers to better loan terms in the private market. At the same time, CMV and *Casa Propia* target groups do theoretically overlap, creating competition between the two. However, because CMV housing tends to be physically less attractive – and has been stigmatised as 'public housing' – the lower income groups are in practice relegated to CMV housing. *Casa Propia* buyers also have an advantage that CMV buyers do not have: that of choosing their apartment from among all those on offer.[4]

Other factors in the *Casa Propia* social cost-benefit analysis

The preceding section identifies the most important shortcoming of the *Casa Propia* programme, i.e. that it is essentially serving middle-income families, the least vulnerable members of the housing deficit group. The following paragraphs highlight briefly some preliminary observations of the other innovative aspects of the programme that may be considered in the overall evaluation of *Casa Propia*.

While *Casa Propia* does appear to have induced the private sector to produce housing for the non-rich, it has not increased the supply of housing for lower-income groups. Nor has the city proved that the market can serve this sector of the population. The conclusion is that *Casa Propia*, together with the existing CMV housing programmes, including 'Villas de Emergencia' (emergency housing) for the destitute, reflects the absence of a unified social housing policy. To its credit, however, Casa Propia's use of private land for public housing purposes may help to dampen land speculation in some parts of Buenos Aires.

Casa Propia's impact on the process of urbanisation in Buenos Aires is generally assessed to have been positive inasmuch as it has successfully encouraged construction in the southern area of the city, following the global strategy of increasing densities there. From a design standpoint, Casa Propia has avoided the look of 'social housing' but it has not received accolades for improving the cityscape. The finishings within the apartments have been criticised for not exceeding the minimum required by the city's housing code. It needs to be pointed out, however, that the programme has resulted only in one huge housing complex. The remaining building projects, though approved, were suspended soon after the model plans had been exhibited. In other words, although Casa Propia was promoted at the highest level and enjoyed much media publicity, the concrete outcomes were very limited.

Residents of the neighbourhoods where Casa Propia buildings have been constructed tend to have a more critical view of their new neighbours. Casa Propia's tall buildings tower over the low-rise housing surrounding them, blocking sunlight and breezes, saturating the infrastructure, bringing increased car traffic and the privatisation of public space. The higher-income neighbours have brought with them security systems, guards, and a desire to segregate themselves from the local community. The renovation of the area stimulated by Casa Propia has increased land prices and rent in the neighbouring areas, forcing the lowest-income inhabitants to move from the area to cheaper locations. This suggests the need to consider whether Casa Propia or other forms of 'social housing' are the proper means for increasing the density of low-income settlements.

The management of Casa Propia has received mixed reviews. On the one hand, it has proved itself to be substantially more efficient at delivering housing than CMV/FONAVI, whose poor co-ordination in the execution of plans has left many projects stalled. Over the 1996–1999 period, FONAVI was able to use only one fifth of the funding allotted to it. In contrast, Casa Propia managed to build 520 of its planned 1148 units before construction was halted by a disagreement between the city and the programme's private lenders. This has tarnished the original claim that Casa Propia would be managed competently and transparently through a board broadly representing all the important stakeholders. The cause for concern is business practices that have occurred under the board's supervision. For example, in some of the buildings containing both 001 and 102 apartments, the construction companies included additional amenities such as swimming pools and saunas that increased both construction and maintenance prices, making the apartments in those buildings less affordable to some lower- and middle-class families.[5] Indeed, charges of malfeasance of this kind lie behind the BACG's refusal to deposit a loan guarantee (fondo fiduiciario) with its lenders, resulting in the litigation that has stalled the project. Problems such as these appear to reflect a deeper problem of public–private co-operation in housing development.

Conclusion

The implementation of sustainable development in cities of the South requires local governments with the capacity to review proposals to achieve this goal critically. Governments without this capacity may be more susceptible than others to 'solutions that have been proven elsewhere'. The use of best practices to disseminate innovations highlights the risk of importing models from different cultural contexts. If certain norms and social policies that have been historically consolidated are crucial to the validity of a model, then it makes little sense to adopt the same model where those conditions do not exist. Before importing *Casa Propia* as a model of best practice, it would be important first to know where, when, and how free market principles have helped a country like Argentina today accomplish the social and environmental objectives set forth by the Mayor of Buenos Aires in 1996.

Because it is not being implemented within a broad strategy to substantially reduce Buenos Aires' housing deficit, *Casa Propia* operates in an isolated manner, supplying housing for the less vulnerable groups in deficit. Over time, and with the insertion of *Casa Propia* into a consolidated social policy framework, it may induce private investors to join schemes that allow lower-income groups better access to housing, while releasing public funds for other uses.

Today, the contradiction the programme represents is the failure to predict that better-off social groups would be the main beneficiaries of the projects and that the free market *per se* is not sufficient to induce investments to generate adequate housing that is affordable to lower-income sectors. More important now is to establish a state subsidy system founded on social equity rather than entirely on our current understandings of financial sustainability.

On the other hand, urban densification under highly permissive standards tends to create conflicts within the urban community. These are often expressed in demands for less drastic social and environmental changes in the urban landscape. High-rise projects like *Casa Propia* are often counter-productive to improving living conditions for the population already settled in the areas chosen for 'renewal'.

Such contradictions should lead to a consideration of sustainable development from the perspective of its target population. It is necessary to work with more than one single paradigm of sustainability. For middle-income groups, this is often 'weak sustainability' or economic sustainability, where the emphasis is upon maintaining the status quo in the allocation of resources, levels of consumption, and financial value. *Casa Propia* embodies this kind of thinking. Were it to be expected to reach low-income groups, *Casa Propia* would need to apply the concept of 'strong sustainability', in which there is little, if any, consideration of the financial or other costs of attaining a city where healthy, sustainable housing was available for all (Bell and Morse 1999). Whether strong or weak sustainability is applied to policies to promote 'social housing' in the 'compact city' in an attempt to achieve sustainable urban development constitutes a crucial question for the government of Buenos Aires.

Acknowledgement

The author is grateful to David Westendorff for his painstaking help in understanding and interpreting an earlier draft of this paper.

Notes

1   In Argentina, *redes de contención social* are provisions or arrangements organised by the state to guarantee universal access to unemployment insurance, basic housing, healthcare, education, and other essential services. The nearest equivalent in English is the traditional provisions of the European welfare state. However, the term *contención social* also has defensive connotations, as though the provision of basic services were viewed as a means of preventing social unrest and being able to govern, rather than as a moral obligation both to pre-empt social exclusion and to promote sustainable social development by reducing the gap between rich and poor.

2   UNCHS best practice principles that could be applied to the analysis of *Casa Propia* include: *Public–private co-operation; impact* in the sense of providing tangible evidence of improving crucial aspects of life; *sustainability*, reflected in changes in legislation, norms, standards, social

and sectoral policies; harmonisation of social economic and environmental strategies; structures and processes in decision making; and efficiency and transparency in management. Other characteristics of best practices proposed by UNCHS are those that promote community empowerment and social inclusion.

3 Version 001b is for a slightly larger and more costly apartment model. However, because the delivery mechanisms of Versions 001a and 001b are virtually identical, no distinction will be made between them.

4 The CMV/FODEVI programme was meant to attract middle- to low-income households, but in practice there was considerable overlap with beneficiaries of *Casa Propia*. The project files reveal that when people found out that the *Casa Propia* programme was to be suspended many of them transferred to the CMV/FODEVI scheme, which offered them almost the same level of accommodation (perhaps slightly more basic) with 100 per cent public finance.

5 The board approved various 'global offers' by construction companies, but as these began to compete with each other, various luxury features were added to the plans, in order to attract customers. Individual members of the board expressed their displeasure, but the board itself never voiced its disapproval. Though they favoured the public–private co-operation idea, they never envisaged the municipality, through *Casa Propia*, taking on the role of a real estate company.

References

Bell, Simon and Stephen Morse (1999) *Sustainable Indicators: Measuring the Immeasurable*, London: Earthscan

Gobierno de la Ciudad de Buenos Aires (GCBA) (1998) 'Plan Urbano Ambiental de la Ciudad de Buenos Aires. Elementos de diagnóstico', Working Paper, Buenos Aires: GCBA

Gobierno de la Ciudad de Buenos Aires (GCBA) (1999) *Programa Habitacional Casa Propia. Manual para compradores*, Buenos Aires: GCBA

Residents' associations and information communication technologies: a suggested approach to international action-research

Cesare Ottolini

How can we measure an elephant?

'Suppose I hire you to measure an elephant. That may sound like a pretty straightforward job description, but think about it for a minute. Do you measure its weight? Height? Length? Volume? Intensity of its grey colour? ... In order to measure this creature, you need to select one or a few characteristics from many possibilities. That choice will be determined by your purpose of measuring.' (Stone 1998) The problem becomes more complex if the elephant moves, changes position, and grows. It becomes almost impossible if the elephant evolves into another species. How can I measure something that is no longer there, or that has even become something else?

Metaphors aside, if we consider the issue of indicators, we can't avoid considering their great variety, the differences in where they come from, and the different reasons for the collection and elaboration of data. From the Organisation for Security and Co-operation in Europe (OSCE) to the IMF, from the World Bank to UNESCO, from the various other UN agencies to government databases, not forgetting the indicators adopted to measure the implementation of Agenda 21 and the Habitat Agenda, a growing number of institutions, especially transnational bodies, are weaving a web of numerical output that cannot be interpreted easily or put to any use. This issue is further complicated if we consider the role of information communication technologies (ICTs). Technological innovation in this field is bringing about a real revolution in the relationships between production and exchange, and is thereby accelerating the processes of globalisation. We are dealing with an unprecedented revolution whose influence permeates right down to the family and the local neighbourhood. But despite this influence, the use of ICTs is not regarded as an indicator of urban development, even though precise and up-to-date statistics are available.

The unequal distribution of ICTs

What can we understand from data concerning that 'tool-cum-symbol' of ICTs, the distribution of the Internet hosts and users throughout the world? In July 1997, there were about 19.5 million hosts on the Internet. For several years, this number doubled every year, yet the distribution by countries and regions didn't change much in this period. The Third World is still participating with a mere 3 per cent, while the USA accounts for about 60 per cent of all the Internet hosts. About 81.5 per cent of Internet hosts worldwide are in the G7 countries, where only about 10 per cent of the world's population lives. On the other hand, some of the most populous countries of the Third World – China, India, Brazil, and Nigeria – together make up a combined total of only 0.6 per cent of all hosts, even though they account for about one third of the world's population. Many countries have only a few Internet connections and there are still some blank areas in Africa and Asia on the Internet map. In January 1997, for example, only four Internet hosts were to be found in Nigeria, a country with a population of 100 million. In developing countries, full Internet connections, with all services, are available only in the capital cities, and beyond their boundaries, sometimes only e-mail is available. In Africa, with the exception of South Africa and Senegal, there are no direct Internet connections in rural areas.

This gap can be explained if we examine the three prerequisites for using the Internet: a telephone connection, a computer and modem, and electricity. Such prerequisites are the exception rather than the norm in the Third World. Lack of access to electricity is in many cases a basic and insurmountable obstacle. Many developing countries experience frequent power failures in their cities while the rural areas lack any power supply at all – which is the case for 70 per cent of all Africans living in rural areas and for over half of their counterparts in the Indian subcontinent.

As for telephone lines, 80 per cent of the world's population doesn't have one. In 49 countries there is not even one telephone mainline for every 100 inhabitants, and 35 of these countries are in Africa. In the USA and in Germany there is a telephone line for every two inhabitants, and the ten richest countries, which represent only 20 per cent of the world's population, have 75 per cent of all telephone mainlines.

On average, developing countries have 5.2 telephone lines per 100 persons while in industrialised countries the corresponding figure is 52.3. In Third World regions most telephone lines are in city areas. In rural Africa, there are only 228,000 lines – one for every 1700 people (CIA 1995).

Last, but not least, is cost. For countries without direct access to the Internet the costs of being connected are especially prohibitive since they are based on international call rates. Monthly fees for an Internet account are often beyond the reach of ordinary people. The average monthly cost of a low-volume Internet account in Africa is about US$65, roughly equivalent to the monthly per capita income of Mozambique. And besides all that, acquiring a computer and a modem is much more expensive in the Third World than in the First World. The average cost of a PC and a modem – let's say, US$2000 – is clearly an astronomical amount of money to most people in developing countries which have an average GNP per capita of US$970, compared with US$16,394 in the industrialised world (UNDP 1996).

These figures tell us something about the North–South divide. The situation is constantly evolving, as reflected in the fact that up to today 78,792 million Internet hosts have been certified worldwide.[1] But this gap will only increase if we consider the costs of cabling, which are prohibitive for countries at risk of bankruptcy because of their foreign debt (Hamelink 1998). In other words, rather than laying out the foundation for a new civilisation, the information revolution seems to be introducing a new and more dangerous form of exclusion (Castells 1998). And it would be difficult to argue that Internet connectivity is a top priority for developing countries that are facing war, famine, unemployment, and pollution.

A possible interpretation of the social use of ICTs

Data alone do not tell us whether and how the ICTs are being used by the various interested parties – public authorities, private sectors, NGOs, and residents' associations – to promote the sustainable development of the city. But let us try to see whether the information revolution has played a prominent role in consolidating democracy and citizens' rights, and in rethinking how the city should function (Afemann 1997). We know that certain transnational institutions have specific programmes for developing ICT use. For example, the World Bank has its Regional Environment Information Management Project (REIMP), which seeks to offer full Internet services to membership countries. It also has its programme for information and development or INFODEV. Likewise, UNESCO has created the Intergovernmental Informatics Programme (IIP), which revolves around the principle of developing human resources to promote comprehensive, sustainable development in developing countries.

The use of ICTs received a strong push, starting from the various UN summits of the 1990s, especially after the 1992 UNCED conference in Rio de Janeiro, whose Agenda 21 mentions the need to collect and use information for sustainable development and for monitoring the Agenda's implementation. This document also calls on UN agencies to make all their information accessible by means of computer networks.

We also know that NGOs are increasingly making use of ICTs. The Association for Progressive Communication (APC) has been a real pioneer in this sector since 1984. This global federation is comprised of 24 non-profit providers covering over 50,000 members in 133 countries. The APC fosters the exchange of experience and the design and implementation of development programmes, while also managing hundreds of e-conferences on topics ranging from AIDS to Zimbabwe. The first experience of globally orchestrated participation by means of computer networks was at Rio, something that has continued at subsequent summits, including the WTO meeting at Seattle.

Throughout such events, NGOs and grassroots associations have woven a network of relations and exchanges, though they are also aware of the risks and limitations of ICTs. The 1994 Declaration of New Delhi refers to the UN Declaration on the Right to Development, the UN Covenant on Civil and Political Rights, the Universal Declaration of Human Rights, the declarations of the MacBride Round Table, and the Quito Declaration.[2] All these declarations emphasise the ever-increasing monopolisation and commercialisation of information and the expansion of a global economy, which have in turn tended to subvert democratic processes and reduce popular participation. The signatories thus call for global democratisation rather than a global supermarket. Everyone has the right to be informed and to inform others, something that modern media could make a real possibility. How? By taxing the use of the Internet for commercial purposes, it would be possible to underwrite the democratic use of ICTs, and to support decentralised forms of organisation while at the same time fostering cultural diversity.

ICTs and urban development: some paths

Such dynamics suggest some paths to follow in looking at how ICTs might help organisations concerned with promoting sustainable urban development. Things have started to become clearer since Habitat II, when Habitat International Coalition (HIC) took on the role of preparing and co-ordinating the participation of popular organisations and NGOs. On that occasion, HIC carried out international action-research, and for the first time used the Internet as a principal tool for acquiring knowledge and exchanging and evaluating the new experiences developed by urban residents themselves in building their cities (HIC 1997). This was around the time that the Dialogues and Documents for Human Progress evolved (DPH 1997), a network to foster the exchange of experience by means of thousands of computerised digests on urban, social, and environmental issues.

Along similar lines, we find some interesting examples that emphasise the disparity between North and South. In the USA, there are now hundreds of local, national, federal, and international associations using the Internet, ranging from the National Coalition for the Homeless to the National Alliance to End Homelessness, from the National Low Income Housing Coalition to Habitat for Humanity. One such example is Neighbourhoods Online, a virtual centre created in 1995 in Philadelphia, serving people involved in the construction and development of neighbourhoods across the USA. This server seeks to provide rapid access to information regarding the various aspects of life in the neighbourhoods, as well as to create a national network of activists and a mechanism through which to link up individual citizens. Another example is the Homeless People Network, a website reserved for the homeless: homeless, maybe, but connected to the Internet and so able to use the services of the member associations or the Internet points.

In the South the situation is much more difficult, even if interesting practical experiences aren't at all lacking. Among these is ENDA-Tiers Monde, an international NGO based in Dakar that focuses on sustainable development in Africa and the developing world. Members of APC are registered with its networking department which has, since the early 1990s, provided connectivity to the larger organisations for its NGO partners in Senegal and francophone West Africa. Between 1992 and 1996, ENDA acted as a local hub for e-mail, which was networked over telephone lines and Fidonet to GreenNet in the UK.

By 1996 ENDA began to provide full Internet services including e-mail, mailing lists, and access to the Web. Its activity derives from the view that South–South exchanges promote development, which is why it seeks to expand the use of ICTs in neighbourhood associations through action-research training projects.

Another example is Fedevivienda (the Federación Nacional de Organizaciones de Vivienda Popular), established in 1982 by five organisations involved in welfare housing projects in Colombia. One of the first to use the Internet, Fedevivienda helped to form Colnodo, a Colombian communications network serving NGOs dedicated to community development. In 1999 Colnodo received the first Internet Columbia Award from the Columbian Chamber of Information and Telecommunications. Colnodo is also involved in a transnational project called Telecentro, which is funded by the International Development Research Centre (IDRC), and aims to provide four Bogotá neighbourhoods with access to the Internet and ICT training courses.

A knowledge and analysis deficit

The Declaration of New Delhi drew a firm line between the diametrically opposed views of the ICT zealots, who suggest that information technology has the capacity to transform society and to eradicate social ills, and of the ICT Luddites, who argue that the new technology has the capacity to enslave society. Popular organisations have tended to be pragmatic in their use of ICTs. However, there is still widespread ignorance of the impact that ICTs can have on their activities, the nature of the relationship with groups who lack telecommunication connections, and ICTs' effectiveness in facing the challenge posed by globalisation and in promoting sustainable development.

Among the few existing analyses, there is the research on 'Gender and technology of information' developed by an *ad hoc* APC programme which singles out some of the general tendencies (*www.gn.apc.org/gn/women*). It has revealed, for instance, that in Europe and in the South there is predominant use of e-mail and of e-group forums, with more attention paid to disseminating the information gathered in this way via other media (photocopies, fax, telephone, radio, etc.). In some countries of Latin America, as well as in the North, there is far greater use of the Web and of search engines.

This lack of real knowledge might well lead not just to a corresponding academic and scientific deficit, but also to a mistaken approach to the whole question. Paradoxically, even if ICTs took off massively in developing countries, this might simply lead to more consumerist or virtual use of ICTs, with no positive implications for sustainable development. The spread of television as the new opium of the people, to take an example of a medium which could well have had a more positive role to play, should serve as something of a warning.

Towards a bottom-up and participatory approach

It would seem particularly important to develop research on ICTs that goes beyond measuring the North–South gap in order to give voice to those who have a direct interest in how ICTs are used. In other words, the aim should be to undertake action-research that actively incorporates the people who are themselves involved in promoting changes in the urban sector, in order to facilitate the use of ICTs in the exchange of experiences, help in changing certain ways of thinking and working, and strengthen their capacity. This type of research should determine specific needs in terms of tools and training in how to use them and will probably call for new kinds of indicators. However, the most important thing for these studies to accomplish is an analysis of the economic, political, and cultural obstacles, and the identification of emerging trends in community-based initiatives and alternative uses of ICTs.

This bottom-up approach might also offer more likelihood of moving from the simple awareness of the problems to their possible solutions as it would probably favour the popular strategies we need in order to bring about the ecologically and socially sustainable urban policies that have, until now, been virtually denied at the local level (Ottolini 1998).

In the final analysis, we are dealing with new and unexplored areas of research – and not only Web based – that could offer to governments, to the transnational institutions, and to other interested bodies, new ideas for how to improve the conventional approach of international aid agencies towards urban development.

Notes

1 Internet Software Consortium, updated on 28 April 2000.
2 The Round Table, a communications rights advocacy group, was created in 1989 to stimulate discussion of issues embodied in the 1980 UNESCO MacBride Report. The MacBride Round Table is an international group of scholars, journalists, NGO representatives, activists, and other communication experts devoted to the examination and monitoring of world communication rights and balances, and reporting findings to community groups, UN agencies, NGOs, and the news media.

References

Afemann, Uwe (1997) *Internet for the Third World: Chance or Threat?*, Osnabrück, Germany: University of Osnabrück Computer Centre

Castells, Manuel (1998) 'Informational capitalism and social exclusion', *UNRISD News* 19

CIA (1995) *The World Factbook*, New York: Central Intelligence Agency

DPH (1997) *Réseau international d'échanges d'expériences et de réflexion utiles à l'action*, Paris: Fondation Charles Léopold Mayer pour le Progrès de l'Homme

Habitat International Coalition (HIC) (1997) *Building the City with the People: New Trends in Community Initiatives in Co-operation with Local Governments*, Mexico DF: HIC

Hamelink, Cees (1998) 'The digital advance: more than half the world's people have never made a phone call. Will ICTs assure us change?', *UN Chronicle* No. 3

Ottolini, Cesare (1998) *Popular Strategies in Historic Urban Centres*, Mexico DF: Habitat International Coalition

Stone, Deborah (1998) *Policy Paradox and Political Reason*, New York: Harper Collins

UNDP (1996) *Human Development Report 1996*, New York: Oxford University Press

Monitoring megacities:

the MURBANDY/MOLAND approach

Carlo Lavalle, Luca Demicheli, Maddalena
Turchini, Pilar Casals-Carrasco, and
Monika Niederhuber

Extensive urbanisation and increasing population growth – especially
in the megacities[1] of developing countries – were recognised as being
of major concern in 1992, when the United Nations Conference on
Environment and Development (UNCED) recommended redressing
the various environmental problems caused by urbanisation, and
promoting economic, social, and ecological dynamics that would enhance
the contribution of the city to sustainable development. More recent
evidence has heightened the urgency of monitoring and understanding
urban dynamics.

Since 1992, and especially in developing countries, urban agglomerations are still attracting migrants from surrounding regions despite
their lack of basic amenities and infrastructure. Consequently, the
urban population is increasing at a much faster rate than the overall
average. This is exacerbating existing habitat problems such as urban
sprawl and the large numbers of people without adequate shelter:
ever more people are living in slums in conditions of poverty,
unemployment, with dangerous levels of air and water pollution, etc..
Furthermore, the largest urban areas, the megacities, are already
affecting the global environment, and have the potential to have still
greater impact. These urban areas therefore also indirectly affect the
non-urban population.

The global process of urbanisation, with all that this means in terms
of migration, traffic, pollution, and natural hazards, is influenced by
many forces and comprises many components. Land values, migration
patterns, and economies, for instance, all need to be carefully
monitored and analysed. Looking at one component of change in
isolation could lead to decisions being taken on the basis of insufficient
information, which might well compromise progress towards
sustainability. Cities in developing countries, in particular the megacities,
typically lack the capacity to obtain the necessary data and to carry out

the comprehensive analyses needed in order to set and achieve sustainability targets.

Understanding urban dynamics is one of the most complex tasks in planning sustainable urban development while also conserving natural resources. The complexity and variety of the different components making up the urban environment, and of the interactions among them, are most pronounced in the megacities. In the South, where available mapping is often outdated or very poor, and where there is a general lack of standard and comparable information on cities, such problems are exacerbated. In this context, it is important to develop uniform systems of monitoring the distribution, changing patterns, and growth of human settlements. This will certainly be facilitated by new technologies, tools, and expertise.

In this paper we describe efforts supported by the European Commission (EC) to improve sustainable development strategies in developing countries with the aid of new methodologies based on hi-tech tools.[2] The study examines the use of the MOLAND approach to assess the dynamics of urban areas in Europe and in a subset of megacities in developing countries. This methodology is based on the analysis of land-use changes combined with different layers of information. The first half of the paper describes the technological framework of the MOLAND Project. This is followed by a brief description of the case studies undertaken in Eastern Europe and several developing countries. We then discuss the implications of the MOLAND Project for urban sustainability and draw some preliminary conclusions about its usefulness.

Background and technological framework

Earth observation (EO) is a modern science that intensively studies the Earth's changing environment, using remote-sensing tools such as satellite imagery and aerial photography. The Earth's physical components, such as the atmosphere, oceans, and land, are therefore studied from a viewpoint that is distinct from those of classical geographical and geophysical approaches. This viewpoint improves our understanding of various natural processes, and the effects of our actions upon the environment. Under the EC's Fourth Framework Programme (1995-98) for Research and Technological Development and Demonstration (RTD), the Centre for Earth Observation (CEO) of the EC's Directorate General Joint Research Centre (DG JRC) was responsible for promoting the overall use of EO.

In 1998, under the umbrella of activities carried out by CEO, a pilot study named MURBANDY (Monitoring Urban Dynamics) was launched. It initially sought to provide a way to measure the extent of urban areas, as well as of their progress towards sustainability, through the creation of land-use databases for various European cities.[3] The project progressed quickly, and raised an unexpected level of interest from both its initial potential customers as well as external audiences. As a consequence, the number of study areas was extended to 25, and the project's objectives broadened. MURBANDY became one element of a new, expanded project – MOLAND (Monitoring Land-use/Cover Change Dynamics).

The MOLAND Project: monitoring urban and regional dynamics

The MOLAND Project seeks to set up and define a specific methodology for monitoring the dynamics of human settlements, and to provide information on a significant set of European cities and a second set of megacities in developing countries. Thus, morphological and structural changes are monitored, evaluated, and analysed, in order to characterise past and future trends of urban landscapes (EEA 1999).

The methodology is based on the creation of an accurate land-use database specifically designed for urban areas. To date, such a database has been created for 25 European cities, which have been ordered according to a single land-use classification scheme in order to obtain homogeneous data. The data were derived from satellite imagery and aerial photography, using remote-sensing and Geographic Information Systems (GIS) technologies. The database is the basis for combining environmental, economic, and social data, in order to improve the understanding of dynamics and characteristics of urban growth and related structural changes, commuting issues, and the status of transport and energy infrastructures.

As part of the extension of MOLAND to non-European cities, a pilot study is currently being carried out in seven urban areas – Buenos Aires, Chongqing, New Delhi, Bangkok, Johannesburg/Pretoria, Mexico City, and Seoul (see Table 1). Unlike the first phase of the project in Europe, local authorities are not yet involved. The next step will be to encourage them to participate so that they can provide additional information.

City	Population size in millions		
	1975	**2000**	**2015**
Bangkok	3.8	7.3	10.5
Buenos Aires	9.1	11.3	12.3
Chongqing	2.4	4.1	5.8
Johannesburg/Pretoria	2.1	3.3	4.9
Mexico City	11.2	16.3	18.7
New Delhi	4.4	11.6	17.5
Seoul	6.7	12.2	13.1

Table 1: Population of developing-country cities involved in the MOLAND Project

Source: UNCHS (Habitat) (1997)

The methodology is based upon three interrelated tasks: *change, understand,* and *forecast.*

The *change* task detects modifications to land use. This involves remote-sensing tools for creating a detailed land-use database. Four datasets are produced for each city over a period of 50 years, at intervals of about 15 years. Four additional datasets, with the road and rail networks of the corresponding years, are included in the database. The dataset for current years (i.e. 1997 or 1998) is the 'reference' set; previous ones are 'historical'. The reference land-use classification is based on recent data from the panchromatic Indian Remote Sensing satellite (IRS Pan) – (for the new area sets it also makes use of IKONOS data). The historical database is created using satellite imagery or aerial photography from the mid-1950s, late-1960s, and 1980s. All the images are geo-coded, and land-use maps are produced at a scale of 1: 25,000. The minimum mapping unit is 1ha for artificial surfaces, and 3ha for non-artificial surfaces. In addition, the road and rail networks, and rivers and canals, are digitised as linear features. After data processing, each dataset is validated in order to guarantee a high quality of land-use classification products. The land-use database is provided in a simple GIS format.

The *understand* task attempts to analyse and explain urban land-use changes. It sets out to derive and calculate indicators to allow a better understanding of the dynamics of urban areas, and of the impact of cities on the global environment. The main task consists of developing a set of spatially referenced indicators, which are expected to help in understanding the complexity of urban problems, providing detailed spatial information at local and national levels, and supporting city managers and decision makers in defining local policies. The MOLAND indicators focus on urban and regional sustainability, and are designed to be robust and long lasting, and flexible enough to accommodate different urban structures. In practice, such indicators are sufficiently standardised to allow comparisons within different urban areas.

A core set of urban indicators for international use, including land-use and socio-economic information, has yet to be developed. One of the aims within the MOLAND Project is to define specific indicators for urban sustainability, since the project is based on the belief that, without accurate spatial information, no set of indicators of urban sustainability can be complete. The MOLAND indicators are divided into (a) spatially referenced indicators providing information on different land uses and changes in them; and (b) cross-sectoral spatially referenced indicators to evaluate more complex processes for landscape changes (e.g. fragmentation). Socio-economic data, prepared in a spatially disaggregated format, are also being combined with MOLAND data. The aim here is to address carrying capacity and other general factors affecting urban sustainability.

For all the cities and regions studied, basic spatial indicators are calculated showing the land-use changes of the three main classes (i.e. artificial surfaces, agriculture, nature) over a 50-year period. In particular, the changes from agricultural and natural areas to artificial surfaces are investigated, documented, and their statistics calculated. In addition, for several cities, changes in the structure (i.e. fragmentation) of the urban landscape are being measured and analysed, using a landscape structural analysis software (FRAGSTATS) that has been modified for the MOLAND database. The trends over time of the various fragmentation metrics (e.g. edge metrics, core area metrics, nearest neighbour metrics, diversity metrics) computed by FRAGSTATS are being interpreted in the light of known environmental and demographic factors for the different urban areas. The land-use datasets are also being combined with socio-economic and environmental statistical information in order to derive urban sustainability indicators. The final product of the *understand* task will be a document with guidelines on how to report on urban sustainability.

The main objective of the *forecast* task is to develop scenarios of territorial evolution for urban and peri-urban areas, by using information derived from both EO and non-space data. The scenarios are produced by using an integrated model of regional spatial dynamics, consisting of a 'cellular automata' land-use model, linked to both a GIS and to regional economic and demographic models.[4] The model allows the input parameters (e.g. the transport network) to be modified, so as to simulate, both quantitatively and qualitatively, the evolution of land use over time. The question of whether a single model can be applied to all cities (with minimal modifications for national, regional, and city-specific factors), or whether different models are necessary, is being investigated. The resulting scenarios will serve as a major input to formulate and evaluate medium- and long-term strategies for the sustainable development of urban areas.

Strategic framework and sustainability implications

The MOLAND Project is currently investigating likely difficulties in exporting the methodology to non-European and developing countries. Meanwhile, several European local authorities have shown such interest in the project that they have even offered to co-fund it in order to have cities and regions under their administrative jurisdiction studied under MOLAND. Workshops have also been organised with representatives from various international agencies, including the United Nations Environment Programme (UNEP), OECD, WHO, and the European Environment Agency (EEA).

Why has the MOLAND Project attracted so much attention? How can one project be of interest to so many diverse organisations? Part of the answer is that the MOLAND methodology requires only a very limited number of highly skilled developers in order to be used. The MOLAND team operates as a 'remote' co-ordinator, so that the methodology can be – and usually is – applied on site by a local partner. Different customers can then assess the outputs at any level of analysis. Such an approach greatly reduces the costs, also because local authorities usually already own the basic material required by the methodology – satellite data, aerial photographs, master plans, statistical information, etc.. When part of this material is not immediately available (e.g. satellite images), it can be easily acquired at a moderate cost.

The initial costs are limited because it is manpower that ultimately determines the cost of applying MOLAND. This means that the cost of studying a certain area in Japan or in Brazil will be proportional to the difference in cost of living in the two countries. Once the database has been prepared, a minimum effort is required to keep it updated. The MOLAND approach has proved to be quite cost-efficient overall. For example, the average cost of the *change* part of MOLAND was about 90 euros per km^2 for the European areas, though this covers considerable variation between one study domain and another. Moreover, European areas tend to be compact, while elsewhere the phenomenon of 'sprawl' is more evident. For example, the core urban area of Munich is 300km^2, while the core urban area of Bangkok is 1000km^2! The larger the area, the higher the cost will be: studying a megacity is expensive. Clearly, even if the level of detail of the Bangkok database is reduced, the size of the study domain is so large that costs cannot be reduced substantially. The land-use fabric also affects the costs. The more dense the urban fabric, for example, the more accurate the analysis required in order to disaggregate it into detailed land-use classes. On the other hand, if a given region contains, for instance, several water bodies or large areas covered almost uniformly with vegetation, the classification exercise is relatively simple. It is also worth noting that the level of detail required to carry out assessments in Europe is probably higher than that needed in developing countries, where priorities are different.

Considering the level of detail needed for studying megacities, the extent of the areas covered, the cost of specialised personnel, and the cost of materials, we can assume that the methodology is not only affordable for local authorities, but also compares very well in cost–benefit terms.

Moreover the MOLAND Project includes support for technology transfer to non-European and developing countries. In the specific case of Latin America and Asia, the project aims to provide the resources to apply the methodology in the partner cities through specific research programmes. Under the EU's Fifth Framework Programme (1998–2002) for Research and Technological Development and Demonstration, the EC finances international projects within its INCO-DEV (International Co-operation with Developing Countries) programme. The programme envisages three levels of research: (a) policy research to determine the conditions of sustainable development; (b) systems research on the complex interactions in the local environment caused by, for example, rehabilitation and management of natural resources or healthcare; and (c) research to generate tools for system management and policies to promote sustainable development. The programme also aims to reduce the isolation of scientists in developing countries by enabling them to work at an international level while based in their own institutions, and to provide training opportunities.

Case studies

Central and Eastern European cities

Around two thirds of Central and Eastern European citizens already live in cities (EEA 1998), and urban population growth continues. This trend is leading to a rapid increase in the proportion of land occupied by urban areas and a decline in agricultural and natural spaces. To measure the impacts of these trends on the environment, health, quality of life, and population security, requires new tools for appropriate urban and environmental planning.

MOLAND focuses on European cities, some of which belong to the so-called European 'less-favoured regions': the former socialist cities of Bratislava (Slovakia), Prague (Czech Republic), and Tallinn (Estonia); the city of Nicosia (Cyprus); and the city of Heraklion (Crete). Each of these cities has a specific history and development pattern, and faces its own problems. Despite these differences they all need to ensure sustainable development to prevent further economic, ecological, and social deterioration.

Within the process of European enlargement, four of the countries mentioned hope to join the EU in the next few years. In this framework, the MOLAND study is a tool for improving knowledge about the development process of new EU member countries. Because the major cities of Eastern and Central Europe play an especially crucial function as the economic core of their regions, it becomes essential to understand the urban environment. In these cities, MOLAND emphasises environmental and transport issues.

Non-European megacities

Cities in developing countries are generally characterised by very rapid growth and extremely rapid changes in land use, both within the city and in the surrounding territories. As cities expand, spontaneous and informal settlements tend to alter typical environments in peri-urban areas, such as agricultural and natural spaces. A correct analysis of these changes and of settlement characteristics is needed in order to establish planning procedures and, in particular, to assess and monitor disaster prevention, environmental impact and risk assessment, air pollution and solid waste management, infrastructure planning, population density and distribution, quality of urban life, etc. The general absence of adequate information in developing countries may thus be overcome with the assistance of new technologies and tools. Using new commercial satellites, it is also possible to watch change as it occurs, even in areas where aerial photographs are not available. Such data may be crucial at the beginning of a dangerous event (flooding, refugee movements, civil wars) and may also be of use to other parties, such as NGOs, which could then establish contingency plans in advance.

The example of the Three Gorges Dam on the Yangtze River in China demonstrates how the MOLAND methodology may make it possible to analyse the impacts of multiple environmental changes occurring simultaneously over a large region. For the Chinese city of Chongqing, the main consequences of the dam are the serious contamination of water by the flooding of old industrial areas, the rising water table (30m), and the relocation of communities displaced by flooding.[5] The MOLAND Project provides objective and reliable information which is particularly useful when the involvement of different parties (the Chinese government, private funders, construction companies, NGOs, etc.) might lead to different perspectives and to the lack of objective evaluations. MOLAND will provide the information needed about physical change: how much arable land will disappear, how many informal settlements will be built, the location of industrial and archaeological sites, what the vegetation is like now (changes will affect climate in the region), what the current extent of the city is (in developing countries, including China, the exact extent of the cities is rarely known). Most of this data is not being collected by those responsible for the Three Gorges project, despite the strong demand for it both within and outside China.

In the case of Bangkok, for example, air and water pollution, the disastrous traffic situation, and subsidence due to the sinking groundwater table can all be measured and analysed more precisely with the MOLAND approach.

Conclusions

The flexibility of the MOLAND methodology makes it possible to monitor urban dynamics in different countries. The methodology has been adapted to meet the urgent needs of megacities in non-European and developing countries, which are markedly different from those of European cities. In the South, even the most basic information is often missing, e.g. the precise extent of the urban area, quantitative information on infrastructure and services, the number and location of legal and illegal landfills, and the amount of agricultural and natural land that is being replaced by artificial surfaces. The MOLAND Project provides such data, as well as a measure of the changes in land use over time. It also offers the opportunity to carry out more in-depth analyses by combining the land-use database with ancillary information, such as socio-economic and environmental data. The level of detail required in setting up the database can be tailored to local needs and to the resources available.

The very high technology adopted in the Project is already commercially available at affordable prices. Moreover, through the financial mechanisms set up by the EC, it is possible to transfer the methodology to those non-European and developing countries that are interested in establishing an accurate and comparable information system. Costs may be further reduced if local authorities own the basic material and information required by the MOLAND methodology, which makes it a relatively cost-efficient approach to data collection and analysis. The response from both local authorities and international organisations has been very positive; the MOLAND Project is co-operating with the EEA, UNEP, the OECD, Eurostat, and several Directorates General of the EC.

The review of seven non-European cities will test how well the MOLAND methodology can be adapted to the challenges posed by megacities. Because of the different methods used by each city or country to collect information, it is extremely difficult to develop common indicators to assess their progress towards sustainable development. The main advantage of this approach is that it permits comparative analysis among cities, and a central database and information system will be held at JRC. International organisations may therefore benefit from MOLAND in their efforts to develop valid common approaches to defining and monitoring progress towards sustainable development. They should also find it easier to develop strategies to do so if they have a harmonised database at their disposal.

Notes

1 We use the term 'megacities' to include large and fast-growing urban areas.

2 This article is a combination of two papers presented at the ESF/N-AERUS annual workshop (Lavalle *et al.* 2000a,b). The authors wish to thank Rachael Mann for weaving the two papers into one.

3 One can measure urban sustainability through the development of appropriate indicators. Indicators can differ between cities, but some core indicators will be the same for every city. We suggest aggregating the core indicators under the territorial dimension in a uniform manner in order to be able to compare the progress of different cities towards sustainability.

4 Cellular automata are computer simulations that try to emulate the ways the laws of nature are supposed to work in nature.

5 The Three Gorges Dam will be the largest hydroelectric dam in the world. It will create a lake 400km long, and 1.5 million people will be relocated. The whole economy of the region will be affected. The environmental problems related to the damming of the river are huge, and have implications for the global environment (it has been calculated, for instance, that such 'megadams' influence the earth's rotation speed).

References

European Environment Agency (EEA) (1998) *Towards Sustainable Development for Local Authorities*, Brussels: European Commission

European Environment Agency (EEA) (1999) *Environment in the European Union at the Turn of the Century*, Brussels: European Commission

Lavalle, Carlo, L. Demicheli, M. Turchini, and P. Casals-Carrasco (2000) 'Monitoring Non-European Megacities: The MOLAND Approach', paper delivered at ESF/N-AERUS Annual Workshop, Geneva, 3–6 May 2000

Lavalle, Carlo, L. Demicheli, M.Turchini, and M. Niederhuber (2000) 'Where Are Cities Going? A Territorial Outlook', paper delivered at ESF/N-AERUS Annual Workshop, Geneva, 3–6 May 2000

UNCHS (1997) *Monitoring Human Settlements with Urban Indicators (Draft) Guide*, Global Urban Observatory, Nairobi: UN Centre for Human Settlements (Habitat)

Technical versus popular language: some reflections on the vocabulary of urban management in Mexico and Brazil

Hélène Rivière d'Arc

From the 1940s to the 1970s, the expansion of cities outside the domain of any form of regulatory control was a phenomenon that had little impact on the urban planning and management jargon. These urban sprawls were regarded as non-cities. A skim through Brazilian architectural journals of the 1940s reveals the then current concern to eradicate 'urban ills', the *favelas* or *mocambos* (informal settlements or shantytowns). But there were no specific technical words to describe or refer to these areas. These were the years of triumphalist planning, which took its new technical vocabulary from the French model, and even more so from the international organisations (Hiernaux 1999; Rivière d'Arc and Schneier 1993). The global vision of a city that could include the peripheral areas, the non-regulated urban sector, had to resort to the key planning term of the era – the regulatory blueprint, or *plano regulador*, also known as *plano director* or *plano metropolitano* – and all municipalities of more than 10,000 inhabitants had one. The advent of such master plans opened up the space for co-operation with the development banks (e.g. the Inter-American Development Bank and the World Bank), which depended upon high-level negotiations with central ministries and was highly normative in its approach.

Mexico and Brazil adopted the idea of technical planning at around the same time. This reflects several influences, including those of CEPAL, for whom the urban question was then posed in the terms defined by Manuel Castells (1973); slightly later, we see the influence of the Charter of Athens, followed by that of Marxist urban sociology. Paradoxically, the voccabulary of the 1960s carried on being used by Brazil's military governments, even after profound changes in what were regarded as the determinant variables in urban planning. It also remained current in Mexico at the beginning of the 1970s, under the leftist government of Echeverría.

In fact, the heyday of *planificación* (in Mexico) or *planejamento* (in Brazil) lasted from 1960 to 1985, when the urban peripheries started to be taken over by new residential developments, often financed by low-income housing programmes (INFONAVIT in Mexico and BNH in Brazil). Massive financial support also poured in from international organisations, though more for training urban planners and managers than for building homes. Thus, two quite distinct doctrines were influential during this period – that of the international organisations versus a welfare state that looked at different sectors of the population as social categories whose shared characteristics helped their members to identify with each other as particular social groups.[1]

The concept of 'human settlement' responds to the UN's vision at the time. During a period of rapid rural–urban migration and in the face of concerns to settle these transient populations, the term 'human settlement' implied the recognition both of changes in population distribution, and of people's right to land, even in the urban context.[2] The 'urban human settlement' was then taken on by those states which still saw their role as that of protecting their citizens. 'Urban human settlements' as applied to the expanding peripheries of cities, and new ways of allocating space within them, represented an extraordinarily sanitised way to refer to the way in which the urbanisation process was evolving at that time. Nonetheless, 'urban human settlements' rapidly found their place within *planos reguladores* and became the basis for new ways to allocate urban areas, whether perceived pejoratively (by most professionals) or in the more sanitised sense (by the population at large) (Ibarra 1997). 'Infra' zones of every kind began to appear, whether they were called Special Social Interest Zones (*Zonas Especiales de Interés Social*, or ZEIS) as in Mexico, or 'sub-normal zones' (*zonas sub-normais*), as in Recife. The people living in these areas were ignorant of such terms, but their use served to mask the stigma attached to them by local urban planners, the welfare state preferred the term *asentamientos habitacionales* (housing settlements), which would then be referred to as *lotes* and *fraccionamientos* (plots or building lots) once construction began.

The *assentamento*, in the Brazilian tradition of collective struggle for access to urban land, followed a different course from that of the Mexican *asentamiento popular* (low-income and often informal settlement). While the Mexicans we surveyed did not belong either to an *asentamiento* or to a formal *fraccionamiento*, they recognised the existence of these categories and assumed that these were more comfortable and more privileged by the state than were their own still informal neighbourhoods (*sus propias colonias*) (Ibarra 1997). On the other hand, the 'settled' population on the outskirts of Recife believed that an *assentamento* was synonymous with *campamento* (camp) and harked back to the roadside settlements of the *Movemento Sem Terra* (Landless Movement) during their land protests.

This period also saw the appearance in Brazil of *conjuntos* (housing estates), the early precursor to the large popular housing developments of the 1970s.[3] The new cityscape they brought into being soon fuelled a fierce debate between technocrats and basistas (pro-poor or populist activists) that characterised the late 1970s and early 1980s among Brazil's professional urban planners. Those favouring the welfare state continued to promote the construction of *conjuntos habitacionais* (available on the basis of various multiples of the minimum wage), foundations (*pe de casa*), or simply just a plan or projection (*embriao*) for the poorest. The activists, on the other hand, attempted to create a direct link with the people already living in the *occupaçoes, invasoes,* and *favelas* (essentially the squatter settlements and shantytowns), with the support of certain professional organisations and NGOs, in order to help them build their own neighbourhoods. Today we are witnessing the pyrrhic victory of the latter approach.

The terms of the debate differed in Mexico because of differences in the regulatory régime. However, these regulations were persistently flouted by middlemen who gave every impression of observing legal processes for land development while in fact ignoring them completely. Known as *promotores* or *fraccionadores*, these middlemen often belonged to underground or illegal networks, and so were obliged to use the sanitised vocabulary in order to conceal what they were actually doing. Thus, the formal housing lots that they delivered to people in their *de facto* settlements appeared to have come about through a legitimate process.

Enter the language of business management and the urban environment

One might assume that in the years following Habitat I (held in Vancouver in 1976), which stressed the importance of addressing the needs of human settlements, that greater attention would have been focused on these issues. The slowdown in the growth rates of major Latin American cities such as Mexico City, Rio de Janeiro, or São Paulo would suggest so, even if they still suffer the consequences of their earlier breakneck expansion. One might further assume, then, that the pressure on urban land had also decreased, and some observers have indeed noted that access to some services in the big cities improved during the 1980s, particularly in Brazil (Ribeiro and Correa do Lago 1994). But the consolidation of peripheral settlements has not prevented a deepening of social segregation and/or of fragmentation of the cities. This is reflected today in the visible and growing poverty in the urban landscape. Around the world we see evidence of deepening social extremes.

How does the experts' language reflect this urban reality? How do urban technocrats and officials use this language? How can one create a vocabulary that facilitates dialogue between local authorities and the marginalised residents who see little point in negotiating with the state, even if the intermediaries between the two – now, more often than not, NGOs – have changed?

First, the term 'good governance' contains two opposing definitions of cities, what Jean-François Tribillon (1999) calls the '*ville-marché*' (urban land, credit, production, publicity, communications, formal employment, competing services, etc.) and the '*ville-cité*', or 'urban-city', a concept which includes poor people, who receive public subsidies so that they can indeed participate as full citizens (Lautier 1999).

The recommendations of international organisations, notably the World Bank, are popularised through a heavily loaded vocabulary that designates not spaces, but functional concepts: competitiveness, 'liveability', good governance, management, and 'bankability', the combination of which amounts to a sustainable city (World Bank 1999). It is then up to each city or town to apply these concepts to urban spaces that are already broadly marked either by their own regulatory frameworks or alternatively by having been built too quickly and without any such regulation. Thus we find ourselves face to face with many terms for which we need to establish a common meaning, but which seem comprehensible only in English: accountability, sustainability, good governance, poverty alleviation, participation, security of tenure, public–private partnership, cost recovery, replicability, third sector, and so on (N-AERUS 1999).

The term *la buena gobernabilidad* (the usual translation into Spanish of 'good governance') originated in the private business world of the USA in the 1920s. It assumes that management can bring the two sides together, while dropping the idea of welfare. This is seen in the new global approach to the city in which special zones are established – for example, in Recife 'The Special Zone of Rigorous Preservation' (ZPR) – that consolidate human settlements (the pyrrhic victory to which we referred above) and render them viable (by cleaning up the environment, cutting down noise and pollution, implementing security measures, etc.), while applying as far as possible what is called 'the true price of services'.[4]

In Mexico, cities managed by the National Action Party (PAN) have enthusiastically adopted this way of envisaging urban management, and the recommendations of good governance should from now on be applied to any new developments (Ward 1998).[5] However, 'edge-cities' or other 'flexi-spaces' have yet to appear. Cities managed by the Institutional Revolutionary Party (PRI), by contrast, remain prisoners of the 'statist' vision and the doctrine of the welfare state. Certain words from the planning era remain the order of the day. In Brazil, the debate on popular participation dating back to the return to democracy after military rule, and the formulation of the 1988 Constitution, is very much alive, especially within the municipalities administered by left-wing parties. In these cities, local government emphasises resource sharing over competition (whether for space or economic benefits for the élite). An excellent example of this is the difficulty of translating into Spanish or Portuguese one of the principal instruments of new urban governance – 'partnership' – a concept that has yet to replace 'participation'.

The popular response: community

Jan Bitoun (1999) shows how inhabitants develop their own vocabulary to use with different interlocutors, in order to give their demands a basis for negotiation. We can also see, when we look at the urban planning documents, that the language of urban administration is itself fluid and volatile. Terms like the ZEIS in Recife or the *fraccionamiento* in Guadalajara have only the appearance of rigour. Thus, the key negotiating term in both Brazil and Mexico is 'community' (*communidade* and *communidad*, respectively). This recalls the idea of inhabitants as participants, while also conveying the sense of a neighbourhood's physical delimitations, within which everyone feels a degree of mutual solidarity. NGOs have clearly encouraged the use of this word. In fact, a range of sociological and local connotations of the words used to refer to one's place of residence are found in both countries. Rather than speaking of belonging to a squatter or irregular settlement (be it an *invasão* in Brazil or a *colonia irregular* in Mexico), inhabitants define themselves to outsiders as a community. It is a term that has for the last 20 years or so served as a magic potion for resolving all kinds of conflict. Unlike the way it is commonly used by French sociologists, 'community' does not sound at all pejorative in Mexico or Brazil.[6] It is used everywhere and everyone knows that it is habitually used for resolving misunderstandings among the different actors involved in various types of intervention (e.g. international bodies, local authorities, the affected populations). Indeed, it is 'the' negotiating term.

However, what communities actually do is extremely contested (Vidal 1999), whether their actions are generally perceived in a positive light as in the cities of Brazil or Mexico, where they are seen as representing collective action, or in a negative one, as obstacles to policies to integrate societies and foster a sense of citizenship, which is how they are often viewed in France. In our view, no word has been so heavily used in order to designate at one and the same time a particular group and how it feels about itself at a given moment. If the community and the place to which it refers are key words in the lexicon of negotiation, will the poor urban peripheries remain non-cities?

This paper has shown, with reference to Brazil and Mexico, how different social groups use and understand certain terms in ways that reflect their different interests and perspectives. The city planners and technical experts use terms to describe informal and low-income housing developments that are not used, or even understood, by the people living in them. In addition, different actors often use the same terms, but apply different meanings or connotations to them. For instance, the people themselves invest the term 'community' with a social and political content, using this as a negotiating tool and as a way to describe their collective identity. For their part, the international agencies often harness the term to a top-down or managerial view of social realities. In each case, these terms not only interpret, but also change, reality by setting the stage for new policies and new social practices.

Notes

1 While a given population group will also identify itself according to other characteristics, it tends also to internalise those attributed to it. For instance, we recall that the social housing built in the 1970s when Camaçari was rapidly industrialising was allocated on the basis of household incomes, some up to the equivalent of two minimum wages (as such a low household income would have made it very difficult to get a foot in the housing market), from two to five times the minimum wage, etc.. Thus, rural immigrants would see themselves as belonging to one of these categories.

2 We can give more meaning to this expression by translating it as a need that is so urgent as to become a right, something we think of today as 'a human right'. Here we do not refer to the more substantial 'residences' or condominiums that became popular with the middle and upper classes, known as *conjuntos fechados*, *conjuntos horizontales*.

3 Elsewhere, we show that the taste of the rich middle classes can be expensive for municipalities and cause headaches for private companies who provide services and claim to practise cost-recovery pricing, based on experiences in Mérida and Guadalajara in Mexico, and Salvador de Bahia in Brazil, among others (Rivière d'Arc 1999).

4 We have seen the introduction of business concepts, such as 'total quality management' (accompanied by internships and training for municipal workers), in Ciudad Juárez on the Mexico–US border, in a municipality governed by the PAN.

Since this kind of language feeds into notions of business efficiency, the local government effectively facilitates private investments by offering the most attractive conditions (Hiernaux 1999).

5 We have seen the introduction of business concepts, such as 'total quality management' (accompanied by internships and training for municipal workers), in Ciudad Juárez on the Mexico-US border, in a municipality governed by the PAN. Since this kind of language feeds into notions of business efficiency, the local government effectively facilitates private investments by offering the most attractive conditions (Hiernaux 1999).

6 Might it have been the omnipresent Catholic Church and its NGO brethren who pushed the term 'community' – as evidenced, for instance, by the Christian base communities of the 1960–85 period of military government in Brazil? Or perhaps it is a translation of a term that international organis-ations have been bandying around for more than 20 years (in phrases such as 'community organisations', 'community groups', or what the Bank calls 'community development')? Or does it have a longer lineage, dating from a time when it designated a territory, i.e. the 'commune' of the French Revolution?

References

Bitoun, Jan (1999) 'Les territoires du dialogue: mots de la ville et enjeu de la gestion participative à Recife', in *Amérique latine: les discours techniques et savants sur la ville dans la politique urbaine*, 'Les mots de la ville' Project, Working Paper No. 37, Paris: MOST-UNESCO

Castells, Manuel (1973) *La question urbaine*, Paris: Maspéro

Hiernaux, Daniel (1999) 'Les mots de la planification du territoire au Méxique', in *Amérique latine: les discours techniques et savants sur la ville dans la politique urbaine*, 'Les mots de la ville' Project, Working Paper No. 37, Paris: MOST-UNESCO

Ibarra, Xochitl Ibarra (1997) 'Palabras, espacio urbano y periferia en Guadalajara (México)', paper delivered at the colloquium 'Les mots de la ville', Paris

Lautier, Bruno (1999) 'Pourquoi faudrait-il donc aider les pauvres? Enoncé de quelques doutes sur la façon dont une banque (mondiale) fut saisie par la morale', paper delivered at GEMDEV, Institut d'Administration Publique, July 1999

N-AERUS (1999) 'Background Paper', delivered at a workshop on 'Concepts and Paradigms of Urban Management in the Context of Developing Countries', held at the Instituto Universitario di Architettura di Venezia, 11–12 March

Ribeiro, Luis Cesar and Luciana Correa do Lago (1994) 'Brésil: evolution métropolitaine et nouveaux modèles d'inégalité sociale', special number in *La Ville et l'Amérique latine, Problèmes d'Amérique latine*, Paris: La Documentation Française

Rivière d'Arc, Hélène (1999) 'Los vocables del consenso "modesto" en la gestión de las grandes urbes en Brasil y en México', *Revista Mexicana de Sociología* No. 4, October–December: 43–54

Rivière d'Arc, Hélène and Graciella Schneier (1993) 'De Caracas à Rio et Buenos Aires: un siècle d'aspiration à la modernité urbaine', in Rivière d'Arc (ed.) *L'Amerique latine au XIXe et XXe siècles. Héritages et territoires*, Paris: Armand Colin

Tribillon, Jean-François (1999) 'La gestion urbaine entre deux modèles, celui de la ville-marché et celui de la ville-cité', paper delivered at a workshop on 'Concepts and Paradigms of Urban Management in the Context of Developing Countries', Instituto Universitario di Architettura di Venezia, 11-12 March

Vidal, Dominique (1999) *La politique au quartier. Rapports sociaux et citoyenneté à Recife*, Collection Brasilia, Paris: Editions de la MSH

Ward, Peter (1998) 'From machine politics to the politics of technocracy: charting changes in governance in the Mexican municipalities', *Bulletin of Latin-American Research* 17(1): 13–28

World Bank (1999) 'A Strategic View of Urban and Local Government Issues: Implications for the Bank', draft document, Washington DC: World Bank

Resources

The evolution of thinking about the role of cities in promoting sustainable development and the application of sustainable development theory and practice to the management of urban settlements have come a long way in the decade and a half since the Brundtland Commission. Indeed, the literature on these subjects is extensive and complex, just as cities have become in the latter half of the twentieth century. The brief set of resources that follows cannot possibly do justice to all aspects of the debate. Rather, it attempts to list some of the newer publications on the subject that discuss the emerging understanding of the main bottlenecks in achieving cities that provide incomes, healthy living conditions, and vibrant cultural life for all sectors of the population. Cities that manage to do this without exporting negative by-products to other regions or following generations are 'sustainable'.

Some of the major themes that are covered the bibliography include those that have been raised in the chapters in this volume:

Major Definitions of Sustainable Urban Development: These are references on existing and emerging definitions of and approaches to sustainable development in an urban context, emphasising, for example, ecological footprints, environmental protection, poverty alleviation, competitiveness, bankability, etc..

Action Towards Sustainable Urban Development: This includes descriptions of projects and activities of the major international and bilateral agencies in the name of sustainable development (including UNDP, UNEP, UNESCO, UNICEF, and the World Bank). Some agencies influence the debate on sustainable urban development primarily through advocacy, while others do so through the provision of technical assistance and/or loans and grants to developing countries. The advice and assistance offered to the same country by different donors can be contradictory.

The Role of Local Authorities/Municipal Governance: The role of local bodies in planning and implementing action for sustainable development, highlighting the changing roles and responsibilities of cities as official players, the relationship of the city government to planning and market forces, current methods of planning for the sustainable city, and the politics of sustainable development at the local level.

Global forces in Sustainable Development: *How are external forces, particularly the integration of local economies into the international economy, constraining and/or promoting sustainable development in urban settlements?*

Other themes appearing in the books in the bibliography were less directly addressed in this volume, but will be useful for those looking for a more comprehensive view of the debate. For example, this volume deals largely with urban sustainable development in and from the perspectives of developing country practitioners. A number of the titles in the bibliography focus on the problems and solutions for achieving sustainable cities in developed countries. Other topics not dealt with explicitly in this Reader but included in some of the entries below examine sectoral issues (water, sanitation, transportation, refuse removal, etc.) in relation to urban sustainable development, whereas others document efforts to build sustainable cities on the basis of neighbourhood or community action.

We chose Habitat II, which took place in Istanbul in June 1996, as the chronological starting point of the bibliography. Readers looking for earlier materials on the same subject will do well to consult the journals listed in the bibliography, some of which published many important articles and reviewed the book-length studies on sustainable development in the urban context that were coming on the market at around the time of Habitat II. The Earthscan Reader on Sustainable Cities (1999), listed below, is also an important reference. Alas, because none of the five contributors to this bibliography was able to lay hands on physical copies of a number of important new books, we were unable to include them in the resources list. For this we offer apologies to both their authors and our readers.

This resource list was compiled and annotated by Katy Agg, Rachael Mann, and David Westendorff (all of UNRISD), with additional input from Deborah Eade and Nicola Frost (Editor and Reviews Editor respectively of Development in Practice*).*

Books

Adrian Atkinson and Adriana Allen: *The Urban Environment in Development Co-operation: A Background Study,* Luxembourg: Office for Official Publications of the Countries of the European Community, 1998.

Environmental degradation is not inevitable; it can be halted, and sometimes reversed, by developing appropriate policies, devising effective management programmes, and applying the right tools. This European Commission (EC) study is concerned with improving the coherence and effectiveness of development co-operation in relation to the urban environment. It identifies the major priorities and needs of developing countries, provides a detailed analysis of all relevant activities and instruments of the EC and an overview of those of related institutions, investigates other forms of international development co-operation, and summarises the most successful policies and best practice.

Adrian Atkinson, Julio D. Davila, Edésio Fernandes, Michael Mattingly (eds): *The Challenge of Environmental Management in Urban Areas,* Aldershot: Ashgate, 1999.

Sustainability is not only about the continuing supply of resources but also about social and economic systems, politics, and culture. It is a challenge that cities in both the South and the North are failing to meet effectively. Chapters from a range of international contributors are grouped under three headings: policy, management and organisation, and politics. They look at sectoral issues (such as waste management or fresh water supplies) as well as the underlying context to the topic and relations among the actors involved.

Joel Audefroy and Cesare Ottolini (eds): *Vivre dans les centres historiques: Experiences et luttes des habitants pour rester dans les centres historiques,* Paris: Editions Charles Léopold Mayer, 2001.

The deterioration of housing conditions in old city centres is a common phenomenon, particularly in the South. Projects to upgrade these centres often result in evicting long-term residents, who are also likely to be among the poorer members of society. Contributors ask how city residents can best collaborate with professional urban developers and politicians so that they can avoid being forced to leave their homes and way of life. The book includes case studies from Bucharest, Dakar, Lima, Mexico, Tuzla, and Venice, which testify to the creative efforts of residents to prevent the decline of old city centres. Its editors are representatives of Habitat International Coalition.

Antoine S. Bailly, Philippe Brun, Roderick J. Lawrence, and Marie-Claire Rey (eds): *Socially Sustainable Cities: Principles and Practices,* London: Economica, 2000.

Arising from the UNESCO Management of Social Transformations programme (MOST), this publication extracts key details from its aim of building an internationally comparable knowledge base for urban management. It takes perspectives from the ten cities in the MOST network (Budapest, Cape Town, Geneva, Lyon, Montreal, Nairobi, Rotterdam, Sâo Paulo, San Salvador, and Toronto) and looks at the central components of socially sustainable urban development. Issues covered include: urban governance, social and cultural policies, public services, city planning and habitat, urban transport and accessibility, and economic revitalisation.

Sheridan Bartlett, Roger Hart, David Satterthwaite, Ximena de la Barra, and Alfredo Missair (eds): *Cities for Children: Children's Rights, Poverty and Urban Management*, London: Earthscan, 1999.

Children want to live among family and friends, to feel safe in their homes and communities, have space to play, and places where they can escape from noise and pollution. This book is intended to help local authorities respond to these basic rights and requirements. The book introduces the history of children's rights and goes on to look at issues such as housing, community participation, working children, health and education services, and juvenile justice. It also discusses wider factors, including economic security, social justice, and environmental management, all crucial to improving children's well-being. The volume includes a resource section, listing relevant publications and organisations.

Hugh Barton (ed.): *Sustainable Communities: the Potential for Eco-neighbourhoods*, London: Earthscan, 2000.

It is widely agreed that sustainable communities are the key to sustainable urban development, but there is little clear idea about how to halt the demise of local neighbourhoods, and re-invent them as the basis for local resource management and community-based decision making. Basing its observations on case studies from the UK, this book examines the practical implications of a commitment to building social capital within urban communities. It highlights some of the operational contradictions inherent in these ideals, such as the fact that, while the re-use of urban brown-field sites is accepted as sensible planning policy, local Agenda 21 groups and neighbourhood associations often oppose development on playing fields and allotments. The book argues for a holistic model that builds on consensus.

Timothy Beatley: *Green Urbanism: Learning from European Cities*, Washington, DC: Island Press, 2000.

This book looks at sustainable cities in Europe and asks what the USA might learn from their experience. The author visited 30 cities in 11 European countries, although the focus is on The Netherlands, Scandinavia, and Germany, as countries or sub-regions that have invested most in this area. The way in which all elements of city planning (finance, taxation, land use regulation, densification, and transportation) have been woven together to tackle environmental issues is examined closely. The book also looks at creative housing and living environments, and at the growth of green commerce. While the city is widely viewed as the cause of, rather than the solution to, many environmental problems, the author argues that the city represents the most compelling opportunities for moving society towards sustainability. By the same author, see also *The Ecology of Place: Planning for Environment, Economy, and Community*, Washington, DC: Island Press, 1997.

Erhard Berner: *Defending a Place in the City: Localities and the Struggle for Urban Land in Metro Manila*, Manila: Ateneo de Manila University Press, 1997.

Far from being victims of urban dynamics, Berner argues that squatters are at the core of the metropolitan dilemma. This study of the slums of Metro Manila emphasises that such developments are the logical results of both globalisation and localisation. The Philippines is not an isolated case as metropolises across the world face similar challenges. Five communities are analysed in terms of an urban theory of strategic groups, localities, and local organisations. Addressed at social scientists, government, and private sector officials, the study concludes that planning should be based on the residents' own existing designs for everyday living.

Jordi Borja and Manuel Castells: *Local and Global: The Management of Cities in the Information Age*, London: Earthscan, 1997.

Profound changes in systems of production, consumption, government, and communication are transforming the patterns of urban development. The authors argue that cities are being reborn as global networks, structured around new principles of technological space. Old community norms are being discarded in order to adapt to the emergent international economic order. Citizens and NGOs are crucial to involving a collective development programme in which strategic plans are rooted in the diverse groupings of the urban area. Unless a dynamic relationship between the local and the global is established, problems of urbanisation will become unmanageable. Both authors are widely respected in the field of urban policy, and this book is aimed at planners and policy makers, as well as academics and students.

Rod Burgess, M. Carmona, and T. Kolstee (eds): *The Challenge of Sustainable Cities: Neo-liberalism and Urban Strategies in Developing Countries*, London: Zed Books, 1997.

This book presents a critical assessment of the development of urban policy in an era of neo-liberal development rhetoric. It explores the implications of current policy and practice for the roles of architects and planners, and compares the varying approaches employed in Africa, Asia, and Latin America. It examines how, in the face of structural adjustment, and under pressure from an increasingly market-oriented civil society, issues such as participation and community enablement can have a positive influence on urban strategies. Policy makers, planners, and urban professionals tend to lose sight of the meaning of macroeconomic, environmental, and political changes, thus overlooking marginal interests and social groups, and the pattern of regulatory processes that shape the relationships between the state, the market, and the built environment.

Michael Carley, Paul Jenkins, and Harry Smith (eds): *Urban Development and Civil Society: the Role of Communities in Sustainable Cities*, London: Earthscan, 2001.

With the shift in emphasis from state-run development to market-driven and public-private sector initiatives, the urban poor have been further marginalised from decision making and implementation. This book argues that 'bottom-up' community initiatives should be placed at the heart of sustainable urban planning, and that the state must engage fully with both the market and civil society in order to develop innovative new approaches to urban management.

Charles Correa: *Housing and Urbanisation*, London: Thames and Hudson, 2000.

This book offers some concrete solutions to inner-city planning. In the first section, architect and planner Charles Correa publishes 450 recent plans and photographs of low-cost urban dwellings in India and Malaysia. The second section identifies and discusses the key issues for a contemporary urban manifesto. Several examples of places where these principles have been applied include government projects for the recycling of urban land in Bombay and the construction of an indigenous township in South India.

Mike Douglass and John Friedmann (eds): *Cities for Citizens: Planning and the Rise of Civil Society in a Global Age*, Chichester: John Wiley, 1998.

This collection of 14 case studies addresses the issues of democratisation, multiculturalism, gender difference, and human flourishing in the field of urban planning. Cities are undergoing a profound identity change: the editors highlight the rising strength of civil society and the emerging local–global setting as key factors behind this transformation. Contributors argue that planning can and should represent an alternative to the uncertainties presented by the global competitive market. In particular, urban planning has the potential to collaborate with those marginalised by the new order. Presentations on policy and practice from cities in South America, Europe, the USA, and Asia are sandwiched between two introductory conceptual chapters on planning and the concluding theoretical debates in this wide-ranging volume on shaping cities for citizens.

Edèsio Fernandes and Ann Varley (eds): *Illegal Cities: Law and Urban Change in Developing Countries*, London: Zed Books, 1998.

The editors identify the role of law in urban growth as a neglected element of development and legal studies. The book collates essays on Africa, Asia, and Latin America, where the poor must step outside the law to gain access to land. It asks why their housing is illegal, why it matters that it is illegal, and what should be done about it. Contributors approach the subject from a socio-legal perspective, emphasising how legal institutions, legislation, and judicial decisions affect the social production of urban space. They offer a basic introduction to the subject through a broad-ranging collection of empirical studies, looking at issues such as property rights and the public control of urban land, land invasions and informal settlements, the deregulation of housing markets, legal pluralism, and security of tenure. Fernandes is also editor of *Environmental Strategies for Sustainable Development in Urban Areas* (Avebury, 1998).

Maria Emilia Freire and Richard Stren (eds): *The Challenge of Urban Government: Policies and Practices*, Washington, DC: World Bank, 2001.

Freire argues that urbanisation is a defining factor of a country's economic growth, and the most efficient means of bringing amenity and civilisation to human lives. This publication is the result of the first course run by the World Bank on urban management, designed to steer cities towards their full potential – as liveable, competitive, well-governed, and bankable entities. The nine chapters relate to the modules of the course, taught by academics and researchers from within and outside the Bank. The chapters cover globalisation and city strategy, financial management and private sector participation, local governance, environmental management, and poverty reduction. The book explores innovative policies and practices for meeting the challenges – increasing in scope and complexity – that cities are facing.

Richard Gilbert, Don Stevenson, Herbert Girardet, and Richard Stren: *Making Cities Work: The Role of Local Authorities in the Urban Environment*, London: Earthscan, 1996.

Two trends – urbanisation and the diffusion of political power – put the responsibility for economic growth and sustainable development squarely on the shoulders of cities and municipal authorities. This publication, written to coincide with the Second United Nations Conference on Human Settlements (Habitat II) held in Istanbul in 1996, argues that local authorities should be at the centre of work concerning the urban environment, and that broad partnerships are needed to achieve sustainable development. With an eye towards future international co-operation, the principal authors, Gilbert and Stevenson, analyse current global mechanisms of collaboration in the field of urban development. They make recommendations on the role of intergovernmental, national, and local agencies in achieving stronger links between municipalities internationally.

Herbert Girardet: *The Gaia Atlas of Cities: New Directions for Sustainable Urban Development*, revised edition, New York: Anchor Books, 1996.

An attractive and accessible look at the future of cities in the face of continually rising urban populations. Girardet takes examples from all over the world to examine trends in architecture, waste and sanitation, housing, cultural life, and social problems such as drug abuse and violence. He explains the forces which both drive and entice people to migrate from rural areas, and argues for the need to (re-)establish a mutually enriching relationship between town and country, and to revive rural community life in order to help deal with the problem of excessive urban growth.

Peter Geoffrey Hall and Ulrich Pfeiffer: *Urban Future 21: A Global Agenda for Twenty-First Century Cities*, New York: Spon Press, 2000.

Prepared for the World Commission on Twenty-First Century Urbanisation conference in July 2000, the authors offer a comprehensive review of the state of world urban development at the millennium and a forecast of the main issues that will dominate urban debates in the next 25 years. Topics covered include demographic change, markets and planning, informal hyper-growth, urban governance, housing policy, transport, infrastructure, and the weakening of mature cities.

Jorge E. Hardoy and David Satterthwaite: *Squatter Citizen: Life in the Urban Third World*, London: Earthscan, 1989.

Arguing that the true planners and builders of Third World cities are the poor, this book seeks to describe the rapid and complex process of urban change in developing countries from the perspective of those who are living through it. The authors question many assumptions about Third World conglomerations and the role and status of 'squatters' within them. They begin by describing the growth of cities in terms of colonialism and go on to review some practical implications of this, such as the failure of government policies to incorporate the 'illegal' elements of their cities, as well as housing, transport, and environmental problems. The final chapter looks at the growth of smaller urban centres, challenging the view that urbanisation is about the development of megacities.

Jorge E. Hardoy, Diana Mitlin, and David Satterthwaite: *Environmental Problems in an Urbanising World: Finding Solutions in Africa, Asia and Latin America*, London: Earthscan, 2001.

This new edition of the 1992 *Environmental Problems in Third World Cities* argues that successful urban planning requires an understanding of the links between the city's economy and built environment, and the physical environment in which it is located. A more inter-disciplinary attitude from professionals will greatly enhance the chances of achieving this. It is argued that, although each city is different, many environmental problems can be improved at relatively little cost; and that environmental problems generally have political solutions.

Mike Jenks and Rod Burgess (eds): *Compact Cities: Sustainable Urban Forms for Developing Countries*, London: Spon Press, 2001.

An addition to the Compact Cities series (*Compact City*, 1996; *Achieving Sustainable Architecture*, 2000), this volume extends the debate about the nature of sustainable cities to developing countries. It examines the merits and defects of compact city approaches in terms of their applicability to urban areas in Africa, Asia, and Latin America. The volume brings together a wide range of papers and case studies from academics and practitioners to review issues of theory, policy, and practice.

William M. Lafferty and James Meadowcroft (eds): *Implementing Sustainable Development: Strategies and Initiatives in High Consumption Societies*, Oxford: OUP, 2000.

This book aims to provide the empirical 'fire' to justify the discursive 'smoke' of many academic publications on sustainable development. It focuses on the concrete progress made by governments in the developed world since the 1992 Earth Summit, showing that sustainable development has influenced a change of direction in governmental response to environmental problems. Each chapter examines the attitude of a different country (Australia, Japan, the USA, and the EU states). In addition, the book provides a political and policy context to the practical programmes reviewed, with introductory and concluding essays by the editors.

Charles Landry: *The Creative City: A Toolkit for Urban Innovators*, London: Earthscan, 2000.

While cities have always been at the centre of cultural expression as well as of wealth creation, they currently face immense economic, social, and infrastructural problems. The author brings together examples of innovation and regeneration from around the world in the form of a toolkit of methods and approaches to solving urban problems in ways that catalyse and capitalise upon the energies residing in them.

Gordon McGranahan, Pedro Jacobi, Jacob Songsore, Charles Surjadi, and Marianne Kjellén: *The Citizens at Risk: From Urban Sanitation to Sustainable Cities*, London: Earthscan, 2001.

The authors argue that current debates on the policy and practice of sustainable development fail to engage with the political and ethical aspects of promoting environmental justice. The international urban environmental agenda has tracked the concerns of cities in developed countries, rather than the 'older' problems experienced by less affluent cities. It has thus moved away from the concern for equity that spurred the promotion of sanitation in Western cities in the nineteenth century, to a concern with environmental pollution and, more recently, to the sustainability of urban lifestyles. The authors argue that there is still much to learn and improve upon on in the area of environmental health, and that traditional solutions are no longer appropriate.

Isabelle Milbert: *What Future for Urban Co-operation? Assessment of Post-Habitat II Strategies*, Bern: SDC, 1999.

This inventory of urban activities undertaken by bilateral and multilateral development co-operation agencies is a sourcebook for international co-ordination and political dialogue in the urban sector. The reversal of rural/urban demographics in the last 30 years has established grounds for the urbanisation of human habitats, lifestyles, and cultural values. International agencies have responded by calling for a new approach to cities, prioritising partnerships between government and civil society. This book, which comes out of the Graduate Institute of Development Studies (IUED) in Geneva, catalogues their efforts as well as analysing the trends and perspectives revealed by the data on urban aid.

Panos: *Governing Our Cities: Will People Power Work?* London: Panos Institute, 2000.

Prepared as a briefing paper for the 2001 Istanbul Plus Five review of Habitat II, this document reviews the model of governance that was endorsed by UN member states, which was supposed to respond to the needs of the poor and the marginalised within cities and so move away from the privatisation of public services favoured by the World Bank as a solution to urban problems. Progress towards this goal has been at best patchy, and undermined by lack of commitment as well as inadequate resources. The case of Porto Alegre, where participatory budgeting has been working for some years, is highlighted as an example of what can be done, given the will to create the mechanisms.

Keith Pezzoli: *Human Settlements and Planning for Ecological Sustainability: The Case of Mexico City*, Massachusetts: MIT Press, 2000.

This describes what happened when residents of a greenbelt zone in Mexico City refused to be relocated, instead proposing that the area be transformed into ecological settlements. The book tackles the fundamental conflict between the human need for shelter and survival, and the scientific necessity of preserving the natural environment. It also looks at the history of human settlement in the area and traces the origins of urban development. The author uses urban and regional planning theory and practice to examine the implications for sustainability raised by the topic.

Meine Pieter van Dijk, Marike Noordhoek, and Emiel Wegelin (eds): *New Institutional Forms in Urban Management: Emerging Practices in Developing and Transitional Countries*, Rotterdam: Institute for Housing and Urban Development Studies, 2001.

The body of knowledge and expertise on innovative forms of urban management is growing rapidly. This book aims to give insight into some of the theoretical and practical aspects of increasingly complex urban issues. The 11 contributors from IHS link their practical experience in a wide range of countries to the international context. In particular, they discuss the changing role of government, decentralisation and new legal frameworks, the impact of new technologies, and the incorporation of cultural diversity into urban management. The evolution of new institutional forms is mapped in order to determine the major actors in this development process.

Janelle Plummer: *Municipalities and Community Participation: A Sourcebook for Capacity Building*, London: Earthscan, 2000.

Throughout developing nations, municipal authorities remain the single most important influence on whether conditions will improve or deteriorate for much of the urban population. But municipalities can only work effectively through partnership with all levels of society. This sourcebook aims to bring about stronger and more sustainable forms of community participation and to offer a strategic framework for working urban partnerships. Illustrative examples document key elements of participatory processes, identify common constraints, and outline effective instruments municipalities can adopt to achieve change. A checklist for action is provided to help translate concepts into tangible form.

Mario Poléses and Richard Stren: *The Social Sustainability of Cities: Diversity and the Management of Change*, Toronto: University of Toronto Press, 2000.

As large cities with tight links to the international economy grow larger and wealthier, they also tend to manifest greater social dislocation in the form of increasing poverty, unequal access to public services, entrenched spatial segregation of different classes and social or ethnic groups, anomie, and crime, etc.. Including case studies from Africa, the Americas, and Europe, this book highlights the importance and impact of the policies that cities adopt to integrate diverse groups and cultural practices in an equitable fashion while contending with a global economy that presses for structural adjustment. The authors conclude that 'policies conducive to social sustainability should...seek to promote fiscal equalisation, to weave communities within the metropolis into a cohesive whole, and to provide transport systems that ensure equal access to public services and workplaces, all within the framework of an open and democratic local governance structure'.

Cedric Pugh (ed.): *Sustainable Cities in Developing Countries: Theory and Practice at the Millennium*, London: Earthscan, 2001.

This volume brings together a wide range of expert opinion on sustainable urban development for a multi-disciplinary review of the major issues. It looks at the application of Local Agenda 21 in cities in the developing world and examines the legal mechanisms, environmental, health, and economic concerns raised by the topic.

The contributors cover key contemporary developments such as the effects of international law and the control of greenhouse gases, and analyse theoretical studies of community environments from the World Bank, WHO, and the United Nations Environment Programme (UNEP). See also by the same author *Sustainability, the Environment and Urbanisation*, London: Earthscan, 1996.

Joe Ravetz: *City Region 2020: Integrated Planning for a Sustainable Environment*, London: Earthscan, 1999.

Drawing on a comprehensive case study undertaken in Greater Manchester, this manual offers guidelines for the integrated strategic management of cities and regions. It presents a 25-year plan for the restructuring of the post-industrial urban system in the West, with a focus on the links between economic, social, and environmental sectors. It includes technical scenarios for land use, energy, and material flows; spatial scenarios for each area and settlement type; lateral thinking on cultural, informational, localisation and globalisation trends; and practical actions for national and local government, business, the voluntary sector, and the general public.

David Satterthwaite (ed.): *The Earthscan Reader in Sustainable Cities*, London: Earthscan, 1999.

This Reader for students and professionals examines how a growing urban population can be compatible with sustainable development goals. It includes published articles and extracts from books from a wide range of sources. The papers come from several perspectives, but many argue that the key issue is not so much the creation of 'sustainable cities' as the generation of an integrated system that fits into the sustainable development of the wider region and, ultimately, the whole biosphere. Defining the boundaries of such a diffuse topic is recognised as a challenge; the conceptual essays present a context to the subject, while sectoral case studies provide examples of programmes at local, national, and global levels. David Satterthwaite is author of several books on the urban environment and founder and co-editor of the journal *Environment and Urbanization*.

Maf Smith, John Whitelegg, and Nick Williams: *Greening the Built Environment*, London: Earthscan, in association with the World Wide Fund for Nature, 1998.

The built environment incorporates homes, workplaces, public facilities, and places of leisure; as such it is the site of many conflicting interests and needs, including space, mobility, production and consumption, pollution, health, and security. The authors note that while cost and similar concerns are of major importance, they should not take precedence over other values that underpin human well-being. Getting the right balance among these competing issues is the only way to build sustainable towns and cities that will in turn facilitate sustainable lifestyles.

UNCED: *Agenda 21*, Geneva: UN Department of Public Information, 1999.

Agenda 21 is the statement of principles on sustainable development adopted by 178 governments attending the Earth Summit held in Rio de Janeiro in 1992. In conjunction with the Rio Declaration, it has become the comprehensive blueprint for an international programme of action to prevent further environmental degradation. Its key thesis is that global partnership is the only way to achieve progress for sustainable development.

It includes relevant chapters on urban topics such as: demographic dynamics and sustainability; promoting sustainable human settlement development; environmentally sound management of solid wastes and sewage-related issues; and local authorities' initiatives in support of Agenda 21.

UN Centre for Human Settlements (Habitat): *Cities in a Globalising World: Global Report on Human Settlements 2001*, London: Earthscan, 2001.

The positive effects of globalisation are its ability to facilitate the diffusion of knowledge and the acceptance of norms of democracy, environmental care, and human rights. However, as Kofi Annan the UN Secretary General states in his foreword, these benefits are distributed unevenly. Cities represent the starkest of these inequalities; they harbour unprecedented patterns of segregation, often generating wealth at the centre while allowing huge populations to live in poverty on the periphery. This report presents a comprehensive review of the world's cities and analyses the impacts of global social, economic, and technological trends on human settlements. Drawing on more than 80 background papers from international specialists, it includes case studies, graphics, and statistical data.

UN Centre for Human Settlements (Habitat): *The State of the World's Cities 2001*, Nairobi: UNCHS, 2001.

This attractively produced report constructs a current picture of urban issues and policies around the world and is the organisation's first attempt to monitor, analyse, and report on the realities that the urban agenda presents policy makers. It provides an overview of areas that are most affected by global trends, whether positively or negatively, before taking a region-by-region look at urbanisation and its implications. The report then covers urban shelter, society, environment, economy, and governance.

Nick Wates: *The Community Planning Handbook: How People Can Shape Their Cities, Towns, and Villages in Any Part of the World*, London: Earthscan, 2000.

It is widely held that local participation is the only way of achieving sustainable societies. A range of methods has been pioneered in different countries, and growing numbers of residents are becoming involved in determining the shape of their local environment. This handbook, concerned particularly with the built environment, features accessible best-practice information on the methods available to communities. Scenarios and possible strategies are worked through, and checklists and tips provided for reference. Based on experience in the UK, it is recommended by an international selection of experts, with the aim of being applicable in communities in any part of the world.

Diane Warburton (ed.): *Community and Sustainable Development: Participation in the Future*, London: Earthscan, 1998.

This UK-based publication features contributions from academics and community-based workers, who offer varied perspectives on the underlying issues of participation and sustainable development. Despite the international consensus on the importance of participation, there are unresolved questions about achieving sustainable development in practice. Can the ideal of collective action compete with pervasive individualism? How can expert knowledge and participation be allied with the diversity of local culture? What are the implications of community action for democracy and wider accountability? Taking the WCED definition of sustainable development, the book looks at the future resources needed to sustain humanity.

Edmundo Werna: *Combating Urban Inequalities: Challenges for Managing Cities in the Developing World*, Cheltenham: Edward Elgar, 2000.

Analysing the relationship between urban management and the unequal pattern of provision in developing countries, this book starts from the premise that socio-economic inequalities constitute a significant development problem. The author argues that inequalities are more harmful to society than poverty itself, and that poverty should be defined as relative, not absolute. This is particularly significant in urban areas, where the divisions between rich and poor are most evident and most real. Werna's concern is with the impact of local government performance and privatisation on relative poverty. The implications for policy making are highlighted throughout, and the argument is illustrated with empirical data from Nairobi, Chittagong, and Sâo Paulo.

Edmundo Werna, Trudy Harpham, Ilona Blue, and Greg Goldstein (eds): *Healthy City Projects in Developing Countries: An International Approach to Local Problems*, London: Earthscan, 1998.

Urban growth has generated a number of health problems for poorer residents, such as pollution and stress in addition to the infectious diseases associated with poverty. The WHO Healthy City Project has helped to highlight this situation and has stressed the importance of integrating public health into management. The book relates experience from a range of cities and suggests ways to make better linkages between urban policy makers, environmentalists, and health professionals.

Kenneth G. Willis, R. Kerry Turner, and Ian J. Bateman (eds): *Urban Planning and Management*, Cheltenham: Edward Elgar, 2001.

A collection of 29 key articles dating from 1991 to 1998 on different aspects of sustainability in urban planning and management, which tease out the conflicting arguments about whether and how sustainability should be achieved. Topics include the life and death of cities, whether cities should be compact or dispersed, sustainable urban policy and energy use, town planning, Local Agenda 21, the sustainable provision of services, and legal property rights and management practices.

World Bank: *Cities in Transition: World Bank Urban and Local Government Strategy*, Washington, DC: World Bank, 2000.

This work crystallises the World Bank's current understanding of sustainable development in the urban context. Cities that fulfill the bill are those that are 'liveable, competitive, well-governed, and bankable'. Despite the inherent contradictions between the means and ends implied in the Bank's approach, this document deserves reading because of the influence the Bank has on policy in many developing countries. The report urges the World Bank to 'view the city holistically while intervening selectively', facilitate city-led development processes and support national urban policy frameworks, as well as investing in education on urban issues. Four chapters look in detail at the need for a new urban strategy, the means to pursue a vision of sustainable cities, and requirements for implementation of such a programme.

World Commission on Environment and Development (WCED): *Our Common Future*, Oxford: OUP, 1987.

This document was commissioned by the UN to construct a 'global agenda for change', in particular to propose long-term environmental strategies for achieving sustainable development by 2000. As such, it is a key document for those reviewing developments since its publication. Under three headings – common concerns, common challenges, and common endeavours – the report considers ways to ensure greater co-operation between nations in order to halt environmental degradation, and methods to implement international agreements more effectively. A real sense of urgency underlies its attempts to construct a definition of environmental priorities, and the project, which was headed by Gro Harlem Brundtland, achieved unanimous backing from all the Commissioners involved.

Journals

City: published three times a year by Carfax, Taylor & Francis. ISSN: 1354-9839. Editors: Ash Amin, Manuel Castells, Bob Catterall, Michael Edwards, Mark Gottdiener, Kevin Robins, Sophie Watson, and Jianfei Zhu.

Publishing analysis of urban trends, culture, theory, policy, and action in the new urban arena, *City* looks at cities and their futures from a multi-disciplinary perspective with contributions from scholars in geography, the social sciences, planning, cultural studies, and the humanities. It aims to tackle policy and action as well as theory and analysis. Recent articles of interest include: Eduardo Mendieta, 'Invisible cities: a phenomenology of globalisation from below', and Adrian Atkinson, 'Surabaya, Indonesia: Local Agenda 21 in the context of radical political reform'.

Development in Practice, published five times a year by Carfax, Taylor & Francis on behalf of Oxfam GB. ISSN: 0961-4524. Editor: Deborah Eade.

Publishing practice-based analysis and research concerning the social dimensions of development and humanitarianism, the journal serves developing professionals worldwide by challenging current assumptions, stimulating new thinking, and seeking to shape future ways of working. Special thematic and guest-edited issues are published regularly. www.developmentinpractice.org

Environment and Urbanization: published twice a year by the International Institute for Environment and Development. ISSN: 0956-2478. Editor: David Satterthwaite.

Designed to encourage experts from Latin America, Asia, and Africa to write about their work, debate issues, and exchange information on their activities and publications. A theme-based journal, there have been three issues on sustainable cities since 1998.

Habitat International: published quarterly by UNCHS (Habitat). ISSN: 0197-3975. Editor: Charles L. Choguill.

Focuses on urbanisation in the developing world, publishing research on the study, planning, design, production, and management of human settlements. It acknowledges, however, that changes in the industrialised world are of growing importance, and the economic, social, technological, and political changes in one region will always affect other regions.

International Journal of Urban and Regional Research: published quarterly by Blackwell Publishers. ISSN: 0309-1317. Editor: Patrick le Gales.

Publishes articles on recent developments in policy, theory, and practice by leading writers in the field. It also includes shorter pieces in its 'debates' section, as well as book reviews, conference reports, and coverage of new mobilisations. Recent articles include: Abdoumaliq Simone, 'Straddling the divides: remaking associational life in the informal African city', and Karl F. Seidman, 'Revitalising inner-city neighbourhoods in the United States'.

Journal of Environment and Development: A Review of International Policy: published quarterly by Sage. ISSN: 1070-4965. Editor: Gordon F. MacDonald.

Seeking to further research and debate on the nexus of environment and development issues at every level, the journal provides a forum that bridges the parallel policy debates among policy makers, lawyers, academics, business people, and NGO activists worldwide.

Local Environment: published quarterly by Carfax, Taylor & Francis. ISSN: 1354-9839. Editors: Julian Agyeman and Bob Evans.

Focusing on local environmental and sustainability policy, politics, and action, the journal aims to be a forum in which to examine, evaluate, and discuss the environmental, social, and economic policies involved in sustainable development. *Local Environment* is associated with the International Council for Local Environmental Initiatives (ICLEI) in evaluating and presenting the methods and tools necessary to achieve local sustainable development worldwide. Recent issues contain guest editorials on themes such as Waste, Youth and Sustainability, and Sustainability's Greatest Challenge.

Regional Development Dialogue: published twice yearly by the United Nations Centre of Regional Development (UNCRD). ISSN: 0250-6505. Editor: Yo Kimura.

Invites critical discussion of regional development matters among academics and practitioners and is particularly aimed at policy makers, government officials, and professional planners worldwide. Recent articles include: Chamniern P. Vorratnchaiphan and Elizabeth C. Hollister, 'Urban environmental management, governance innovation and the UNDP LIFE programme'; Emiel A. Wegelin, 'Urban poverty and local actions towards its reduction'; and Wang Huijiong, 'Urban poverty alleviation and development'. The first issue of 1999 runs on the theme of poverty alleviation in the context of urban and regional development.

Third World Planning Review (TWPR): published quarterly by Liverpool University Press. ISSN: 0142-7849. Editors: Bill Gould, Chris Pycroft, and Katie Willis.

Publishes papers on urban and regional planning in the developing world, stressing the social, cultural, economic, and political relationships that underlie and inform planning practice. Issues covered include the use and development of resources and energy; technical co-operation and planning policy, shelter, transport, communications and other infrastructure, planning techniques and methodology, rural development, demographic change, education, and finance for development. Recent articles include: Victor F.S. Sit, 'A window on Beijing: the social geography of housing in a recent period of transition' and Paul W.K. Yankson, 'Accommodating informal economic units in the urban built environment: Accra Metropolitan Area'.

Town and Country Planning: published monthly by the Town and Country Planning Association Journal. ISSN: 0040-9960. Editor: Nick Matthews.

The journal of the UK-based Town and Country Planning Association publishes articles on planning policies that promote sustainable development as a means of conserving natural resources and reducing pollution. These are inspired by the belief that effective planning is good for economic well-being and that the needs and aspirations of the local communities should be reflected in planning policies. Although focusing on the UK, it also draws on relevant worldwide issues.

Urban Studies: published 13 times a year by Carfax, Taylor & Francis. ISSN: 0042-0980. Editors: W.F. Lever and Ronan Paddison.

Deals with a broad range of urban and regional problems susceptible to the analysis of social science. These include issues such as urban housing, employment, race, politics, and crime, and problems of regional investment and transport. Most articles deal with European and North American societies, but those addressing less developed nations are published regularly. Relevant special issues published recently are: Anne Haila, *Asia's Global Cities*; Joos Droogleever Fortuijn, Sako Musterd, and Wim Ostendorf, *Ethnic Segregation in Cities: New Forms and Explanations in a Dynamic World;* and Cedric Pugh, *Habitat II.*

Organisations

The Development Planning Unit (DPU), University College London is an international centre specialising in academic teaching, practical training, research, and consultancy in the field of urban and regional development, planning, and management. It is concerned with promoting sustainable forms of development, understanding urbanisation processes, and encouraging innovation in all aspects of responding to the economic, social, and environmental development of cities and regions, especially in Africa, Asia, and Latin America. Contact details: 9 Endsleigh Gardens, London WC1H 0ED, UK. E-mail: dpu@ucl.ac.uk. **www.ucl.ac.uk/dpu/**

Institute for Housing and Urban Development Studies is an international education institute dedicated to strengthening local capacities in housing, urban management, and urban environmental management, with the overall objective of improving urban quality and reducing urban poverty. Besides developing and conducting training and education programmes in The Netherlands, IHS is engaged in various advisory and technical assistance projects for clients including the multilateral agencies. Contact details: PO Box 1935, 3000 BX Rotterdam, The Netherlands. E-mail: ihs@ihs.nl. **www.ihs.nl**

International Council for Local Environment Initiatives (ICLEI) is an association of over 340 local government offices dedicated to the prevention and solution of local, regional, and global environmental problems through local action. ICLEI was launched in 1990 as the international environmental agency for local governments under the sponsorship of the United Nations Environment Programme (UNEP), the International Union of Local Authorities (IULA), and the Center for Innovative Diplomacy. The Council's strategic objectives are achieved through ICLEI's international campaigns, which generate widespread political awareness and recruit local governments to make formal commitments to the priority issues identified by ICLEI's members. **www.iclei.org**

International Development Banks
The African Development Bank (AfDB) runs urban projects and makes loans to programmes throughout Africa for the re-development of cities and slums. The percentage of annual lending to urban spheres, however, is minimal in comparison to other fields. **www.afdb.org** The Asian Development Bank (AsDB) has a less consolidated approach to urban development, but is moving towards more emphasis on urban policy and lending in response to increasing strain on urban centres in Asia. **www.adb.org** The Inter-American Development Bank (IDB) has a history of urban development lending and grants for projects in Latin America, but focuses heavily on investment in infrastructure and has a less developed idea towards sustainable urban development. **www.iadb.org** The World Bank offers a large database of information regarding its lending in the urban development sector. This is based on urban project assessment documents for specific projects. **www.worldbank.org**

International Institute for Environment and Development (IIED)
The Human Settlements programme represents the IIED's policy research work in urban areas undertaken in partnership with NGOs and academic institutions. It focuses on the reduction of poverty and improvement of health and housing conditions in low-income urban groups (in mainly Africa, Asia, and Latin America) while promoting more ecologically sustainable patterns of urban development. It also concentrates on urban environmental quality and planning, urban governance, and urban change. It seeks to influence government and aid agencies, strengthen influence of researchers and professionals in the South, and network. The work includes evaluation, technical policy assistance, seminars, publications, and training. Contact details: 3 Endsleigh Street, London WC1H 0DD, UK. E-mail: humans@iied.org. **www.iied.org**

Research Institute for the Built Environment (Institut de Recherche sur l'Environnement Construit, IREC) was founded in 1971 as an interdisciplinary team of researchers analysing the built environment and urban phenomena in regional, national, and global development plans. Through courses and publications, as well as direct exchanges with city builders and managers, IREC sensitises architects and engineers (academic and professional), public opinion, and the political environment to ongoing transformations and likely outcomes in the urban context. Contact details: Institut de Recherche sur l'Environnement Construit (IREC), Ecole Polytéchnique Fédérale de Lausanne, CH-1015 Lausanne, Switzerland. **www.epfl.ch**

Network-Association of European Researchers on Urbanisation in the South (N-AERUS) is a network of researchers and experts working on urban issues in developing countries which works in association with counterpart researchers and institutions in the South. It seeks to mobilise and develop European institutional and individual research and training capacities on urban issues in the South with the support of institutions and individual researchers with relevant experience in this field. E-mail: naerus@naerus.org. **www.naerus.org**

Instituto PÓLIS (Formaçao e Assessoria em Políticas Sociais) is a Brazilian NGO dedicated to research, training, technical assistance, and advocacy in the areas of citizens' rights and democracy in relation to local governance as well as local government. In addition to a substantial database on participatory local government, Pólis has a range of publications including the journal *Revista Pólis*, abstracts from which are available on its website. Contact details: Rua Cônego Eugênio Leite 433-Pinheiros, 05414-010 São Paulo SP, Brazil. E-mail: polis@polis.org.br. **www.polis.org.br**

Rooftops Canada Foundation/Abri International is an international development organisation dedicated to improving housing conditions and building sustainable communities in Africa, Asia, Latin America, and the Caribbean, and Eastern Europe. Founded by the Co-operative Housing Federation of Canada, Rooftops Canada is now a leading authority in this area, and was the NGO liaison and global NGO secretariat for Habitat II. Contact details: 2 Berkeley Street, Suite 207, Toronto, Ontario, Canada M5A 4J5. **www.chf.ca**

United Nations agencies with programmes on sustainable urban development include: UNCHS – The Sustainable Cities Programme based in Nairobi, which focuses heavily on the Environmental Planning and Management (EPM) approach. **www.undp.org/un/habitat/scp/** UNESCO – The Management of Social Transformations Programme (MOST), which promotes international comparative social science research, a main theme of which is urban development and governance. UNESCO is also involved in the Campaign on Cities as Messengers of Peace. **www.unesco.org/most/most2.htm** UNICEF runs the Child-friendly Cities Campaign. **www.unicef.org** WHO – Healthy Cities Programme seeks to enhance the physical, mental, social, and environmental well-being of the people who live and work in cities. **www.who.dk/healthy-cities/welcome.htm**

United Nations Research Institute for Social Development (UNRISD) engages in multi-disciplinary research on the social dimensions of contemporary problems affecting development. Its work is guided by the conviction that, for effective development policies to be formulated, it is crucial to have an understanding of the social and political. Through an extensive international network, UNRISD aims to promote original research and strengthen research capacity in developing countries. Two recent publications include: **Solon Barraclough**, *Towards Integrated and Sustainable Development?*, Geneva: UNRISD, 2001; and **Jaime Joseph**, *Lima Megaciudad, democracia, desarrollo y descentralización en sectores populares*, Lima: Centro Alternativa and UNRISD, 1999. Contact details: Palais des Nations, 1211 Geneva 10, Switzerland. E-mail: info@unrisd.org. **www.unrisd.org**

Urban Sector Network (USN) is an umbrella group of nine autonomous South African NGOs that are involved in development and governance issues, focusing on the involvement of the poor in decision-making processes, particularly in relation to housing and service needs, sustainable human settlements, and transformation of local government. Their members provide a range of technical assistance programmes and research and documentation services, with publications ranging from self-help manuals to information on social housing and formal submissions to government committees. Contact details: PO Box 146, Wits 2060, South Africa. E-mail: info@usn.org. **www.usn.org.za**

Addresses of publishers

(addresses for organisations are listed under individual entries)

Anchor Books
1540 Broadway, New York, NY 10036, USA

Ashgate Publishing
Gower House, Croft Road, Aldershot, Hants GU11 3HR, UK.
E-mail: info@ashgate.com

Ateneo de Manila University Press
Bellarmine Hall, Katipunan Avenue, Loyola Heights, Quezon City, PO Box 153, 1099 Manila, Philippines. Fax: +632 920 7215

Blackwell Publishers
108 Cowley Road, Oxford OX4 1JF, UK. Fax: +44 (0)1865 791347

Earthscan Publications
120 Pentonville Road, London N1 9JN, UK. E-mail: earthinfo@earthscan.co.uk

Economica
9 Wimpole Street, London W1M 8LB, UK.

Editions Charles Léopold Mayer
38 rue Saint-Sabin, F-75011 Paris, France. E-mail: diffusion@fph.fr

Edward Elgar Publishing
Glensanda House, Montpellier Parade, Cheltenham GL50 1UA, UK.
E-mail: info@e-elgar.co.uk

International Institute for Environment and Development
3 Endsleigh Street, London WC1H 0BD, UK. E-mail: humans@iied.org

Institute for Housing and Development Studies
PO Box 1395, 3000 BX Rotterdam, The Netherlands. Fax: +31 10 404 1523

Island Press
1718 Connecticut Avenue NW, Suite 300, Washington, DC 20009, USA.
E-mail: info@islandpress.org

MIT Press
Five Cambridge Center, Cambridge, MA 02142-1493, USA.
E-mail: mitpress-orders@mit.edu

Office for the Official Publications of the Countries of the European Community
57 rue des Romains , L-2444 Luxembourg. E-mail: claire.noel@seid.com

Oxford University Press
Great Clarendon Street, Oxford OX2 6DP, UK. E-mail: enquiry@oup.co.uk

The Panos Institute
9 White Lion Street, London N1 9PD, UK. E-mail: panos@panoslondon.org.uk

Sage Publications
6 Bonhill Street, London EC2A 4PU, UK. E-mail: info@sagepub.co.uk.

Spon Press
11 New Fetter Lane, London EC4P 4EE, UK. E-mail: info.sponpress@sponpress.com

Swiss Agency for Development and Co-operation (SDC)
Industry, Vocational Education and Urban Development Service, CH-3003 Bern,
Switzerland

Taylor & Francis
11 New Fetter Lane, London EC4P 4EE, UK. E-mail: journals.orders@tandf.co.uk

Thames & Hudson
181a High Holborn, London WC1V 7QX, UK. E-mail: sales@thameshudson.co.uk

Town and Country Planning Association
17 Carlton House Terrace, London SW1Y 5AS, UK. E-mail: editor@tcpa.org.uk

John Wiley & Sons
Baffins Lane, Chichester, West Sussex PO19 1UD, UK. Fax: +44 (0)1243 843296

UNCHS (Habitat)
Publications Unit, PO Box 30030, Nairobi, Kenya
E-mail: habitat.publications@unchs.org

United Nations Centre of Regional Development (UNCRD)
Nagono 1-47, Nakamura-ku, Nagoya 450-0001, Japan. E-mail: rep@uncrd.or.jp

United Nations Publications
Sales Office and Bookshop, CH-1211 Geneva 10, Switzerland.
E-mail: unpubli@unog.ch

University of Toronto Press
5201 Dufferin Street, North York, Ontario M3H 5T8, Canada.
E-mail: utpbooks@utpress.utoronto.ca

World Bank
1818 H Street NW, Washington, DC 20433, USA. E-mail: books@worldbank.org

Zed Books
7 Cynthia Street, London N1 9JF, UK. E-mail: sales@zedbooks.demon.co.uk

Index

economic sustainability, defined 16
employment, urban, India, becoming
more informal 141
employment, Mar del Plata
decrease in industrial employment
23
effects of competition 22–3
fishing industry one of main
sources 21–2
labour flexibilisation strategy 23, 34
women 24
workers' rights 24
ENDA-Tiers Monde, providing
Internet communication for
organisations in West Africa 301–2
engineering, high-quality, for slum
networking projects 54
environment, and sustainability 103
environmental conditions,
deterioration in, Mar del Plata
26–7, 35
environmental costs, externalisation
of, Mar del Plata 27
environmental degradation, Metro
Manila 125
environmental infrastructure, focus
on by APUSP 208–10, 215–16
environmental management, India
147–8
environmental movements, urban,
India
basic approaches 151–2
still nascent 153
Environmental Planning and
Management (EPM: UNCHS and
UNEP) 66, 138–9
adoption agreement with Dar es
Salaam 66
encourages partnership and power-
sharing 78–9
implies cross-sectoral
co-ordination and consensus-
building 83
institutionalising process 65–88
leading role for local governments
in implementation 84
potential value of stakeholder
participation 84

relationship with should be defined
83–4
use of working groups 66–7
environmental problems, in cities of
the South 139
environmental regulations, avoidance
of, Mar del Plata 23
environmental sustainability 177
EPM see Environmental Planning and
Management (EPM: UNCHS and
UNEP)
ESAP see Economic Structural
Adjustment Programme (ESAP),
Zimbabwe
ESAs see external support agencies
(ESAs)
ethical domination, imposition of the
one-thought world 109–10
ethical systems, 'alternate' 110
ethics, and development 105–6
European Community (EC), Fourth
Framework Programme for
Research and Technological
Development and Demonstration
306
European companies, fishing in
Argentine Sea 26
European Union (EU)
annulment of agreement with
Argentina 34
Fifth Framework Programme for
Research and Technological
Development and
Demonstration 311–12
trawler subsidies, freezer trawlers
in Argentine Sea 26
expertise, parasitic 131
external assistance agencies 5
external support agencies (ESAs) 5, 201n
bilateral
assistance for co-operation
projects 195–6
producing policy documents
181–2
early support for rural projects
178
funding gone into Agenda 21
programmes 187–8

technological approach
inappropriate 282–3
'too little, too expensive'(Baross)
232
see also low-income housing; self-
help housing; social housing
Housing by People, John Turner 227
housing, low-cost, India 170–2
innovative building designs 172
low-cost materials developed
170–2, 171
housing poverty
determined by land supply and
allocation 229–30
UNCHS definition 228
see also informal settlements
housing settlements, plots/building
lots 317
Human Development Report (UNDP:
1996) 104
human rights 103
human settlement(s)
concept of 317
monitoring dynamics of with
MOLAND 307
urban human settlements 317
human society, of the twenty-first
century 101
Hyderabad City 7, 149
EPM and *Master Plan* 2011 145
incremental development scheme
'Khuda ki Basti' (KKB) 240–1
imitates illegal development
strategies 240

ICTs *see* information communication
technologies (ICTs)
illegal settlements
demolitions and evictions, an
unsustainable policy 230–1
see also informal settlements
India
74th Amendment to the
Constitution 205–6
decentralisation in government
44
decentralisation of urban
governance 142

a landmark in power
transferance 48
not working efficiently 174
powers and functions of civic
bodies defined 166
revolutionary changes for urban
bodies 165–7
Air Pollution (Prevention and
Control) Act (1981) 143
Andhra Pradesh *see* Andhra
Pradesh Urban Services for the
Poor (APUSP)
Bio-Medical Waste (Managing and
Handling) Rules (1998) 143
British city government model 165
building of urban/'environmental'
infrastructure, effects of 152
Centre for Technology
Development 146
cities
difficult to assess
improvement/deterioration in
service quality with
subcontracting 53
entering into management
contracts for basic services 50,
51, 52
experience of financing
infrastructure 3
disturbing features of the urban
experience 160–4
growth patterns of cities 161–2,
161
effects of resource crisis in the
economy 61
efforts towards sustainable cities 144
Environment Protection Act (1986)
143
FIRE project 46, 146, 149
framing of urban problem and
finance 147
Ganga Action Plan (cleaning
R. Ganga), result of a PIL 149
Government does not recognise all
pillars of sustainable
development 148–9
government failure to address
urban environmental issues 137

International Council for Local
Environmental Initiatives (ICLEI),
Manual for Local Planning for
Agenda 21 (1996) 107
International Development Council
(IDRC: Canada), financial
arrangements 187
International Institute for
Environment and Development
(IIED) 182
international organisations
money for Brazil and Mexico 317
recommendations, language of
popularisation 319
Internet 289–90, 298–9

Kenya 257

labour relations, 'flexibilisation' of,
Argentina 20,23,34
LAC region *see* Latin America and the
Caribbean
land
for low-income housing,
Zimbabwe 267
shortage of, Buenos Aires 287
standards and regulations for
individual plots 260–1
land issue, rarely taken into account in
housing provision 230
landscape structural analysis software
(FRAGSTATS) 309
language, technical versus popular
316–23
Latin America and the Caribbean
changes in city government 3–4
democracy and social participation
in cities 89–101
difficulties in resolving problems
of cities and the urban habitat 92
poverty a great problem 95
Latin American cities
an alternative form of management
for 95–9
challenges for: obstacles and
opportunities 94
problems of, demands and
challenges created by 91–3

Lesotho 249, 254
Lima 102, 108, 112–16
local development, guiding principles
for 91–2
local governments 92, 133–5
low-income housing
Brazil 317
Harare 267–8
Mexico 317

Madras *see* Chennai (Madras)
Mali, processing of proposals 257
management contracts for basic
service provision, India 50, 51, 52
many fall into serious difficulties
50
Manila 4–5
MAPP *see* Municipal Action Plan for
Poverty Reduction
Mar del Plata, Argentina
adoption of Exclusive Economic
Zone 20
commercial fishing, history of
19–20
conflict between formal and
informal processing sectors
31–2
effects of internationalisation of
fishing industry 2
evolution of fishing industry 32, 33
expansion of local firms 20
impact of restructuring process
21–9
local government 34–5
policy decision to decentralise
fishing to Patagonia 20–1
reasoning behind lack of
government help 35
reasoning behind reorganisation
into co-operatives 34
restructuring transformed the local
fishing industry 19, 32
Mar del Plata, Argentina, restructuring
of the fishing industry 12–42
conflicts in aftermath of the
restructuring process 29–36
the 'Fish War' 29–32
the fishing industry 18–21

Nairobi, Dandora projects, existing
standards too high 249
National Institute for Research and
Fishing Development (INIDEP:
Argentina) 20
warning of unsustainability of hake
fisheries 25–6, 39
National Slum Development
Programme (NSDP) 217
natural sustainability 16
neo-liberalism 110
Network Association of European
Researchers on Urbanisation in the
South (N-AERUS) 183
NGOs
as catalysts 152
making use of ICTs 300
part of the fragmentation of issues
and actors 109
problems and traps to grapple with
109–11
work in Latin American cities 93
working in urban areas, some
funding for 185
see also ENDA-Tiers Monde
Northern towns/cities, twinning with
Southern towns/cities 186, 195

Our Common Future (Brundtland
Report) 103

parasitic development 122–4
participation 106–7, 186
participatory approaches, in urban
projects 185–7, 195–7
participatory democracy, seen as a trap
110
participatory planning appraisal
(PPA), Andhra Pradesh 210–12
Pasig River rehabilitation, Metro
Manila 128–30
Peru 254, 257, 258
petty trading *see* informal trading
activities
Philippines, the
Community Mortgage Programme
6–7, 127, 133–4, 135n, 237–9
housing policies, Marcos régime 237

unsustainable development 122–35
challenges ahead 132–5
Pasig River rehabilitation
128–30
patterns of parasitism in cities
124–5
role of foreign aid agencies
130–2
physical sustainability 16–17
PILs *see* Public Interest Litigations
(PILs), India
planning and decision making, role for
civil society 99
planning regulations 248, 250–1
planning standards 252–3
political culture, and development
119–20
political sustainability 17
pollution, sea and beach, Mar del Plata
27
poor *see* urban poor
popular participation
in community development and
management programmes,
criteria for 100
and democratic urban
management 97–8
population
India 140–1, 160
Metro Manila 124–5
urban, growing 305
Central and Eastern European
cities 312
developing countries 305
Harare 267–8
Latin American cities 318–19
poverty
in the LAC region 95, 96
urbanisation of 226–30
poverty alleviation
a governance issue 184
legal obligation, Indian
municipalities 205–6
poverty alleviation programmes 152–3
not seen to lead to sustainable
urban development 148
Swarna Jayanti Sheri Rojgar Yojana
(SJSRY) 142

sewerage provision, in Slum
Networking Projects 54-5, 55–6
Singapore, social housing 231, 244n
sites and services provision 231
Hyderabad 240–1
projects from international
agencies 249
in remote peripheral locations,
unacceptable 232
Slum Networking Projects (SNP),
India 53–61
slum up-grading 231
slumlordism 236
slums, continue to grow 305
small businesses, survival of 108
social costs, of inadequate housing
267
social housing 231
the compact city and private-public
partnership 287–96
social infrastructure, not non-
productive investment 95
social movements, and corruption 185
social policies, and caring government
133
social segregation/fragmentation 319
social and spatial segregation, Latin
American cities 96
social sustainability 16
solid waste 145,163
management 52–3, 145, 147–8, 198
South-South twinning 196
squatter settlements 228, 252, 267
squatters, the Philippine 'Community
Mortgage Programme' 237
squatting 248
squatting syndicates, strategies of
235
stability, a social, political and
economic process 114–17
State, the
adopting private sector orientation
towards profitability, results of 99
rethinking and reforming of 116
society's regulatory agent 98–9
streamlining of 90
Stockholm Environment Institute
(SEI) 182

Strong, Maurice 107–8
structural adjustment 106, 131
India 43, 62
programmes 226
adverse impacts of 137, 188
India 140–3
see also Economic Structural
Adjustment Programme
(ESAP), Zimbabwe
structural reforms, needed in Latin
American cities 95–6
structured debt obligations (SDOs)
57–8, 61
sustainability 103, 106
as an essential part of development
104
a camouflaged trap 106–7
environmental definition 164
pragmatic and realistic definition
164
spontaneous efforts towards, India:
fragmented efforts 149–52
a stable structure for 114–17
treacherous for urban policy
(Marcuse) 106
sustainable cities
change in macro-development
climate needed 155
concept of 136,138
conflicting situation to be
addressed 154–5
India
inclusive and synergetic
approach 154–5
limited vision of official
programmes 143–9
philosophy and context 164–5
international co-operation in
pursuit of 177–203
regional experiences in achieving
sustainability 3–5
in the South 137–40
inclusive approach based on
four pillars 140, 155
need for inclusive and
synergetic approach 154–5
Sustainable Cities Programme
(UNCHS and UNEP) 136

Development in Practice Readers

Development in Practice Readers draw on the contents of the acclaimed international journal *Development in Practice*.

'The great strength of the Development in Practice Readers is their concentrated focus. For the reader interested in a specific topic ... each title provides a systematic collation of a range of the most interesting things practitioners have had to say on that topic. It ... lets busy readers get on with their lives, better informed and better able to deal with relevant tasks.'

(Paddy Reilly, Director, Development Studies Centre, Dublin)

The series presents cutting-edge contributions from practitioners, policy makers, scholars, and activists on important topics in development. Recent titles have covered themes as diverse as advocacy, NGOs and civil society, management, cities, gender, and armed conflict.

There are two types of book in the series: thematic collections of papers from past issues of the journal on a topic of current interest, and reprints of single issues of the journal, guest-edited by specialists in their field, on a chosen theme or topic.

Each book is introduced by an overview of the subject, written by an internationally recognised practitioner, researcher, or thinker, and each contains a specially commissioned annotated list of current and classic books and journals, plus information about organisations, websites, and other electronic information sources – in all, an essential reading list on the chosen topic. New titles also contain a detailed index. *Development in Practice Readers* are ideal as introductions to current thinking on key topics in development for students, researchers, and practitioners.

For an up-to-date list of titles available in the series, contact any of the following:

- the Oxfam Publishing website at www.oxfam.org.uk/publications
- the *Development in Practice* website at www.developmentinpractice.org
- Oxfam Publishing by email at publish@oxfam.org.uk
- Oxfam Publishing at 274 Banbury Road, Oxford OX2 7DZ, UK.

'This book [Development, NGOs, and Civil Society] will be useful for practitioners seeking to make sense of a complex subject, as well as for teachers and students looking for a good, topical introduction to the subject. There is a comprehensive annotated bibliography included for further exploration of many of the issues.'

(David Lewis, Centre for Civil Society at The London School of Economics, writing in *Community Development Journal* 36/2)

Development in Practice

'A wonderful journal – a real "one stop must-read" on social development issues.'

(Patrick Mulvany, Intermediate Technology Development Group, UK)

Development in Practice is an international peer-reviewed journal. It offers practice-based analysis and research on the social dimensions of development and humanitarianism, and provides a forum for debate and the exchange of ideas among practitioners, policy makers, academics, and activists worldwide.

Development in Practice challenges current assumptions, stimulates new thinking, and seeks to shape future ways of working.

It offers a wide range of content: full-length and short articles, practical notes, conference reports, a round-up of current research, and an extensive reviews section.

Development in Practice publishes a minimum of five issues in each annual volume: at least one of the issues is a 'double', focused on a key topic and guest-edited by an acknowledged expert in the field. There is a special reduced subscription for readers in middle- and low-income countries, and all subscriptions include on-line access.

For more information, to request a free sample copy, or to subscribe, write to Oxfam Publishing, 274 Banbury Road, Oxford OX2 7DZ, UK, or visit: www.developmentinpractice.org, where you will find abstracts (written in English, French, Portuguese, and Spanish) of everything published in the journal, and selected materials from recent issues.

Development in Practice is published for Oxfam GB by Carfax, Taylor and Francis.

'Development in Practice *is the premier journal for practitioners and scholars in the humanitarian field who are interested in both practical insights and academic rigour.*'

(Joseph G Block, American Refugee Committee, USA)